*Workers*

# WORKERS:
## Worlds of Labor

*Eric Hobsbawm*

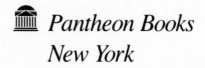 *Pantheon Books*
*New York*

Library of Congress Cataloging in Publication Data

Hobsbawm, E. J. (Eric J.), 1917–
Workers: worlds of labor

Includes index.
1. Labor and laboring classes—History. 2. Labor and laboring
classes—Great Britain—History.
I. Title.
HD4851.H63    1985        305.5'62'09        84-18946
ISBN 0-394-54300-9
ISBN 0-394-72896-3 (pbk.)

*Manufactured in the United States of America*
*First American Edition*

# Contents

# Illustrations

*The illustrations follow page 98.*

The author would like to acknowledge the following sources:

Jean François Millet, *Liberty* (photo courtesy of the Courtauld Institute of Art)

Eugène Delacroix, *Liberty on the Barricades* (Musée du Louvre, Paris)

Félicien Rops, *Peuple* (courtesy of the Victoria and Albert Museum, London)

Banner of the Southend branch of the National Union of General Workers (photo, John Gorman Collection)

Vera Mukhina, *Worker and Collective Farmer* (Novosti Press Agency)

Constantin Meunier, *Woman of the People* (courtesy of A.C.L., Brussels)

Richard Earlom (after Joseph Wright of Derby), *An Iron Forge* (Thomas Agnew and Son)

Aleksandr Terent'evich Matveev, *October* (1927) (photo courtesy of the Courtauld Institute of Art)

# Acknowledgements

Chapter 1, 'Labour History and Ideology', first appeared in the *Journal of Social History*, Summer 1974.

Chapter 2, 'Notes on Class Consciousness', is reprinted from I. Meszaros (ed): *History and Class Consciousness*, Routledge and Kegan Paul, London, 1971.

Chapter 3, 'Religion and the Rise of Socialism', is reprinted from *Marxist Perspectives*, Spring 1978.

Chapter 4, 'What is the Workers' Country?', first appeared in *Saothar* (Journal of the Irish Labour History Society), No. 8, 1982.

Chapter 6, 'Man and Woman: Images on the Left', first appeared in *History Workshop Journal*, 1978.

Chapter 7, 'Political Shoemakers', was co-written with Joan W. Scott and is reprinted with the permission of the Past and Present Society from *Past and Present: A Journal of Historical Studies*, No. 89, November 1980. World Copyright: The Past and Present Society, Corpus Christi College, Oxford, England.

Chapter 8, 'The Nineteenth-Century London Labour Market,' is reprinted from *London: Aspects of Change*, MacGibbon and Kee, London 1964.

Chapter 15, 'The 1970s: Syndicalism without Syndicalists?', first appeared in *New Society*, 5 April 1979.

Chapter 16, 'Should Poor People Organize?', first appeared in the *New York Review of Books*, 3 March 1978.

# Preface

This is a further volume of studies in the history of labour. It follows, after a lengthy interval, the collection first published in 1964 under the title *Labouring Men*.

The major theme of these studies is the formation and evolution of working classes in the period between the late eighteenth century and the mid-twentieth, and the relation between the situation they find themselves in society, and the 'consciousness', ways of life and movements they generated. As in *Labouring Men*, I am not so much concerned with labour and socialist organizations, ideologies and policies as such (though I believe them to be an essential dimension of working classes) but with their roots in working-class reality; including that of working-class militants. Some of those I write about have names which are known to the wider world; most of them have not. Still, they were all part of a wider world, and I have tried to take account of their relation to it. The history of any one class cannot be written if it is isolated from other classes, from the states, institutions and ideas that provide their framework, from their historical heritage – and, obviously, from the transformations of the economies that require industrial wage-labour and have therefore created and transformed the classes of those who perform it.

I have found it helpful to divide the history of the relation of the working classes to the rest of society into three broad phases: a transitional phase of early industrialism when an industrial working class with an independent way and view of life emerges from the former 'lower orders' or 'labouring poor'; a phase of highly developed 'separatism', and a phase of relative decline of separateness (cf. my 'The formation of the industrial working classes: some problems' in *Third International Conference of Economic History*, Munich 1965, pp. 175–80). The studies in this book deal essentially with the first two, but especially the second, of these phases. They only touch the fringes of the contemporary developments in the working classes of the older industrialized countries, i.e. those since the 1950s.

Since the general theme, in one way or another, runs through most chapters, their subject-matter is not always clearly separable. I have done my best to eliminate duplications which are to be found in the papers as originally written or published, except when a little occasional repetition seemed useful in underlining some points or arguments of importance. Nevertheless, the book falls into three main parts. The first seven chapters are general and comparative. They deal with the ideological assumptions of those who write labour history and with the specific nature of working-class consciousness as distinct from that of other social groups. These chapters are followed by more specific comparative discussions of the relation between socialist movements and religion (or rather irreligion), of labour and nations, and the transformations of labour ritual and iconography. Another chapter explores the links between social existence and consciousness in the case of a particular occupation traditionally and internationally type-cast as workshop intellectuals and radicals: the shoemakers. It is written jointly with Professor Joan Wallach Scott, who has kindly consented to its publication here.

Chapters 8 to 15 deal essentially with the British working class, though chapter 9 sees it in comparative perspective. Chapters 10, 11 and 14 form the core of this part, since they attempt to survey important aspects of the development of the British working class as a whole, or of crucial parts of it, over a lengthy period. This part also takes up two themes explored in *Labouring Men* which are relevant to working-class development in general, and which happen to have given rise since 1964 to further historical research and lively debates: the 'new unionism' and the 'aristocracy of labour'.

The final two chapters reflect on the connection between the existence of working classes, their struggles, and the ideas implicit in them.

Labour history has been transformed since the 1950s, when most of the essays in *Labouring Men* were written. It is no longer true to say that 'there has been comparatively little work about the working classes as such (as distinct from labour organizations and movements).' On the contrary. Every aspect of the study of working classes has flourished as never before, both in Britain and abroad. What is more to the point, it has produced a number of historical works of major importance, without which the present book could not have been written. The past twenty years have undoubtedly been a golden age for labour history. The present volume cannot therefore hope to do as much pioneering as its predecessor. Nevertheless, some of the ground it covers may still not be universally familiar.

About half the studies have not previously been published, at least in English, or are (like chapter 13) expanded and rewritten so extensively as to constitute new texts. They were given originally as lectures or papers to various conferences or at various universities. The rest were published in the *Journal for Social History*, *Marxist Perspectives*, *Saothar* (the journal of the Irish Labour History Society), *History Workshop Journal*, *Past & Present*, *New Society*, *The New York Review of Books*, and in two books: chapter 2 in I. Meszaros (ed.), *Aspects of History and Class Consciousness* (Routledge & Kegan Paul 1971) and chapter 8 in *London, Aspects of Change* (Macgibbon & Kee 1964). I am grateful for permission to reprint. Where it seemed necessary, the published papers have been brought up to date. The dates of original composition and publication are given.

I am much indebted to Dr Ronald Avery and especially Susan Haskins for help in research.

With the exception of chapter 10, which was written for a French public and therefore assumes little or no prior knowledge, all papers were originally addressed to an academic public. Nevertheless, I hope they will be comprehensible to, and may perhaps be read with enjoyment by, people who have no professional interest in labour history, or possibly in any kind of history.

*Workers*

# *1:* Labour History and Ideology

Labour history is today flourishing in most countries as never before, at least quantitatively. As to quality, it is difficult to judge the present against the past, and some of us would not be too happy to step into the ring with, say, Sidney and Beatrice Webb or Gustav Mayer, but we are fortunately not obliged to confront them face to face, since we can stand on their shoulders. The expansion of labour history as a field of study has overwhelmingly – but by no means entirely – taken the form of its transformation into an academic field. The typical labour historian is a university researcher or teacher, though this is also not universally true. As such he or she stands at a point of junction between politics and academic study, between practical commitment and theoretical understanding, between interpreting the world and changing it.

For labour history is by tradition a highly political subject, and one which was for long practised largely outside the universities. All the studies of labour were of course political since the subject began to arouse systematic scholarly interest, say in the 1830s and 1840s with the various enquiries into the condition of the new proletariat. When practised by academics (i.e. social scientists) they were essentially 'problem-solving', the problem being what to do about the workers. But though the academic study of labour problems, e.g. in late nineteenth-century Germany, produced a substantial fall-out of historical work, its basic orientation was not historical; and conversely, the academic historians until, say, World War II – at least in the developed European countries – took little interest in labour during the industrial period, though substantially greater interest in subjects relevant to labour history in the pre-industrial period – e.g. journeymen, guilds and suchlike. The bulk of the labour historians, whether or not they were or eventually became academics, came from within, or from the close proximity of, the labour movements themselves. Initially a great many of them were not in fact academics at all, even when their scholarship and erudition were impeccable: the Webbs in Britain, Mehring, Bernstein and Mayer in Germany, Deutsch in Austria, Dolléans in France. It is worth remembering that as late as 1963 a major non-university work appeared in our field – E.P. Thompson's *Making of the Working Class* – for Thompson produced it while he was a teacher in the working-class adult education movement and did not become a university teacher until after its publication. Of course the great majority of labour historians are even today members of or sympathizers with the labour movement, and represent one or other of the ideological or political tendencies within it; the major exception being the historiography of communist parties and the labour movements of the Third World, which generated an enormous output of anti-Red research, mostly practised or financed by the USA from the period of the Cold War on. But most of us are both on the left and academics. And perhaps one might add that, with the gradual ideological or political disintegration of the great socialist movements – whether social-democratic or communist – in most of Europe, even the more committed historians of this kind now have more room for scholarly manoeuvre than before.

Labour history 'from within the movement' and largely outside the universities tended to have certain characteristics. In the first place it tended to identify the 'working classes' with 'the labour movement', or even with a specific organization, party and ideology. It thus tended to identify labour history with labour movement history, if not actually with the history of the ideology of the movement; and the stronger and more unified the movement was in a country or period, the greater the temptation of such identification. Until very recently Italian labour history has had this characteristic to a marked degree and still has to some extent. It thus neglected the history of the working classes themselves, insofar as they could not be subsumed under that of their organizations or even the rank-and-file as against their leaders. This was a substantial gap.

In the second place, as with other essentially 'patriotic' fields – provincial history, the history of jazz or railway buffs, business history, even national histories – labour history from within the movement tended to be both a little antiquarian and preoccupied with giving to labour movements the importance which nobody else seemed to accord to them. Both are understandable motives, and the second was justified. For if those who don't live in Ipswich (Eng. or Mass.) cannot understand that foreigners do not find *all* facts about their town as fascinating as they do, it is undeniable that orthodox history paid quite insufficient attention to labour movements, let alone to the working class. And yet, two somewhat undesirable results followed from this attitude: 1) It led to a failure to distinguish the relatively important from the relatively trivial. For example, the British *Socialist League* of the 1880s was a small and impermanent organization among other small but more permanent ones, and hardly deserves the very heavy weight of scholarship which has been placed upon it; it briefly attracted a few important personalities, it acted as a pioneer of socialism in a few provincial towns, and it broke up rapidly and was never heard of again. But because it was associated with Engels, with William Morris and other notable figures, it has been given historical attention quite out of proportion to its importance. To some extent this applies to most other socialist bodies. Labour movement historiography is full of monographs of the sort of organization of which we have all had some experience – small sects which never get beyond that role, groups, journals or whatnot which live and die within a decade without ever playing much of a part. The ones that do have not necessarily been treated with greater attention than the ones which don't. The little group of British De Leonites, for instance (the SLP), deserves more attention than the Socialist League because of its function as an activator of industrial militancy in Scotland. 2) It leads to a certain self-isolation of labour movement history from the rest of history, which incidentally makes it easier to lump the important and the trivial together without discrimination. For instance, it seems clear that in the 1880s British bourgeois observers of the new socialist movements were not particularly worried about Karl Marx and his followers – at all events until these started to agitate among the unemployed – rather less so than about the anarchists. They were mistaken, though not much; for if there was no anarchist movement of significance at the time, there was not much of a Marxist movement either. But if we are to see the labour movement in the setting of the class struggle, which is

a two-sided relationship, or in the broader setting of national history, we cannot treat it as though it operated in isolation. In short,
classical labour movement history tended to produce an esoteric
version of history.

In the third place – and this follows from what has already been
said – classical labour movement history tended to produce both a
model and an accepted version of history, both national and international, which ranged from an informal but not very flexible to a
formal and highly inflexible orthodoxy. We need not concern ourselves much with the more formal and inflexible versions, though
they are of decisive importance to historians in some socialist countries – and the political element in historical interpretations associated with particular parties or organizations is not to be underestimated, even when it reflects not political judgement but the
prejudices, personal memories or self-defence of particular leaders.
Even in the pre-1914 German Social Democratic Party the question
of Lassalle and Schweitzer was one which historians found sensitive. Nobody stopped Mehring and Mayer, but Bebel himself intervened to criticize at least the latter. However, even the informal
orthodoxies must be recognized for what they are. I myself pointed
out long ago that the traditional 'model' of the development of the
labour movement was a (partly loaded) selection from the facts,
classifying some as central and relegating others to the margin or
excluding them. Even today students still tend to pick their research
subjects in labour movement history from among the accepted ones
and according to the accepted periodization, thus producing those
long queues of applicants competing for thesis subjects somewhere
within the over-exposed areas of the Revival of Socialism in the
1880s, Chartism, the militant movements of World War I – or their
equivalents in other countries. I do not say that the orthodoxy is
entirely wrong. If it did not reflect a good deal of what really
happened, it could hardly have established itself. Nevertheless it is
a historically evolved construct. For example, the Independent Labour Party is still taken largely at its own valuation – as the first
independent working-class party – though in fact an impartial view
would suggest that it failed quite dramatically to become anything
of the kind. Conversely, the old radical-democratic type of labour
politics – Chartist rather than Lib–Lab – which were far from
negligible in the 1890s tend to be overlooked. And yet when it was
launched on what turned out to be its brief career, the National

Democratic Convention of 1899 started under most impressive auspices and for a time looked like a strong rival to the new Labour Representation Committee (the later Labour Party). For every student who has even heard of the NDC there must be fifty who can write an essay on the ILP.

Finally, and perhaps somewhat surprisingly, traditional labour movement historiography was technically and methodologically rather orthodox. It produced a great deal of traditional narrative and institutional history; only its subject matter was unusual. A striking example of this is P. Spriano's *Storia del Partito Comunista Italiano*, which is an admirable and highly impressive piece of scholarship, unlike most other histories of communist parties, either official or hostile. Yet it reads very much like any other piece of first-rate political history. It is the history of party policy and its political activities; of its ideological debates; of its leadership and its peripeties; of its relations with the Comintern, and of all manner of interesting and important things. But the whole story is seen from above: we only glimpse occasionally what the rank-and-file militant or supporter thought or how he/she conceived the movement.[1] We are told very little about who these members and supporters were, or what their relations were with non-communist militants or with non-militants, or about the role and function of the movement and the party in particular cities and regions. The sort of things that we now know about, say, the Guesdists in France (to cite a monograph by an orthodox CP historian in that country[2]), we are not told. I make these remarks with no intention of diminishing the value of a really first-class and indeed epoch-making work, but to point out the difference between one kind of labour history and another.

II

The growing academicism of labour history has corrected some of the biases of traditional labour history, and the changing political conjuncture on the left has corrected others. Getting a PhD today implies a competence in research and a capacity to thread one's way through a large literature of varied views, which was simply not mandatory in the old days, and exposes the writer to considerably more varied criticism. Some trade union histories are still written, at least in Britain, in the old way, but they are exceptional. Tradi-

tional historical myths are today weaker in many labour movements and hence defended with less emotional commitment, except
when still within living memory – as the 1930s still are. At the same
time the change in the situation of organized movements has tended
to widen the perspectives of labour historians. They are increasingly preoccupied with the rank-and-file as well as with the leaders,
with the unorganized as well as with the organized, with the 'conservative working man' as well as with the radical or revolutionary:
in short with the class rather than the movement or party. This is
a good thing.

Nevertheless, the force which has expanded labour history has
remained largely political: the radicalization of generations of students and (in due course) junior professors in the 1960s. In Britain,
in the USA, in West Germany (where there has been a remarkable
revival in such studies), in Italy among the new left, and doubtless
elsewhere, radicalization has produced a substantial crop of new
labour historians, whose interest in the subject is basically that of
political commitment though their competence as researchers may
be greater and their scope somewhat wider. They all produce something of interest, but the approach of some of them is disappointing
and of others open to question. To dip into the past for inspiring
examples of struggle or the like is to write history backwards and
eclectically. It is not a very good way of writing it. I don't wish to
enter into the debates about American 'new left' history, but to
some of it at least these strictures apply. Again, to recapture what
we can of the ways in which the labouring poor lived, acted and
thought, is important, and insofar as it is now producing a spate
of 'oral history' or even (as with the History Workshop publica-
tions) memoirs actually written by men and women from the working class, an essential widening of our perspective. And yet these
things are not ends in themselves, however excited we may feel at
discovering what has been hitherto unknown. If we do not formulate questions first and look for the material in the light of these
questions, we risk producing merely a left-wing version of antiquar-
ianism, work which is the equivalent of that of amateur folklore
collectors. I do not wish to discourage such work, though if it is
done, it had better be done with as much system as Child collected
his ballads or Nettlau his anarchist materials. It has evident political value, especially when the material is such as to appeal to a
non-academic public. Recapturing a forgotten, inspiring or memor-

able past is a fit task for historians. Who would not wish to have
a book like Studs Terkel's *Hard Times*?[3] But when a recent reprint
of J.T. Murphy's *Preparing for Power* (1934),[4] a book which
throws light on the militants of a certain period of British labour,
but is not a good history of the labour movement, is justified on
the ground that it is the sort of thing that trade union militants
today would understand and like, a red light should be flashed.
There is a difference between history and inspirational or propagandist material, though good history may be both.

It is equally dangerous to fight old ideological battles over again,
a temptation which few who have written about the ideological
history of socialism and about communist movements have resisted. Not because all such disputes are unimportant or obsolete,
though some of them are, but because they may need to be refor-
mulated, and placed into a new setting, if they are to be sensibly
discussed by historians. Thus the celebrated debate on Bernstein's
'revisionism' retains its interest and practical significance today, at
any rate for Marxists. Yet it must be misunderstood if it is divorced
from its contemporary ideological and political context. It was not
a simple deviation from true Marxism, to be approved or rejected
according to taste, but a moment in the formulation of 'Marxism'
itself, out of the heritage of the founders, which simultaneously
created both 'orthodoxy' and its corollary, 'heresy'. Moreover
both, at least in the developed countries of Europe, attempted to
cope with a specific situation, an apparently stable, flourishing and
expanding capitalist economy and stable political structures, thus
diverging from the Marxism of regions in which economies and
regimes were neither. Such considerations are by now commonplace for the period of the Second International, partly owing to
the excellent work of Georges Haupt in Paris,[5] mainly because the
controversies of that era are no longer politically incendiary. But
the history of labour movements since 1917 is still discussed in a
less historical spirit.

One special word of warning may be useful. The old ideological
battles have always been fought historically not only in a priori
ideological terms, often read into the record retrospectively (e.g.
the conceptions of 'centrists' into the pre-1914 International), but
also by means of a loose and highly speculative version of
'counter-factual' history. I need merely mention such discussions
as those about the pros and cons of anarchists and communists in

the Spanish civil war, about the reasons for the failure of the German revolution in 1918-19, about whether the French Popular Front government of 1936 'ought to have' settled the mass strikes of that year or whether the French or Italian partisans ought to have made a bid for revolutionary power in 1944-5. All these arguments, like the more formalized exercises of the cliometricians, rest on the assumption that we can estimate or calculate how different the history of the world would have been if Cleopatra's nose had been an inch longer. Now two things may be said confidently about counterfactual (or 'if my grandmother had wheels she'd be a Greyhound bus') history. First, that its interest lies entirely in methodology and/or in the present and future. History is what happened, not what might have happened. The railroads *were* built, the German revolution of 1918 failed. The interest in thinking about what might have happened if these things had not happened lies in clarifying what hypotheses can properly be formulated about historical events, and in deciding between alternatives which are real and not imaginary – e.g. whether it is more efficient *today* to develop nuclear or non-nuclear energy, or how to choose *tomorrow* between alternative policies of labour movements. A third proposition may be also suggested, namely that in our field, unlike the narrower field of cliometrics, counterfactual speculations are not theoretical exercises but pretend to investigate actual alternatives, and that we rarely know enough to do so convincingly. Fogel never supposed that not building the American railroads was a genuine possibility, but when we speculate about what the effects of a German Soviet revolution might have been, we are assuming that such a development might have taken place. Now sometimes the probabilities are so high that we can speculate with some realism, normally about what couldn't have happened rather than what could. For instance, in assessing the development of the British labour movement since the 1880s we can exclude the possibility that a mass Marxist party could have developed instead of something like the Labour Party, before or after 1920, and we can therefore criticize the SDF or the CP not for what they could not seriously hope to have achieved, but within the limits of what it was not so impracticable for them to achieve – e.g., greater success in local government elections. However, sometimes there is no consensus about probabilities (or more likely improbabilities), and then we are in danger of drifting into endless and fruitless retrospective argument. Thus Staughton Lynd in a recent article[6] suggests that the American CP would have done better to maintain its line of independent revolutionary unionism after 1934 instead of putting its energy into the policy which was to produce the CIO. We may or may not sympathize with his view, but there are two basic things wrong with it. In the first place it is formulated in terms far too vague and imprecise for all of us to know clearly what exactly it is that is being discussed. In the second, and even if it were formulated in a more satisfactory manner, I cannot see any way of settling this argument. Doubtless all of us will go on applying the question 'if only' to labour or any other history. But when we do so we ought to be very lucidly aware of just what we are doing, why we are doing it, and what we can hope to achieve by it.

III

The dangers and temptations of the committed left-wing historian of labour movements are different from those which beset the academic technician. I will not dwell on those which are also ideological, though often – perhaps generally – concealed behind the assumptions, methods and jargons of some academic specialism. Enough has been written about the ideology implicit, and sometimes explicit, in certain schools of the social sciences, notably those which prevailed in the USA in the 1950s, and in such terms as 'integration' or 'modernization'. The ones I am concerned with are due chiefly to inexperience and unclarity.

Like all history, labour history has widened enormously in both scope and method, partly through an extension of its field from the narrowly political, ideological or even economic to social history in the broadest sense, partly through the consequent necessity to exploit entirely new sources by means of apposite, and largely novel techniques, partly through contact with the social sciences, from whom it has borrowed freely. This does not mean that traditional methods are exhausted, even in countries in which they have long flourished. (In countries without a serious tradition of labour history, or where the subject has been largely mythologized, the scope for even the most old fashioned straight historian is still enormous.) Nothing could be more ultra-traditional than G. Neppi Modona's *Sciopero, potere politico e magistratura 1870–1922* (Bari, 1972), a simple attempt by a historically trained lawyer to trace the changes in Italian law on strikes and in the attitudes of government and judges to trials arising out of labour conflicts. It does not contain so much as a single table of statistics. Yet it adds considerably to our understanding of that neglected aspect of labour history, the other side of the class struggle, because nobody had hitherto done this simple job. Indeed, some of the most impressive pieces of labour history in the past ten years are technically rather traditional, e.g. Peter Nettl's *Rosa Luxemburg*, Royden Harrison's *Before the Socialists* or J.F.C. Harrison's *Robert Owen and the Owenites.*[7]

Still, much of labour history – especially the social history of the working class – must use new methods and techniques, e.g. any work which touches on historic demography. Much of it has indeed launched itself with more or less enthusiasm into new, and especially quantitative techniques, notably in the USA and France. These provide three temptations. The first is to become ends in themselves rather than tools. Little need be said about this. The second is to exaggerate the value of the data to which the new techniques can be applied and neglect those to which they can't. This is a great danger in quantified comparative labour history, which selects out what is statistically comparable and tends to omit what is not. Thus a great deal is comparable about miners in different countries. Yet it is relevant to, say, Indian miners in the Andes that going to work in mines is one of the few methods available for peasants to accumulate cash for the purchase of land in their villages, and that therefore: a) they may be originally recruited from among the peasant proprietors rather than the landless peasants; and b) that ex-miners may become *kulaks*. This is evidently not relevant to English miners in the nineteenth century.

The third temptation is to overlook the ambiguities and conceptual difficulties of the data. Consider the presently fashionable studies in public disorder and violence, which can be readily quantified. This is based on the application of two convergent assumptions: a) that there is a sharper distinction between 'violent' and 'non-violent' acts than within each category; and b) that certain kinds of violence are singled out for attention – mostly on administrative, legal, political or moral grounds *by the authorities or the upper classes.* Now these assumptions and criteria may be quite external to the events they measure, and may therefore completely mislead us as to their nature. Thus if we were to take the point of view of moderate miners on strikes we would apply quite different criteria. The worst offence would be scabbing, and there would be no substantial moral difference between peaceful picketing, the pressure of public opinion and physically stopping scabs going down the pit. Beating up a scab or two would be relatively venial and might be inevitable, but an uncontrolled riot of the *Germinal* type might be regrettable, and sabotaging the pumps or the safety arrangements would be generally condemned. Some kinds of violence would be classified with non-violent actions, since they would become distinct from them only because of outside intervention in an otherwise peaceful activity. The crucial criterion would be the distinction not between force and non-violence, but between different kinds of force or violence, and the crucial variable not the miners' willingness to use force, but the employers' or the authorities' determination to resist strikes and the means they were prepared to use. Only when this has been separated out would we be in a position to assess the curve of the miners' own violence, i.e. to distinguish between different national or regional propensities to violence, or between different phases of the miners' movements.

The application of new concepts, generally drawn from the social sciences, is also dangerous, *if we are not clear in our own minds what we are trying to discover and explain*; or if you prefer the jargon, what our model is. The danger is all the greater, because (as Ernst Gombrich has recently pointed out) the nature of the academic profession is such as to put a premium on originality and fashionableness. The most implausible views can be certain of making all subsequent footnotes and bibliographies, if they are new enough, however easily they may be dismissed. It is only a question of time before someone analyses craft unions in the light of the anthropological discussions on artificial kinship, if they have not already done so; and I daresay someone has already analysed labour unions as systems of patron-client relationships. Obviously some such borrowings are likely to be rejected for ideological reasons – e.g. the analysis of relationships within labour movements as a form of market (political scientists have played about with this), and others will at the moment seem irrelevant, but might one day become fashionable, e.g. the application of Lévi-Strauss' binary opposites to working-class language. But in *all* cases, the test of new concepts and ideas is not simply that they are new, or seem interesting, but that they are relevant to our own basic questions.

This implies knowing what these are. And, as so often in this paper, I have once again to insist that labour historians have frequently lacked methodological and conceptual clarity. I do not wish to impose any particular model or theory on them, Marxist or otherwise, but merely to suggest clarity about whatever our approach happens to be. Nevertheless, whatever this is, I suggest that we shall all go wrong unless we bear in mind three important considerations:

1) The history of labour is part of the history of society, or rather of particular societies which have specifiable things in common. Class relationships, whatever the nature of class, are relationships *between* classes or strata, which cannot adequately be described or analysed in isolation, or in terms of their internal divisions or stratifications. This implies a model of what societies are and how they work.

2) The history of labour is a multi-layered affair, though the levels of reality or analysis form a whole: workers and movements, rank-and-file and leaders, socio-economic, political, cultural, ideological and 'historical' both in the sense that they operate within a context given by the past and in the sense that they change over time in certain specifiable ways. We cannot abstract one or more from the rest (except for purposes of temporary convenience), nor can we practise an excessive reductionism. The political level of analysis cannot simply be subsumed under the socio-economic: even at the most elementary level there is a difference in working-class life between capitalist economies virtually lacking a state social security system and those which have one, and the nature of this system may be equally important.

3) Some aspects of our subject are quantifiable, others are not, at any rate in comparable terms. The problem of labour history (as of any other social history) is how to combine different kinds of quantification with qualitative statements. Some time ago a team of Swedish workers, who are preparing an ambitious and comprehensive study of the working class in nineteenth-century Stockholm, put this problem to me concretely. They said: We are producing a series of quantitative studies of everything for which material is available, from demography, family reconstitution, crime, prostitution, wages and economic fluctuations to strikes, riots and labour organization. But how can we fit into this picture what it was actually *like* to be a bricklayer in nineteenth-century Stockholm? What workers thought and felt and why? In other words, how can we find a common denominator for what one

might call labour history as E.P. Thompson writes it and as Stephan Thernstrom writes it? All except those most brainwashed by the dream of being some kind of retrospective 'behavioural scientists' are aware of the problem, but can we say that it has been adequately solved?

Clearly the solution is to some extent a matter of scale. If we have as much scope as, say, a French state doctoral thesis, we can do both, as Rolande Trempé has shown in her magnificent study of the miners of Carmaux.[8] But probably the days of the academic blue whales are numbered and works on the scale of this, or of Edward Thompson's great book, will in future necessarily be the work of teams. And teams by the nature of their work tend to break up rather than synthesize research. (The problem is particularly acute for comparative studies.) But even if in the future there may be a greater division betwen researchers and synthesizers, the difficulty will not disappear. Perhaps it is an essential difficulty of all history and all historians. It is about human beings, and we cannot abstract from their humanity.

These remarks are moderately platitudinous, but perhaps there is room for an occasional reassertion of platitudes, because they are easily forgotten. Let me conclude with yet another. Labour history, like all the social sciences, is concerned with changing as well as with interpreting the world. (If they were not, economics would be merely a sub-branch of mathematics.) Now there are two things to be said about the relation between interpreting and changing the world. In the first place, the interpretation must be objectively valid, whether or not it suits us, or rather it must be communicable to anyone. There is no such thing as a labour history which can only be written or understood by manual workers, any more than – I am sorry this has to be said – there is an Irish, black or chicano history which is only valid when written by Irishmen, blacks or chicanos, or accessible to them. That people who feel directly identified with it will load their own history with an emotional weight which others do not find there is quite another question; itself also distinct from the fact that they will be more tempted to misread it. The history of the miracle-working practices of the kings of France and England will have a meaning for a French legitimist or a British Jacobite which it cannot have for us, but the late Marc Bloch who wrote it cannot be criticized because he was a French republican but only, if at all, because he got it wrong.

In the second place, and more importantly, we ought to know what we mean by changing the world. The wrong kind of social scientists, including de facto labour historians, have tried to change the world in a bad way, as witness Vietnam, where a lot of policy was based on certain theories about the nature of urbanization, or the heavily-financed American attempts in the 1950s to break up one form of labour movement in numerous countries and substitute others. Were these bad because the theories were wrong, or were the defects of the theories due to the desire to implement bad policies, or both? At all events, there was and is a direct relation between academic theory and policy intentions. It is easy to see this when we have no sympathy for either the theories or the policies, and especially when the results are as horrifying as in Southeast Asia. It is less easy to detect the analogous dangers in our own interpretations. Yet they exist, even though obscured by our own bias and the autonomous operations of the academic mechanism in which we are enmeshed. In what ways and directions do we want to change the world, or do our researches imply changing it? Are we in danger of forgetting that the subject and the object of our researches are people? We ought not to be, since people – not 'labour' but real working men and women, though often ignorant, shortsighted and prejudiced men and women – is what our subject is about. For many of us the final object of our work is to create a world in which working people can make their own life and their own history, rather than to have it made for them by others, including academics.

(1974)

# 2: Notes on Class Consciousness

The title of this paper is taken from the well-known but largely unread book by George Lukács, *History and Class Consciousness*, a collection of studies published in 1923, strongly criticized within the Communist movement, and virtually unobtainable for some thirty or forty years thereafter. In fact, since no English version of it was in print until recently, it is still little more than a title to most people in this country.

I want to reflect, as a historian, on the nature and role of class consciousness in history, on the assumption that we are all agreed about one basic proposition: that social classes, class conflict and class consciousness exist and play a role in history. We may well disagree on what role they play, or on its importance, but for the sake of the present argument further general agreement is not necessary. Nevertheless, in fairness both to the subject and to the thinker whose name is so obviously associated with it, I ought perhaps to begin by explaining where my own reflections connect with Lukács's own extremely interesting argument (which is, of course, derived from Marx) and where they do not.

As most people with a moderate acquaintance with Marxism know, there is a certain ambiguity in Marx's treatment of social classes, which is perhaps due to the fact that he never wrote systematically about this subject. The manuscript of *Capital* breaks off at the very point where this systematic exposition was due to begin, so that Chapter 52 of Volume III of *Capital* on classes cannot even be considered an outline or torso. Elsewhere Marx used the term 'class' in two rather different senses, according to context. First, it could stand for those broad aggregates of people which can be classified together by an objective criterion - because they stand in a similar relationship to the means of production -

and more especially the groupings of exploiters and exploited which, for purely economic reasons, are found in all human societies beyond the primitive communal and, as Marx would argue, until the triumph of proletarian revolution. 'Class' is used in this sense in the celebrated opening passage of the *Communist Manifesto* ('The history of all hitherto existing society is the history of class struggles') and for the general purposes of what we might call Marx's macro-theory. I do not claim that this simple formulation exhausts the meaning of 'class' in the first sense of Marx's usage, but it will at least serve to distinguish it from the second sense, which introduces a subjective element into the concept of class – namely, *class consciousness*. For the purposes of the historian, i.e. the student of micro-history, or of history 'as it happened' (and of the present 'as it happens') as distinct from the general and rather abstract models of the historical transformations of societies, class and the problem of class consciousness are inseparable. Class in the full sense only comes into existence at the historical moment when classes begin to acquire consciousness of themselves as such. It is no accident that the *locus classicus* of Marx's discussion of class consciousness is a piece of contemporary history, dealing in years, months, or even weeks and days – namely, that work of genius, *The Eighteenth Brumaire of Louis Bonaparte.* The two senses of 'class' are not, of course, in conflict. Each has its place in Marx's thought.

Lukács's treatment, if I understand him correctly, starts with this duality. He distinguishes between the objective fact of class and the theoretical deductions from this which could be and/or which are drawn by men. But he makes a further distinction: between the *actual* ideas which men form about class, and which are the subject matter of historical study[1] and what he calls 'ascribed' (*zugerechnetes*) class consciousness. This consists of 'the ideas, sentiments, etc., which men in a given situation of life *would* have, *if they were able to grasp in its entirety* this situation, and the interests deriving from it, both as regards immediate action and as regards the structure of society which (would) correspond to those interests'.[2] In other words, it is what, let us say, an ideally rational bourgeois or proletarian would think. It is a theoretical construct, based on a theoretical model of society, and not an empirical generalization about what people actually think. Lukács further argues that in different classes the 'distance' between actual and ascribed class consciousness is larger or smaller, and may be so large as to constitute not only a difference of degree, but one of kind.

Lukács derives some very interesting ideas from this distinction, but these are not my concern here. I do not say that the historian *qua* historian must only be concerned with the actual facts. If he is a Marxist or indeed if he tries to answer any of the really significant questions about the historical transformations of society in any way, he must also have at the back of his mind a theoretical model of societies and transformations, and the contrast between actual and rational behaviour cannot but concern him, if only because he must be concerned with the historical effectiveness of the actions and ideas he studies, which – at least up to and including the era of bourgeois society – do not normally correspond to the intentions of the inviduals and organizations which undertake them or hold them. For instance, it is important to note – as Lukács and Marx did, incidentally – that the class consciousness of peasants is normally quite ineffective, except when organized and led by non-peasants with non-peasant ideas; and why this is so. Or it is important to note the divergence between the actual, i.e. observable class consciousness of proletarians, which is programmatically rather modest, and the kind of wider class consciousness not merely 'ascribable' (in the Lukácsian sense) to them, but actually embodied in the working class through the socialist labour movements which this class developed. However, though historians cannot overlook such matters, they are naturally more concerned professionally with what actually happened (including what might under specified circumstances have happened), than they are with what ought really to happen. I shall therefore leave aside much of Lukács's discussion as irrelevant to my purpose, which is the rather modest one of the historian.

The first point I wish to make is one which was also made by both Marx and Lukács. While classes in the objective sense can be said to have existed ever since the break-up of a society based essentially on kinship, class consciousness is a phenomenon of the modern industrial era. This is familiar to historians, who have often traced the transition from the pre-industrial concept of 'rank' or 'estate' to the modern one of 'class', from such terms as 'the populace' or 'the labouring poor' to 'the proletariat' or 'the working class' (via the intermediate 'the working classes'), and the, historically slightly earlier, formation of such terms as 'middle class' or 'bourgeoisie' out of the old 'middle rank(s) of society'. In Western Europe this change occurred roughly in the first half of the nineteenth century, probably before 1830-40. Why is class consciousness so late to emerge?

In my view Lukács's argument is persuasive. He points out that economically speaking all precapitalist societies have incomparably less cohesion as a single entity than the capitalist economy. Their various parts are far more independent of one another, their mutual economic dependence far less. The smaller the role of commodity exchange in an economy, the more parts of society are either economically self-sufficient (like the parts of the rural economy) or have no particular economic function except perhaps parasitic consumption (as in classical antiquity), the more distant, indirect, 'unreal' are the links between what people actually experience as economy, polity or society, and what actually constitutes the wider economic, political, etc. framework within which they operate.[3]

Contrariwise, one might add, the relatively few and numerically small strata whose actual experience coincides with this larger framework may develop something like a class consciousness much sooner than the rest. This is true, for instance, of nobility and gentry, who are few in number, interrelated, and who function in part through their direct relationship to institutions which express or symbolize society as a whole – such as king, the court, parliament, etc. I note in passing that some historians have used this phenomenon as an argument against Marxist interpretations of class and class struggles in history. As will be evident, it is in fact specifically provided for in Marxist analysis.

In other words, under capitalism class is an immediate and in some sense a directly *experienced* historical reality, whereas in pre-capitalist epochs it may merely be an analytical construct which makes sense of a complex of facts otherwise inexplicable. This distinction must not, of course, be confused with the more familiar Marxist proposition that in the course of capitalist development class structure is simplified and polarized until, in extreme cases such as Britain at some periods, one can operate in practice with a simple two-class system of 'middle class' and 'working class'. This may also be true, but that is part of another line of thought. Incidentally, it does not imply, and Marx never suggested that it implied, a perfect homogeneity of each class. For certain purposes we need not trouble about their internal heterogeneities, as, for instance, when defining certain crucial relations between classes, such as that between employers and workers. For other purposes we cannot leave them out of account. Neither Marx nor Engels neglected the social complexities, stratifications, etc., within classes in their directly historical writings or their analyses of contemporary politics. However, this is by the way.

If we try to look at the consciousness of social strata in the pre-capitalist epochs, we therefore find a situation of some complexity. At the top we have groups such as the high aristocracy which come close to class consciousness on the modern scale, i.e. on what, using an anachronism, we might call the 'national' scale (the scale of the large state), or even in some respects the international scale. However, it is highly likely that even in such cases of 'class consciousness' the criterion of self-definition will be primarily non-economic, whereas in modern classes it is primarily economic. It may be impossible to be a noble without holding land and dominating peasants, and abstaining from manual labour, but these characteristics could not be enough to define a noble to the satisfaction of a medieval society. This would require also kinship ('blood'), special legal status and privileges, a special relationship to the king, or various others.

At the bottom of the social hierarchy, on the other hand, the criteria of social definition are either too narrow or too global for class consciousness. In one sense they may be entirely localized, since the village community, the district, or some other limited area is in fact the only *real* society and economy that matters, the rest of the world making only remote and occasional incursions into it. So far as men living in such circumstances are concerned, the man from the next valley may not be merely be a foreigner, but an enemy, however similar his social situation. Political programmes and perspectives are by definition localized. I was once told by a political organizer in Latin America who worked among Indians: 'It is no use telling them the tiller has a right to the soil. What they understand is only this: "You have a right to this piece of land which belonged to your community in your grandfather's day and which has since been stolen from you by the landlords. Now you can claim it back."' Yet in another sense these criteria may be so general and universal as to exclude any properly social self-classification. Peasants may be so convinced that all the world, except for a marginal few, consists of them, that they may merely define themselves as 'people' or (as in Russian language) 'Christians'. (This leads to unconscious historical ironies, such as that of the revolutionary atheist libertarian leader in Andalusia who told his defeated comrades, 'Every Christian had better hide in the hills' or the Red Army sergeant who was overheard during the last war addressing his platoon as 'True Believers'.) Or else they may simply define themselves as 'countrymen' against the cities (*campesinos, contadinos, paysans*). One might argue that the well-known affinity of peasants for millennial or messianic movements reflects this social reality. The unit of their organized action is either the parish pump or the universe. There is no in between.

Once again confusion must be avoided. What I have been talking about is the absence of a specific class consciousness. This is *not* the same as that low degree of class consciousness which Marx and other observers have noted, e.g. among the peasantry in the capitalist era. Marx ascribed this, at any rate in the case of nineteenth-century France, to the fact that being a peasant implied being exactly like a great many other peasants, but lacking mutual economic relationships with them.[4] Each peasant household is, economically speaking, largely isolated from the others. This may well be true under capitalist conditions, and it may help to distinguish peasants as a class from workers as a class, for concentration in groups of mutual co-operation is the basic social reality of proletarian existence. Marx's argument suggests, in my view correctly and fruitfully, that there are degrees of class cohesion. As Theodore Shanin once put it,[5] the peasantry is a 'class of low classness', and conversely one might say that the industrial proletariat is a class of extremely high 'classness'. (It is, after all, the only class which has developed genuine political mass movements held together specifically and primarily by class consciousness, e.g. as 'parties of the working class' – Labour parties, *Partis Ouvriers*, etc.)

However, the point I have noted about pre-capitalist societies is not this, but a different one. In such societies, it may be suggested, the social consciousness of the 'lower ranks' or subaltern classes will be fragmented into local or other segments even when their social reality is one of economic and social co-operation and mutual aid, as is the case in several kinds of village community. There will frequently be not high or low 'classness', but, in the sense of consciousness, no 'classness' at all, beyond the miniature scale. Alternatively, it may be suggested, the unity felt by the subaltern groups will be so global as to go beyond class and state. There will not be peasants, but 'people' or 'countrymen'; there will be not workers, but an indiscriminate 'common people' or 'labouring poor', distinguished from the rich merely by poverty, from the idle (whether rich or poor) by the compulsion to live by the sweat of their brow, and from the powerful by the unspoken or explicit corollary of weakness and helplessness.

Between the top and the bottom of the pre-industrial social hierarchies, we find a conglomerate of local, sectional and other groups, each with its multiple horizons, and far too complex for cursory analysis, or for that matter for more than the rarest common action on the 'national' scale. Within a locality, such as a city state, these may in fact be profitably analysed in terms of class and class struggles, as indeed contemporaries and historians have habitually done from the days of the ancient Greek cities. However, even here the realities of socio-economic stratification are likely to be overlaid, in the minds of men, by the non-economic – e.g. the legal – classifications which tend to prevail in such societies. This is obvious where the new reality of a society divided frankly by economics comes into conflict with the old models of an hierarchically stratified society, the reality of socio-economic transformation with the ideal of socio-economic fixity. Then we can see the conflicting criteria of social consciousness locked in battle, e.g. the declining corporate or guild consciousness of journeymen craftsmen and the rising class consciousness of proletarians, skilled or otherwise. How far such consciousness of status (which is, of course, itself economic, insofar as legal or quasi-legal privilege implies economic advantage) persists or can revive under modern capitalism is an interesting subject for enquiry, which I cannot pursue. Lukács has a few suggestive observations on this point, to which I draw your attention.[6]

Can we therefore say that class consciousness is absent from pre-capitalist societies? Not entirely, for even if we leave aside the history of small and locally enclosed communities such as city states, and the special case of ruling classes, we encounter two types of social movement which plainly operate on a more than local and less then ecumenical scale. These are, first, those of the 'common people' or 'labouring poor' against the 'top people' ('When Adam delved and Eve span, who was then the gentleman?') and, second, the phenomenon of peasant wars, sometimes actually recognized and named as such by contemporaries. The absence of class consciousness in the modern sense does not imply the absence of classes and class conflict. But it is evident that in the modern economy this changes quite fundamentally.

How? Let me begin with a general but very significant observation. The scale of modern class consciousness is wider than in the past, but it is essentially 'national' and not global: that is to say it operates within the framework of the territorial states which, in spite of the marked development of a single interdependent world economy, have remained to this day the main units of economic development. In this sense our situation is still analogous to that of pre-capitalist societies though on a higher level. The decisive aspects of economic reality may be global, but the *palpable*, the experienced economic reality, the things which directly and obviously affect the lives and livelihoods of people, are those of Britain, the United States, France, etc. It is not impossible that we may today be entering the era of a directly global economy. Some numerically small strata of the population do indeed already function internationally, subject to linguistic limitations, as, for instance, scientists and some other types of academics, a fact both expressed and symbolized by their rapid movement between jobs in different parts of the world. However, for most people this is not yet the case, and indeed in important ways the increasing management of the economy and of social affairs by governments has intensified the national character of social consciousness. To this extent global classes are still the same sort of theoretical constructs as they were in pre-capitalist days, except at rare moments of global revolutionary ferment. The real and effective classes are national. The links of 'international solidarity' between French and British workers, or even between their socialist movements, are far more tenuous than the links which bind British workers to one another.

Within these limits, what of the consciousness of the different classes? I do not want to go through the list of the classes and strata which historians and sociologists might or might not agree to recognize as the major ones. Instead, I wish to draw your attention to two aspects of the problem.

The first is the question of the relation between class consciousness and socio-economic reality. There are 'class' slogans and programmes which have very little chance of realization, because they run dead against the current of history, and others which are more practicable, because they run with it. Peasant movements and those of the classical petty bourgeoisie of small artisans, shopkeepers, petty entrepreneurs, etc., belong to the first kind. Politically these strata may be extremely formidable, because of their numerical strength or for other reasons, but historically they are inevitable victims, even when they ensure the victory of whatever cause they attach themselves to. At most they may become powerful sectional vested interests of negation, and even these have rather limited strength in countries where the dominant economic or political forces are extremely dynamic. The immense political strength of the North American farmers and small towns has not significantly slowed down the decline of either the farmers as a class, or the economic concentration against which the Populists fought so strenuously. The Nazis, who were to borne to power on the mass mobilization of such strata, and some of whom actually tried to some extent to realize their programme, turned out to be a régime of monopolist and state capitalism, not because they set out to be, but because the programme of the 'little man' was simply a non-starter. If the socialist perspectives of the working-class movement are excluded, then the only alternative in western industrial states is a régime of big business-cum-big government.

The relation between peasant movements and the régimes they have brought to power in the twentieth century is analogous. These revolutions, as Eric Wolf has pointed out, have been victorious primarily because they have mobilized the peasantry, and above all the most traditionally-minded strata of the peasantry.[7] Yet the actual social outcome of these transformations has been very different from the aspirations of the peasants who made them possible, even when they received the land. History has more than confirmed the Marxists against the Narodniks: post-revolutionary systems have not been constructed on the foundations of the pre-capitalist village communities, but on its ruins. (However, it is only fair to add that they confirmed the Narodniks against some of the Marxists on another point: the most effective rural revolutionaries have been neither the proto-capitalist *kulaks* nor the proletarianized village labourers, but the middle peasantry.)

More interesting than such cases of what might be called blind-alley class consciousness is the situation of classes whose relation to social reality changes. The case of the bourgeoisie is both instructive and familiar. Around, say, 1860, bourgeois class consciousness, even in an unsophisticated form, did in fact reflect and – at a very superficial level – explain the reality of bourgeois society. In 1960 this was plainly not so any longer, even though our society can still be described as capitalist. We can still read the sort of opinions which every good Liberal *paterfamilias* took for granted at the time Lincoln was assassinated, mostly in the leader columns of the *Daily Telegraph* and the speeches of a few back-bench Conservative MPs.* They are indeed still taken for granted in good suburban homes. It is patent that today these views have about as much relation to reality as the speeches of William Jennings Bryan about the Bible. Conversely, it is today evident that the pure programme of nineteenth-century economic liberalism, as put forward, say, in the Presidential campaign of Barry Goldwater in 1964, is as un-realizable as the peasant or petty-bourgeois utopias. The difference between them is that the Goldwater ideology did once serve to transform the world economy, but no longer does so, whereas the other ideologies of the 'little men' never did. In brief, the develop-ment of capitalism has left its former carrier, the bourgeoisie, be-hind. The contradiction between the social nature of production and the private nature of appropriation in this system has always existed, but was (economically speaking) secondary up to a certain point. Unrestricted competitive private enterprise by owner-man-aged family firms and state abstention was not merely an ideal, or even a social reality, but at a certain stage the most effective model for the rapid economic growth of industrial economies. Today the contradiction is dramatic and obvious. The capitalism of vast corporations intertwined with vast states remains a system of private appropriation, and its basic problems arise from this fact. However, even in its ordinary business operations it finds the economic liberalism of the nineteenth century quite irrelevant, and the class which carried it, the classical bourgeoisie, unnecessary.

The point I wish to make is this. Some forms of class conscious-ness, and the ideologies based on them, are, as it were, in tune with historical development, and others not. Some, having once been in tune, cease to be. Who, if any, are today the rising classes whose

---

* Since this was written such backwoodsmen have formed governments in both the United States and Britain.

consciousness and ideology point to the future? The question is important not only in political terms, but (if we follow Marx) for our understanding of epistemology, at least in the social sciences. I cannot, however, pursue it further here.

The second aspect I want to discuss concerns the relation between class consciousness and organization. Let me begin with some obvious historic differences between bourgeois or 'middle-class' and working-class consciousnesss. Bourgeois movements were based on a very powerful class consciousness. In fact, we can probably still say that the class struggle is normally fought or felt with much greater or more consistent bitterness on the bourgeois side of the front (where the menace of revolution is the dominant sentiment) than on the proletarian side (where hope, a civilized emotion, is at least as important as hatred). However, they were rarely *explicit* class movements. The few parties which have called themselves specifically 'middle-class' parties, or by some similar title, are normally pressure groups for particular and generally modest purposes, such as keeping down rates and taxes. The bourgeois movements waved liberal, conservative, or other ideological banners, but claimed to be socially classless or all-embracing even when they were visibly not. Proletarian movements, on the other hand, are based on explicit class consciousness and class cohesion. At the same time bourgeois movements were organized much more loosely and informally, often apparently for limited purposes, and involved much less loyalty and discipline than working-class ones, though in actual fact their political perspectives might be very ambitious. In this respect the contrast between the Anti-Corn Law League, the prototype as it were of bourgeois-class movements, and the Chartists, the prototype of mass-proletarian ones, is instructive.

As we have noted, the difference is not necessarily in the scope of the political objectives pursued. Both may be equally ambitious in so far as they aimed at the overthrow of one kind of society and its replacement by another. The difference may lie in the nature of the social experience of the classes or strata, their composition, and their social function. This point could be formulated in various ways. The bourgeoisie or 'upper middle class' was or is an élite group of cadres, not because its members are specially selected for ability or enterprise (as they always felt sure they were), but because it consists essentially of people who are, at least potentially, in positions of command or influence, however local; of people who can make things happen as individuals or in small numbers. (This statement does not apply to the petty bourgeoisie or lower middle class as a group.) The characteristic 'campaign' of the modern British professional strata – against the location of an airport, the routing of a motorway, or some other piece of administrative steam-rollering – is effective out of all proportion to the number of persons involved in it for this reason. On the other hand, the working class, like the peasantry, consists almost by definition of people who cannot make things happen except collectively, though, unlike peasants, their experience of labour demonstrates every day that they must act collectively or not at all. But even their collective action requires structure and leadership to be effective. Without a formal organization for action, except under certain circumstances at the place of work, they are unlikely to be effective; without one which is capable of exercising hegemony (to use Gramsci's phrase), they will remain as subaltern as the common people of the pre-industrial past. The fact that history may, as Marxists argue, have cast them as the grave-diggers of an old and the foundation of a new society (although this requires some rethinking or at least reformulation) does not change this characteristic of their social existence here and now. In other words, bourgeois or middle-class movements can operate as 'stage armies of the good'; proletarian ones can only operate as real armies with real generals and staffs.

The matter may be put another way. Each class has two levels of aspiration, at least until it becomes politically victorious: the immediate, day-by-day specific demands and the more general demand for the kind of society which suits it. (Once it is victorious this second demand turns into conservatism.) There may, of course, be conflicts between these two levels of aspiration, as when sections of the nineteenth-century bourgeoisie, whose general demand was for government abstention from economic interference, found themselves appealing to government for specific aid and protection. In the case of a class like the bourgeoisie both these levels of aspirations can be pursued with only relatively loose or *ad hoc* kinds of organization, though not without a general ideology to hold them together, such as economic liberalism. Even the nineteenth-century class parties of liberalism were not mass parties or movements (except insofar as they appealed to the lower orders), but coalitions of notables, of influential individuals or small groups.*

On the other hand, working-class consciousness at both levels implies formal organization; and organization which is itself the carrier of class ideology, which without it would be little more than a complex of informal habits and practices. The organization (the 'union', 'party' or 'movement') thus becomes an extension of the individual worker's personality, which it supplements and completes. When working-class militants or party supporters, faced with some novel political situation, refuse to express their own opinion and send visiting journalists to 'the union' (or whatever else the title of the organization may be), it expresses not the abdication of their private judgement before some superior authority's, but the assumption that the 'union's' words are their words; they are what they would say if they had the private capacity to say it.†

Nevertheless, the types of consciousness and organization which correspond to each of the two levels are normally distinct, though sometimes linked or combined. The lower level is represented by what Lenin called (with his usual sharp and realistic eye for social realities) 'trade union consciousness', the higher by 'socialist consciousness' (or possibly, but much more rarely, some other consciousness which envisages the total transformation of society). The former is (as Lenin also observed) the more spontaneously generated, but also the more limited. Without the latter the class consciousness of the working class is incomplete, historically speaking, and its very presence as a class may, as in the USA, be – quite mistakenly – questioned. Without either, the workers may, for political purposes, be completely negligible, indeed 'invisible', like the very substantial mass of 'Tory working men' who have always existed in Britain, without affecting, in more than the most fleeting

---

*Once again, this does not apply to parties of the lower middle class, which tended and tend to be mass movements, though, reflecting the socio-economic isolation of the members of these strata, mass movements of a particular kind. Marx's prophetic insight into the relation of the French peasants with Napoleon III is relevant here: 'They cannot represent themselves, they must be represented. Their representative must at the same time appear as their master, as an authority over them.'

† The most striking instances of such identifications are normally found in the comparatively early stages of labour organization, before labour movements have become part of the official political system of operations, and at times or in places where the movement consists of a single organization which represents, i.e. literally 'stands for', the class.

and marginal way, the structure, policy and programme of the Conservative Party, which could not win a single election without them.

Once again the distinction between proletariat and peasants must be made. The latter, also a historically subaltern class, require even the most elementary class consciousness and organization on the national (i.e. the politically effective) scale to be brought to them from outside, whereas the more elementary forms of class consciousness, class action, and organization tend to develop spontaneously within the working class. The development of significant trade union movements is almost universal in societies of industrial capitalism (unless prevented by physical coercion). The development of 'labour' or socialist' parties has been so common in such societies that the infrequent cases where they have not developed (as in the United States) are commonly treated as in some sense exceptional, and requiring special explanation. This is not so with autonomous peasant movements and even less with so-called 'peasant parties', whose structure is in any case rather different from that of 'labour parties'. Proletarian movements have a built-in potential for hegemony, which peasant movements lack.

'Socialist consciousness' *through* organization is thus an essential complement of working-class consciousness. But it is neither automatic nor inevitable, and what is more, it is not class consciousness in the obvious sense in which spontaneous 'trade-unionist' consciousness is, whether in its moderate reformist or in its politically less stable and effective radical, even revolutionary 'syndicalist' form. And at this point the problem of class consciousness in history turns into an acute problem of twentieth-century politics. For the necessary mediation of organization implies a difference, and, with greater or smaller probability, a divergence, between 'class' and 'organization', i.e. on the political level, 'party'. The further we move from the elementary social units and situations in which class and organization mutually control one another – e.g. in the classic case, the socialist or communist union lodge in the mining village – and into the vast and complex area where the major decisions about society are taken, the greater the potential divergence. In the extreme case of what left-wing discussion has baptized 'substitutionism', the movement replaces the class, the party the movement, the apparatus of functionaries the party, the (formally elected) leadership the apparatus, and, in well-known historical examples the inspired general secretary or other leader of the central committee. The problems which arise out of this, to some extent, inevitable divergence affect the entire concept of the nature of socialism, though it may also be argued that, with the increasing irrelevance to contemporary capitalism of the old type of nineteenth-century entrepreneurial bourgeoisie, controlling significant quantities of the means of production *as individuals or families*, they may also be arising within the present system. They are problems, partly of the apparatus of administration, planning, executive and political decision, etc., which any complex modern society must possess, and especially one of economic and social planning and management under present circumstances (i.e. problems of 'bureaucracy'), and partly of the nature of societies and régimes arising out of the labour and socialist movements. These are not the same, though the loose and emotional usage of such terms as 'bureaucracy' in left-wing discussion tends to confuse them: they are congruent only where a formal bureaucracy is *ex officio* a ruling 'class' in the technical sense, as perhaps among the imperial Chinese scholar-gentry, or today among the senior managers of corporate capitalism, whose interest is one of ownership as well as salaried management.*

The crucial problem for socialists is that revolutionary socialist régimes, unlike bourgeois ones, arise not out of class, but out of the characteristic combination of class and organization. It is not the working class itself which takes power and exercises hegemony, but the working-class *movement* or *party*, and (short of taking an anarchist view) it is difficult to see how it could be otherwise. In this respect the historical development of the USSR has been quite logical, though not necessarily inevitable. The 'party' became the effective and formal ruling group, on the assumption that it 'stood

* A ruling group may or may not be bureaucratized, though in European history it has rarely been so; it may operate with or through a bureaucratized administrative system, as in twentieth-century Britain, or an unbureaucratized one, as in eighteenth-century Britain. The same, allowing for the different social status – ruling parties are not classes – may be true in socialist societies. The CPSU is bureaucratic, and operates through a very bureaucratized state and economic administration. The Maoist 'cultural revolution' has, if I understand it correctly, attempted to destroy the bureaucratization of the Chinese CP, but it is a fairly safe bet that the country continues to be administered by means of a bureaucratic system. It is not even impossible to discover examples of a bureaucratized ruling group with a non-bureaucratic, i.e. without an effective, administrative system, as perhaps in some ecclesiastical states of the past.

for' the working class. The systematic subordination of state to party has reflected this. In due course, equally logically, the party absorbed and assimilated the effective individual cadres of the new society as they emerged – its officers, administrators, executives, scientists, etc. – so that at a certain point of Soviet history success in almost any socially significant career implied the invitation to join it. (This did not imply that these 'functional' recruits acquired an equal possibility to form policy with the old members for whom politics was a career, but then there was an analogous difference in the bourgeoisie between those recognized as belonging to the ruling class and those within this body who belonged to the *governing* group.) The fact that the original social basis of the party, the small industrial proletariat of Tsarist Russia, was dispersed or destroyed during the Revolution and Civil War, obviously facilitated this evolution of the Communist Party. The fact that, after a generation of the new régime, the individual cadres of the new society were largely recruited from men and women of worker or peasant origins, who had made their career entirely in and through it, and only in a rapidly diminishing proportion from the members or children of former bourgeois and aristocratic families, whom the régime naturally tried to exclude, speeded the process up further. Nevertheless, it may be suggested that a process of this kind was implicit in the 'proletarian revolution', unless systematic countermeasures were taken.*

The moment when 'proletarian revolution' is successful is therefore the critical one. It is at this moment, when the formerly reasonable assumption of a virtual identity between class and organization opens the way to the subordination of the former to the latter, that 'substitutionism' becomes dangerous. So long as the organization continues to maintain its *automatic* general identity with the class, and denies the possibility of more than the most temporary and superficial divergences, the way to extreme abuses, up to and including Stalinism, lies wide open. Indeed, some degree of abuse is hardly to be avoided, for the organization is likely to assume that its views and actions represent the *real* views (or in Lukácsian terms, the 'ascribed' consciousness) of the class, and where the actual views of the class diverge from it these divergences are due

---

*I am not discussing the possible developments which might lead large numbers of the individual cadres, in particular historical circumstances, to prefer *not* to join the formal organizations of 'top people', i.e. the party.

to ignorance, lack of understanding, hostile infiltration, etc., and must be ignored if not suppressed. The stronger the concentration of party-cum-state power, the greater the temptation to ignore or suppress; and conversely, the weaker this concentration, the greater the temptation to strengthen it.

Hence problems of political democracy, of pluralist structures, freedom of expression, etc., become *more* important than before, a statement which does not imply that the solution of such problems must or should be those of bourgeois liberalism. To take an obvious example. If under socialist systems trade unions lose their old functions and strikes are outlawed, then, whatever the general justification and the possible overall gains for the workers, these have lost an essential means for influencing the conditions of their lives, and unless they acquire some other means for the purpose theirs is a net loss. The classical bourgeoisie could defend the equivalent of its 'trade-union-conscious' interests in various more or less informal ways, where they conflicted with the wider interests of the class as interpreted by governments. The working class, even in socialist systems, can do so only through organization, i.e. only through a political system of multiple organizations *or* through a single movement which makes itself sensitive to the views of its rank-and-file, i.e. through effective internal democracy.

But is this exclusively a problem of proletarian revolutions and socialist systems? As we have already noted in passing, similar problems are arising out of the changing structure of the modern capitalist economy itself. Increasingly the constitutional, legal, political and other devices by means of which people were traditionally supposed to ensure some influence over the shaping of their lives and their society – if only negative influence – are becoming ineffective. This is not so merely in the sense in which they have always been ineffective for the 'labouring poor' in any but a trivial manner, but in the sense that they are increasingly irrelevant to the actual machinery of technocratic and bureaucratized decision. 'Politics' are reduced to public relations and manipulations. Decisions as vital as war and peace not merely by-pass the official organs for them, but may be taken – by a handful of central bankers, by a president or prime minister with one or two backroom advisers, by an even less identifiable interlocking of technicians and executives – in ways which are not even formally open to political control. The classical machinery of nineteenth-century 'real' politics increasingly revolves in a void: the leading articles of the 'heavy' news-papers are read by back-bench MPs whose opinions are negligible or by ministers who are dispensable; and their respective speeches are only a little less insignificant than their private *démarches* with those who actually take decisions, assuming they can be identified. Even the members of 'the Establishment' (or ruling class) may as individuals be little more influential than the shareholders in whose interests capitalist firms are still (in legal theory) conducted. Increasingly the real members of the ruling class today are not so much real persons as organizations; not the Krupps or Rockefellers, but General Motors and IBM, not to mention the organization of government and the public sector, with whom they readily interchange executives.*

The political dimensions of class consciousness and especially the relation between members of the class and organizations are therefore rapidly changing. The problems of the relations of the proletariat with working-class states, or even the large-scale organizations of their movement under capitalism, are only a special case within a more general situation, which the imperatives of technology and large-scale public or corporate management have transformed. This observation should not be used merely to score debating points. Nothing is more futile and infuriating than pots calling kettles black and assuming that in so doing they have solved the problem of blackness. Classes continue and have consciousness. It is the practical expression of this consciousness which is today in question, given the changes in its historic context. But at this point the historian may fall silent, not without relief. His professional concern is not the present or future, though he ought to throw some light on it, but the past. What is likely to happen, and what we can or ought to do about it, cannot be discussed here.

(1971)

* At a lower level, it also seems that the difference between formally liberal-democratic and other political systems may be diminishing sharply. Neither President de Gaulle, whose constitution guaranteed him against excessive electoral or parliamentary interference, nor President Johnson, who was not so safeguarded, were significantly affected by the pressures recognized in liberal systems. Both were vulnerable only to quite different pressures, operating outside such systems.

# 3: Religion and the Rise of Socialism

The modern working-class socialist movement has developed with an overwhelmingly secular, indeed often a militantly anti-religious, ideology. The first condition of membership of the Communist League, even before Marx joined it, was 'freedom from all religion, practical independence from any church association or any ceremonies not required by civil law'.[1] Conversely, religio-political versions of socialism and communism have always been marginal and generally not very important phenomena: perhaps forerunners of the movement, like Wilhelm Weitling; perhaps on its eccentric fringes, where the vegetarians, the advocates of free love, and the other enthusiasts for what we would today call counter-culture and commune living flourished. There were indeed a few labour movements, notably the British, whose activists largely came from or passed through Protestant sectarianism and nonconformity, and some parts of which show an interesting confluence of religion and class struggle. But these movements also have the marks of archaism, and in any case, there was no important working-class Christian socialism, merely the standard socialism, elaborated by secular thinkers and translated into the familiar biblical terminology.[2]

Now, secularization appears strange at first sight, for in the world in which the modern labour movement was born, religion remained inseparable from the ideology of common people and provided the main language for its expression. We should expect the attempts to formulate new social programmes in religious terms to be at least as prominent as social heresies and radical sects had been in earlier centuries, and still were in many rural areas. Were not many workers villagers themselves or peasants' children? Would we not expect them to be open to archaic ideological arguments like that secretary of a Komsomol cell in the Soviet Russia of the 1920s, who was convinced by 'evangelists' that Christianity had been distorted by the priests for the sake of gain, and that the gospel was really socialism preached by Jesus, and who thereupon took his whole cell to church and read the gospel there?[3] Conversely, would we not expect men and women brought up in an atmosphere imbued with religion to show considerable resistance to movements so visibly, and often militantly, godless?

In fact, we do often find such mass resistance. The anti-Jacobin popular insurrectionaries of Naples who, we may recall, believed that 'the man who has bread and wine, must be a Jacobine' sang:

> Naples won't stay a republic
> Here's an end to equality.
> Here's an end to liberty
> Long live God and his Majesty.[4]

A major peasant war was waged in Mexico in the 1920s in the name of Christ the King against the godless city revolutionaries. And the universally free-thinking left in Moslem countries discovered, as Rodinson recalls, that 'attacks on religion were in general useless or even harmful'. They have often been tempted to make use of the ideology which they were attacking.[5] Yet even in the traditionalist peasant zones and among the traditionalist *menu peuple* of the ancient big cities, godless movements sometimes made dramatic progress: in the rural areas of Spain captured by the anarchists; in former Catholic-monarchist southern France after 1830; in Catholic Vienna after 1870. In short, religious ideology proved recessive, secular ideology dominant, even though once the labour and socialist movement had conquered the mass of those who did not seriously resist its secularism, it discovered the mass of those – mostly nonproletarians – who did, and rather effectively. The problem before us is why the movement itself tended generally to be committed to irreligion, and why the active or passive resistance of the masses to this irreligion was not stronger. This raises the wider problem of secularization in the modern world.

The process of secularization is as yet far from clearly understood. Its most obvious symptom or result is the decline in the (voluntary) membership of religious bodies and in participation in their rites and activities. We know something about this decline in quantitative terms, though only patchily for the nineteenth century, especially outside France. But quite apart from gaps in our information, what does it mean? Does the sometimes impressive fashion for civil marriages in parts of Victorian Britain tell us something about popular attitudes to religious rites of passage or merely about the technical difficulties of nonconformist marriages?[6] To take a more dramatic case: in France civil burial was plainly a major break with traditional Catholicism. Proudhon claimed that 'burial outside the Church is the symbol of social resurrection'.[7] That is, in spite of the ambivalence of the phrase, he saw it, in the manner of later militants, as a gesture of secularism. (But how far can we regard the desire for cremation as a deliberately secularist gesture, even though German Social-Democrats clearly saw it in this light?)[8] Yet the genesis of civil burial appears to have been more complex in early nineteenth-century Provence.[9] The Church refused religious burial to unbelievers as to other sinners. But in the eyes of the people, at this stage far from secularist, death in itself requires solemnization and every man has equal right to the religious ceremonies normally supplied by the Church. It was wrong of the Church to refuse this right on grounds of doctrine or morality – at least to respected members of the community.

Consequently, the people supported non-religious burial in the absence of religious ceremony, and thus the secular ritualization of what was to become a militantly anti-religious demonstration began in Provence. The initiative in secularization came from the Church which 'defended the modern position that Catholicism is one option among others, while its adversaries, ancestors of the modern secularist left, demanded that it provide a universal public service'. The popular attitude was not secular. It rather implied that 'the real religion was the cult of the dead, whereas the Church was a ceremonial machine, more particularly one designed to produce ritual funerals'. In fact, a crack opened in the traditional syncretism of popular religion and doctrinal Christianity into which the wedge of secularism could henceforth be inserted.

We need hardly add that secularists were quick to widen this crack. No social occasion radiated more powerful and solemn vibrations, and concentrated the mind more intensely on the human condition, than the ceremonials of death and its commemoration – especially the commemoration of leaders and martyrs. Even if some secular revolutionaries, like the Blanquists, had not systematically used the civil burial movement to get access to the Parisian working class, eventually developing the political cult of the dead into a flourishing revolutionary ritual,[10] the potential of death for collective manifestations, did not take much discovering. If death was no longer everyone's right but only of those approved by official religion, it could also express other ideological options, such as those of the motto of the Austrian social-democrats' Cremation Society 'The Flame': 'Proletarian in life, proletarian in death, and buried in the spirit of cultural progress'. Probably more than anything else, the emergence of secular ceremonials of death which could be associated with secular movements, allowed secularist labour and socialist movements to acquire the ritual dimension to which their rank-and-file was accustomed.

We should therefore beware of crude facts and statistics alone. What we require are indications of attitudes – for instance towards the major religious holidays, some of which survived secularization unscathed (perhaps, like Christmas, through conversion into private family festivals) while others, like the two spring festivals,[11] showed signs of ideological reinterpretation before turning into simple vacations. As so often in social history, new questions reveal or create their own sources. They may be qualitative, like Obelkevich's pioneer investigation of nineteenth-century Lincolnshire; or quantitative, like Vovelle's important analysis of Provençal wills and funeral inscriptions, or the study of onomastics, which has only just begun. Thus, Agulhon has made an interesting start by discovering that among the numerous social clubs of the Var in 1830–48 those with saints' names were already exceeded in number by those with secular names: generally not so much ideological or political as literary, humorous, absurd.[12] In short, the historian of this difficult subject must, for the time being, proceed with caution.

Still, membership of religious bodies and participation in rites must be a main indicator, whatever exactly it means. There is little doubt that from the middle or perhaps the late nineteenth-century religious practice declined everywhere, although there were occasional or localized recoveries in the zeal for religious vocations.[13] Even the British nonconformists, after a period of rapid growth from the mid-eighteenth century, lost ground relatively from the late nineteenth century before declining absolutely in the twentieth.[14] The extent of religious non-participation before the mid-nineteenth century is obscure, though in some areas it was substantial, as in Paris where by 1875, 12 per cent of children were unbaptized, and 12.6 per cent of marriages and 21 per cent of funerals nonreligious.[15] De-Christianization was patchy, with large variations in religious practice, though in the twentieth century even some of the most pious grew apathetic.[16]

The decline in religious practice should not be confused with formal conversion to 'unbelief', which always remained a minority phenomenon confined mainly to the political left for which it was a symbol of commitment. A substantial atheist minority is an almost certain sign of a strong local left-wing tradition, as in Emilia, in Solingen (with just under 14 per cent atheists in 1950), or in parts of The Netherlands.[17] The opposite is not necessarily true: in the Basso Mantovano, one of several regions in which agrarian class struggle has tended to de-Christianize the rural proletariat – Friesland, the Alemtejo, and Andalusia are others[18] – the Christian–Democrat Party did not even succeed in getting the vote of all practising Catholics.[19] However, the figures of official atheism, even when available, are generally below actual unbelief, as indicated by opinion surveys; the 1.6 per cent of Austrians declaring themselves non-religious in 1934 clearly do not represent the extent of unbelief in the notably atheist Austrian Socialist Party. We may note in passing that the period of most rapid growth for official atheism coincides with the heyday of the Second International, 1890–1914. The percentage of freethinkers in Denmark, The Netherlands, and Italy roughly doubled between 1900 and 1910, and more than trebled in Norway. (In absolute numbers it was large only in Italy and The Netherlands.[20])

A few generalizations about this decline can be made with confidence. It was invariably far more marked among men than among women, so that the degree of 'feminization' of religious rites provides an excellent indicator of the degree of religious indifference, but not of the progress of free thought. Men and women seem to have been converted to secularism together.[21] For whatever reason, it was probably earlier and more marked in cities, and more marked in large towns than in smaller ones.[22]

The question of working-class religion becomes confused, partly because the characteristic workers of proto-industrialization (hand-loom weavers, journeymen artisans, miners, etc.) were much given to religious excitement or heterodoxy, partly because much of industrialization took place in villages and small towns. Yet 'beyond any possible doubt'[23] workers in cities took less part in formal religious practice than others, and relative working-class indifference or irreligion is recorded by practically all enquiries at all dates.

Thus, in Spain, factory workers were at the bottom of the ranking table in both areas of high and of low religiosity.[24] In short, we can agree with the nineteenth-century clergymen who had no doubt that 'the introduction of a factory brings de-Christianization',[25] though this was not always true of the mine, until class consciousness took miners into movements associated with irreligion. Migration, normally from country to city, and contact with the city, led to a decline in religious practice, in certain cases even among the peasantry.[26]

This generalization amounts to little more than that in traditional societies religion forms part of the structures of both authority and community which are disrupted, destroyed, or transformed by the development of modern capitalism. As Allum shows, Neapolitan religiosity even today mirrors the failure of *Gesellschaft* to replace *Gemeinschaft*.[27] This change does not in itself produce a growth of secularism and rationalism among the masses, except to the extent that religion ceases to have the virtual monopoly of forming and communicating ideas among the common people. It does lose this monopoly, but, however historically inevitable, secularization is not spontaneous. It occurs both because of changes in the authority structure (e.g., the substitution of a bourgeois for a feudal state); by changes within community, society, and ways of life that bring secular languages of ideas closer to the common people (e.g., through literacy and secular writings); and through collective experiences that precipitate changes in popular ideology (e.g., revolutions). Where these do not occur the erosion of religion is not automatically accompanied by active scepticism.

Consider the possible centres of critical independence and alternative ideas within the ranks of the common people. There are always some potential centres of this kind, apart from those merely outside the structure of community and authority and therefore not likely to influence it: travelling people and other marginals. Thus, in eighteenth-century France there were the innkeepers (*cabaretiers*), the natural 'anti-curés of the village' because they were in competition for the same customers at the same time. Since Puritanism goes with temperance, they were not normally so significant in countries with a sectarian-radical tradition such as Britain, but very important for the socialist movement in both Germany and France. Twenty-seven per cent of Marxist (Guesdist) militants in Roubaix, and two-thirds of the local socialist counsellors in the mid-1890s were *cabaretiers*.[28] There were the wine-growers, so permanently associated with free thought that piety in these quarters caused surprise: 'The men of Sancerre', said one of Le Bras' clerical informants, 'used to be very fervent, even though they were wine-growers.'[29] Catholicism is undoubtedly weak in all major French wine-growing areas. We may read what we wish into this correlation, which does not, by the way, seem to hold good in other countries.

More generally, there were the artisans, notoriously independent of landlord control in the village,[30] and especially what Maitron called 'the sedentary crafts which allow a man to "philosophize" while he performs familiar tasks',[31] notably of course those well-known worker-intellectuals and dissidents, the shoemakers. We do not know when they exchanged religious speculation *à la* Jacob Boehme for atheism, but their interest in the natural sciences was already a joke in Metternich's Austria. And it was only natural that when such men were potential nuclei of the anti-establishment, they would be attracted to doctrines and movements specifically criticizing authority in the religious form that rather naturally seemed to them inseparable from its other forms. Sebastien Faure, speaking for all rank-and-file anarchists, reminds us that 'in society today authority takes three principal forms which produce three forms of coercion: (1) the political form: the state; (2) the economic form: capital; (3) the moral form: religion.'[32] Tom Paine, as we know, was by no means an atheist. It was not God but churches and religious institutions he regarded as 'engines of power' and devices attempting 'to terrify and enslave mankind, and monopolize power and profit'.[33] Still, the distinction was not very clear to many. Whether the activists and leaders of plebeian and labour movements were secularists or religious dissidents, they were almost by definition critics of the establishment in both its lay and its religious forms.

Yet we cannot simply treat such men and groups in isolation from the rest of society. Class is not merely a relationship between groups, it is also their coexistence within a social, cultural, and institutional framework set by those above. The world of the poor, however elaborate, self-contained, and separate, is a subaltern and therefore in some senses incomplete world, for it normally takes for granted the existence of the general framework of those who have hegemony, or at any rate its inability for most of the time to do much about it. It accepts their hegemony, even when it challenges some of its implications because, largely, it has to. Ideas, models, and situations in which action becomes possible tend to reach it from outside, if only because the initiative that changes conditions on a national scale comes from above or because the mechanisms for diffusing ideas are generated outside. Only in the nineteenth century did the working class itself generate, or become identified with, a potentially hegemonic force – the organized labour and socialist movement – with the potential, for instance, to transform itself into a system of national rule, as in the case of communist parties after revolutions. This is an historic novelty. Yet even this potential hegemony, though it rests, at least before the transfer of power, on the mobilization and active support of the masses, derives its ideology, its programmes, and strategies primarily from people and sources outside the world of the subaltern classes: from mostly bourgeois intellectuals like Marx and Engels, from German philosophy, British political economy, and French socialism. The reasons need not concern us here.

When we analyse the process of secularization, we must bear in mind both the significance of decisions from above, which change the scenery among which the subaltern classes form their opinions; the role of the elites in the hegemonic system; and the role of hegemonic culture and ideology. Thus secularization in Sesto Fiorentino, the first socialist commune in Tuscany, depended closely on national unification – the creation of the national state, in which the mass of the inhabitants was not much actively involved. As its historian, the late Ernesto Ragionieri, has put it:

The first approach to this change came from the liberal bourgeoisie. Though it did not impede the clergy in its ideological control over the popular classes, it could hardly not undermine it. Having constituted the national state and bourgeois state, the bourgeoisie could not help but provide an initial and decisive stimulus for the disintegration of parochial life, whether deliberately or, more often, involuntarily.[34]

For instance, by the reinforcement of the autonomous authority of secular organizations such as the municipality, symbolized for example, by the new town hall and the transfer of the markets from the church square to a new square. In the mid-nineteenth century the priests of the Orléans diocese were in constant friction with such lay institutions, simply because these – though by no means secularist – resented Church interference in their affairs: with the municipalities, the musical societies, the Fire-Brigade.[35] Such bodies were, as it were, functionally anticlerical. Or to take a more dramatic example: secularization took a spectacular turn upwards in France during the years when anticlericalism dominated French politics – from 1880 on – and especially during the years that culminated in the separation of Church and State. In the diocese of Limoges – a notoriously de-Christianized area – there were only 2.5 per cent of non-baptized children, 5.75 per cent of civil burials, and 14 per cent of civil marriages in 1899. In 1907 there were 25 per cent of non-baptisms, 23 per cent of civil burials, and 48.5 per cent civil marriages, after which the figures settled down somewhat.[36] We may well argue that the Limousin was ready for de-Christianization; but it is evident that a series of national, not local, events precipitated the mass defection.

Again the influence of the elites is significant and may be decisive, particularly in the countryside, as Agulhon demonstrates very clearly for the Var. At a later stage the French bourgeoisie was largely re-Catholicized, but by then the class conflict and consciousness reinforced the anticlericalism of its workers. The influence of or deference to elites should not, however, be confused with the other reasons that drew plebeian and middle-class culture together.

More generally the popular classes fall under the influence of the hegemonic culture because it is in a sense the only culture that operates as such through literacy – the very construction of a standard national language belongs to the literate elite.[37] The very process of reading and schooling diffuses it, even unintentionally. The most traditional repertoire of popular literature inevitably contains thick deposits of upper-class origin, as in the Bibliothèque Bleue of the seventeenth and eighteenth centuries.[38] Menocchio, the village atheist of the sixteenth century, whose story has been brilliantly told by Carlo Ginzburg,[39] is interesting precisely because as a literate he could 'bring books into confrontation with the oral tradition in which he had grown up'. Books, especially the *Voyages of Mandeville*, Ginzburg begins, were for him primarily the catalyst of his own ideas drawn from the popular tradition. Yet in fact the most important popular function of books was not thus to fertilize a few lonely and original autodidacts, who are impressive but rarely influential. Most popular readers, like most readers of any class, are followers. I am far from claiming that this makes all high culture an agency of class propaganda; that books are, as it were, bourgeois by their very nature. Rather, popular ideas cannot be understood without recalling the hegemony of high culture. Take, for instance, the phenomenon which Ragionieri for his Tuscan village dates in the last decades of the nineteenth century and above all the first fifteen years of the twentieth: the practice of abandoning Catholic first names for secular ones, which has obvious ideological and political implications. True, the militants sometimes hung well-known political manifestos round their hapless children's necks: Spartacus, Galileo, Benito Mussolini or – to remind you of another particularly ironic case – Walt Whitman Rostow and Eugene V. Debs Rostow. But mainly they chose names from opera, drama, and literature: Rigoletto and Rigoletta, Aida, Tosca, Torquato, Dante. Significantly, high culture becomes the medium for the break with ancient tradition at the grass roots.

This possibility exists only because nineteenth-century bourgeois culture is, at least in theory, open to all, and indeed an invitation to be shared by all. The famous village freethinker Konrad Deubler in the remoteness of Goisern, Upper Austria, would not have had Shakespeare in his well-stocked bookcase if bourgeois culture had not insisted on translating him.[40] It was not only possible but inviting for men who shared the ideology of new times for which tradition was an obstacle – i.e., the values of the Enlightenment. To the extent that they shared with the bourgeoisie and the educated elites a common goal and a common adversary in 'reaction', 'privilege', and 'aristocracy' – in short, until the discovery that the employer was the worker's main adversary, and perhaps even beyond this point, this alliance remained strong, perhaps decisive. To cite the case of Deubler again: this radical village miller and later innkeeper was both the friend and correspondent of bourgeois-radical writers, scientists, and philosophers – the aged Feuerbach spent his holidays with him – the patron of the early saltworkers' organizations that soon became social-democrat, and the friend of the Kautskys. He thus confirms, incidentally, Agulhon's observation about the significance of the 'intermediate milieux (artisans, petty intellectuals), the intermediate status-groups (property-qualified and municipal electors), and the networks of intermediate influence (for instance, the activities of voluntary associations)'.[41]

Traditional peasants on the whole spurned the new ideology, not only because they were traditional, but because the new times – and those who were the carriers, like townsmen – appeared to bring nothing except trouble. One might even argue that women were less tempted by secularization, for the new bourgeois world was primarily male-dominated.[42] Conversely, workers, and especially skilled artisans, responded positively because tradition offered them only disruption and misery; because the new world was the only one they lived in; or because, in spite of everything, their hopes had to lie not in a return to some idealized model of a past, which had no place for people like themselves, but in the future.

The working classes were nonetheless interested in the new ideology not for itself, but only as part of a package that included the struggle for a better life – i.e., through something like the labour movement. Men did not become freethinkers but 'worker freethinkers'. Just so certain left-wing villages in Provence 'do not practise religion because they are Republicans. They claim that in some way it is impossible for them to be both for the Republic and for religion.'[43]

Ideologically, socialist and bourgeois rationalist ideas therefore converged, though for the mass of ordinary people these had to be mediated through political commitment, action, and organization. The two were linked not only through a common ideology, but through the belief underlying it – in progress, education, science, and the need to overcome a tradition that stood in the way of both personal and collective liberation. No doubt these meant divergent things in bourgeois and working-class minds: Jules Ferry, the anticlerical, thought of science and democracy as a pair of twins,[44] Marxists thought the same way about science and socialism, and anarchists, convinced that everything could be achieved 'with a pistol and an encyclopaedia',[45] included the immediate abolition of the state. All shared the confidence in science and enlightenment as against conservatives deeply suspicious of both; and all (notably Charles Darwin) shared a belief in the same science, about whose incompatibility with theology an American professor wrote a celebrated and massive book;[46] they shared the same faith in science, in print, and in education. English socialists, mainly from dissenting backgrounds, shared this attitude with the German social-democrats, all officially Marxist. Caxton, Gutenberg, and Darwin were among the great world liberators. Not for nothing was a non-socialist anticlerical work like Dodel's *Moses or Darwin* more widely read in German social-democratic libraries than anything by Marx or even Kautsky. It recurs in many a German worker's intellectual autobiography.[47]

To join a movement of emancipation – of self-liberation through class liberation – therefore implied a militant antitraditionalism, whether or not that movement was atheist in ideology. There is much less difference between the reading of the British and German labour militant about 1900 than one might suppose. Since movements sought to change personal lives and hopes here and now, as well as to achieve political and economic ends, it had to be so. Labour movements, whatever else they were, were also 'cultural revolutions' of this kind, and nowhere more so than among the rural anarchist labourers of Spain or in the villages of France and Italy. What was the effect of that which Agulhon rightly calls 'the relevation' of the Republic among the cork workers of the mountains behind the French Riviera? Among other things, a mass participation of women workers in politics; the refusal by the women to let their children learn the catechism; and that symptom of cultural revolution we have already noted in Sesto Fiorentino – the naming of children with secular and militant names.[48] So I would suggest that the rise in atheism, noticeable in so many places before 1914, was perhaps accelerated but not explained by such events as the separation of church and state in France. It was both the by-product and, so far as many of the militants were concerned, an essential content of the rise of the labour movement.

Conversely, the visible decline of organized religion in the mid-twentieth century also led to a slackening of militant anticlericalism on the left. Even in 1948 a French observer noted that 'declarations of faith in atheism, atheist behaviour, are disappearing in the milieux of the extreme left in the cities'. As the piety of right-wing zones declines to little more than the level of de-Christianized left-wing ones, left-wing ones abandon demonstrative non-baptism.[49] Religion and anti-religion cease to be the criteria of commitment. When God is dying, He can no longer be the great enemy of progress.

There had always been limits to secularist militancy, for practical politicians were not content to leave potential supporters with 'religious prejudices' or relics of ancient faith to the reactionaries.[50] Parties like the German SDP played down atheist propaganda, although without abandoning their rationalist convictions. For socialists the shift came, in theory, all the more easily since secularism for Marxists was not an end in itself; and they were rightly convinced that workers became rationalists not through godless propaganda as such, but through joining their class movement. Yet in fact, personal as well as social emancipation from tradition was what many militants got from joining the movement. Militant secularism grew from the grass roots where socialism, or especially anarchism, was seen not so much as a political programme than as a personal conversion and 'cultural revolution'. Faith was there to be destroyed on principle, not conciliated. That this intransigence sometimes isolated the activists did not matter.* More significant, militantly godless movements had no difficulty in gaining mass support both among the workers and in some rural areas, though by that very fact they left other regions and groups which resisted in the hands of those who waved the banners or truncheons of God.

Though irreligion might attract plebeian cadres, there is no evidence that in itself it had any special appeal to the masses. Moreover, though it may be argued that certain environments such as the big city inevitably tended to erode formal religious practices based on village and small-town community structure, much industrial development took place in small-scale communities far from unfavourable to religion, as is proved by the persistent tendency towards pietism and sects of many types of industrial outworkers, or even – although sometimes concealed by their massive adherence to godless labour movements – of miners.[51] In any case, even in the big city the constant influx of rural migrants should have counteracted de-Christianization, but clearly did so only momentarily. The argument that immigrants are de-Christianized by culture shock is so far unproven,[52] and remains doubtful, though the removal of the tight social control of the village has an obvious effect. Our problem is not so much the positive appeal of irreligion as the feeble resistance of religion. Admittedly, the greater the religious apathy or indifference of an environment, the less resistance we may expect to actively irreligious ideologies, though extremely apathetic groups, such as the lowest labouring and sub-proletarian strata, may by that very token be resistant to any ideology at all.

* Cf. a Belgian, answering the enquiry summarized by Poulat: 'Social revolutions are always made by a minority. Only afterwards will the masses understand.'

First, official, theological/church religion was always weak among the masses – as distinct from the unofficial ritual/magical religion which the churches either incorporated, accepted, or over-looked 'in order to prevent the formation of two religions'.[53] To become militant, this religion had to be once again welded to both the official Church – as the Catholic Church but not the Church of England succeeded in doing from the 1860s on – and to political resistance to parties that could be identified, among other things, with irreligion. This was not a spontaneous process, though historic tradition might facilitate it.[54] There are enough examples of pious, not to say superstitious or even classical populations voting for a 'godless' left – 40 per cent of people in Sicily and Sardinia in the polarized 1950s saw no incompatibility between Catholicism and communism[55] – for us to beware of simple equations. But we cannot assume that the sceptical and sometimes ferociously anti-clerical elements within this popular subreligion bring it closer to the secularists. The Sicilian proverb: 'Priests and friars: we go to mass and kick them in the kidneys'[56] has nothing to do with mod-ern rationalism.

Second, by the nineteenth century, in Western Europe at least, the religious ideology of revolt had already become recessive rather than dominant, perhaps because its communitarian (*gemeinschaft-lich*) ideal had increasingly little specific political relevance. Reli-gious revolt in defence of past against future, however revolu-tionary its implications, remains capable of mobilizing considerable rural masses, as with the Sanfedist, Carlist, or Cristero movements: but in the form of 'the good old religion'. Religio-ideological 're-formation' or dissidence, in the form mainly of sectarian growth, or specific religio-socialist bodies, can form and mobilize cadres, though their political attitude has nothing distinctively religious about it, but rarely masses.[57] The phenomenon of occasional mass revivalism is largely outside politics. Conversions to Protestantism in Catholic industrial society, though not absent,[58] are of minor importance. Religious socialism or communism is a marginal phen-omenon. Modern concepts may be translated into religious lang-uage ('Christ was the first socialist') to make them acceptable or comprehensible, but remain stubbornly modern. The most notable example of genuine religio-ideological recreations of society since the French Revolution have, like the Mormons, no links with the secular or any other left.

Third, the hold of traditional churches slackened as soon as (1) the community they embodied, and therefore the class relations within it, were disrupted,[59] and (2) when therefore religion could be identified with the rulers, exploiters, and oppressors, unless, in countries with a strong sectarian-radical tradition, dissidence took the form of sectarianism. That is how the Vienna artisans, famous in the 1850s for their piety, explained their defection in the 1890s.[60]

These very threats to the Church's position from a society identified with 'progress, liberalism, and modern civilization' and, increasingly, from loss of state power, led it into alliance with the political right, which automatically drove anyone on the political left into an alliance with anticlericalism and, in Catholic countries, irreligion. Even people without any prior commitment became hostile to the faith because it was hostile to their cause, or because their cause was hostile to it.[61]

Thus, by the nineteenth century, if once the social fabric on which traditional religion rested grew frayed, religion itself had little effective means for protecting itself against mass movements that happened to bring secularism with them, although history and – as with the Irish and Poles – national identity helped. Where such movements had no secularist colour, the question was simply not important. Though the religious origins and commitments of British labour activists have much interest for historians, there is no evidence that trade unionists or labour voters, unless disciplined Catholics, took much notice of whether their representatives were believers or agnostics. Wesley and Marx marked degrees of radicalism rather than attributes to God.

These tendencies are now receding into the past, at least in Christian countries. The Churches are left free to move left, for neither the right nor state support can any longer protect them against erosion. Some Christians may thus hope to retain or, more doubtfully, to regain the support of masses believed to be identified with the left. It is a surprising development. Conversely, parties of the Marxist left, seeking to widen their support, are more inclined to abandon their traditional identification with active irreligion. And yet whatever the political attitudes of religious people or bodies, religion remains mainly a conservative force – with a small *c*. Even the popular subreligion of the masses was always conservative, for it embodied the defence of custom – the way things had been done in the past. The strongest religion remains the old-time religion.

The tension between religion and progress persists where religion remains strong and where progress is believed to require those dramatic changes in personal behaviour and social values which the mass of people are unwilling to make – or at least unwilling to make when required by their leaders. Thus, irreligion and anticlericalism seem to be matters of life and death in countries launching upon rapid modernization as, in a sense, so many nineteenth-century bourgeoisies felt themselves to be doing: particularly so in countries in which progress comes through revolution, and governments feel themselves powerful enough to force the evident truth upon the more backward citizens. All the more so if their own activists have fought their way free from the darkness and superstition in which their fathers lived. In nineteenth-century Britain the most passionate secularists tended to come from the most strongly religious families.[62] There are no more ferocious destroyers of tradition than men and women – say, peasant cadres formed in some revolutionary army – who know the force of what they are trying to destroy, and hate it with both a personal and a social hatred.[63] The spirit of the anti-Church militant, hammer of tradition, may be dying in Western countries with the spirit of the Church militant. But there are places such as China in the 1960s and 1970s where it is still very much alive.

(1978)

# 4: What is the Workers' Country?

If it is wrong to assume that workers have no country, it is equally misleading to assume that they have only one, and that we know what it is. We talk of the French, German or Italian working classes, and in doing so we indicate, quite rightly, that much the most important forces defining any particular working class are those of the national economy of the state in which a worker lives, and the laws, institutions, practices and official culture of that state. An Irish labourer migrating to Boston, his brother who settled in Glasgow, and a third brother who went to Sydney would remain Irish, but become part of three very different working classes with different histories. At the same time, and as this example suggests, it is also wrong to assume that the members of such national working classes are or ever were homogeneous bodies of Frenchmen, Britons or Italians, or, even when they saw themselves as such, that they are not divided by other communal demarcations, or that they are *exclusively* identified with the state which defines their effective existence as a class and an organized movement. It is equally wrong to assume that such an identification is eternal and unchanging. These assumptions are based on the myths of modern nationalism, a nineteenth-century invention. Though they are not entirely fictitious, they are not much more realistic than the opposite assumption that national or communal identity are irrelevant to the proletariat.

No doubt it is possible to discover countries in which the working class is nationally homogeneous in this sense – perhaps in Iceland, with its 250,000 inhabitants – but for practical purposes such cases may be neglected. All national working classes tend to be heterogeneous, and with multiple identifications, though for certain purposes and at certain times some may loom larger than others. An Indian shop steward in Slough may see himself for one purpose as a member of the British working class (as distinct from his brother who remained in India), for another as a coloured person (as distinct from the whites), for another as an Indian (as distinct from the British or Pakistanis), for yet another as a Sikh (as distinct from Christians, Hindus or Muslims), as a Punjabi (as distinct from a Gujerati), probably also as someone from a particular area and village in the Punjab, and certainly as a member of a particular network of kinship. Of course some of these identifications, however important for everyday purposes (e.g. in arranging the marriage of sons and daughters), are politically rather subordinate.

Moreover, one identification does not exclude the others. The Andalusians, Basques and Catalans who fought Napoleon did so as Spaniards, without in the least losing the sense of the differences which separated them from each other. What is more, such identifications change over time, as well as with the context of action. Sicilian and Calabrian labourers went to America and became Americans, but in doing so they also came to see themselves – as they probably had not done before – as Italians who belonged, to some extent, not only to the old country but also to a nation whose members were scattered across the world from Argentina and Brazil to Australia. Conversely, workers who once saw themselves primarily as Belgians, in spite of talking two quite different and mutually incomprehensible languages, today identify themselves primarily as Flemings and French-speaking Walloons.

These multiple identifications give rise to something like a 'national' problem within working classes only when they seriously get in each other's way. So far as one can tell there was no serious national problem before 1914 in the mines of South Wales where English immigrants, English - and Welsh - speaking Welshmen, a handful of Spaniards and doubtless a few other minorities worked together, joining the South Wales Miners' Federation and supporting Labour. There was in the Ruhr, where a mass of immigrant Polish miners, separated from the Germans by language and from the freethinking Social Democratic Party by Catholicism, showed a marked reluctance to support the party of their class. Again, to take the extreme case of the United States, where the working class consisted largely of immigrants incapable initially of understanding either the language of the country or of other groups of immigrants: their national and linguistic differences undoubtedly made the formation of a working-class consciousness more difficult, though they did not entirely inhibit it, and certainly did not prevent the formation of a general political consciousness of the immigrant poor – the 'ethnic Americans' who, much as they fought with each other collectively formed the basis of the Democratic Party in the big cities. But they certainly created no major political problems for the country which officially welcomed them and was neutral about their religions. The very same people who in their home states – as Irishmen in the United Kingdom, as Poles in Russia and Germany, as Czechs in Austria – constituted a 'national problem' which threatened the political unity or even the existence of these states were of little more significance across the ocean than in the choice of candidates for municipal elections.

Indeed, the example of the Irish in Britain illustrates the same point. Most of them were both workers and, very consciously, Catholic and Irish. Until the twenty-six counties separated from the United Kingdom, most of them found a formula which combined national and class identification by supporting, or allying with, parties and movements which claimed to be in favour of both, or at any rate hostile to both. (Few Irish Nationalist candidates stood in Britain, and outside the Scotland division of Liverpool, none was elected.) Unions with a strong Irish tinge – the National Union of Dock Labourers was commonly known as 'the Irish union' – behaved much like other unions. No doubt this was facilitated by the fact that the movement which claimed to stand for 'the people' or the working class – Liberals, Labour and Socialists – opposed the oppression of Ireland, joined in protests against it, and indeed supported the Irish nationalist demand for Home Rule for a united Ireland. After Irish separation had been achieved, the bulk of the Catholic Irish in Britain, insofar as they organized and voted at all, undoubtedly gravitated to the parties of their class. Nor did the fact that they enjoyed dual political rights seem to create any major difficulties: even today Irishmen who vote Labour in Britain will not necessarily feel obliged to vote for a Labour or working-class party when they return to the Republic of Ireland.

The relatively smooth integration is all the more striking when we recall that at the grassroots anti-Catholic and anti-Irish sentiments were powerful and sometimes savage in Britain – and by no means only in Liverpool and Glasgow. Moreover, in the case of Ulster or British Orange workers, Protestant identification unquestionably cut across both class and national identification. Nevertheless, for the majority group among the Irish, perhaps just because they were so evidently a majority, the double identification as Irish and (when in Britain) British workers, seems to have been relatively unproblematic.*

Thus practically all so-called 'national' working classes consist of a jig-saw of heterogeneous groups. On the one hand, historical development has tended to weld these together into more or less nation-wide blocks, so that differences between Kerrymen and Tipperary men are subordinated to a general Irishness (except, perhaps, for purposes of sporting contests), or between Catholic and Lutheran Germans into a general German-ness (except for purposes of electoral identification). Such nation-wide 'national consciousness' is historically recent, though some examples (perhaps 'Englishness') date back rather longer. But on the other hand the mobility and the shifting of people in contemporary society, which may be essentially described as a world on the move, create new bonds and new frictions breaking up these blocks.

Thus mass migration into the mines of South Wales, mainly from England, created a strongly Welsh working class, but one which ceased to speak Welsh, thus intensifying the silent tensions between the English-speaking majority of the Welsh and the regionally concentrated and diminishing Welsh-speaking minority. A much smaller migration into North Wales - but one not absorbed into the fabric of the local social structure - has, as we know, produced considerable friction between the Welsh and the English in that region, and, in some parts, a transfer of political loyalties from the all-British Labour Party (inheritor of the all-British Liberal Party) to Plaid Cymru. Similarly, even without migration, changes in the economy, in society and in politics may disturb the established stable pattern of relations between different groups, with unpredictable and sometimes catastrophic results. We have seen this happen in recent years in Cyprus, where Greeks and Turks had long co-existed, and in the Lebanon, a notorious jig-saw puzzle of Maronite, Orthodox and variously Catholic Christians, Sunni and Shiite Muslim, Arabs, Armenians, Druzes and various others.

*The problem of the Republican militants in Britain who saw or see themselves exclusively as anti-British Irish, as of the 'spoiled Catholic' Irish, often on the most militant wing of British labour movements, would need to be considered separately. But, at least since the 1880s, this problem concerns numerically small minorities.

Still, the major disturbances have almost certainly come from mass mobility, our economic and social transformations implying mass migration within and between states. Neither capitalist nor socialist industrialization is conceivable without it. And this produces the special problems of 'strangers' or 'foreigners' – a problem already created in many regions by pre-capitalist patterns of settlement and colonization. This clearly affects the working class very directly.

There are two aspects to the intermingling of different communities, of which the relation between 'natives' and immigrants is a particularly clear example.

First, there is the fourfold pattern of the balance between the two. We may neglect case (a), a country without working-class emigration or immigration as too rare to be significant. Case (b), a country with little emigration but significant immigration, is comparatively rare, though France might fit the bill. The French, while receiving masses of foreign workers since industrialization, have never moved outside their frontiers themselves. Case (c) is rather more common: countries with little immigration but a good deal of emigration: in the nineteenth century Norway and the territory of the present Republic of Ireland were obvious examples. Case (d), which is probably the most common in industrial Europe, consists of countries with both substantial emigration and immigration – as in nineteenth-century Britain and Germany. Both immigration and emigration have a bearing on the history of national working classes for, as every Irishman knows, emigration does not snap the links between the exiles and the home country, not least in the history of its labour movement. Tranmael, the leader of the Norwegian labour movement during and after World War I, had been in the Industrial Workers of the World in the United States, whither the Norwegians migrated. Tom Mann migrated to Australia and returned to Britain. As for the Irish movement, its history is filled with returned emigrants: Davitt, Larkin, Connolly.

The second aspect concerns the complexity of the pattern of migration and the distribution of migrant groups. Emigrants from one state or national group may either flow in a single stream to one region and nowhere else, as the peasant from the Creuse in central France moved as building labourers to Paris, or they may fan out to produce a temporary or permanent diaspora which may be worldwide. Wherever there was hard-rock mining on the globe in the nineteenth century, groups of Cornishmen were to be found.

The converse of this phenomenon is even more relevant for our purposes.

In some regions or countries, the game of 'foreigners' has only two players: Poles and Germans in the Ruhr, Basques and Spaniards in the Basque country. More commonly the working class contains an immigrant sector composed of a variety of 'strangers' of different kinds, divided among themselves as well as separated from the natives, and in the extreme case the working class is predominantly composed of immigrants, as in the United States, Argentina and Brazil during the major period of mass migration before 1914. Yet, whether the number of players in the game is greater or smaller, the pattern which usually develops is one of occupational specialization, or a sort of national stratification.

Thus in 1914 there were few mines in the Ruhr which did not have a majority of Polish miners, and even today everyone in Britain expects construction sites to be full of Irishmen. What tends to set one national or religious or racial group of workers against another, is not so much occupational specialization in itself, as the tendency for one group to occupy, and seek to monopolize, the more highly skilled, better paid and more desirable jobs. Such divisions and stratifications occur even in nationally homogeneous working classes, but it is certain that they are enormously exacerbated when they coincide with divisions of language, colour, religion or nationality. Belfast is an unhappy and obvious case in point.

Yet communal differences alone have not prevented labour movements from organizing workers successfully across such divisions. A powerful Social Democratic Party in Vienna united Czech and German workers. Before 1914 the differences between Flemish and Walloon workers in Belgium were politically so insignificant that a standard work on socialism in Belgium by two leaders of the Labour Party there did not bother to so much as mention the 'Flemish question'. Today, when all Belgian parties are linguistically divided, the motto 'Workers of all Lands, Unite' incised in Flemish on the Labour Hall in Ghent remains as a melancholy reminder of this lost unity. Highly unified working classes with a powerful class consciousness have been forged out of a mixture of natives and various immigrant groups, as in Argentina. Single working-class movements have even been created, as in India, out of a conglomerate of mutually hostile and linguistically incomprehensible castes, language groups and religions. For that matter, even in Ulster men who feared for their lives from Catholic or Protestant proletarians outside the shipyard or dock gates were – and perhaps still are – prepared to act together inside them for purposes of industrial disputes. The historical as well as practical problem is to discover under what circumstances such class unity can come into being, work, or cease to work.

Three circumstances may be suggested, in which natural or communal divisions may fatally disrupt working classes. Such disruption may arise from the influence of nationalist or other political movements outside the working class; from rapid and major changes in the composition of that class (or more generally, in society) which established patterns cannot absorb; and from the attempt to maintain disproportionately favourable conditions by strict limitations of entry into the working class.

The last case is probably the least common, for while the tendency to form 'labour aristocracies' is fairly general, blanket exclusion is rather uncommon, except on the grounds of colour and sex, two barriers which, because of their visibility, are very difficult to cross. Still, where such blanket exclusion operates or has operated, as in the White Australia policy, the Chinese Exclusion Laws in the United States and anti-black discrimination in South African industry, it has certainly come primarily from within the unusually favoured local working class, afraid of losing its exceptionally advantageous conditions. Where exclusion is totally successful, there is no split in the working class, since the excluded are kept out altogether. Where the favoured and the unprivileged co-exist, as in South Africa, in practice two parallel and perhaps mutually hostile working classes tend to develop. However, in capitalist and probably also socialist industrialization it is rare for labour to be consistently so favoured or so strong as to impose permanent blanket exclusiveness. Consequently even labour movements based on the attempt to create congeries of labour aristocracies, as in mid-nineteenth-century Britain, aimed at labour movements which were inclusive, that is they recognized that they ought ideally to achieve the organization of all workers, and certainly of all who were likely to penetrate into the enclosure they reserved for their trade or occupation. Within such a comprehensive movement, the special advantages of labour aristocracy ought, of course, to be safeguarded.

Changes in the social composition of the working class may be divisive, insofar as they disturb established social patterns and allow rivalries within the class to be nationally or communally coloured, or class lines to coincide with national or communal lines. This has been the danger in regions like Catalonia and, even more, the Basque country, where industrial development leads to a mass influx of Spanish workers, slow to learn to speak Catalan and even slower to learn Basque, and rather despised by native Catalans or feared by native Basques. Nobody acquainted with the problems of the coloured minorities in Britain would want to under-estimate the consequent sense of mutual hostility and even fear between different groups of workers. This is all the more dramatic, since traditionally organized labour movements have actively dis-couraged national, racial or religious prejudices. At the same time one may doubt whether these frictions, *by themselves*, are of de-cisive significance. It is chiefly when the state and its institutions are involved, as by demands for a linguistic monopoly, or for legal equality, or for autonomy or separatism, that they become explo-sive – as they unfortunately have in Ulster. In fact, traditionally national and regional minority groups in states, especially when composed of workers, have, other things being equal, tended to support the mass party on the progressive wing of the majority nation's politics as being the most likely to defend their minority interests. Even today American blacks and white ethnics, between whom no love is lost, both tend to vote for the Democratic Party, while in Britain Asian and West Indian workers tend to vote La-bour in spite of the racialism of many white working-class Labour voters.

However, the most powerful divisive forces, in the form of pol-itical parties and movements such as those inspired by nationalism, come from outside the working classes. Historically such move-ments have hardly ever originated within them, though they have often sought to appeal to them. They were divisive, not only because they naturally accentuated the linguistic, religious, physi-cal and other distinctions between 'their' sector of a heterogeneous working class and the rest, but also because their objects were by definition at odds with those of class consciousness. They sought to substitute the dividing line between 'the nation' (including both its exploiters and exploited) and 'the foreigners' (including all workers classifiable as such) for class lines. Moreover, in the early stages of nationalist movements, nationalists either took little interest in the issues which preoccupied workers as workers – organized or unorganized – or regarded the solution of such problems as conditional on the prior achievement of the nationalist objectives.The discovery that national and social liberation must go together, was not usually made by the pioneers of nationalist movements, which is why some of the most effective nationalist parties and organizations emerged out of socialist agitations (e.g. the Polish Socialist Party whose leader, Pilsudski, became the head of independent Poland after World War I, and labour Zionism, which became the real architect of Israel). Even when the discovery was made within nationalist movements, activists who gave too high a priority to social liberation were difficult to digest. The nationalist reputation of Michael Davitt has suffered accordingly.

Historically it has proved difficult to deny and prevent class consciousness, since it arises naturally and logically out of the proletarian condition, at least in the elementary form of 'trade union consciousness', that is to say the recognition that workers as such need to organize collectively against employers in order to defend and improve their conditions as hired hands. Thus Catholic trade unions were formed not because most 'social Catholics' at the end of the nineteenth century favoured them – they regarded them, in Albert de Mun's words, as 'the specific organization of the war of one group against another' and preferred mixed associations of employers and workers – but because the latter did not meet the trade union needs of Catholic workers. In France 'social Catholics' accepted them, with more or less reluctance, between 1897 and 1912. Again, even in countries with strong national loyalties among workers, trade unionism tended to resist the fragmentation of unions along national lines. Czech workers certainly did not think of themselves as the same as German workers, but while they were inclined to vote for Czech political parties rather than non-Czech or all-Austrian ones, the pressure to split the Austrian trade union movement along national lines did not come from within the labour movement. It arose some time after the split into national sections of the Social Democratic Party had become effective, and was resisted more strongly by the all-Austrian unions. Indeed, even after the split had taken place, the majority of Czech unionists remained in the all-Austrian organizations, where, of course, they were entitled to form their own Czech branches and had their own Bohemian leadership. Similarly today, while the parties of the left in Spain have split along national or regional lines, there has been no comparable tendency to divide the all-Spanish trade union movements. The reasons are obvious. The unity of all workers is an evident asset when they go on strike for economic reasons, and even though for other purposes they may think of themselves chiefly as Catholics or Protestants, black or white, Poles or Mexicans, it is advisable to put these distinctions aside for such purposes as asking for higher wages.

Nevertheless, it is equally clear that if class consciousness cannot be eliminated, it certainly neither excludes nor, usually, dominates national sentiments. The collapse of the Second International in 1914 into socialist parties and trade-union movements – most of which supported their belligerent governments, is familiar. What is less familiar, since the internationalism of labour historians has not insisted on it, is the strong current of chauvinism which is found in some politically radical working classes. Thomas Wright, the 'Journeyman Engineer' who reported on the English working class of the 1860s, notes specifically that the older, radical and Chartist generation of workers combined a passionate distrust of all who were not workers with a John-Bullish patriotism. In itself, strong national sentiment may not be of great political consequence. English and French workers, who almost certainly did not like what they thought they knew about one another's country, have never since 1815 been expected to fight against their neighbours across the Channel. At times social-revolutionary or anti-war sentiment may override patriotism, as in the last years of World War I. Even at such times patriotism may not be negligible. It has been suggested that in France (unlike Britian) the growth of mass working-class support for the Russian Revolution was distinctly slow until it became clear it would not jeopardize the chances of victory in the West. A similar phenomenon may be observable in the Habsburg Empire. While the famous wave of anti-war strikes in January 1918, which began in the armaments works near Vienna, rapidly spread throughout the engineering factories of ethnic Austria and Hungary, it did *not* spread to the Czech areas of Bohemia. It has been suggested that anti-war mobilization was inhibited here by the policy of the nationalist movement (by this time echoed among many Czech workers), which relied on an Allied victory for the achievement of its aim – the independence of what was shortly to become Czechoslovakia.

In certain circumstances the appeal of nationalism or patriotism to workers was likely to be particularly effective. One of these occurred when they could identify with an existing nation-state *as citizens* rather than mere passive subjects, i.e. where their integration into the political and hegemonic system of their rules was underway, not least through that major agent of conscious socialization from above, a public system of elementary education. Class and private discontent did not prevent most English, French or German workers from seeing Britain, France and Germany as in some sense 'their country', as, say, Austrian ones in 1914 did not (because there was no nation-state), or Italian workers and peasants did not, since few even spoke and even fewer could read Italian, and hardly any of them had enjoyed the right to vote for more than a year. Another occurred, where nationalist agitation, often building on memories of a former political state or autonomy, or organizations embodying the separateness of a nationality (e.g. the Catholicism of the dependent people as against the Protestantism or Orthodoxy of the ruling state) were in existence before an industrial working class developed. This was the case among people like the Irish, the Poles and the Czechs. However, as already suggested, what made national sentiments explosive and capable of destroying the cross-national unity of the working class was that they were intertwined with issues directly affecting the state and its institutions. Thus linguistic nationalism becomes explosive when language ceases to be merely a medium of communication between people, but one language or dialect rather than another becomes 'official' – e.g. the language of law courts, schools, and public notices.

All this implies that working-class consciousness, however inevitable and essential, is probably politically secondary to other kinds of consciousness. As we know, where it has come into conflict in our century with national, or religious, or racial consciousness, it has usually yielded and retreated. It is clear that, for certain limited purposes, working-class consciousness and the labour movements it generates – at all events at the elementary 'trade-unionist' level – are very strong indeed. They are not indestructible, for sheer force has frequently destroyed such movements, but even these are potentially permanent and revivable. We have recently seen such consciousness and such movements revive in the very different circumstances of two rapidly industrializing countries, Brazil and

Poland. They may well be the decisive lever for major political changes, as looked likely in 1980-1 in Poland. But historians must note that it is equally clear that working-class consciousness alone co-exists with other forms of collective identification and neither eliminates nor replaces them. And, as Lenin rightly observed, while it will spontaneously and everywhere generate 'trade-unionist' practices and (where it is allowed to) organizations or other movements for corporate pressure and self-defence, it does not automatically generate mass parties with a socialist consciousness.

That such parties were generated almost as a matter of course during a certain historical period, mainly between the 1880s and 1930s, is significant, but requires more historical explanation than it has generally received. These parties, or their lineal successors, are still in being and often influential, but where they did not already exist, or the influence of socialists/communists was significant in labour movements before World War II, hardly any such parties have emerged out of the working classes since then, notably in the so-called 'Third World'. This may have implications for traditional socialist expectations about the role of the working class and working-class parties in bringing about socialism, which need not be discussed here.

What bearing has all this on the making of the Irish working class? The major fact which requires explanation, at least for outsiders, is why labour as an independent political force has in the past been relatively negligible in Ireland, compared with the countries of the United Kingdom. Neither in North nor South have class movements of the workers made a more than marginal political mark. This is not adequately explained by the lack, until recently, of much industrialization in the twenty-six counties. It is certainly not explained by any lack of industrialization in Ulster. Moreover from the days when Dublin was a stronghold of trade societies to the period before World War I, when both Belfast and Dublin were the scene of some of the largest and most dramatic industrial disputes in the United Kingdom, Ireland has been familiar with labour battles. The most obvious explanation is that – except at moments or for rather limited trade unionist purposes – the potential Irish constituency for such working-class movements have identified themselves in politics as Catholic nationalists or Protestant unionists rather than as 'labour'. It is difficult to think of any other country in western Europe in which this has been so marked and persistent a characteristic of the working class.

Without pushing the analogy too far, a comparison of Ireland with Belgium, a more recently partitioned country and working class, may be instructive. As north-east Ulster and the rest of Ireland followed their divergent economic evolution, so did Wallonia and Flanders. Wallonia industrialized heavily, while Flanders, though containing a major port (Antwerp) and a significant industrial centre (Ghent), remained predominantly agrarian and saw itself as underprivileged. As old-fashioned nineteenth-century basic industries lost their firm footing in Ulster and Wallonia, so Flanders and to some extent the Republic of Ireland, have become more industrialized and prosperous; but not, like the old zones, as part of the British or – *de facto* – the French industrial economies, but within a European and transnational framework. As Catholics and Protestants are inseparable in Belfast, so Flemings and French-speakers are inseparable in Brussels.

Yet Belgium, though occupied from time to time, has long been independent of its immediate neighbours (France and The Netherlands) and, since 1830, it has been an independent state, whereas the connection with Britain clearly dominated Irish affairs throughout, and still dominates those of Ulster. In the Belgian working class the two groups hardly mixed, since the language border is rather clearly marked. Where they did mix as in Brussels, the city grew slowly enough – from say 6 per cent of the population in the early nineteenth century to about 9 per cent in 1911 – for Flemish immigrants to be assimilated, as it seemed they were willing to be, facing little real resistance. On the other hand Belfast grew from very little to about a third of the population of the six counties during the century, at first by a mass influx of Ulster Catholics which, around the middle of the century, looked as though it might swamp the Protestants, later by a mass growth of Ulster Protestants, which reduced the Catholics to a permanent and embittered minority. By 1911 Belfast was disproportionately more Protestant than the rest of the province, and Catholics were far more systematically excluded from the city's skilled trades than they had been in 1870.

The Belgian labour movement grew up from the 1880s as a strong, single and unified body operating across language lines, and largely engaged, before 1914, in the struggle for universal male suffrage, which minimized internal divergences within the working class. It was not seriously split linguistically until after World War II. Not so in Ireland, where the official commitment to a single all-Irish labour movement often concealed an essentially nationalist orientation struggling against the trade-union movement of skilled workers who were quite content with the usual autonomy within an all-UK organization. Moreover, the established dominance of the national issue (Home Rule or Independence from Britain) deprived labour of a unifying issue of political mobilization, such as the fight for electoral democracy provided in Belgium.

The paradox of the Irish situation in the period when a major labour movement might have been expected to emerge – from the end of the 1880s to 1914, the era of 'new unionism' and 'labour unrest' – is that three factors converged to tie Catholic workers to Fenian nationalism. Mass nationalist mobilization and Orange resistance equated political Irishness with Catholicism. The old craft unionism of skilled workers (concentrated in industrial Ulster) would in any case not have been much use to unskilled workers, but the increasingly systematic exclusion of Catholics from skilled Ulster trades intensified the tensions between the two sectors of the working class. Finally, the very radicalism, or even the socialist and revolutionary convictions, of the 'new' union leaders and organizers, who wanted to break with the caution and 'reformism' of the old unions, had political implications in Ireland which it did not have in Britain; for in Ulster, at least, organized skilled workers were not only 'old' unionists but also tended to be Orangemen. In short, both political mobilization (National and Unionist) and the class mobilization of hitherto unorganized and unorganizable workers, united to divide the working class. A labour movement which was both *political* and *industrial* and which united Protestant and Catholic, Orange and Green, skilled and unskilled, became impossible. It would have been possible only if divisions between sections of workers had not coincided with divisions between Catholic and Protestant (which increasingly implied between Green and Orange), as they did in Belfast, the test of any united Irish labour movement. In any case, such a movement would have been possible only by overlooking the separation from Britian, i.e. by regarding the issues around which Irish politics revolved as irrelevant to Labour as such. It is not impossible to conceive of this, but the prospect hardly seemed realistic between 1880 and 1921. The most that could be expected of a political labour movement neutral as between Orange and Green, but many of whose members were far from neutral as individuals, would have been a pressure group for the specific interests of trade unionists, or for legislation of specific interest to wage-workers: in fact something like an all-Irish Labour Representation Committee. Yet even in Britain itself, the Labour Representation Committee, though in theory operating outside the field of political dispute between Liberals and Conservatives, which was distinctly less impassioned than that between Nationalist and Unionists, actually had great difficulty until after World War I in emancipating itself from the political loyalties of so many organized workers to one of the two parties, and the suspicion of those who supported the other.

This, then, was the dilemma of Irish labour leaders. It was independent of their personal convictions. A case can be made for James Connolly's choice of the 'Green' option, on the grounds that most Irishmen were Catholics, and that in any case the dour and respectable 'old unionists' (and Unionists) of Protestant Belfast hardly looked like promising material for social revolution. Yet if the Catholic labouring masses seemed to offer better prospects for revolutionaries – after all, even Jim Larkin who was not an Irish nationalist in the sense Connolly was, or became, had his greatest triumphs among them – the Green option automatically excluded that united movement of all Irish workers of which Connolly dreamed. But Connolly's decision for an Irish labour movement which would not merely appeal essentially to Southerners and Catholics in practice, but was nationalist in aspiration, had even more serious consequnces. It meant the subordination of southern Irish labour to nationalism. Marxist parties have sometimes succeeded in transforming their societies after taking the lead of movements of national liberation, but hardly ever, if at all, in competition with previously established and strong national movements under other leadership. In spite of Connolly's efforts and his leadership in 1916 it was the IRA and not the Citizens' Army which took over the green flag. Connolly lives on in official memory as a Fenian martyr rather than as a Marxist revolutionary. Perhaps this was inevitable. One cannot confidently say otherwise. Nevertheless it meant that a strong and independent political movement of labour developed neither in the north nor in the south, though it is possible that today the conditions for such a movement are better in the south, because partition is *de facto* no longer a significant issue in the Republic. In the north, as we know, it still is.

Does this mean that Ireland contained not one but two working classes or even, as some enthusiasts hold, not one but two nations? In the literal sense this is obviously not so. Catholics and Protestants in Ulster no more formed separate working classes in any economic or operational sense than they did on Clydeside. Such questions arise chiefly because it is often assumed, without much thought, that working classes, or any other large classes, do not 'exist' except as monolithic blocks, as it is assumed that a nation is not 'real' unless each member, living on its territory, who is not a certified foreigner or a defined 'minority', is uniformly coloured right through with whatever is considered the accepted national dye. Today this is usually language, though the Irish have learned the hard way that this dye does not always take. In a few European countries and many more Afro-Asian ones it is still religion. Right-wing Americans think it is a set of conventional practices and beliefs, lacking which a person in 'un-American'. This is not so. The unity of classes and nations is defined by what they have in common as against other groups, and not by their internal homogeneity. There is no state which does not contain regional, sectional, or other differences among its population, and these are potentially disruptive, as the recent rise of separatist movements in western Europe proves. The only difference in principle between Ireland and Bavaria is that the Catholic-Protestant difference in Ireland has proved disruptive, whereas the attempt to prove that the Protestant minority in the northern part of Bavaria (Franconia) is oppressed by the Catholic majority is at present confined to a lunatic fringe of ultra-left ex-students. Similarly, all working classes contain internal conflicts, though usually they remain subordinate.

On the other hand the course of history can both merge and split societies, and therefore the classes within them. It has divided Ireland. Given that there now exist separate political units and economies in north and south, it becomes impossible any longer to speak of a single Irish working class any more than a single Bengali or German working class, to name but two other partitioned nations. Separate states are powerful definers of economy and society. This does not mean that the two Irelands cease to have much in common as have the two Germanies – not least kinfolk and culture. We may speculate about what might happen if both were united

– given the widening divergences it is increasingly difficult to say 're-united' – but in both cases the question is at present academic. To this extent history has up to the present led to the making of two Irish working classes.

Of these, the Ulster working class suffers particularly, indeed one is tempted to say uniquely, acute divisions. The only parallel one can readily think of is the Hindu-Moslem communal tension on the Indian subcontinent. For these reasons no general conclusions about working class and nation can be drawn from Ulster. Ireland remains resolutely unique in this respect. So, no doubt, does every other country or nation, once historians concentrate their attention sufficiently upon it. However, unfortunately the uniqueness of Irish historical development has manifested itself – so far – largely at the expense of the making of its working class and its labour movement.

(1982)

# 5: The Transformation of Labour Rituals*

I

Ritual is a fashionable subject among historians today. Nevertheless, it is worth asking why we should study its transformations in
labour movements, as distinct from anywhere else. Like all groups
of human beings, collectivities of workers, whether officially organized or not, occasionally indulge in formalized practices associated
with appropriate objects and symbols. Antiquarians, collectors and
folklorists, as well as students of ritual in general, are naturally
interested in such practices, especially when their material relics are
collectable. They have generated a substantial body of literature
over the past two decades. We have only to think of British trade
union banners and emblems, which were almost totally neglected by scholarship before the 1960s, though in 1947 Klingender
had drawn attention to labour iconography in his pioneer study of
*Art and the Industrial Revolution.*[1] But what, apart from the concern of preservationists, is the point of investigating labour rituals
as distinct from any others? I suggest that it has three peculiarities
which are of interest to the historian.

In the first place, modern labour movements, however profoundly rooted in the practices of labour and the traditions of the
past, and linked with institutions associated with these, are historically new, if only because modern industrial society has no historic
precedent. This novelty is such that early labour historians, most
of whom were, of course, associated with labour movements, either
tended to neglect the heritage they derived from the past or even,
like the Webbs, to deny any continuity with pre-industrial movements and organizations.[2] This is no longer so. Indeed, some of

* This chapter was given as a lecture at the Anglo-American Historians' Conference in London in 1982.

the most interesting recent work in the field operates precisely in the gap between pre-industrial labour and the nineteenth-century (skilled) workers.[3] Nevertheless, the novelty is not to be denied. While some labour rituals were derived from pre-industrial ones, others, particularly in the socialist period, were and had to be new.

In the second place, some forms of labour movement carry an emotional charge of quite exceptional force, which encourages ritual expression. This is not unusual in itself – we need only think of religion – but labour movements are peculiar precisely because, by and large, traditional religion generally played a small and diminishing role in their development, even when their members did not actively reject it. Moreover, the novelty of the class they represented, and of their social aspirations at least as formulated in the various ideologies typically associated with labour movements, was such as to make it difficult or impossible to fit into the ritual structuring of a traditional universe and of the human place in it, to which most earlier ritual systems were dedicated. But let there be no doubt about the profundity of the emotions involved. In 1873 the socialist workers of Breslau (Wroclaw), then in Germany, ten years after the death of the pioneer workers' leader Lassalle, dedicated a new red flag. On the front it bore a painting of an oak wreath and ribbon, two clasped hands, the inscription 'May 23 1863, Ferdinand Lassalle', surmounted by the motto 'Liberty, Equality, Fraternity', and, at the foot, 'Unity is Strength'. On the back it bore the inscription 'The social-democratic workers in Breslau 1873'. During Bismarck's anti-socialist law the flag was smuggled into Switzerland. Under Hitler, between 1933 and 1945, it was carefully kept, first buried in an allotment garden, later in the cellar of a plumber, who refused to give it up to the Red Army officers who came to salute it in 1945. When Breslau became Polish and was renamed Wroclaw, the keeper of the flag transported it to West Germany to hand it over to the Social-Democratic Party which, presumably, still has it.[4] This was and is an object for which ordinary men and women have more than once risked liberty and even life.

In the third place – and this is in some ways the most interesting aspect of the question – such ritualization developed in a movement which was in some respects not merely indifferent to ritualism but actively hostile to it as a form of irrationalism, or in Marx' terms, 'superstitious authoritarianism'.[5] Insofar as labour ritual de-

veloped, as it were, against the grain of strongly rationalist movements, it may throw light on the circumstances which generate such
formalization or 'invention of tradition'.[6]

But how has it been transformed? Its first and major secular
transformation is that it has declined. There is, quite simply, much
less of it, and what remains is truncated, vestigial, sometimes disguised as something else. Its iconography, symbolism and other
ceremonial furniture have been impoverished over time. As the late
J.E. Williams pointed out, the transformation of the council chamber of the Derbyshire miners in 1954 was symbolic. 'As if to symbolize the change from the nineteenth to the twentieth century, the
old banner of the Derbyshire Miners' Association which had
adorned the wall behind the platform was replaced by a plaque
depicting modern mining scenes and bearing the inscription
"N.U.M., Derbyshire Area".'[7] There is, of course, one major exception to this trend of secular decline. Revolutionary movements
which become governments, as has happened from time to time
since 1917, have tended to develop public ritualization in an almost
byzantine manner, though, once again, on the basis of a symbolic
and iconographical language which, by comparison with the past,
is drastically reduced. Or at least, which employs a ritual language
that appears to have little use for the ancient vocabulary. Such
tendencies are also observable in what might be called 'labour city
states' such as Vienna between 1918 and 1934.[8] These phenomena
will not be considered here, except incidentally.

Nevertheless, it will not do to see the history of labour ritual
simply as one of secular decline, even though this decline is certain.
What occurred was also a change of ritual and symbolic language,
for instance, among other things, the substitution for a traditional
vocabulary of symbolism and allegory, of the idiom of the shorthand 'trade-mark' or 'logo', which has symbolic meaning chiefly,
or only, by association. And what we have to reconstruct is not a
history of gradual disappearance, until nothing remains of this kind
of Cheshire Cat except a disembodied smile – old banners without
those who once bore them, rescued by lamenting scholars from
mildewed union cellars. We have, for instance, to explain a new
flowering of sometimes old and sometimes new ritual, which might
be more elaborate than in the past, in the three decades before
1918. In short, we are concerned with history and not merely
socio-anthropological generalization.

II

Collective manual labour is by tradition a rather ritualized activity, deeply intertwined with the ritual structuring of personal lives and social collectivities, the cycles of the seasons, beginnings and endings, the rites of passage and the rest. Workplaces and work-groups are both structured and often cohesive. So we might expect labour movements, insofar as they derive from or continue ancient and long-established labour processes – as in building and printing – to absorb much of the formal and informal rituals associated with them. Some of these have no special affinity with labour movements, for instance the innumerable 'fines and footings' in the workshop which were celebrated – to the grief of nineteenth-century temperance advocates – with a social drink, or even several.[9] Others were both ritual and utilitarian. Thus the old London coopers wore moleskin aprons which needed to be aired and dried daily before starting work, 'a ritual which gives coopers a chance to engage in general chit-chat or serious discussion for which they have no time once they have commenced work'.[10] In just such a way we are told that in the much less traditionalist South Wales mines, the spell at the bottom of the pit-shaft while miners adapted from daylight to dark, came to be a regular period for the discussion of politics and union matters.[11]

Organized pre-industrial corporate trades, mostly of skilled craftsmen, had developed an entire world of such ritual practices about which students have written at length. Those of craft apprentices and journeymen naturally included a large element of what might be called proto-trade-unionism. Insofar as nineteenth-century unionism grew directly out of such craft tradition or organization, such ritual was also likely to penetrate it. How far it did so remains a matter of debate. My own view is that the connection on the continent was probably indirect; the handicrafts remained largely separate from the industrializing sector and journeymen's organizations like the French *compagnonnages* existed side by side with, and were gradually pushed onto the margin by, modern forms of labour struggle and organization.[12] Nevertheless, the men who formed labour organizations were largely skilled craft workers, educated and socialized in the craft tradition, and to this extent these traditions helped to shape those of modern labour. Let us not forget that the bulk of activists in central European social democracy at the end of the nineteenth, and even in the early twentieth century, were still apprenticed journeymen who had often done their highly formalized and ritualized *Wanderjahre* stint as travellers.[13] In Britain I would argue, following Leeson and others, that the connection is quite direct. Journeymen's organizations, formal or informal, were transformed into trade societies. Indeed, to the extent that craft tradition and vocabulary survive at all in this country, other than in the street- and indoor-theatre of City Livery Companies, it is in and through the skilled trade-union movement, even in the ritual address of members as 'Dear Sir and Brother'. This is not merely evident in the practices of printers' chapels, often described[14] and apparently little changed over the centuries – though printing has been transformed since the 1880s – but more generally in the elaborate ritual furniture of British nineteenth-century unionism and popular politics and sociability.

Not all of this was ancient. A good deal was expressed in the ritual and symbolic language prevalent in the eighteenth century, which in turn adapted an older vocabulary to an ideology of enlightenment and progress. The relations of labour movements, as distinct from corporate craft bodies, with formal churches or even dissenting sects, were problematic,[15] quite apart from possible mutual suspicion or hostility. Even among the religious Yorkshire and Derbyshire miners, whose banners in 1873 were still often painted with biblical scenes,[16] the hymns with which their annual demonstrations opened ceased to hold the attention of the public after 1889.[17] So, in spite of the prevalence of 'superstitions' – some of which have recently attracted learned attention[18] – in spite of the well-known taste of miners, farm-labourers and fishermen for Primitive Methodism and other sects, and in spite of the Catholic labour movements which later sprang up in competition with the secular ones, the basic ritual and symbolic language of early labour movements was, and perhaps could not but be, different from that of its members' religion.

Iconographically it used the emblematic and allegorical language so dear to Warburgian scholars, ritually in forms similar to and perhaps derived from Freemasonry, which continued to overlap with building workers' organizations even in the early nineteenth century.[19] Probably in Britain the link was made chiefly via such basically plebeian friendly orders as the Oddfellows who, by their own statement, imitated Masonry.[20] This, it may be suggested, had two advantages. In the first place the ideology of the Enlightenment was one which had a strong appeal to working-class activists and militants from the American Revolution onwards. In the second place Masonry, though secret, was also influential, respectable and hardly ever actually banned. At all events the elaborate visual imagery of early organizations, which has been most fully analysed in Dr Müller's monograph on the Certificate of the Amalgamated Society of Engineers,[21] was a version of the accepted secular public vocabulary of symbolism and allegory in this era.

The actual ritual of a masonic type clearly played a less significant part in early labour movements, unless we include the friendly orders and *compagnonnages* in them. It enters our field only insofar as such bodies were secret because illegal, or insofar as they were believed to require binding together by means of solemn or menacing initiation ceremonies and oaths, and needed to secure efficient conduct of business – rather like armies – by means of a strict, formalized and easily ritualized routine of meetings. How far they did so is not clear. My own view is that oaths and the like were no longer of great significance by the 1840s, but that they were still widely believed to be significant by outsiders in the early 1830s. They may well have been habitual at that time. At all events an interesting debate arose on this subject among the Lancashire Catholic priesthood, given the ecclesiastical commination of secret oaths. The priests who sympathized with the desire of their flocks to defend wages and conditions collectively, assumed as a matter of course that joining unions implied taking oaths: hence the problem. Were they well informed? We do not really know yet.[22]

Labour movements with such a background – and we are de facto speaking almost exclusively of Britain – were thus likely to develop a fairly elaborate set of ritual equipment adapted and developed from past tradition. They would include formalities of initiation, meeting and procedure, of communication with brothers from other parts, such as those long associated with the tramping system. They would include rituals of public presentation such as processions on ceremonial occasions shading over into modern demonstrations, such as the marches of trade societies which were integrated into the Preston guild processions which took place every twenty years, or the Nantwich Crispin's Day procession of 1833 organized by Thomas Dunning's union.[23] They would certainly include the usual conventions of public dinners and toasts, of official congratulation or commiseration at funerals whose public significance was evident.[24] They would include a large store of ritual paraphernalia. The banners which are so characteristic of British unions and public demonstrations – among Yorkshire miners they are recorded from at least 1819[25] – are now the best known of such objects, and their considerable expense – between £30 and £60 in the early 1870s[26] – demonstrates either the financial strength of branches or the sacrifices they were ready to make for ritual, or both. But they would also include the elaborate clothing, for private ritual or public procession – the 'white cotton gloves and flashy waistcoats' worn by the Derbyshire miners on their annual demonstration in the 1870s[27] – the rosettes, ribbons and sashes, popular, it seems not only among miners but transport workers and among union officials generally,[28] the badges – which began to spread from 1860 on,[29] the fobs for the watch-chains of prosperous artisans, and presumably the jugs, Stafford-shire figures or other ceramic tributes to radical sentiment. They would also include a plethora of more or less utilitarian printed matter, ranging from tramp certificates, membership cards and let-terheads, usually with some symbolic decoration, to those allegor-ical certificates which Leeson and Müller have surveyed.[30] These are not to be confused with membership cards, for they were neither compulsory nor an actual proof of membership, but were bought, to be framed and put up on the walls of zealous unionists' parlours as demonstrations of pride and attachment.

The ritual furniture of such movements was thus large and var-ied. One has only to compare the elaboration of British union banners and certificates (often accompanied by exegetical leaflets) with the much simpler banners which proliferated in, say, Italian labour organizations.[31] These consist overwhelmingly of simple red and sometimes black pieces of cloth bearing only the name of the organization, a motto or slogan, and perhaps a suitable but sim-plified symbol. One might even hazard the guess that the wealth of this British iconographical tradition, as well as the influence of the arts-and-crafts movement and the talent of Walter Crane, explain why so much of the international iconography of the early social-democratic movement – notably of May Day – came for a time to be inspired by the otherwise negligible British socialist movement. Of course, in the socialist era new ideological themes required new visual symbols of anti-capitalist struggle and socialist hope, which were drawn from the ancient iconographic storehouse, though now presented in new William-Morris style.[32]

I shall merely mention two obvious occasions for such ritual: mass political demonstrations and union festivals, both long associated (if only via friendly-society influence) with bands, banners, ceremonial marches, speeches and popular sociability. There is little doubt that these became institutionalized in the middle decades of the century among the miners, though they may have been declining among the older trade societies and later, among friendly orders. The first of the great annual regional demonstrations of miners, of which the Durham miners' gala is the last survivor, seems to have been in Yorkshire in 1867.[33] They were highly elaborate, with each lodge gathering at an allotted billet – generally a pub – from where they formed up – four abreast, as the rules insisted – to take their place in the procession, all miners marching and none watching except the womenfolk who, at least in South Yorkshire, were specifically excluded from the march.[34] They may have become more elaborate as the years went by. In 1891 the Derbyshire officials 'wore handsome gilt badges' with the motto 'United We Stand, Divided We Fall', and the members of the executive wore red sashes. At their peak each lodge of the Durham miners probably had three to four large banners – and the sight and sound of this sea of banners and Niagara of brass bands demonstrated the power of labour to all.

The Great Depression of the 1870s and 1880s took its toll, but in the late 1880s the movement revived, now reinforced by new unions and new ideologies, and it may well be that the last decades before 1914, and especially the 1890s saw the height of this fashion for iconography and public ceremony, now – as befits the character of British labour – sometimes combining non-socialist and socialist imagery. There are obvious similarities with what Agulhon has called 'statuomania' in Europe and which reached its peak in this period.[35] Nevertheless, as the old allegorical and symbolic language ceased to be understood, or perhaps became both unnecessary and less attractive, its popularity declined and its imagery was transformed and impoverished. While in 1889 more than half the members of the ASE had owned a certificate, in 1916 only 20 per cent did so – and of the 43,000 who joined in 1917 only perhaps 750 to 800 bought one.[36] They were no doubt replaced by the more modern membership badge, another non-utilitarian object – except among such bodies as the Mersey Quay and Railway Carters[37] – but this also became iconographically much simplified. Leeson has already noted that the later union certificates could not be identified as belonging to a *labour* union without the actual name of the organization and inscribed motto or text. Increasingly they become sheets illustrating various industrial processes in a naturalistic, sometimes a photographic, manner.[38] It is of course true, as we shall see, that simple conventional shorthand symbols – more political than trade unionist – now come to replace the old symbolism: the red flag itself, the rising sun of socialism, the hammer and sickle (which is much the best known of these), and occasionally truncated versions of old images, such as the anti-militarist symbol of the broken sword on Italian labour flags.*[39] Nevertheless, we are entering a different and more sparsely furnished ritual world. As so often in the case of labour practices, the transformation is accelerated by economic and political fluctuations. The decline of the great era of banners was accentuated by defeat and slump – their production fell sharply after 1930 and, in spite of some postwar revival, has continued to decline. The firm of George Tutill, which made about three-quarters of all known banners, produced none at all in 1967.[40] More modern union banners have also, incidentally, tended to shy away from elaborate pictures and portraiture, let alone allegory.

III

The new simplicity happened to fit in with some aspects of the new or socialist phase of labour ritual. In spite of the force of the historic environment from which no one can escape, the bulk of modern labour movements – including much of the British ones after 1889 – were new in their membership, forms of organization, strategy and aspirations. The mass parties whose membership could reach into the hundreds of thousands by 1914; the mass electorates which could give between 30 and 40 per cent of the national male suffrage to such parties by then;[41] the mass membership of stable labour unions itself have no precedents before 1870; probably not even in Britain. What is equally to the point, the ideological activ-

* It is found in a more elaborate form – the skilled smith refusing to repair the broken sword presented by Mars – on the ASE certificate.

ists who inspired them were (with a few exceptions like Lassalle) anti-ritualist even in their ritualism. German social democrats were suspicious of miners' festivals.[42] Anarchists were suspicious of any formality whatever. They were puritans – far from naturally inclined to those commemorative dinners at which British militants, even after World War II, recalled, preserved and absorbed the tradition of past battles, victories and defeats and linked them to present and future.[43] The funeral of the revolutionary miner Jack Lavin of Warsop (Nottinghamshire) in 1919 was a relatively simple affair: coffin draped in red flag, with 'a wreath of crimson blooms and bunches of roses', borne by comrades with red ribbons in their coats; a long eulogy, and various speeches and tributes; a song at the graveside as he was lowered into the earth amid cries of 'Poor Old Jack'.[44] There have been – there still are – political and labour funerals which exploit the possibilities of this traditionally ceremonial occasion more elaborately.[45]

The new labour ritualism thus developed spontaneously and in an unplanned way, though it was sometimes taken over by organizations. I shall mention three aspects of it by way of illustration.

The first is the red flag itself, whose rise as the symbol of social revolution and later labour appears to be overwhelmingly spontaneous: from February 1848 when it emerges on the barricades everywhere,[46] to the French strikes of 1871-90, where 'red, when it appears is almost always by way of improvization' to the First of May demonstration which – in France at least – institutionalized the red flag.[47] As we shall see May Day is itself a grassroots phenomenon.

The second is what one might call the ritualization of procedure at meetings, which is closely associated with organization. Here, in both France and Britain, the influence of the local political tradition – republican in one country, parliamentary in the other – is undoubtedly important. Citrine insists that British labour practice is or should be an adaptation of parliamentary procedure,[48] and Perrot points out that French meetings develop '*un rituel inspiré des pratiques parlementaires*'.[49] We now have the appointment of chairman and secretary (equipped with the indispensable bell), or of the 'bureau' or platform, installed behind a table on a dais or platform. The chairman (who must be addressed formally) occupies the centre – he 'should be raised above the others slightly' in Citrine's opinion.[50] There is – in Britain at least – the constitutionalist ballet of minutes, motions, amendments, references back, suspensions of standing orders and the rest which have been the delight of generations of labour activists. There are the endless votes, formal and substantial – typically, in labour organizations, by show of hands. The rationale of all this may be strictly utilitarian, and yet there is no escaping the impression that the formality itself provides a certain ritual satisfaction. One cannot indeed go as far as Perrot who describes the function of such public meetings as 'less to decide than to create communion'.[51] Yet is Citrine entirely utilitarian when he describes how to start a meeting: 'The chairman looks round, sees the door is closed, clears his throat and declares the meeting open'?[52] Nobody who has attended a TUC or Labour conference even before the ritual singing by the enemies on the platform will doubt that it is more than a way of getting through business.

The international May Day, which dates back to 1889, is perhaps the most ambitious of labour rituals.[53] In some ways it is a more ambitious and generalized version of the annual combined labour demonstration and festival which we have seen emerging for one highly specific group of workers and confined to single regions in the miners' demonstrations and galas of two decades earlier. It shared with these the essential characteristic of being a regular public self-presentation of a class, an assertion of power, indeed in its invasion of the establishment's social space, a symbolic conquest. But equally crucially, it was the assertion of class through an *organized movement* – union or party. It was the labour army's annual trooping of the colours – a political occasion unthinkable without the slogans, the demands, the speeches which, even among the self-contained pitmen increasingly came to be made by national figures representing not the union but the movement as a whole.[54] At the same time, since the class as such was involved, it was also like subsequent gatherings of the same kind – one thinks of the national festivals of *L'Humanité* in France or *Unità* in Italy, a *family* occasion and a popular festival – though one which, in spite of an ample supply of beer and skittles, prided itself on its demonstration of self-control. Just as the Durham miners in 1872 were proud to disappoint the respectable who trembled at the invasion of the black barbarians[55] – we recall the white gloves of the marchers – so a few years ago the Neapolitans took pride in a rather more startling achievement. Nothing, they claimed, had been stolen and nobody cheated during the national festival of *Unità*, when it took place in that notoriously ingenious and light-fingered city.

But the miners' galas were planned as annual occasions and even at the first tentative one in Durham in 1871 three prizes were offered for the band contest and 'liberal money prizes for various athletic sports.'[56] May Day was planned simply as a one-off simultaneous international demonstration for the Legal Eight Hour Day. How much of its force, like that of the red flag, was due to this sense of internationalism, we can only speculate, but certainly a good deal. Annual repetition was imposed on the parties and the International by public demand from the grassroots. Moreover, it was through public participation that a demonstration was turned into a holiday in both the ritual and the festive sense. Engels only came to refer to it as a *Maifeier* or celebration instead of a demonstration in 1893.[57] On the contrary: the ideologically purer revolutionaries were actually suspicious of merrymaking as politically diversionary, and of folkloric practices as a concession to the spirit of superstition.[58] They would have preferred more glum and militant protest marches. Leaders with a better sense of the masses, like Adler, Vandervelde and Costa, were better tuned to the wavelength of the masses. As Costa said in 1893: 'Catholics have Easter; henceforth workers will have their own Easter.'[59] The Italians, mobilizing a traditional and largely illiterate class, tended to be unusually sensitive to the force of symbol and ceremony.[60] What is more, the specific demand of the original May Day soon dropped into the background. It increasingly turned into an annual assertion of class presence - most successfully so where, against the advice of cautious socialist and union leaders which prevailed in Britain and Germany, it underlined that presence by a symbolic assertion of the fundamental power of workers, the abstention from work by a one-day strike. In many Latin countries it came to be seen as a commemoration of martyrs - the 'Chicago martyrs', and is still sometimes so regarded.

The ritual element in the workers' May Day - which was, as someone observed, even among radical and revolutionary anniversaries the *only* one associated exclusively with the proletariat - was immediately recognized by the artists, journalists, poets and versifiers who, on behalf of their parties, produced badges, flags, posters, May Day periodicals, cartoons and other suitable material for the occasion. Their iconographic language echoes the imagery of spring, youth and growth which was spontaneously associated with the day. Flowers were an important part of this imagery and immediately came to be worn, we hardly know how: the carnation in Austria and Italy – eventually it became *the* flower of May Day – the red (paper) rose in Germany, sweet briar and poppy in France, as well as the may; but not the lily-of-the-valley which later came into non-political symbiosis with May Day in France. What popular memory associated with the Fusillade de Fourmies, the shooting down of such a procession in 1891, was the image of a young girl carrying such a flowering branch.[61] A good deal of this was doubtless due to the historical accident which led the International to choose this emotionally and traditionally charged date for its demonstration. Much was certainly due to its initiation at one of the notable moments of international labour awakening, growth and expansion. It was a celebration of renewal and hope at a season of renewal and hope, and might well not have established itself so permanently had it been initiated at a less optimistic moment in labour's history.

What did this day signify for the workers? Fortunately we are not quite in the dark about this, for the organizers of a recent Italian exhibition of labour banners showed the appropriate ones to a few ancients, who immediately associated them with the First of May. Let me quote Pietro Comollo, a Torinese in his late seventies:

> The banners were educational. Everybody used to say: 'It's our festival – it's the workers' festival.' We knew vaguely that it was in memory of those who'd fought for the Eight Hours, the Chicago Martyrs. So that was a symbolic fact, that had become symbolic for the workers . . . And then, well, it was just a holiday: there were the red carnations. It was a fighting demonstration, not only because they had extorted May Day through their organizations, but because we were all there together and united. Even the anarchists turned up.[62]

It was the ritual of class, community, struggle and union.

The strength of the workers' emotional attachment to this occasion is indicated by the efforts of the movement's opponents to annex it. After the Bolsheviks it was Hitler who, in 1933, turned it into an official national holiday of labour, subsequently followed by the EEC. Moreover, just as Hitler consciously combined the red of the socialist flag with the very different symbol of the swastika, so we can see the Nazis in the 1930s deliberately transforming the symbolic imagery of the day from one of class struggle to one of class cooperation in the national cause.[63]

How far have such ritualizations of the new socialist labour movements survived and developed since the 1890s? It it difficult to generalize. Since they were essentially *public* rituals, they could only flourish in countries where labour movements were legal, and especially, I would suggest, where politics left sufficient scope for mass mobilization. Elsewhere they were the symbolic property of small underground groups or secret revolutionary organizations, whose rather colourful ritual history I have written about elsewhere. I merely repeat my conviction that such left-wing bodies – but not right-wing or nationalist ones – shed their ritualism almost completely, a process accelerated, where necessary, by the ban on masonic membership imposed by the communist movement between the wars. Probably the new public rituals reached their peak in the period of the united – except for the anarchists – and, it seemed, the inevitably triumphant socialist labour movements before 1914, but the national and regional divergences after 1917 are such that there may be exceptions. They were certainly carried by hope and confidence rather than conflict. Retreat and economic depression have time and again enfeebled them, and conversely advances – as in France in 1936, over much of Europe in 1944–5, have revived them.

There are movements, even after 1945, which still show the old apparatus of ritualization in good working order, transforming such apparently utilitarian occasions as the annual exchange of party cards,[64] or the raising of funds, which is the primary justification of branch fêtes and the great pyramid of French and Italian festivals in aid of the party newspapers. But on the whole, what has survived best are the handful of elementary symbols which are least dependent on large organizations capable of mobilizing large bodies of working men and women: the colour red, which completed its conquest of socialist movements after 1917*, the *International*, which became the world anthem of the movement in the early 1900s[66] and a few other symbolic songs – the *Red Flag*, *Bandiera Rossa* – and a few symbols and gestures, some of obscure but almost certainly post-1917 origin like the clenched fist. These

---

* In Italy it finally vanquished the traditional black-bordered red in that period, as witness the song *Bandiera Rossa*.[65]

were easily learned or taken up by spontaneous, unorganized re-
vivals of militancy such as the student movements of the late 1960s.

For with some notable exceptions, the great class movements of
the classical era of mass socialist workers' parties have not very
successfully survived the extraordinary economic, social and cultural transformations of the 1950s and 1960s, at least in the western
industrial countries. The working class is not the same any more
and neither is society. To put it in the simplest terms – those of an
old Italian lady who carried her first banner in 1920 at the age of
twelve, less than a month after starting work in the cotton-mill:
'They're all *signori* nowadays, those who go out to work, they have
everything they ask for; I never asked for anything, because there
wasn't anything to be had.'[67] It is little wonder that the old tend
to talk about May Day in the past tense.

The rituals I have tried to sketch were essentially self-assertions
and self-definitions of a new class *through class organization;* and
within it, of a large cadre of militants drawn from that class or
identified with it, asserting their own capacity to órganize, to practise politics as well as the old élite, to demonstrate their own rise
through that of their class. Where labour movements go back beyond the socialist era, these rituals moved from the self-assertion
of the whole 'trade' or occupation, to that of the wage-workers
within the trade, and, as in the miners' movements, the class community as a whole, as part of a wider movement of all workers.
Where they coincide with the socialist era, the identification of
class, party and the hope of a new world based on both, prevailed
from the outset. The ritual occasions and the ritual language were
transformed, perhaps after an initial period of transition, as between
the 1880s and the October Revolution, when the new socialist labour movements or (as in Britain) the older movements growing
towards class movements committed to socialism, combined the
symbolisms of the old and the new on their banners and emblems.
They were also simplified, as the old and elaborate symbolical and
allegorical vocabulary ceased to be understood, and perhaps also
because poverty implied simplification. One recalls that even in
1874, when the workers of Breslau commemorated the tenth anniversary of Lassalle's death – the rituals of death, as we have seen,
maintained their ancient significance and their capacity to crystal-
lize the structure of the individual's relation to the community and
the world – the men wore red and green sashes, but few of the

women, who were supposed to wear black, could do so, because they did not own black dresses....[68] In any case the major form of public ritual in modern mass societies, increasingly tended to be a sort of public drama, in which the distinction between participants and spectators, actors and spear-carriers, was attenuated, and where the mass itself acted as its own symbol.* Modern governments have exploited this form of public spectacle to good effect. This was not a development peculiar to labour movements, though their mass organizations and parties, being among the first of their kind, may have pioneered some of this transformation. However, such reflections take us far beyond an essay on labour rituals.

Nevertheless, except for certain public purposes, ritual has undoubtedly declined. And in labour movements this is not very surprising. For even at the peak of its development, its role in the era of mass labour movements and parties was marginal, unlike its role in, say, nationalist movements. For the identification of workers with their movement, profound though it often was, was neither achieved nor even really symbolized by ritual. It took place by the mere assertion of class which implied organization, an organization which was far more than a merely utilitarian device. Hence the contempt of those used to the unionism of the old miners' lodges for the 'penny-in-the-slot' unions of later years. The very word 'labour' or 'worker' could be enough to establish this emotional identification, as among the 200,000 or so members of (social-democratic) Workers' Choral Societies in 1914 Germany, the 130,000 or so 'worker cyclists',[69] the 'worker stamp collectors' who still met, no doubt rather elderly and much reduced in numbers, in a Viennese public house in the 1970s. It is true that there was even then a disproportion between the dedication of militants and the matter-of-fact formalities associated with it; a disproportion which would have been incomprehensible to early journeymen societies or for that matter to priests. It was in this space that modern labour ritual grew up to supply colour, emotional structure and ceremony. The space was large. In his recent memoirs an elderly East German poet has reflected how strange it is that the signing of a small and crumpled piece of paper, presented by a young worker on a Berlin street corner in 1931, he still feels as binding him to the party he

---

* It was actually suggested that on the route of the mass demonstrations in Vienna ramps should be constructed, so that the marchers, temporarily raised above street level, should be able to *see* the masses of which each file was a part.

then joined as a schoolboy.[70] It is not really puzzling. In signing, he signed away his life to a cause and a dream, as people did in those days.

Yet the disproportion remains. The space was never systematically filled by ritual. What movement, playing so central a part in the history of the nineteenth and twentieth century, and destined to conquer an area of the world larger than that of Islam and with greater rapidity than did the disciples of Mohammed, has done so – at least until its transformation into states and regimes – with less ritual baggage than the socialist movement? It derived its emotional force and legitimacy from its identification with a class, the working class, whose historical triumph it believed to be certain and inevitable. That seemed enough. The historian can only observe the phenomenon. He is not obliged to enquire how far this belief was, or is likely to be, justified.

(1982)

# 6: Man and Woman: Images on the Left

Women have often pointed out that male historians in the past, including Marxists, have grossly neglected the female half of the human race. The criticism is just; the present writer accepts that it applies to his own work. Yet if this deficiency is to be remedied, it cannot be simply by developing a specialized branch of history which deals exclusively with women, for in human society the two sexes are inseparable.[1] What we need also to study is the changing forms of the relations between the sexes, both in social reality and in the image which both sexes have of one another. The present paper is a preliminary attempt to do this for the revolutionary and socialist movements of the nineteenth and early twentieth centuries by means of the ideology expressed in the images and emblems associated with these movements. Since these were overwhelmingly designed by men, it is of course impossible to assume that the sex-roles they represent express the views of most women. However, it is possible to compare these images of roles and relationships with the social realities of the period, and with the more specifically formulated ideologies of revolutionary and socialist movements.

That such a comparison is possible, is the assumption which underlies this paper. It is not suggested that the images here analysed directly reflect social realities, except where they were specifically designed to do so, as in pictures intended to have documentary value, and even then they clearly did not only reflect reality. My assumption is merely that in images designed to be seen by and to have an impact upon a wide public, e.g. of workers, the public's experience of reality sets limits to the degree to which they may diverge from that experience. If the capitalist in socialist cartoons of the *Belle Epoque* were to have been *habitually* presented not as a fat man smoking a cigar and in a top hat, but as a fat woman, these permissible limits would have been exceeded, and the caricatures would have been less effective; for most bosses were not only conceived as males but were males. It does not follow that all capitalists were fat with top hats and cigars, though these attributes were readily understood as indicating wealth in a bourgeois society, and had to be understood as specifying one particular form of wealth and privilege as distinct from others, e.g. the nobleman's. Such a correspondence with reality was evidently less necessary in purely symbolic and allegorical images, and yet even here they were not completely absent; if the deity of war had been presented as a woman, it would have been with the intention to shock. To interpret iconography in this manner is naturally not to make a serious analysis of image and symbol. My purpose is more modest.

Let us begin with perhaps the most famous of revolutionary paintings, though one not created by a revolutionary: Delacroix' *Liberty on the Barricades* in 1830. The picture will be familiar to many: a bare-breasted girl in Phrygian bonnet with a banner, stepping over the fallen, followed by armed men in characteristic costumes. The sources of the picture have been much investigated.[2] Whatever they are, its contemporary interpretation is not in doubt. Liberty was seen not as an allegorical figure, but as a real woman (inspired no doubt by the heroic Marie Deschamps, whose feats suggested the picture). She was seen as a woman of the people, belonging to the people, at ease among the people:

> C'est une forte femme aux puissantes mamelles,
> à la voix rauque, aux durs appas qui ...
>
> Agile et marchant à grands pas
> Se plaît aux cris du peuple. ...
> Barbier, *La Curée*
>
> (A strong woman, stout bosom'd,
> With raucous voice and rough charm ...
> She strides forward with confidence,
> Rejoicing in the clamour of the people. ...
> *The Bandwagon*)

She was for Balzac, of peasant stock: 'dark-skinned and ardent, the very image of the people'.[3] She was proud, even insolent (Balzac's words), and thus the very opposite of the public image of women in bourgeois society. And, as the contemporaries stress, she was sexually emancipated. Barbier, whose *La Curée* is certainly one of Delacroix' sources, invents an entire history of sexual emancipation and initiative for her:

> qui ne prend ses amours que dans la populace,
> qui ne prête son large flanc
> qu'à des gens forts comme elle

> (who takes her lovers only from among the masses,
> who gives her sturdy body only to men as strong as herself)

after having, *enfant de la Bastille* ('child of the Bastille'), spread universal sexual excitement around her, tired of her early lovers and followed Napoleon's banners and a *capitaine de vingt ans* ('20-year-old captain'). Now she returned,

> toujours belle et *nue* [my emphasis, EJH]
> avec l'écharpe aux trois couleurs

> (still beautiful and *naked* with the tricolour sash)

to win the 'Trois Glorieuses' (the July Revolution) for her people.[4]

Heine, who comments on the picture itself, pushes the image even further towards another ambiguous stereotype of the independent and sexually emancipated woman, the courtesan: 'a strange mixture of Phyrne, fishwife and goddess of freedom'.[5] The theme is recognizable: Flaubert in *Education Sentimentale* returns to it in the context of 1848, with his image of Liberty as a common prostitute in the ransacked Tuileries (though operating the habitual bourgeois transition from the equation liberty = good to that of license = bad): 'In the ante-chamber, bolt upright on a pile of clothes, stood a woman of the streets posing as a statue of liberty'. The same note is hinted at by the reactionary Félicien Rops, who had actually represented 'the Commune personified by a naked woman, a soldier's cap on her head and sword at her side',[6] an image which came not only to his own mind. His powerful *Peuple* is a naked young woman, in the posture of a whore dressed only in stockings and a night cap, possibly hinting at the Phrygian bonnet, her legs opening on her sex.[7]

The novelty of Delacroix' *Liberty* therefore lies in the identification of the nude female figure with a real woman of the people, an emancipated woman, and one playing an active – indeed a leading – role in the movement of men. How far back this revolutionary image can be traced is a question which must be left to art historians to answer.[8] Here we can only note two things. *First*, its concreteness removes it from the usual allegorical role of females, though she maintains the nakedness of such figures, and this nudity is indeed stressed by painter and observers. She does not inspire or represent: she *acts*. *Second*, she seems clearly distinct from the traditional iconographic image of woman as an active freedom-fighter, notably Judith, who, with David, so often represents the successful struggle of the weak against the strong. Unlike David and Judith, Delacroix' *Liberty* is not alone, nor does she represent weakness. On the contrary, she represents the concentrated force of the invincible people. Since 'the people' consists of a collection of different classes and occupations, and is presented as such, a general symbol not identified with any of them is desirable. For traditional iconographic reasons this was likely to be female. But the woman chosen represents 'the people'.

The Revolution of 1830 seems to represent the high point of this image of Liberty as an active, emancipated girl accepted as leader by men, though the theme continues to be popular in 1848, doubtless because of Delacroix' influence on other painters. She remains naked in Phrygian cap in Millet's *Liberty on the Barricades*, but her context is now vague. She remains a leader-figure in Daumier's draft of *The Uprising* but, once again, her context is shadowy. On the other hand, though there are not many representations of the Commune and of Liberty in 1871, they tended to be naked (as in the design of Rops mentioned above) or bare-breasted.[9] Perhaps the notably active part played by women in the Commune also accounts for the symbolization of this revolution by a non-allegorical (i.e. clothed) and obviously militant woman in at least one foreign illustration.[10]

The revolutionary concept of republic or liberty thus still tended to be a naked, or more likely bare-breasted, female. The Communard Dalou's celebrated statue of the Republic on the Place de la Nation still has at least one breast bared. Only research could show how far the revelation of the breast retains this rebellious or at least polemical association, as perhaps in the cartoon from the Dreyfus period (January 1898) in which a young and virginal Marianne, one breast exposed, is protected against a monster by a matronly and armed Justice over the line: 'Justice: Have no fear of the monster! I am here'.[11] On the other hand the institutionalized Republic, Marianne, in spite of her revolutionary origins, is now normally though lightly, clothed. The reign of decency has been re-established. Perhaps also the reign of lies, since it is characteristic of the allegorical female figure of Truth – she still appears frequently, notably in the caricatures of the Dreyfus period – that she should be naked.[12] And indeed, even in the iconography of the respectable British labour movement of Victorian England, she remains naked, as on the emblem of the Amalgamated Society of Carpenters and Joiners, 1860,[13] until late Victorian morality prevails.

Generally, the role of the female figure, naked or clothed, diminishes sharply with the transition from the democratic-plebeian revolutions of the nineteenth century to the proletarian and socialist movements of the twentieth. In a sense, the main problem of this paper consists in this masculinization of the imagery of the labour and socialist movement.

For obvious reasons the working woman proletarian is not much represented by artists, outside the few industries which were predominantly female. This was certainly not due to prejudice. Constantin Meunier, the Belgian who pioneered the typical idealization of the male worker, painted – and to a lesser extent sculpted – women wage-workers as readily as men; sometimes, as in his *Le retour des mines* (Coming back from the mines) (1905) working together with men – as women still did in Belgian mines.[14] However, it is probable that the image of woman as a wage-worker and an active participant together with males in political activity[15] was largely due to socialist influence. In Britain it does not become noticeable in the trade union iconography until this influence is felt.[16] In the emblems of pre-socialist British trade unions, uninfluenced by intellectuals, real women appear mainly in those small images by which unions advertised their fraternal help to members in distress: sickness, accident and funeral benefit. They stand by the bedside of the sick husband as his mates come to visit him adorned with the sash of their union. Surrounded by children, they shake hands with the union representative who hands them money after the death of the breadwinner.

Of course women are still present in the form of symbol and allegory, though towards the end of the century in Britain union emblems are to be found without any female figures, especially in such purely masculine industries as coal-mining, steel-smelting and the like.[17] Still, the allegories of liberal self-help continue to be

largely female, because they had always been. Prudence, Industry
(=diligence) Fortitude, Temperance, Truth and Justice presided
over the Stone Masons' Friendly Society in 1868; Art, Industry,
Truth and Justice over the Amalgamated Society of Carpenters and
Joiners. From the 1880s on one has the impression that only Justice
and Truth, possibly supplemented by Faith and Hope, survive
among these traditional figures. However as socialism advances,
other female persons enter the iconography of the left, though they
are in no sense supposed to represent real women. They are goddesses or muses.

Thus on a banner of the (left-wing) Workers' Union, 1898–1929,
a sweet young lady in white drapery and sandals points to a rising
sun labelled 'A better life' for the benefit of a number of realistically
painted workers in working dress. She is Faith, as the text below
the picture makes clear. A militant figure, also in white draperies
and sandals, but with sword and buckler marked 'Justice & Equality', not a hair out of place on her well-styled head, stands before
a muscular worker in an open shirt who has evidently just defeated
a beast labelled 'Capitalism' which lies dead on the ground before
him. The banner is labelled 'The Triumph of Labour', and represents the Southend-on-Sea branch of the National Union of
General Workers, another socialist union. The Tottenham branch
of the same union has the same young lady, this time with flowing
hair, her dress marked 'Light, Education, Industrial Organisation,
Political Action and Real International', pointing out the promised
land in the shape of a children's playground to the usual group of
workers. The promised land is labelled 'gain the Cooperative Commonwealth', and the entire banner illustrates the slogan 'Producers
of the Nation's Wealth, Unite! And have your share of the
world.'[18]

These images are all the more significant because they are obviously linked to the new socialist movement, which develops its
own iconography, and because (unlike the old allegorical vocabulary) this new iconography is in part inspired by the tradition of
French revolutionary imagery, from which Delacroix' *Liberty* is
also derived. Stylistically, in Britain at least, it belongs to the progressive arts-and-crafts movement and its offshoot, *art nouveau*,
which provided British socialism with its chief artists and illustra-
tors, William Morris and Walter Crane. Yet Walter Crane's widely
popular image of humanity advancing to socialism – a couple in

loose summery clothes, the man carrying a child on his shoulder – like so many of his designs still reflects the debt to 1789 in the presence of the Phrygian bonnet.[19] The earliest of the First-of-May badges of the Austrian social-democrats make the connection even more obvious. They represent a female figure with the motto: Fraternity, Equality, Liberty and the Eight-Hour Day.[20]

Yet what is the role of the women in this new socialist iconography? They inspire. The emblem of the *Labour Annual*,[21] published from 1895, is T.A. West's *Light and Life*. A lady in flowing robes, half-visible behind an escutcheon, blows a ritual trumpet for the benefit of a handsome boy with open-necked shirt and sleeves rolled up beyond the elbow, carrying a basket from which he sows the seed of, presumably, socialist propaganda; rays, stars and waves form the background to the design. Insofar as human women appear in this iconography, they are part of an idealized couple, with or without children. Insofar as each is symbolically identified with some activity, it is the man who represents industrial labour. In Crane's couple he has beside him a pick and a shovel, while she, carrying a basket of corn, and with a rake by her side, represents nature or at most agriculture. Curiously enough, the same division occurs in Mukhina's famous sculpture of the (male) worker and the (female) *kolkhoz* peasant on the Soviet Pavilion at the Paris International Exposition of 1937: he the hammer, she the sickle.

Of course actual women of the working classes also occur in the new socialist iconography, and embody a symbolic meaning, at least by implication. Yet they are quite different from the militant girls of the Paris Commune. They are figures of suffering and endurance. Meunier, that great pioneer of proletarian art and socialist realism – both as realism and as idealisation – anticipates them, as usual. His *Femme du Peuple* (Woman of the People) (1893) is old, thin, her hair drawn back so tightly as to suggest little more than a naked skull, her withered flat chest suggested by the very (and untypical) nakedness of her shoulders.[21] His even better-known *Le Grisou* (Firedamp) has the female figure, swathed in shawls, grieving over the corpse of the dead miner. These are the suffering proletarian mothers best known from Gorki's novel or Kaethe Kollwitz' tragic drawings.[23] And it is perhaps not insignificant that their bodies become invisible under shawls and headcloths. The typical image of the proletarian woman has been desexualized and hides behind the clothes of poverty. She is spirit, not body. (In real life this image of the suffering wife and mother turned militant is perhaps exemplified by the blackclad eloquence of *La Pasionaria* in the days of the Spanish Civil War.)

Yet while the female body in socialist iconography is increasingly dressed, if not concealed, a curious thing is happening to the male body. It is increasingly revealed for symbolic purposes. The image which increasingly symbolizes the working class is the exact counterpart to Delacroix' *Liberty*, namely a topless young man: the powerful figure of a masculine labourer, swinging hammer or pick and *naked to the waist*.[24] This image is unrealistic in two ways. In the first place, it was by no means easy to find many nineteenth-century male workers in the countries with strong labour movements labouring with a naked torso. This, as Van Gogh recognized, was one of the difficulties of an era of artistic realism. He would have liked to paint the naked bodies of peasants, but in real life they did not go naked.[25] The numerous pictures representing industrial labour, even under conditions when it would today seem reasonable to take off one's shirt, as in the heat and glow of iron-works or gasworks, almost universally show them clothed, however lightly. This includes not merely what might be called broad evocations of the world of labour such as Madox Ford's *Work*, or Alfred Roll's *Le Travail* (1881) – a scene of open-air building work – but realistic paintings or graphic reporting.[26] Naturally bare torsoed workers could be seen – for instance among some, but by no means all, British coal-face workers. In such cases workers could be realistically presented as semi-nudes, as in G. Caillebotte's *Raboteurs de Parquet* (Floor-polishers),[27] or in the figure of a coal-hewer on the emblem of the Ironfounders' Union (1857).[28] In real life, however, these were all special cases. In the second place, the image of nakedness is unrealistic because it almost certainly excluded the vast body of skilled and factory workers, who would not have dreamed of working without their shirts at any time, and who, incidentally, in general formed the bulk of the organized labour movement.

When the bare-torsoed worker first appears in art is uncertain. Certainly what must be one of the earliest sculptured proletarians, Westmacott's slate-worker on the Penrhyn monument, Bangor (1821)[29], is dressed, while the peasant girl near him is, perhaps semi-allegorically, rather decolletée. At all events from the 1880s on he was familiar in sculpture in the work of the Belgian, Constantin

Meunier, perhaps the first artist to devote himself wholeheartedly to the presentation of the manual worker; possibly also of the Communard Dalou, whose unfinished monument to labour contains similar motifs. Obviously he was much more prominent in sculpture, which had, by long tradition, a much stronger tendency to present the human figure nude than painting. In fact, Meunier's drawings and paintings are much more often realistically clothed, and, as has been shown for at least one of his themes, dockers unloading a ship, were only undressed in the three-dimensional design for a monument of labour.[30] Perhaps this is one reason why the semi-nude figure is less prominent in the period of the Second International, when the socialist movement was not in a position to commission many public monuments as yet, and comes into his own after 1917 in Soviet Russia, where it was. Yet, though a direct comparison between painted and sculptured image is therefore misleading, the bare male torso may already be found here and there on two-dimensional emblems, banners and other pictures of the labour movement even in the nineteenth century. Still, in sculpture he triumphed after 1917 in Soviet Russia, under such titles as *Worker, The Weapons of the Proletariat, Memorial of Bloody Sunday 1905* etc.[31] The theme is not yet exhausted, since a statue called 'Friendship of the Peoples' of the 1970s still presents the familiar topless Hercules swinging a hammer.[32]

Painting and graphics still found it harder to break the links with realism. It is not easy to find any bare-torsoed workers in the heroic age of the Russian revolutionary poster. Even the symbolic painting *Trud* (Toil) presents a design of an idealized young man *in working clothes*, surrounded by the tools of a skilled artisan,[33] rather than the heavy-muscled and basically unskilled titan of the more familiar kind. The powerful hammer-swinger engaged in breaking the chains binding the globe, who symbolized the *Communist International* on the covers of its periodical from 1920, wore clothes on his torso, though only sketchy ones. The symbolic decorations of this review in its early numbers were non-human: five pointed stars, rays, hammers, sickles, ears of grain, beehives, cornucopias, roses, thorns, crossed torches and chains. While there were more modern images such as stylizations of smoking factory chimneys in the art-nouveau fashion* and driving bands of

---

* In Russia this motif occurs as early as 1905–7.

transmission-belts, there were no bare-chested workers. Propaganda photographs of such men do not become common, if they occur at all, before the first Five-Year Plan.[34] Nevertheless, though the progress of the two-dimensional bare torso was slower than might be thought, the image was familiar. Thus it is the symbol decorating the cover of the French edition of the *Compte Rendu Analytique* of the 5th Congress of Comintern (Paris, 1924).

Why the bare body? The question can only be briefly discussed, but takes us back both to the language of idealized and symbolic presentation and to the need to develop such a language for the socialist revolutionary movement. There is no doubt that eighteenth-century aesthetic theory linked the naked body and the idealization of the human being; often quite consciously as in Winckelmann. An idealized person (as distinct from an allegorical figure) could not be clothed in the garments of real life, and – as in the nude statues of Napoleon – should if possible be presented without garments. Realism had no place in such a presentation. When Stendhal criticized the painter David, because it would have been suicidal for his warriors of antiquity to go into battle naked, armed only with helmet, sword and shield, he was simply drawing attention, in his usual role as provocator, to the incompatibility of symbolic and realistic statement in art. But the socialist movement, in spite of its profound attachment in principle to realism in art – an attachment which goes back to the Saint-Simonians – required a language of symbolic statement, in which to state its ideals. As we have seen, the emblems and banners of the British trade unions – rightly described by Klingender as 'the true folk-art of nineteenth century Britain'[35] – are a combination of realism, allegory and symbol. They are probably the last flourishing form of the allegorical and symbolic language outside public monumental sculpture. An idealized presentation of the subject of the movement, the struggling working class itself, must sooner or later involve the use of the nude – as on the banner of the Export Branch of the Dockers' Union in the 1890s, where a naked muscular figure, his loins lightly draped, kneels on a rock wrestling with a large green serpent, surrounded by suitable mottoes.[36] In short, though the tension between realism and symbolism remained, it was still difficult to devise a complete vocabulary of symbol and ideal without the nude. On the other hand, it may be suggested that the total nude was no longer acceptable. It cannot have been easy to overlook the absurdity of the 1927 'Group: October'[37] which consists of three muscular men, naked except for the Red-army cap worn by one of them, with hammers and other suitable paraphernalia. Let us conjecture that the bare-torsoed image expressed a compromise between symbolism and realism. There were after all *real* workers who could be so presented.

We are left with a final, but crucial question. Why is the struggling working class symbolized exclusively by a *male* torso? Here we can only speculate. Two lines of speculation may be suggested.

The first concerns the changes in the actual sexual division of labour in the capitalist period, both productive and political. It is a paradox of nineteenth-century industrialization that it tended to increase and sharpen the sexual division of labour between (unpaid) household work and (paid) work outside, by depriving the producer of control over the means of production. In the pre-industrial or proto-industrial economy (peasant farming, artisanal production, small shopkeeping, cottage industry, putting-out, etc.) household and production were generally a single or combined unit, and though this normally meant that women were grossly overworked – since they did most of the housework and shared in the rest of the work – they were not confined to one type of work. Indeed, in the great expansion of 'proto-industrialism' (cottage industry) which has recently been investigated the actual productive processes attenuated or even abolished the differences in work between men and women, with far-reaching effects on the social and sexual roles and conventions of the sexes.[38]

On the other hand in the increasingly common situation of the worker who laboured for an employer in a workplace belonging to the employer, home and work were separate. Typically it was the male who had to leave home every day to work for wages and the woman who did not. Typically women worked outside the home (where they did so at all) only before or, if widowed or separated, after marriage, or where the husband was unable to earn sufficient to maintain wife and family, and very likely only so long as he was unable to do so. Conversely, an occupation in which an adult man was normally unable to earn a family wage was – very understandably – regarded as underpaid. Hence, the labour movement quite logically developed the tendency to calculate the desirable minimum wage in terms of the earnings of a single (i.e. in practice male) breadwinner, and to regard a wage-working wife as a symptom of an undesirable economic situation. In fact the situation was often undesirable, and the number of married women obliged to work for wages or their equivalent was substantial, though a very large proportion of them did so at home – i.e. outside the effective range of labour movements.[39] Moreover, even in industries in which the work of married women was traditionally well established – as in the Lancashire textile region – its scope can be exaggerated. In 1901 38 per cent of married and widowed women in Blackburn were employed for wages, but only 15 per cent of those in Bolton.[40]

In short, conventionally women aimed to stop working for wages outside the house once they got married. Britain, where in 1911 only 11 per cent of wage-working women had husbands and only 10 per cent of married women worked, was perhaps an extreme case; but even in Germany (1907) where 30 per cent of wage-working women had husbands the sex-difference was striking. For every wife at wage-work in the age-groups from 25 to 40 years, there were four wage-working husbands.[41] The situation of the married woman was not substantially changed as yet by the tendency – rather marked after 1900 – for women to enter industry in larger numbers, and by the growing variety of occupations and leisure activities open to unmarried girls.[42] 'The trend towards a larger number of married women having a specified occupation had not been firmly established at the turn of the century.'[43] The point is worth stressing, since some feminist historians, for reasons difficult to understand, have attempted to deny it. Nineteenth-century industrialization (unlike twentieth-century industrialization) tended to make marriage and the family the major career of the working class woman who was not obliged by sheer poverty to take other work.[44] Insofar as she worked for wages before marriage, she saw wage-work as a temporary, though no doubt desirable, phase in her life. Once married, she belonged to the proletariat not as a worker, but as the wife, mother and housekeeper of workers.

Politically the pre-industrial struggle of the poor not only produced ample room for women to take part beside men – neither sex had such political rights as the right to vote – but in some respects a specific and leading role for them. The commonest form of struggle was that to assert social justice, i.e. the maintenance of what E. P. Thompson has called 'the moral economy of the crowd' through direct action to control prices.[45] In the form of action, which could be politically decisive – we recall the march of the women on Versailles in 1789 – women not only took the lead, but were conventionally expected to. As Luisa Accati rightly states: 'in a large number of cases (I would almost say in practically all cases) women have the decisive role, whether because it is they who take the initiative, or because they form a very large part of the crowd'.[46] We need not here consider the well-known pre-industrial practice in which rebellious men take action disguised as women, as in the so-called Rebecca Riots of Wales (1843).

Furthermore, the characteristic urban revolution of the pre-industrial period was not proletarian but plebeian. Within the *menu peuple*, a socially heterogeneous coalition of elements, united by common 'littleness' and poverty rather than by occupational or class criteria, women could play a political role, provided only they could come out on the streets. They could and did help to build barricades. They could assist those who fought behind them. They could even fight or bear arms themselves. Even the image of the modern 'people's revolution' in a large non-industrial metropolis contains them, as anyone who recalls the street scenes of Havana after the triumph of Fidel Castro will testify.

On the other hand the specific form of struggle of the proletariat, the trade union and the strike, largely excluded the women, or greatly reduced their visible role as active participants, except in the few industries in which they were heavily concentrated. Thus in 1896 the total number of women in British trade unions (excluding teachers) was 142,000 or something like 8 per cent; but 60 per cent of these were in the extremely strongly organized cotton industry. By 1910 it was above 10 per cent but though there had been some growth in trade unionism among white-collar and shopworkers, the great bulk of the expansion in industry was still in textiles.[47] Elsewhere their role was indeed crucial, but distinct, even in small industrial and mining centres where place and work and community were inseparable. Yet if in such places their role in strikes was public, visible and essential, it was nevertheless not that of strikers themselves.

Moreover, where men's work and women's work were not so separate and distinct that no question of intermixture could arise, the normal attitude of male trade unionists towards women seeking to enter their occupation was, in the words of S. and B. Webb, 'resentment and abhorrence'.[48] The reason was simple: since their wages were so much lower, they represented a threat to the rates and conditions of men. They were – to quote the Webbs again – 'as a class, the most dangerous enemies of the artisan's Standard of Life', though the men's attitude was also – in spite of the growing influence on the left – strongly influenced by what would today be called 'sexism':[49] 'the respectable artisan has an instinctive distaste for the promiscuous mixing of men and women in daily intercourse, whether this be in the workshop or in a social club'.[50] Consequently the policy of all unions capable of doing so was to exclude women from their work, and the policy even of those unions incapable of doing so (e.g. the cotton weavers) was to segregate the sexes or at least to avoid women and girls working 'in conjunction with men, especially if (they are) removed from constant association with other female workers'.[51] Thus both the fear of the economic competition of women workers and the maintenance of 'morality' combined to keep women outside or on the margins of the labour movement – except in the conventional role of family members.

The paradox of the labour movement was thus that it encouraged an ideology of sexual equality and emancipation, while in practice discouraging the actual joint participation of men and women in the process of labour as workers. For the minority of emancipated women of all classes, including workers, it provided the best opportunities to develop as human beings, indeed as leaders and public figures. Probably it provided the only environment in the nineteenth century which gave them such opportunities. Nor should we underestimate the effect on the ordinary, even the married, working-class women of a movement passionately committed to female emancipation. Unlike the petty-bourgeois 'progressive' movement which, as among the French Radical Socialists, virtually flaunted its male chauvinism, the socialist labour movement tried to overcome the tendencies within the proletariat and elsewhere to maintain sexual inequality, even if it failed to achieve as much as it would have wished.[52] It is not insignificant that the major work by the charismatic leader of the German socialists, August Bebel – and by far the most popular work of socialist propaganda in Germany at that period – was his *Woman and Socialism*.[53] Yet at the same time the labour movement unconsciously tightened the bonds which kept the majority of (non-wage-earning) married women of the working class in their assigned and subordinate social role. The more powerful it became as a mass movement, the more effective these brakes on its own emancipatory theory and practice became; at least until the economic transformations destroyed the nineteenth-century industrial phase of the sexual division of labour. In a sense the iconography of the movement reflects this unconscious reinforcement of the sexual division of labour. In spite of and against the movement's conscious intentions, its image expressed the essential 'maleness' of the proletarian struggle in its elementary form before 1914, the trade-union struggle.

It should now be clear why, paradoxically, the historical change from an era of plebeian and democratic to one of proletarian-socialist movements should have led, iconographically, to a decline in the role of the female. However, there may be another factor which reinforced this masculinization of the movement: the decline of classical pre-industrial millennialism. This is an even more speculative question, and I touch on it with caution and hesitation.

As has already been suggested, in the iconography of the left, the female figure maintained herself best as an image of utopia: the goddess of freedom, the symbol of victory, the figure who pointed towards the perfect society of the future. And indeed the imagery of the socialist utopia was essentially one of nature, of fertility and growth, of blossoming, for which the female metaphor came naturally:

> Les générations écloses
> Verront fleurir leurs bébés roses
> Comme églantiers en Floréal
> Ce sera la saison des roses ...
> Voilà l'avenir social
>     E. Pottier[54]

> (The budding generations
> Will see their rosy babies flower
> Like briars in the spring.
> It will be the season of roses ...
> That's the people's future.)

Eugène Pottier, the Fourierist author of the *Internationale*, is full of such images of femaleness, even in its literal sense of the maternal breast:

pour tes enfants longtemps sevrés
reprends le rôle du mamelle
    (L'Age d'Or)
Ah, chassons-la. Dans l'or des blés
Mère apparais, les seins gonflées
à nos phalanges collectives
    (La fille du Thermidor)
Du sein de la nourrice, il coule ce beau jour
Une inondation d'existence et d'amour.
Tout est fécondité, tout pullule et foisonne
    (Abondance)
Nature – toi qui gonfles ton sein
        pour ta famille entière
    (La Cremaillère)

(To your children, though weaned long ago,
Give once again your breast.
    *The Golden Age*
In the golden meadows come to us Mother,
Your breasts full for the collective hosts.
    *Daughter of Thermidor*
This beautiful day flows from the nurse's breast,
A flood of life and love.
All is fruitfulness, everything swarms and abounds.
    *Abundance*
Nature – you whose breast has swell'd
To feed your entire family . . .
    *Celebration*)

So, in a less explicitly physical way, is Walter Crane who, as we
have seen, was largely responsible for the themes of socialist imagery in Britain from the 1880s on. It was an imagery of spring and
flowers, of harvest (as in the well-known 'The Triumph of Labour'
designed for the 1891 May Day demonstration), of girls in light
flowing dresses and Phrygian bonnets.[55] Ceres was the goddess of
communism.[56]

It is not surprising that the period of socialist ideology most
deeply imbued with feminism, and most inclined to assign a crucial,
indeed sometimes a dominant, role to women, was the romantic-
utopian era before 1848. Of course at this period we can hardly
speak of a socialist 'movement' at all, but only of small and atypical
groups. Moreover, the actual number and prominence of women
in leading positions in such groups was far smaller than in the

Millet: *Liberty on the Barricades*

Delacroix: *Liberty on the Barricades* (detail)

Félicien Rops: *Peuple*

National Union of
General Workers banner.

Mukhina: *Sculpture on the Soviet Pavilion*

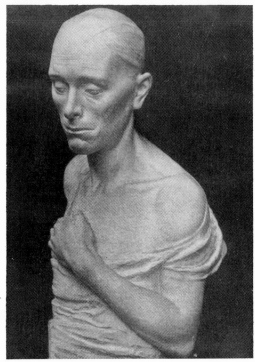

Constantin Meunier: *Woman of the People*

Richard Earldom after
Joseph Wright of Derby:
*An Iron Forge*

Alexandr Terent'evich
Matveev: *October* (1927)

years of the non-utopian Second International. There is nothing to compare in the Britain of Owenism and Chartism with the role of women as writers, public speakers and leaders in the 1880s and 1890s, not only in the middle-class ambiance of the Fabian Society, but in the much more working-class atmosphere of the Independent Labour Party, not to mention such figures as Eleanor Marx in the trade-union movement. Moreover, the women who then became prominent, like Beatrice Webb or Rosa Luxemburg, did not make their reputation because they were women, but because they were outstanding irrespective of sex. Nevertheless, the role of women's emancipation in socialist ideology has never been more obvious and central than in the period of 'utopian socialism'.

This was partly due to the crucial role assigned to the destruction of the traditional family in the socialism of that period;[57] a role which is still very clear in *The Communist Manifesto*. The family was seen as the prison-house not only of the women, who were not on the whole very active in politics, or indeed as a mass very enthusiastic about the abolition of marriage, but also of young people, who were much more attracted to revolutionary ideologies. Moreover, as J.F.C. Harrison has rightly pointed out, even on empirical grounds the new proletarians might well conclude that 'their rude little homes were a restrictive and circumscribing influence, and that in community they would have a means of breaking out of this: "we can afford to live in palaces as well as the rich ... were we only to adopt the principle of combination, the patriarchal principle of large families, such as that of Abraham".'[58] It has been the consumer-society, combined – paradoxically – with the replacement of mutual aid by state welfare, which has weakened this argument against the privatized nuclear-family household.

Yet utopian socialism also assigned another role to women, which was basically similar to the female role in the chiliastic religious movements with which the utopians had much in common. Here women were not only – perhaps not even primarily – equal, but superior. Their specific role was that of prophets, like Joanna Southcott, founder of an influential millennial movement in early nineteenth-century England, or the '*femme-mère-messie*' (woman-mother-messiah) of the Saint-Simonian religion.[59] This role incidentally provided opportunities for a public career in a masculine world for a small number of women. The foundresses of Christian Science and Theosophy come to mind. However, the tendency of the socialist and labour movements to move away from chiliasm towards rationalist theory and organization ('scientific socialism') made this social role for women in the movement increasingly marginal. Able women, whose talents lay in filling it, were pushed out of the centre of the movement into fringe religions which provided more scope for them. Thus Annie Besant, secularist and socialist, found fulfilment and her major political role after 1890 as high priestess of Theosophy and – through Theosophy – an inspirer of the Indian national liberation movement.

All that remained of the utopian/messianic role of women in socialism was the image of the female as inspiration and symbol of the better world. But paradoxically this image by itself was hardly distinguishable from Goethe's '*das ewig weibliche zieht uns hinan*' ('the eternal feminine raises us to the heavens'). In actuality it could be no different from the bourgeois-masculine idealization of the female in theory, which was only too readily compatible with her inferiority in practice. At most the female image of the inspirer became the image of a Joan of Arc, easily recognizable in Walter Crane's designs. Joan of Arc was indeed an icon of women's militancy, but she did not represent either political or personal emancipation, or indeed activism, in any sense that could become a model for real women. Even if we forget that she excluded the majority of women who were no longer virgins – i.e. women as sexual beings – there was, by historic definition, room for only a very few Joans of Arc in the world at any given moment. And, incidentally, as the increasingly enthusiastic adoption of Joan of Arc by the French right-wing demonstrates, her image was ideologically and politically undetermined. She might or might not represent Liberty. She might be on the barricades, but she did not – unlike Delacroix' girl – necessarily belong there.

Unfortunately it is at present impossible to continue the iconographic analysis of the socialist movement beyond a point of history which is already fairly remote. The traditional language of symbol and allegory is no longer much spoken or understood, and with its decline women as goddesses and muses, as personifications of virtue and ideals, even as Joans of Arc, have lost their specific place in political imagery. Even the famous international symbol of peace in the 1950s was no longer a woman, as it would almost certainly have been in the nineteenth-century, but Picasso's dove. The same is probably true of masculine images, though the

hammer-wielding Promethean man survived longer as the personi-
fication of movement and struggle. The iconography of the movement since, say, World War II, is non-traditional. We do not at
present have the analytical tools to interpret it, e.g. to make symbolic readings of the main modern iconographic medium, which is
ostensibly naturalistic, the photograph or film.

Iconography can therefore not throw significant light at present
on the relations between men and women in the mid-twentieth-
century socialist movement, as it can for the nineteenth-century.
Still, it can make one final suggestion about the masculine image.
This, as has already been suggested, is in some senses paradoxical,
since it typifies not so much the worker as sheer muscular effort;
not intelligence, skill and experience, but brute strength. Even, as
in Meunier's famous Iron-puddler, physical effort which virtually
excludes and exhausts the mind. One can see artistic reasons for
this. As Brandt points out, in Meunier 'the proletariat is transformed
into a Greek athlete',[60] and for this form of idealization the expression of intelligence is irrelevant. One can also see historical reasons
for it. The period 1870–1914 was above all the period in which
industry relied on a massive influx of inexperienced but physically
strong labour to perform the very large proportion of labour-intensive and relatively unskilled tasks; and when the dramatic environment of darkness, flame and smoke typified the revolution in man's
capacity to produce by steampowered industry.

And yet, as we know, the bulk of the militants of organized labour
in this period consisted, if we leave aside the admittedly important
contingent of miners, essentially of skilled men. How is it that an
image which omits all the characteristics of their kind of labour,
established itself as the expression of the working class? Three
explanations may be suggested. The first, and perhaps psychologi-
cally the most convincing, is that for most workers, whatever their
skill, the criterion of belonging to their class was precisely the
performance of manual, physical labour. The instincts of genuine
labour movements were *ouvrieriste*: a distrust of those who did not
get their hands dirty. This the image represented. The second is
that the movement wished to stress precisely its inclusive character.
It comprised all proletarians, not merely printers, skilled mechanics
and their like. The third, which probably prevailed in the period of
the Third International, was that in some sense the relatively unskilled, purely manual labourer, the miner or docker, was consi-

dered more revolutionary, since he did not belong to the labour aristocracy with its penchant for reformism and social-democracy. He represented 'the masses' to whom revolutionaries appealed over the heads of the social-democrats. The image was reality, insofar as it represented the fundamental distinction between manual and non-manual work; aspiration insofar as it implied a programme or a strategy. How realistic it was in the second respect is a question which does not belong to the present paper. But it is nevertheless not insignificant that, as an image, it omitted much that was most characteristic about the working class and its labour movement.

(1978)

# 7: Political Shoemakers*

## Co-written with Joan W. Scott

He had gone deeper into Arminianism and politics than any of his fellows. The *Methodist Magazine* and the *Weekly Dispatch* were regularly sent to him by his brother. He always had plenty of shoemaking, and was more independent than either the farmers or labourers. He used to make uncivil remarks about the land-lords and the House of Lords, the House of Commons, the new poor law, bishops, parsons, Corn laws, the church, and class legislation.[1]

A very curious thing is that each trade develops in the artisans practising it, a specific character, a particular temperament. The butcher is generally serious and full of his own importance, the house painter is thoughtless and a rake, the tailor is sensual, the grocer stupid, the porter curious and prattling, the shoemaker and cobbler, finally, are gay, sometimes even lively, with a song always on their lips ... Despite the simplicity of their tastes, the makers of new and old shoes are always distin-guished by a restless, sometimes aggressive spirit and by an enormous tendency to loquacity. Is there a riot? Does an orator emerge from the crowd? It is without doubt a cobbler who has come to make a speech to the people.[2]

I

The political radicalism of nineteenth-century shoemakers is pro-verbial. Social historians of a variety of persuasions have described the phenomenon and assumed it needed no explanation. A his-torian of the German revolution of 1848, for example, concluded that it was 'not accidental' that shoemakers 'played a dominant role in the activities of the people'. Historians of the 'Swing' riots in England referred to the shoemakers' 'notorious radicalism' and Jacques Rougerie accounted for the shoemakers' prominence in the Paris Commune by referring to their 'traditionally militancy'. Even so heterodox a writer as Theodore Zeldin accepts the common view

*We would like to thank William Sewell Jr., E.P. Thompson and Alfred Young for their helpful comments.

on this point.[3] The present paper attempts to account for the remarkable reputation of shoemakers as political radicals.

To say that shoemakers or any other trade, have a reputation for radicalism may, of course, mean one or more of three things: a reputation for militant action in movements of social protest, whether confined to the trade in question or not; a reputation for sympathy or association with, or activity in, movements of the political left; and a reputation as what might be called ideologists of the common people. Though very likely to be associated, these are not the same. Apprentices and unmarried journeymen in traditional corporate crafts were likely to be mobilized readily, without any necessary connection with whatever counted at the time as political radicalism. French *universitaires* have, at least since the Dreyfus period, had a reputation for standing well to the left of their students. This did not necessarily imply, though it did not exclude, militant collective action. Australian sheep-shearers, though often both militant and associated with the left, are not generally thought of as greatly interested in ideology,* whereas village schoolteachers often are.

Shoemakers as a trade had, in the nineteenth century, a reputation for radicalism in all three senses. They were militant both on trade matters and in wider movements of social protest. Though shoemakers' unions were limited to certain sections or localities of a very large trade, and only intermittently effective, they were organized on a national scale rather early in both France and Switzerland, not to mention England where the London union, founded in 1792, was said to extend nationally in 1804. Shoemakers and carpenters were the first members of the Federation of Workers of the Argentine Region (1890), the first attempt at a national union body for that country. They occasionally struck on a large scale and were among the most strike-prone trades in France during the July monarchy. They were also prominent in revolutionary crowds. Their role as political activists can be documented amply. Of the persons active in the British Chartist movement .whose

---

* The late Ian Turner of the Australian National University, Canberra, cited the case of a large number of these men, arrested after the October Revolution for holding a meeting in favour of insurrection and soviets. A careful search for subversive literature produced no printed matter of any kind, except a leaflet which a number carried in their pockets. It read: 'If water rots your boots, what will it do to your stomach?'

occupations are known, shoemakers formed much the largest single group after the weavers and unspecified 'labourers': more than twice the number of building-trade workers and more than 10 per cent of all occupationally described militants. In the taking of the Bastille, or at least among those arrested for it, the twenty-eight shoemakers were exceeded only by the cabinet-makers, joiners and locksmiths – and in the riots of the Champ de Mars and in August 1792 by no other trade.[4] Among those arrested in Paris for opposing the *coup d'etat* of 1851, shoemakers were most numerous.[5] The workers involved in the Paris Commune of 1871 who suffered the highest proportion of deportations after its defeat were, as Jacques Rougerie observes, 'of course, as always, the shoemakers'.[6] When rebellion broke out in the German city of Konstanz in April 1848, the shoemakers provided by far the largest single component of the rioters, almost as much as the next-most riotous trades (the tailors and joiners) put together.[7] At the other end of the world, the first anarchist ever recorded in a provincial town in Rio Grande do Sul in Brazil was an Italian shoemaker in 1897, while the only craft union reported as participating in the first (anarchist-inspired) Workers' Congress of Curitiba (Brazil) was the Shoemakers' Association.[8]

Militancy and left-wing activism alone, however, do not distinguish shoemakers as a group from some other craftsmen, who were at times at least as prominent in these respects. Among the casualties of the March revolution of 1848 in Berlin, joiners were more than twice as numerous, and tailors distinctly more numerous than shoemakers, though the trades were of comparable size.[9] Carpenters and tailors were as 'strike-prone' as shoemakers during the July monarchy. French revolutionary crowds included proportionately more printers, joiners, locksmiths and building workers than were in the Parisian population. If eleven shoemakers formed the largest group among the forty-three anarchists arrested in Lyon in 1892, construction workers were not far behind.[10] Tailors are associated with shoemakers as typical activists in the 1848 revolution in Germany, and if both were prominent among the German travelling journeymen who made up the bulk of the Communist League ('the workers' club is small and consists only of shoemakers and tailors', Weydemeyer wrote to Marx in 1850),[11] it seems clear that the tailors were more prominent. Indeed the apparently large number of shoemaker activists may sometimes merely reflect the size of a trade which, in Germany and Britain, constituted much the largest single artisan occupation.[12] The collective actions of the group do not therefore account for the shoemakers' radical reputation.

There can be little doubt, however, that as worker-intellectuals and ideologists shoemakers were exceptional. Once again, they were obviously not unique although, as we shall see, in rural villages and small market towns they had less competition from other settled artisans. Certainly their role as spokesmen and organizers of country people in nineteenth-century England is clear from any study of the 'Swing' riots of 1830 or of rural political radicalism. Hobsbawm and Rudé report that in 1830 the average riotous parish had from two to four times as many shoemakers as the average tranquil one.[13] The local shoemaker quoting Cobbett – John Adams in Kent, William Winkworth in Hampshire – is a familiar figure.[14] The craft's character as 'red-hot politicians' was proverbial. In the shoemaking centre of Northampton, election days were celebrated as 'traditional holidays' as much as the spring and autumn race meetings.[15] Yet the striking fact is the connection between politics and articulate literacy. Who says cobbler surprisingly often says journalist and versifier, preacher and lecturer, writer and editor. This impression is not easy to quantify, though shoemakers form the largest single group – three – in a sample of nineteen French 'worker-poets' of the period before 1850, all of radical views[16]: Sylvain Lapointe of the Yonne, who stood as a candidate in 1848; Hippolyte Tampucci, the editor of *Le grapilleur*; and Gonzalle of Rheims, the editor of *Le républicain*.[17] The list could be easily added to – one thinks of Faustin Bonnefoi, editor of the Fourierist newspaper in Louis Philippe's Marseille,[18] of the autodidact 'Efrahem', who wrote pamphlets urging 'an association of workers of every *corps d'état*[19], and of citizen Villy, a boot-maker who spoke at the first Communist Banquet in 1840 and who had published a pamphlet on the abolition of poverty.[20]

Of course nobody would claim that all, or even the majority among shoemaker activists, were artisan intellectuals. Indeed we have examples of militant shoemakers who were distinctly *not* great readers, at least in their days of activity, such as George Hewes, the last survivor of the Boston Tea Party.[21] Though as a craft shoemakers seem to have been more literate than the average, a fair percentage of bad readers would not be surprising in so large a trade containing so many proverbially poor men.[22] The less literate shoemaker may even have become more common as the trade expanded and was diluted during the nineteenth century. And yet the existence of an unusually, perhaps a uniquely, large number of shoemaker intellectuals is impossible to deny, even if it may be supposed that such persons would draw special attention to themselves in a largely non-literate society. When ideology took a primarily religious form, they pondered the Scriptures, sometimes coming to unorthodox conclusions: it was they who brought Calvinism into the Cevennes,[23] who prophesied, preached (and wrote) messianism, mysticism and heresy.[24] In the secular era the majority of the (largely Spencean communist) Cato Street conspirators were shoemakers, and their attraction to anarchism was notorious. Émile Pouget's *Le Père Peinard* symbolically carried on its cover the picture of a cobbler in his workshop.[25] More generally there is, at least in English, a substantial literature of collective shoemaker biography in the nineteenth century, such as, to our knowledge, exists for no other craft.[26] The overwhelming majority of its subjects are commemorated for intellectual achievements. Their success in this field may explain the appearance of such compendia in the age of self-improvement.

It may even be argued that such proverbs as 'Shoemaker stick to your last', which are found in many countries from antiquity to the Industrial Revolution, indicate precisely this tendency of shoemakers to express opinions on matters which ought to be left to the officially learned – 'Let the cobbler stick to his last and let the learned men write the books'; 'Preaching cobblers make bad shoes'; and so on. Certainly similar proverbs are distinctly less common with reference to other crafts.[27]

Even if we leave such indirect evidence aside, the number of shoemaker-intellectuals is impressive. They were not necessarily radicals, though their eighteenth- and nineteenth-century eulogists preferred to dwell on their achievements in fields which would impress socially superior readers – learning, literature and religion – while not concealing their reputation as folk-politicians. Still, the historians will not fail to note that the religion in which shoemakers distinguished themselves when not associated with anticlericalism and atheism,[28] was often heterodox and radical by contemporary standards. One thinks of Jakob Boehme, the mystic, persecuted by the Lutheran church of his city, and George Fox, the Quaker. One also notes the combination of radicalism and literary activities, as in Thomas Holcroft, the ex-shoemaker playwright and English Jacobin, in Friedrich Sander, the founder of the Vienna Workers' Union in 1848, who also wrote poems,[29] and in the anarchist Jean Grave, shoemaker turned printer, and editor of magazines with a distinct literary-artistic bent.[30]

We cannot of course allow the shoemakers a monopoly of plebeian intellectual activities. Samuel Smiles, always the apostle of self-help, in an essay on 'Astronomers and Students in Humble Life: A New Chapter in the "Pursuit of Knowledge under Difficulties"' lists examples from other trades also.[31] Nevertheless the fact that 'in country places, it is very common to find the situation of parish clerk held by a shoemaker' suggests an uncommon degree of literacy.[32] In any case the intellectualism of shoemakers as a trade impressed more than one observer, and could not readily be explained. Both W. E. Winks and the *Crispin Anecdotes* confessed themselves baffled by it, but agreed 'that more thinking men are to be found shoemakers, as a fraternity, than most others'.[33] In his autobiography the radical shoemaker John Brown commented that: 'Persons possessing the advantages of a more refined education would hardly guess what an amount of knowledge and book-learning is to be met with amongst the members of my ancient trade.'[34] In France shoemakers were said to be 'thinkers ... [they] think about things they have seen or heard ... they fathom more than most the concerns of the workers'.[35] In England an eighteenth-century verse recorded that:

> A cobbler once in days of yore
> Sat musing at his cottage door.
> He liked to read old books, he said,
> And then to ponder, what he'd read.[36]

In Russia a character in a work of Maxim Gorki is described as 'like so many other shoemakers, easily fascinated by a book'.[37]

The shoemaker's reputation as popular philosopher and politician pre-dates the era of industrial capitalism and extends well beyond the typical countries of the capitalist economy. Indeed one has the sense that the nineteenth-century radical shoemakers were fulfilling a role long associated with members of their trade. The patron saints of the craft, Crispin and Crispinian, were martyred because they preached unorthodoxy to their customers in their workshop in Soissons – in this instance Christianity under the pagan emperor Diocletian.[38] In Act 1 of Shakespeare's *Julius Caesar* a cobbler appears leading a crowd of protesters through the streets. The journeymen in Dekker's *Shoemaker's Holiday*, an Elizabethan exercise in public relations on behalf of the 'gentle craft' of London, appear characteristically militant: they threaten to leave their master if a travelling journeyman is not given a job. Almost contemporary with these theatrical allusions, we find the following reference to the shoemakers Robert Hyde and a certain Lodge of Sherborne:

And he further sayeth that a little before Christmas one Robte Hyde of Sherborne shomaker seinge this depont passinge by his doore, called to him & desyered to have some conference with him and after some speches, he entered into these speches. Mr Scarlet you have preachett vnto vs that there is a god, a heaven & a hell & a resurreccion after this Liffe, and that we shall geive an accompte of or worckes, and that the soule is immortall; but nowe sayeth he here is a companye aboute this towne that saye, that hell is noe other but povertie & penurye in this worlde; and heaven is noe other but to be ritch, and enioye pleasueres; and that we dye like beastes, and when we ar gonne there is noe more rememberance of vs &c. and such like. But this Examint did neither then demande whome they were; neither did he deliuer any particulers vnto him And further saieth That it is generally reported by almost euery bodye in Sherborne, and the sayd Allen & his man aforesayde ar Atheistes. And alsoe he sayeth there is one Lodge a shomaker in Sherborne accompted an Atheiste.[39]

The shoemaker, as what the poet Gray called a 'village Hampden', is commemorated in an engraving of Timothy Bennett (died 1756) of Hampton-Wick, Middlesex. He challenged the king's closing of a right of way through Bushy Park by threatening to bring a prosecution – and won. The engraving represents him in 'a firm and complacent aspect, sitting down in the attitude of his conversation with ... [Lord Halifax]' (the ranger of the royal park), symbolizing a democratic confrontation with, and triumph over, privilege.[40] Another source describes a shoemaker walking 'from village to village with his kit in a basket on his back. On getting a job he would drop down on the doorstep, and while at work, he and his customer would strike up with a song, or talk politics'.[41] The notoriety of shoemakers as leaders led Sir Robert Peel to ask some shoemakers, who had come to him to press the demands of their trade society: 'How is it ... that you people are foremost in every movement? ... If there is a conspiracy or political movement, I always find one of you in it.'[42] E.P. Thompson quotes a Yorkshire satirist's 1849 portrait of a 'Village Politician':

He is, typically, a cobbler, an old man and the sage of his industrial village: 'He has a library that he rather prides himself upon. It is a strange collection ... There is the 'Pearl of Great Price' and 'Cobbett's Twopenny Trash' ... 'The Wrongs of Labour' and 'The Rights of Man', 'The History of the French Revolution' and Bunyan's 'Holy War' ... It warms his old heart like a quart of mulled ale, when he hears of a successful revolution, – a throne tumbled, kings flying, and princes scattered abroad ...'.[43]

Englishmen believed, moreover, that French shoemakers shared these traits. More than one account of the French Revolution described 'cobblers ... haranguing under the splendid domes of the Valois and the Capets' and then leading crowds to torture and murder the king.[44] In France as well as in England the shoemaker was known for his love of liberty and his role as village politician. Shoemakers were admired for 'independence of their opinions'. 'The freedom of the people', said one writer, 'is expressed in their demeanour.'[45] The revolt of the Maillotins in 1380 was said to have been sparked by a shoemaker, whose empassioned oration inflamed a crowd.[46] And the downfall of Concini, the Italian statesman, in 1617, was said to have been assured by one Picard, a shoemaker and popular orator, who insulted the admiral when he was alive and defiled him when dead by roasting and eating his heart.[47] Anthropophagy is not a characteristic usually associated with shoemakers, unlike a taste for strong drink, but the shoemakers' reputation for radicalism was deserved and it was not limited to France.

II

To what extent was the shoemaker as philosopher and politician a product of his craft? There seem to be two aspects of this question, one having to do with literacy, the other with independence.

The question of literacy and the shoemaker's proverbial fondness for books and reading is difficult to explain, as there is nothing in the nature of the craft to suggest any occupational connection with the printed word – as among printers. The desperate guesses that their skills with leather were often called upon to bind or repair books, and that sometimes their stalls adjoined those of booksell-

ers, appear to be unsupported by any evidence.[48] Moreover, so far
as we can tell, there is nothing in the customs and traditions of the
craft journeymen which stresses or even implies a special interest
in reading; and though Hans Sachs of Nuremberg was, as every
opera-lover knows, the most famous of the *Meistersinger*, there is
no evidence that shoemakers were disproportionately represented
among these poetic artisans. The link between shoemakers and
books could not have been established before the invention and
popularization of printing, since the written word could hardly
have been directly accessible to the poor before then. The general
character of the shoemakers' journeymen customs suggests that
they have been largely formed by this time.[49] It may, of course, be
argued that once books were available, they were naturally likely
to attract a profession given to speculation and discussion. Nevertheless the question remains.

It may be that the relatively primitive division of labour in shoemaking allowed or compelled vast numbers of shoemakers to work
entirely alone. Certainly Mayhew surmised that it was 'the solitude
of their employment developing their internal resources' which
accounted for their being 'a stern, uncompromising and reflecting
race'.[50] Itinerant cobblers were, of course, isolated workers. But
even in his workshop, the lonely shoemaker was typical. In Germany in 1882 two thirds of them employed no assistants at all.

Yet even the single cobbler was not culturally isolated. He might
receive his training in a small establishment. The master, a few
journeymen and one or two apprentices, as well as the master's
wife, seems to have constituted the ideal-typical artisan establishment. In the most traditional regions of nineteenth-century Germany there were on average only 2.4 or 2.6 journeymen per apprentice.[51] The rapid turnover of journeymen, however, would
widen both the masters' and the apprentices' horizon, and journeymen were notorious and prolonged travellers. A Swabian rural
shoemaker describes their impact on him as an apprentice: 'There
were much-travelled and intelligent people among the journeymen.
So I heard and learned a good deal'. And he in turn worked in
seventeen establishments in fifteen different places between finish-
ing his apprenticeship and setting up as a small master and social-
democratic activist.[52] If, as was the case in Jena, journeymen stayed
only six months on average in a shop, the typical apprentice would,
in the course of three years, have close contact with perhaps fifteen

widely travelled men, and the typical travelling journeyman with a
great many more.

The journeymen would meet each other not only in workshops
but on the road and in the inns which functioned as houses of call,
where jobs and relief, asked for and received in highly ritualized
form,[53] were to be found. There was plenty of occasion for discussing the problems of the trade, the news of the day, and the
diffusion of information generally. In larger cities shoemakers, like
most other tradesmen, might live and work in specialized shoemakers' rows or streets. In centres of market shoemaking, urban or
rural, there was no shortage of others in the trade. Since the work
took little space, several semi-proletarian outworkers or garret-
masters might share a workshop together. Even the loneliest cobbler had probably been socialized in the culture of the 'gentle craft'
at some time.

That 'shoemaker culture', which Peter Burke has recently described as stronger than any other craft culture except the weavers',[54] was unusually marked and persistent. In Scotland, for instance, its Catholic patron saint survived the Calvinist reformation
as 'King Crispin', and in England St Crispin's Day was celebrated
as a shoemakers' holiday, often with processions of the craft, until
well into the nineteenth century, or was revived by journeymen for
political purposes, as in Norwich in 1813. It was still alive or
remembered in some purely rural areas at the end of the century.
The early decline of organized gilds and corporations in England
makes such survivals all the more impressive.[55]

Yet there appears to be nothing in the formal or informal craft
traditions that linked shoemakers specifically to intellectualism, or
even to radicalism. They stressed pride in the trade, based largely
on its indispensability to high and low, young and old. This is the
commonest theme of journeyman shoemakers' songs.[56] They
stressed independence, especially journeyman independence, as
proved by the shoemaker's control over his time of work and leisure – his capacity to celebrate Saint Monday and other holidays
as he chose.[57] Since social leisure and drink were inseparable, they
also stressed drinking, an activity for which shoemakers were celebrated, and that other by-product of bar-room culture, settling
disputes by fighting. 'Look for the best beer where carters and
shoemakers drink', says a Polish proverb. Johann Nestroy's farce
*Lumpazivagabundus* (1836), which follows the fortunes of three

ideal-typical journeymen, presents its shoemaker both as an amateur astronomer (his interest in comets may be inspired by the reading of almanacs) and a spectacular and quarrelsome soak. But these are not particularly intellectual associations.

Perhaps the most plausible explanation of the trade's intellectualism derives from the fact that a shoemaker's work was both sedentary and physically undemanding. Probably it was physically the least taxing labour for men in the countryside. As a result small, weak or physically handicapped boys were habitually put to this trade. Such was the case of Jakob Boehme, the mystic,[58] of Robert Bloomfield, author of *The Farmer's Boy*,[59] of William Gifford, later editor of the *Quarterly Review*, who was 'put ... to the plough' but 'soon found ... too weak for such heavy work', of John Pounds, pioneer of the 'Ragged Schools', who became a shoemaker when an accident maimed him and drove him out of his original trade as a shipwright,[60] of John Lobb, founder of a celebrated firm in St James's which still exists,[60] and almost certainly of numerous others. In Pomeranian Loitz 'almost the only people who devote themselves to this trade are crippled or unsuited to agricultural or industrial work'. Hence the tendency of village shoemakers unable to make ends meet by their craft to take (as in the town of Heide, Schleswig) such second jobs as night-watchmen, school caretakers, messengers, waiters, town criers, assistants to the pastor, or assistant postmen and street sweepers.[6] American naval recruiting order in 1813 insisted on recruiting 'none but strong, healthy, able men. Landsmen may be entered as ordy. seamen ... but on no account ship Tailors, Shoemakers or Blacks [sic] as these from their accustomed occupations rarely possess physical force.'[63]

The number of deformed shoemakers and tailors ('crooked, hump-backed, lame') in the Italian corporate processions of these crafts was noted by Ramazzini.[64] Unlike the tailors, however, the shoemakers were not proverbially associated with feebleness, an observation supported by nineteenth-century statistics of British occupational mortality.[65] On the other hand the *lame* cobbler is recorded as early as the Latin dramatist Plautus. Perhaps the frequency of rural shoemakers who combined their trade with agricultural activities is relevant here. Nevertheless the craft was at least to some extent selected by boys incapable of competing with other labouring men of their age in the conventionally valued physical activities. This may have provided an incentive to acquire other kinds of prestige. And here the semi-routinized nature of much of their work, which could readily be combined with thinking, watching and conversation, may have suggested intellectual alternatives. Shoemakers working together in larger workshops were among those crafts (tailors and cigar-makers are others) which developed the institution of the 'reader' – one of the men taking turns to read newspapers or books out aloud, or an old soldier being hired to read, or the youngest boy having the duty to fetch and read the news. (George Bloomfield, a minor shoemaker-poet, not unreasonably suggested that this was the point to which 'those who say that "Shoemakers are politicians" might trace the solution of their wonder'.)[66] Such quiet and undemanding indoor occupations existed in towns, but in the villages it is difficult to think of others – certainly not the blacksmiths or the wheelwrights.[67]

The shoemaker's work thus permitted thinking and discussion while working; his frequent isolation during working hours threw him on his own intellectual resources; he was selectively recruited from boys with a likely incentive to compensate for their physical handicaps; the training of apprentices and the tramping of journeymen exposed him to the culture of the trade and to the culture and politics of a wider world. We may perhaps add that the lightness of his tool-kit actually made it easier than in some other trades to carry books with him – a fact for which there is also some evidence. Whether all this provides an adequate, still more a testable, explanation of his bookishness, we cannot be certain. Nevertheless three things are clear.

First, the more literate artisan crafts shoemakers, as we shall shortly see, were unusuual in being widely distributed in predominantly illiterate rural and small-town environments, where they could become unofficial clerks or labourers' intellectuals. They had little competition. Secondly, once the popular image of the shoemaker as intellectual and radical existed (as it undoubtedly did) it must have affected reality in several ways. Every time a shoemaker fitted the role, he confirmed popular expectations. As a result shoemakers' behaviour in this role was probably more often noted, recorded and commented upon. The popular image may have attracted young men with literary or philosophical tastes and political interests; or conversely, boys brought into contact with philosophic and radical cobblers might acquire an interest in these matters. Finally, the culture of the trade might develop some of these traits among its practitioners not only because material conditions facilitated them, but because its mores did not stand in the way. In many occupations a 'reading man' would have such tastes knocked or mocked out of him. Among shoemakers they might be more easily accepted as one version of behaviour compatible with group norms.

The shoemaker's independence was clearly tied to the material conditions of his trade and from it stemmed his ability to be a village politician. In addition the humble status of the trade and the relative poverty of its recruits, at least in the nineteenth century, help to explain its radicalism.

The two characteristics are linked. The trade was essentially based on leather, whose preparation (skinning, cleaning, tanning, and so on) is noisome and dirty, and therefore often confined to persons of low social status or outcasts (as in India and Japan). In their origins shoemakers and tanners were closely linked, since shoemakers often tanned their own leather, as they still did until the mid-nineteenth century in the Pomeranian shoemaker community of Loitz.[68] In Leipzig the tanners and shoemakers originally formed a single gild.[69] The low status of shoemakers and the contempt in which they were often held in antiquity – at any rate by writers[70] – may be partly due to this association with 'uncleanness' or the memory of it. Conversely it is not unreasonable to suppose that the craft (which emphasized its indispensability and gentility) was inclined towards radicalism by resentment. Certainly an element of low status seems to have persisted, possibly also influenced by the shoemaker's reputation for physical neglect, possibly a reason for this reputation. Even in the late nineteenth century an author could write of the traditional (pre-factory) trade: 'As a class ... the common shoemakers were neither clean nor tidy in their habits and persons, and the calling was looked down upon as one of low social grade; a fitting employment to which to apprentice the boy inmates of workhouses.'[71]

Moreover, as the costs of apprenticeship were minimal, families which could not afford to bind their sons to a more prosperous, exclusive (and more costly) trade could scrape together the fees required for learning shoemaking. Indeed the association of the craft with poverty was also proverbial.[72] 'All shoemakers go barefoot', goes a Yiddish saying. 'The shoemaker always wears torn shoes.' A mixture of leftover scraps of food was known, around Hamburg, as 'shoemaker's pie'.[73]

The coexistence of independence and poverty in the trade is partly due to its peculiar ubiquity. It was organized early in both town and country, at least in temperate zones where it had long been recognized that 'there's nothing like leather' for tough outdoor labouring footwear. The shoemakers, often of humble origin themselves, served a clientele which included large numbers of humble people. The making and repairing of leather footwear requires specialists of some kind, unlike a good deal of other making and mending. At the end of the nineteenth century there were still shoemakers who specialized in going round the Alpine farms of Austria (*Störschuster*) to make and mend the year's footwear from the hides and leather provided by the farmers.[74] Shoemakers and cobblers were therefore not only a craft organized as such at an uncommonly early date (they are among the earliest documented craft gilds in both England and Germany),[75] but one of the most numerous and widely distributed crafts in town and country. In eighteenth-century Seville, as in nineteenth-century Valparaiso, they exceeded in numbers all other crafts.[76] So did they in Prussia in 1800 (followed by tailors and smiths). In Bavaria in 1771 they were exceeded in numbers only by weavers, but in market villages they were first, followed by brewers and weavers.[77] In rural Friesland in 1749 there were 5.79 of them per 1,000 inhabitants, compared to 4.53 weavers, 4.48 carpenters, 3.70 bakers, 2.08 smiths, 1.76 clergymen, 1.51 innkeepers and 1.45 tailors; shoemakers were to be found in 54 per cent of all settlements, carpenters in 52 per cent, smiths in 40 per cent and innkeepers in 32 per cent.[78] It seems clear that people found it harder to manage without specialized shoemakers and menders within close reach than without other specialized craftsmen and services.

The shoemaker's trade, though it extended over a very wide range of skill and specialization, remained sufficiently primitive in technology and division of labour, and with a sufficiently homogeneous product, to continue essentially as a single craft. There is no equivalent in it to the growing fragmentation of metalworking into specialized separate crafts so often found in the medieval gild economy. Broadly speaking, once the trade had separated from the tanners, leather-sellers and other producers and suppliers of its raw material, its main internal fissures were commercial – between shoemakers and shoe-merchants (whether or not these also made shoes). There was also a division between those who made and those who merely repaired shoes, defined in various ways – cordwainers and cobblers (*savetiers*, *Flickschuster*, *ciabattino*), though it must be noted that the merchants developed essentially from among the cordwainers. The separation between makers and menders was sometimes institutionalized in separate gilds, though cobblers' gilds had difficulty in emancipating themselves completely from cordwainers' control or in remaining viable.

Cobbling was clearly the inferior branch, and the term (in English) is used for any work of poor quality. However, the line between the two was and had to be unclear, especially in times and regions (like eighteenth-century Germany) where fairly static demand confronted growing supply in the towns.[79] To live only by *making* shoes was hardly possible for more than a few. In fact it was assumed that makers cobbled. Thus to reach a 'decent' income (91 gulden a year) it was claimed, no doubt rhetorically, that a master 'would have to work up one pair of new shoes or three pairs of soles and patches every day, and in addition rely on customers paying'. It is thus not surprising that in the eighteenth and nineteenth centuries the terms seem to have become interchangeable in English,[80] while in French the word *cordonnier* came to mean both maker and mender, as *Schuster* did in popular German usage, in spite of the tendency for the more high-class *Schuhmacher* to gain ground at its expense.[81] And indeed, outside strongly gild-controlled cities, which were becoming weaker, how was it possible to keep the making and mending of shoes strictly apart?

The widespread demand for specialized shoemakers and menders made it impossible for corporate cities to monopolize the craft. Village shoe-mending could hardly be banned, and though this type of countryside cobbling was (no doubt inevitably) free of gild control and qualifications, it had almost always to be learned from some kind of shoemaker. There was no way of preventing the local cobbler from also supplying the local demand for shoes, especially of the rough working kind, until the rise of large-scale production and distribution. So journeymen with poor chances of becoming masters in the controlled trade of the city might well prefer to set up on their own in some village or country town. Indeed a growing tendency to do so in Germany was noted as late as the nineteenth century. When in 1840 the prohibition on rural shoemakers (as distinct from cobblers) was finally lifted in the countryside of Saxony, a single master (without apprentices) being henceforth permitted per village, a considerable number of rural shoemakers immediately appeared.[82] It is a good guess that many of them had simply changed their official title.

On the other hand, if there was no sharp line between the best and most specialized shoemaker and the most modest cobbler, the enormous size of the trade suggests that it must generally have included an unusually large section of the marginal, who could not live by their craft alone, especially as shoe-mending – from which German village cobblers might draw half their income – was notoriously unremunerative. Pre-industrial data are hard to find, but a calculation for a Swabian village in the nineteenth century suggests that because of insufficient demand a shoemaker there could not, on average, have made more than seven pairs of footwear in a year,[83] so that for most of them the craft could not have been more than a source of supplementary earnings, possibly taken up as such. The reputation of the trade for poverty thus had a sound base, though the reasons for its overcrowding are not quite clear. Perhaps this is partly explained by the cheapness of the basic equipment and the possibility of practising it at home; perhaps also by the fact that shoemakers were recruited externally, outside the ranks of practising craftsmen and their families. Printers and glass-workers restricted recruitment to their sons, relatives and a few privileged outsiders; shoemakers could rarely do so.* As a result shoemakers controlled neither entry into nor the size of their trade, hence its overcrowding.

The trade was therefore far from homogeneous. Yet so long as it remained essentially a manual artisan trade – and until the 1850s not even the domestic sewing-machine entered it – the divisions within it were vague and shifting. Hence, though there were 'aristocrats' or favoured sectors among shoemakers as among tailors (for example, in the high-class bespoke trade of the cities), neither trade as a whole stood high in the pecking order of the crafts, as the artisan communist Wilhelm Weitling observed.[84] For both, and especially the shoemakers, were unusually numerous, and therefore contained an unusually high proportion of the marginal and unprosperous. Among the hundreds of journeymen artisans who flocked into industrializing Wiener Neustadt in the 1840s and ap-

---

* We are informed, however, that among eighteenth-century London cordwainers inter-generational continuity in the trade was unusually high.

plied for permission to stay there, no less than 14.7 per cent (17 per cent of those from Bohemia) were shoemakers, followed at some distance by 10 per cent (14.6 per cent among Bohemians) of tailors and 8.3 per cent (9.1 per cent among Bohemians) of joiners.[85]

The village shoemaker was self-employed. His business required little capital. Equipment was cheap, light and portable, and he only required a modest roof over his head to work and live, in the worst case in the same room. While this made him unusually mobile, it did not distinguish him from a number of other crafts. What did distinguish him was his contact with large numbers of humble people and his independence from patrons, wealthy clients and employers. Farmers depended on landlords; wheelwrights and builders relied on orders from farmers and persons of substance; tailors served the wealthy since the poor made their own clothes. The shoemaker also served the wealthy, since they needed him; but his main clientele must, in most cases, have been among the poor, since they could not do without him either. That fact is undeniable, even if we know less than we might about the actual use of leather footwear among the poor, which was certainly more restricted than in our prosperous times.* Indeed there is evidence that, as wealthier villagers in the later nineteenth century advanced to store-bought shoes manufactured elsewhere, if not to high-class bespoke foot-wear, the village shoemaker became increasingly dependent on the custom of those who needed tough footwear for outdoor labour.

He could thus express his opinions without the risk of losing his job or his customers – if he were good enough, even his respectable customers.[86] Moreover he was closely linked with his clients by bonds of confidence. This was in part because they were likely to be his debtors, since farm-workers and perhaps peasants could only pay at rare intervals when they received lump sums, for example, after the harvest (pay-day in Pomerania was St Crispin's Day, 25 October)† or between Easter and Whitsun, when annual hirings were renewed. He had to trust his clients, but they had no reason to distrust him. Unlike so many with whom the poor had dealings – the miller, the baker, even the tavern-keeper, who could give

---

* We need to know more, in particular, about the extent of the practice of going barefoot (widespread among women and children) and the use of alternative foot-wear – clogs, felt or bast boots and shoes, and the like.

† Is there a connection between this agricultural rhythm and St Crispin's Day on 25 October?

short weight or measure – the shoemaker produced a new or
mended shoe which could be readily judged, and variations in quality were most likely due not to cheating but to variations in skill.[87]
The shoemaker thus had licence to express his opinions, which
there was no reason to distrust.

That these opinions were heterodox and democratic should cause
no surprise. The village shoemaker's life was akin to that of the
poor, not the rich and powerful. He had little use for hierarchy and
formal organization. There was little enough in his trade, and in
many cases he found work outside and in spite of gild or craft
regulation. He knew the value of independence and had ample
opportunity to compare his relative autonomy with that of his
clients. How far this ability to articulate independent views was
confined to the minority of relatively successful craftsmen rather
than the (presumable) majority of marginal part-time cobblers, we
cannot say, since it is difficult or impossible to compile a representative sample of the radicals in the craft. The question must be left
open. However, in the specific context of the late eighteenth and
early nineteenth centuries it is natural to find radical shoemakers
reading Cobbett, who cried out against the demolition of all small
tradesmen and who denounced a system which replaced 'master
and man ... every one was in his place and every one was free'
with 'masters and slaves'.[88] Nor is it surprising to find them in the
ranks of sansculottes and later of anarchists. In all cases the insistence on modest means, hard work and independence as solutions
to problems of injustice and poverty were within the experience of
village shoemakers.

Much of this argument might also apply to other village artisans.
But while, say, the blacksmith's shop was noisy and his labour
made conversation at work difficult, the shoemaker was strategically well-placed to pass on city ideas and mobilize action. His
village shop provided an ideal setting for the purpose, and articulate men who worked alone most of the time might grow loqua-
cious in company, and could do so while they worked. The rural
shoemaker was always present, his eyes on the street, and he knew
what went on in the community, even when he did not happen to
double as parish clerk or in some other municipal of communal
capacity. Moreover their quiet workshops in villages and small
towns were social centres second only to the inn, open and ready
for conversation all day. Not surprisingly in the French countryside

of 1793–4 shoemakers, together with tavern-keepers, 'seem to have had had a veritable vocation for revolution'. Richard Cobb stresses:

the role of the shoemakers, those village revolutionaries who, installed as mayors by the revolutionary upsurge of summer 1793, or at the head of the committees of surveillance, led the sansculotte minorities against *les gros* ... On the lists of 'terrorists to be disarmed' which were drawn up in the year III in the countryside, they formed a majority. We have here an undeniable social phenomenon.[89]

Of course the cobbler's shop and the tavern differed as meeting-places in one important respect. Men gathered to drink in groups, but in cobbler's shops in ones and twos. Taverns were only for adult males, but women, or more likely children, had access to the village intellectual. In how many village and small-town lives did the shoemaker as educator play a role! Thus Hone's *Every-Day Book* recalls 'an honest old man who patched my shoes and my mind, when I was a boy ... my friend the cobbler, who, though no metaphysician, was given to ruminate on "causation"'. He lent the boy books 'which he kept in the drawer of his seat, with ... the instruments of his "Gentle Craft"'.[90] And as late as the 1940s a future distinguished Marxist labour historian was introduced to politics in boyish conversations in a small-town cobbler's workshop in his native Romania.[91]

The shoemaker was thus a key figure in rural intellectual and political life: literate, articulate, relatively informed, intellectually and sometimes economically independent, at least within his village community. He was constantly present in the places where popular mobilization was likely to take place: on the village street, at markets, fairs and feasts. Whether this is sufficient explanation for his frequently attested role as crowd-leader is not so clear. Under the circumstances, however, we are hardly surprised to find him on occasion in such a role.

III

Among social historians the reputation of shoemakers as radicals is associated mostly with the late eighteenth and early nineteenth centuries, the period of the transition to industrialism. We cannot measure whether or not there was an increase in the number of

militant shoemakers, but it seems likely that two developments
stimulated an intensified radicalism. The first stemmed from the
slow decline of shoemaking as an essentially artisan occupation
and a consequent period of extreme tension within the trade.
Specific problems varied from place to place (relations betwen masters and journeymen were different in Northampton and London)
but it is undeniable that the trade as a whole was politicized. Thus
a young journeyman experienced strikes and participated in discussions of alternate political and economic systems as he acquired his
skills. Those who ended up in small village shops knew about
Jacobinism and carried radical ideas from cities to small towns.
The second development was tied to the growing discontent of
village populations as they faced the consequences of the growth
of agricultural capitalism. Villagers were increasingly open to the
ideological formulations for their grievances which shoemakers
were in a position to provide. The combination of trade and village
circumstances could readily turn the village philosopher into a village politician, as it most certainly did during the 'Swing' riots.

What changes affected the shoemaking trade during the period
which extended, roughly, from 1770 to 1880?

The first point to recall is the sheer numerical size of the trade
which, until mechanization and factory production transformed it,
grew with urbanization and population. The number of shoemaking workers in Vienna (where factories were negligible) more than
trebled between 1855 and 1890, most of this increase occurring before the early 1870s.[92] In Britain the number of adult males in the
trade grew from 133,000 to 243,000 between 1841 and 1851, when
there were more shoemakers in the country than miners.[93] Between
1835 and 1850 an annual average of between 250 and 400 shoemakers
entered Leipzig and, since the city was growing, a somewhat
smaller number left each year. Over this fifteen-year period there
was a minimum number of 3,750 arrivals and 3,000 departures.[94]

The second point to note is the spread of manufacture for the
market as distinct from individual clients and the ubiquitous
repair-work. The 'market shoemaker', making rough ware for sale
on local and regional markets, might in many places still have as
close a relationship with his clients as the bespoke shoemaker, since
he could be found regularly at his stall on market day by men and
women he knew well and who knew him. His was probably a closer
relationship than that of his growing rival, the shoemaker-hawker,

who went from house to house.[95] Both these arrangements, however, lent themselves to various forms of putting-out system – hence the development of both rural and urban shoemaking communities, which might range from agglomerations of traditional craft workshops with minimal workshop division of labour to larger centres which were, in effect, unmechanized factories working with operatives confined to special processes supplemented by urban or village outworkers with their own subdivision of labour.[96] Here large-scale production for export or army and navy contracts could be undertaken. It is possible that many such semi-skilled handworkers came to the trade untrained or unsocialized in the craft, especially when drawn from agriculture.[97] It may well be that apprentices at this period were largely drawn from the rural poor. In Europe, however, the nucleus of apprenticed shoemakers around whom this semi-skilled labour force grew was substantial. This is suggested even for factory operatives in (the radical) J.B. Leno's handbook of shoemaking, and certainly in Erfurt, one of the main German centres of mechanized factory production, one-third of a sample of 193 workers had learned the trade, and half of these were the sons of shoemakers.[98] Since, outside the United States and a little later Britain, no technical innovation other than the small sewing-machine (which spread between the mid-1850s and the early 1870s) was of significance until very late in the nineteenth century, this is not surprising.[99]

The third point is that the press of numbers and the proliferation of putting-out manufacture (referred to by honourable craftsmen as 'dishonourable' or 'junk' work) undermined the independence of the trade and also depressed wages. An inquiry into employment in Marseille in the 1840s revealed that shoemakers were the largest occupational group, notoriously underpaid. They earned an average daily wage of only 3 francs, and an average annual wage of 600 francs, which placed them lower in earnings than many unskilled labourers.[100] The worker-poet Charles Poncy protested in 1850 to St Crispin:

Hunger harnesses us to its black wagon: our wages are so reduced. For bread and rags we burn the midnight oil.

My children, piled pell-mell on ancient bedding, have sucked dry their mother's scrawny breast. We eat the seed-corn that should grow food for the young.[101]

The English shoemaker John Brant attributed his part in the Cato Street conspiracy to low wages and the loss of independence that entailed. His statement suggests that he sought to strike back at those in power, asserting his ability to think and act independently:

He had, by his industry, been able to earn about £3 or £4 a-week, and while this was the case, he never meddled with politics; but when he found his income reduced to 10s a-week, he began to look about him ... And what did he find? Why, men in power, who met to deliberate how they might starve and plunder the country ... He had joined the conspiracy for the public good.[102]

The spread of manufacture for a remote market rather than known clients affected the trade in different ways. At one extreme it might, at least temporarily, lead to a reassertion of the values and claims of the craft as such, shared by both masters and journeymen, against slopwork or 'dishonourable' work locally or in large-scale manufacturing centres like Northampton. At the other extreme, journeymen or proletarianized small masters who perceived that they had become permanent wage-workers, might find their way to trade unionism and conflict with employers, which sharpened the edge of shoemaker radicalism. Thus the Parisian shoemaker 'Efrahem' spoke of the day when 'on the signal being given, all workers will simultaneously leave their workshops and abstain from labour in order to obtain the rise in the price-list they have demanded from the masters'.[103] As already observed, shoemakers took rapidly to forming militant unions. In Britain, at least, the roots of unionism went deep. James Hawker, who occupies a modest place in history as a brilliant and politically conscious poacher and village radical in Leicestershire, was the son of a poor tailor, apprenticed to the Northampton shoe trade. In the intervals of joining and deserting from the army, he drifted into any job he could in the eastern midlands. Yet he joined a union whenever one was available: 'I ran home as quick as I Could and Drew my Travelling Card. For by this time I was a Trade unionist – almost before I knew what it Meant ... Had I not been a union man I might have been compelled to Beg or Steal.'[104]

The line between craft and wage-work, between economic and political militancy, was as yet vague enough to discourage excessive classification. Not until 1874 did traditional shoemakers and manufacturing operatives diverge sufficiently in Britain for the latter to break away from the Amalgamated Cordwainers' Association to form the National Union of Boot and Shoe Rivetters and Finishers – the future National Union of Boot and Shoe Operatives. The union of 1820 contributed to the cause of the defendants in the Cato Street conspiracy. And the unions in putting-out and manufacturing centres drew on the old craft tradition in their protests. At Nantwich in Cheshire, for example, a strong union of this sort celebrated St Crispin's Day in 1833 with:

a grand procession – King Crispin on horseback attired in royal regalia … attended by train-bearers in appropriate costume. The officers were attired in vestments suitable to their rank, and carrying the Dispensation, the Bible, a large pair of globes, and also beautiful specimens of ladies' and gents' boots and shoes … Nearly 500 joined in the procession, each one wearing a white apron neatly trimmed. The rear was brought up by a shopmate in full tramping order, his kit packed on his back and walking stick in his hand.[105]

The union's banner, 'emblematical of our trade, with the motto "May the manufactures of the sons of Crispin be trod upon by all the world" …' was much admired.[106] A gild procession would not have looked very different.

However, the lines leading to our village radicals in the late eighteenth and early nineteenth centuries originate more often from contexts like London, where masters and journeymen shared Jacobin positions such as those articulated by the London Corresponding Society and members of the Cato Street conspiracy, or Paris, where shoemakers were among the most numerous followers of Étienne Cabet. The village shoemaker shared with honourable urban shoemakers the cause of the independent small artisan. In defence of that cause he offered a critique of the economy and the government which could focus the grievances of other workers and spur them to action. The call to action rested upon the assumption that men like himself were capable of action; indeed it assumed that small groups of intelligent 'citizens' could act to remedy injustice independently – without the leadership of more learned men or the support of central formal organizations.

Nevertheless, if changes in the trade itself heightened the awareness of its members to the inequities of society, we cannot simply say that shoemaker radicalism emerged in the late eighteenth century as a response to early industrial capitalism. As we have tried to show, the cobbler as a labouring man's intellectual and hetero-dox philosopher, as the common people's spokesman, as a trade militant, long antedates the Industrial Revolution – at least if the argument of this paper is accepted. What the early stages of indus-trialization or pre-industrialization did was to broaden the base of shoemaker radicalism by increasing the numbers of shoemakers and menders and by creating a large body of at least intermittently pauperized semi-proletarian outworkers. Many craft journeymen were forced out of the traditional framework of corporate artisan activities and expectations, and towards the trade union militancy of skilled workers.

But what this period did above all was vastly to increase both the tool-kit of political radicalism and its repertoire of ideas, de-mands and programmes. Secular democratic, Jacobin, republican, anticlerical, co-operative, socialist, communist and anarchist ideo-logies of social and political criticism multiplied, and supplemented or replaced the ideologies of heterodox religion which had pre-viously provided the main vocabulary of popular thought. Some had greater appeal than others, but aspects of all of them spoke to experiences of shoemakers, old or new. The media for popular agitation and debate also multiplied: newspapers and pamphlets providing greater scope for the writing of labouring intellectuals could be read and discussed in the shoemaker's shop. And as the philosophic or heretical shoemaker turned into the politically radical shoemaker, the emergence of movements of protests and social liberation, of a world turned upside down by great revolutions attempted, achieved and anticipated, gave him a vastly increased public ready to listen, perhaps to follow, in town and village. No wonder that the century beginning with the American revolution was the golden age of shoemaker radicalism.

IV

There is a final question which should be asked. What eventually happened to the radicalism of the gentle craft? We have been con-cerned overwhelmingly with the period before shoemaking became a fully mechanized and factory industry and before the rise of the modern socialist and communist working-class movements. During this lengthy period shoemakers were associated with virtually any and all movements of social protest. We find them prominent among religious sectarians and preachers, in republican, radical, Jacobin and sansculottes movements, in artisan co-operative, socialist and communist groups, among atheist anticlericals, and not least among the anarchists. Were they equally prominent among the socialist movements in the new era?

The answer is no. In Germany they were indeed among the six groups of skilled workers who provided at least two-thirds of the social democratic worker-candidates for the Reichstag elections before 1914: together with woodworkers, metalworkers, printers, cigar-makers and, later, building workers. Nevertheless by 1912 they were well behind all these (except the builders) in elected members, and very far indeed behind metalworkers, builders and woodworkers, though level with the much smaller printers and ahead of the smaller cigar-makers in providing candidates. (See Table.) The shoemakers' union, though as usual early off the mark as an organization, declined from the eighth position in size-ranking in 1892 to ninth in 1899 and twelfth in 1905-12. In the German Communist Party after 1918 they were negligible, for out of 504 leading members only 7 were apprenticed shoemakers. Among the 107 skilled trades (omitting the overwhelmingly predominant metal trades) they were far behind printers (17) and woodworkers (29), though on the same level as tailors (7), bricklayers (7) and plumbers (8). Apart from the unskilled and unapprenticed shoe factory worker Willi Münzenberg, the great propagandist, the German Communist Party contained no eminent shoemaker.[107]

**Reichstag election of 1912: occupational groups as a percentage of candidates and deputies***

| Occupational group | Candidates | Deputies |
| --- | --- | --- |
| Metalworkers | 15.6 | 15.5 |
| Woodworkers | 14.8 | 10.9 |
| Builders | 12.8 | 3.6 |
| Printers | 6.6 | 7.3 |
| Shoemakers | 6.6 | 4.5 |
| Tobacco-workers | 3.8 | 6.4 |
| Tailors | 2.7 | 4.5 |
| Textile-workers | 0.8 | 2.7 |

* Note and source: W.H. Schröder, 'Die Sozialstruktur der sozialdemokratischen Reichstagskandidaten, 1898-1912', in *Herkunft und Mandat: Beiträge zur Führungsproblematik in der Arbeiterbewegung* (Frankfurt and Cologne, 1976), pp. 72-96. All figures are percentages.

In France the shoemakers were clearly somewhat over-represented in the Parti Ouvrier Français of the 1890s compared to their
share in the occupied population (3.6 per cent), with 5.3 per cent of
party members and 7.7 per cent of party candidates (1894-7), but
local data do not show them unduly prominent except in a few
localities.[108] Nobody would have chosen them, as seemed reasonable for the anarchists, to symbolize the militants of the socialist
movement. Indeed the most prominent left-wing shoemakers were
certainly Jean Grave the anarchist and Victor Griffuelhes the revolutionary syndicalist, both with their trade's characteristic bent for
political writing. There is not much doubt that the role of the
shoemaker diminished as the movement's centre of gravity shifted
to the large-scale industries and public sector employment. Though
the most prominent communists in 1945 contained two former
joiners and a former pastry-cook, shoemakers were absent from
the list, whose centre of gravity lay in metals and railways. Among
the fifty-one former artisans elected to the French chamber in 1951
there was only one shoemaker (a socialist).[109]

If any occupations were typical of Austrian Socialist Party activists, they were those of locksmiths/mechanics and printers.[110]
Prominent shoemakers are hard to find in this party, and though
the Spanish Socialist Party had Francisco Mora, a shoemaker, at
one time as its secretary and eventually (and characteristically) its
historian, the occupation that clearly dominated that body of
craftsmen was the printing trade. We can no doubt discover a few
prominent shoemakers in lesser socialist parties such as the Hungarian, where two of them, not unexpectedly, became editors of its
newspaper, and in the (Marxist) Social Democracy of the Kingdom
of Poland and Lithuania, where cobblers 'remained throughout its
history, the main stronghold' of its support.[111]. But the only
brands of modern socialism and communism in which the radical
cobbler seems genuinely to have been prominent are those which
notably failed to become mass parties, or even typical parties of
the industrial working class. The general secretary of the tiny Austrian Communist Party and its (symbolic) presidential candidate
were both former journeymen shoemakers from provincial Carin-
thia and Bohemia respectively, and much the most eminent shoemaker radical of the twentieth century is doubtless President Ceau-
sescu of Romania, whose party, at the time he joined it, probably
contained a mere handful of ethnic Romanians.

In industrialized Britain the shoemakers, so prominent between the days of the London Corresponding Society and the election of the atheist radical Charles Bradlaugh for the shoemaking constituency of Northampton in 1880, played no marked role in the era of the Labour Party, except in their own union. They were barely represented among Labour MPs, nor were they especially visible in other ways. The only man with some (unskilled) shoemaking experience early in his chequered career, who became at all prominent, is the transport workers' leader Ben Tillett.[112]

There seems little doubt that, on the whole, the role of the radical shoemaker was no longer as prominent in the era of the socialist mass labour movements as it was before them. No doubt this is partly due to the transformation of shoemaking from a numerically large artisan or semi-artisan craft into a numerically much smaller industry distributing its products through shops. There were no longer so many members of the most characteristic of 'those sedentary crafts which allow a man to "philosophize" while carrying on with familiar tasks of work' among whom the anarchists found so many of their supporters.[113] Most men and women manufacturing shoes increasingly became a sub-species of the factory operative or outworker of developed industrialism; most who sold shoes had no connection with their making. The radical shoemaker as a type belongs to an earlier era.

His period of glory lies between the American revolution and the rise of the mass socialist working-class parties, whenever that occurred in any particular country (insofar as it did). During this period his bent for democratic and self-confident thinking, talking and preaching, hitherto expressed chiefly through religious heterodoxy and radicalism, found theoretical formulations in secular egalitarian revolutionary ideologies, and his practical militancy in mass movements of social protest and hope. The association with such specifically political ideologies of radicalism turned the age-old 'philosophic cobbler' into the 'radical cobbler' – the poor village intellectual into the village sansculotte, republican or anarchist.

The combination of ubiquity with occasional large concentrations of semi-proletarianized craftsmen gave the shoemaker his universal and prominent role as poor man's advocate, spokesman and leader. He was rarely in the front rank of national movements as an individual. Even among manual workers who gained a reputation as theorists and ideologists, people like Tom Paine the stay-maker, Weitling the tailor, Proudhon and Bray the printers, Bebel the wood-turner, Dietzgen the tanner are more likely to be remembered than any shoemaker. His strength lay at the grass roots. For every Thomas Hardy or Mora or Griffuelhes, there were hundreds of men whom even the specialist in the history of radical and labour movements has difficulty in rescuing from the anonymity of the local militant, for little is known about them except that they spoke and fought locally for other poor men: John Adams, the Maidstone cobbler in the 1830 farm-labourers' riots; Thomas Dunning, whose determination and ingenuity saved the Nantwich shoemakers from what might well have been the fate of the Dorchester labourers; the lone Italian shoemaker anarchist who brought his ideas into a Brazilian provincial town. His milieu was that of face-to-face politics, of *Gemeinschaft* rather than *Gesellschaft*. Historically he belongs to the era of workshop, small town, city neighbourhood and above all village, rather than that of factory and metropolis.

He did not disappear totally. One of the authors of this paper still recalls as a student attending Marxist classes given by an admirable Scottish member of the species, and first had his attention drawn to the problem of shoemaker radicalism in the workshop of a Calabrian cobbler in the 1950s. There are no doubt still places where he survives, not least to inspire the young to follow the ideals of liberty, equality and fraternity, as the shoemaker uncle of Lloyd George taught his nephew the elements of radical politics in a Welsh village of the 1880s. Whether or not he is still a significant phenomenon in the politics of the common people, he has served them well. And he has, collectively and through a surprisingly large number of individuals made his mark on history.

(1980)

# 8: The Nineteenth-Century London Labour Market

This paper deals with the peculiar duality of London, considered as a place where people's wages and labour conditions are determined. For centuries London has been regarded as a labour market distinct from the rest of the country, the main distinction being normally that metropolitan money wage rates were (and still generally are) the highest in the British Isles. Indeed, it is the most tenacious of all the country's local labour markets, for even today, when wage-determination has been nationally standardized and institutionalized, and the number of local wage rates has been much diminished, most industries still distinguish between a London and a provincial standard wage rate. The 'London' of one occupation was and is not necessarily that of another, nor does it necessarily coincide with the various other 'Londons' which exist in the files of administrative authorities or in the minds of ordinary inhabitants; but it has always been a distinct geographical and economic entity, and one that aspired to uniformity. The ideal of the London plumber was and is a state of affairs where the same work will be done under equal conditions and for equal pay in Woolwich and Acton; or to be more precise, where no work will be done under conditions or at rates inferior to an ideal standard for the whole metropolis. At the same time London has never been as homogeneous as this ideal demanded. Its vast size, the nature of its expansion, its lack of any single urban centre, have tended to create and preserve a good deal of localization. To this day, to cross the river is to enter an area whose transport system is organized in a wholly different way (the Underground has by far the greater part of its network in the north), or to change – nationalized – gas suppliers. To cross from Islington to Stoke Newington was, in the 1960s, to change the local cinema programme. The object of this essay is to draw attention to the interplay of these standardizing and localizing tendencies in the London labour market. My discussion deals with the nineteenth century, which conventionally includes the years up to 1914, partly because the period interests me as a historian, partly because this was a period when the pattern of the London economy developed with very little planned interference by public authorities.[1]

I

A special London wage rate existed and still exists in most occupations. Employers and workers – the latter more than the former, for they were more anxious to establish higher London wages – therefore had to establish a defined metropolitan 'district' to which the rate applied. No doubt this represented an aspiration rather than a reality for all but the most tightly and successfully organized trades, but even such aspirations are of interest to the student of urban development. Indeed, the very existence of the concept of a single all-London district is significant. Other large nineteenth-century conurbations, though geographically no larger than Greater London and economically more homogeneous, never developed it. Though employers considered the South-East Lancashire Conurbation a single urban zone from at least the 1850s,[2] it was still a mosaic of local trade-union districts with distinct local rates as late as 1906. Tyneside, in 1906, was divided into three districts of the Amalgamated Society of Engineers and five of the relevant semi-skilled union, while London remained a single district with a single (theoretical) rate for each trade.[3] No doubt this difference is not unexpected: a conurbation which arises out of the expansion of a single town is much more likely to regard itself as such than one which arises from the merger of a number of neighbouring towns and villages. Nevertheless, such consciousness of metropolitan unity deserves to be recorded, for it arose in an area which had no kind of municipal unity, and was, administratively speaking, sub-divided to the point of chaos.

How was the 'London district' to be defined? There were, in the early and mid-nineteenth century, few administrative guides, and those available conflicted with one another: the London of the Metropolitan Police and the Registrar-General, which aimed to define, broadly speaking, the continuously built-up area, or the somewhat different areas covered by the Metropolitan Commission of Sewers (the ancestor of the Metropolitan Board of Works, and more remotely of the LCC) and the London District Post.[4] Whether any of these guided trade unionists or employers' associations, is difficult to say. Normally the trade-union 'district' was defined as a circle of a given radius from a given centre – mostly Charing Cross – rather than in more precise ways. Its size varied from trade to trade, but tended to grow as the century drew on. The London tailors in 1834 accepted a radius of four miles from Charing Cross or Covent Garden,[5] but by the middle of the century most unions seem to have taken a rather larger one, up to twelve miles, i.e. distinctly larger than the built-up area as defined for census and police purposes, which was then comprised, approximately, in a circle of six-mile radius. The bricklayers had enlarged their radius to twelve miles by 1877.[6] The London compositors by 1865 claimed jurisdiction over a fifteen-mile radius and over such additional places as paid London rates. And in the early 1900s they proposed to meet home counties' competition by creating an outer London zone of between twenty-five- and forty-mile radius, though this was to be ruled by slightly lower rates.[7] By 1949 only five trades any longer maintained the twelve-mile radius. Fourteen had a radius of fifteen miles, twelve from sixteen to twenty miles, three from twenty-one to thirty, while seventeen trades adopted the Metropolitan Police Area and three, the London Postal Areas as their 'district'.[8]

That the 'district' tended to expand in size is natural enough, for London itself kept growing. That it tended normally to exceed the built-up area is also understandable. The main problem for unions lay at the periphery, where London work expanded into villages and small towns, whose employers would naturally prefer to apply the lower country rates, or in the home counties, whither employers might migrate – printing is a good example – in order to avoid the high metropolitan rates. Trades which did not face these contingencies were likely to have smaller metropolitan districts than those which did. The tailors were content with a compact area; even in 1949 the top rates for retail bespoke tailoring were paid in an area defined as the London postal districts EC 1–4, W1, WC1 and 2 and SW1, which might well have constituted a 'London' district a century earlier. Printing, on the other hand, has always been exceedingly concerned to expand the metropolitan district.[9] Naturally the actual size of the London district depended, to some extent, on the relative bargaining strength of employers and unions; the former normally interested in keeping the area of top-rate wages small, the latter in extending it.

The standard London district therefore represented, at least in the nineteenth century, when it was backed by nothing more than the unions' bargaining strength, an ideal rather than a reality. It was the area within which unions would wish standard London wages and conditions to apply, rather than the one in which they actually applied. It was intended to include the fortress of effective metropolitan unionism, but also its glacis, though there were no doubt mobile and occasionally well-organized trades, such as some of the builders, who might establish London rates even at the periphery, assuming that no strong local rates applied there, and that the suburban building boom gave them a bargaining advantage. (In such cases they might even succeed in establishing rates higher than the central metropolitan ones.) Nevertheless, it is clear that the area within which London rates actually applied also tended to expand. Thus the central nucleus of the London bricklayers comprised thirteen branches in 1868; twenty-nine in 1880. (The depression and union weakness reduced it to twenty-four by 1890.[10]) The London standard area of the exceptionally efficient carpenters in 1860 already extended into the southern suburban fringe, where building was booming (Norwood), but by 1866 it reached westwards into Ealing, northwards into Wood Green, south-east to Greenwich and Forest Hill. By 1876–7 it included Croydon in the south, Woolwich, Bromley and Chislehurst in the south-east, Barnet and Tottenham in the north.[11] (What normally happened in these outlying suburbs was that rates were fixed locally, but that, after a short delay, they tended to equal or even to surpass the official metropolitan rates.) By 1880 standard working hours seem to have been established throughout London in the engineering and printing trades, but not yet in building, though the successive editions of the builders' 'working rules', the first of which were officially adopted in 1873, reflect a tendency towards the enlargement of the standardized area in this as in other respects.[12]

However, even in unorganized occupations a certain broad recognition of London as a uniform labour market, and a certain tendency towards standardization may be observed, though in the absence of institutional definitions, we cannot describe it very accurately. Among employers the concept of a 'district rate' for unskilled labour in the metropolis was familiar.[13] Indeed, it was obviously to some extent a reality. Thus Mayhew provides us with information about the wages of street cleaners and rubbish carters in the middle of the century, which shows that the better paid of such workers, foremen or gangers and carters, tended to be paid eighteen shillings a week, though the wide variations between local authorities and firms show that there was no formal 'fair rate' such as the labour movement subsequently sought to impose on public authorities by electoral and trade union pressure. Thus sixteen of the twenty-nine parishes and highway boards paid their foremen scavengers eighteen shillings, the rest being divided among four other rates. Out of 180 cartage firms recorded, 127 paid their carters eighteen shillings; the rest being divided among five other rates.[14] A metropolitan level of wages and conditions undoubtedly existed, and the area in which it operated almost certainly tended to grow, though obviously level and area differed from one occupation to another, as did the extent to which it operated in practice.

II

Nevertheless, London was clearly too large for a uniform short-term labour market and was bound to contain major local subdivisions and variations. The chief reason for these lay in the extraordinary short-term immobility of the nineteenth-century worker, which was due partly to ignorance, partly to the virtual absence of cheap or widespread public transport until the last decades of the century. It is worth reminding ourselves that cheap working-class transport from home to work was not the object of railways and omnibus companies, and was provided on a large scale only very late, and then partly as the result of radical and working-class agitations, such as those of the London Trades Council in the 1870s and 1880s,[15] and of pressure from social reformers and town planners, such as are reflected in the Royal Commission on the Housing of the Working Classes of 1884–5, which discussed the matter at length. Cheap and plentiful transport was sufficiently revolutionary for Haydn's *Dictionary of Dates* to make a special point of recording the great increase in the number of buses and the 'daily additions with cheap fares, some 1d and $\frac{1}{2}$d' in 1889.[16]

No railway company appears to have operated workmen's trains in London before the Metropolitan did so in 1864, but thereafter it was usual for all railways which provided new stretches of line in the built-up area to be required by Parliament to provide such trains. The Cheap Trains Act of 1883 gave the Board of Trade extensive powers to oblige companies to increase such traffic if the need seemed to demand it. However, it seems clear that before the middle 1880s the Great Eastern, sending more than 8,000 daily from such stations as Ilford, Forest Gate, Edmonton and Walthamstow, had the largest workmen's traffic of any London railway (1884). The total of such tickets in south London appears to have been a modest 25,671 in 1882. The massive increase clearly occurred between 1880 and 1900. By 1894 there was a total of 6,750,000 fares in south London, undoubtedly encouraged, as in other parts of the metropolis, by the settlement of workers in hitherto marginal areas like Vauxhall, Battersea and Clapham – and also facilitating such settlement. The Great Northern and Great Eastern, keenest on this traffic, maintained their lead, while the Great Western showed least enthusiasm, though the suburbs in its area were served by the North London railway, essentially a commuter line with seven million workmen's fare journeys in 1890.[17]

At all events it is quite clear that the habit of undertaking long journeys to work increased markedly in the 1880s and especially the 1890s, though it was generally agreed that the habit was mainly acquired by skilled and relatively well-paid artisans.[18] At all events even among such workers it was sufficiently novel for the Amalgamated Society of Carpenters and Joiners to draw special attention to the fact that the members of its Hammersmith area got jobs all over London.[19] Still, the journey to work by public transport was available. The radius of workmen's tickets, though under eight miles in south-west London and eight-and-a-half in south-east London, was eleven miles in north, twelve miles in west and twenty-one miles in east London. More to the point, in south London the 2d fare was available within the limits of Battersea Park–Clapham Junction–Clapham Common–Herne Hill–South Bermondsey–Southwark Park–Surrey Docks, and the 4d fare from as far as Catford, Greenwich Park and Plumstead in the south-east, Selhurst and Crystal Palace in the south, Tooting, Putney and Southfields in the south-west.

Even had he been more mobile, the nineteenth-century London worker could rarely have regarded the entire metropolis as his labour market, since he had only the sketchiest means of finding out what jobs it contained. If skilled, employers might conceivably advertise for him, or the union would act as a labour exchange, though in trades which were not themselves highly localized within the metropolis even the union would only give him very general guidance – say, a list of reports of the 'state of trade' in the different branches, such as was common in the building trades; or permission to spend an increasing number of days in London looking for work without losing relief, as among the stonemasons.[20] If unskilled, all that lay beyond a tiny circle of personal acquaintance or walking distance was darkness. The unemployed labourer could make the rounds of the local works and yards, though his best chance, as is amply attested, was to get himself attached to the vague entourage of some foreman or ganger who, if he had jobs going, would find it convenient to have a number of workers to lay his hands on; or who might give preferential treatment to a familiar face.[21] In fact, both skilled and unskilled workers depended largely on hearsay, or on tips provided by or through personal contacts, both of which tended to favour localized patterns of the labour market. A Bermondsey labourer was not likely to look for, or to get, many jobs outside his immediate area; a Bermondsey bricklayer was more likely to get outside jobs, but even he would hear of jobs in south-east London rather than in, say, Paddington or Hackney. Thus a bricklayer, whose biography we possess,[22] was the son of a Kentish bricklayer who migrated, presumably – since that is where most Kentish immigrants tended to go – to southeast London. In 1860–2 he worked round Croydon, the Crystal Palace and Woolwich. In the 1860s he founded and led the Woolwich branch of his union, though he also worked for a time in west London. In the 1880s he was secretary of his Greenwich branch. Clearly, south-east London remained his home-base throughout. A carpenter, born in Harrow (1849) was apprenticed in Notting Hill and joined the Ealing branch of his union in 1869, later transferring to Hammersmith, where he stayed until elected to the General Secretaryship in 1888.[23] Clearly, he was primarily a west Londoner.

There is plenty of evidence of this short chain of distance which normally bound the worker to his place of work; not least in casual occupations or irregular and jobbing work, which obliged him to be virtually 'within call' on pain of losing opportunities of employment. 'In London,' wrote John O'Neil, a shoemaker who has given us one of the few full-scale life histories of a worker for the first half of the century,[24] 'generally speaking, poor people cannot select their lodgings, being obliged in a great manner to accommodate themselves to the circumstances in which they are placed through their employment and other contingencies.' He was explaining why he, a respectable man and teetotaller, was then living in a rookery. 'What', said R.L. Jones before an inquiry in 1846,[25] 'has been the cause of all the hundreds and thousands of small houses in Blackwall and Poplar and all those places? The docks, which have brought the labour there. The labourer will not go away from where the manufactory is, however bad the occupancy of the dwelling may be; he still will be near his work.' Such statements could be multiplied, for instance from the evidence of the Royal Commission on the Housing of the Working Classes in the 1880s, which, as we have seen, put this localization down largely to the absence of cheap public transport. For practical purposes the worker was tied to a radius of 'walking distance' from his home, that is, to one of at most three to four miles.[26]

What sorts of localized patterns existed in consequence of all this within the metropolis? There were, in the main, two: the pattern of 'districts' – it is misleading to call them 'neighbourhoods', for they varied in size – i.e. of the areas in which the worker lived and moved about freely, to which he belonged; and the much looser pattern of London 'regions'. Woolwich is a good example of the first, the 'district', though perhaps an untypical example, for few London districts had so clearly distinct local wage rates and hours (normally lower and longer than elsewhere)[27] and such a clearly distinct economic and social structure: it was one of the two London areas in which cooperation took deep root with the Royal Arsenal Co-operative Society. (The sub-area was in fact for certain purposes rather larger than Woolwich, but that need not detain us.) South London is the clearest example of the second, the 'region'.

The 'district' had at least a rough institutional equivalent of its labour market in the trade-union branch. As Appendix I shows, the same localities provide names for the branches of a variety of trade unions, for instance, Chelsea and Kensington in west London; Lambeth, Greenwich, Woolwich, Camberwell, Battersea in south London; Stepney, Shoreditch, Poplar in east London. The connection between the union branch and the 'district' was indirect and sometimes tenuous, but insofar as the branch reflected anything of the surrounding area of the town, one may claim that it reflected the existence of a known major and often traditional nucleus of working-class life, distinct from its neighbours.[28] The 'region' was unrecognized in theory, though in practice it kept breaking through.[29]

The three main regions reflect a triple division of London which goes back a long way – perhaps it echoes that between London, Westminster and Southwark – and persists to this day: that between the north and west, the north and east, and the south. Thus three gas companies arose in the early nineteenth century to serve London: the 'Gas Light and Coke', whose area ran from Temple Bar in the east to Brompton in the west and Tottenham Court Road in the north; the 'City and London' which served all points between Temple Bar in the west, Whitechapel in the east and St John's Clerkenwell, in the north; and the 'South London'.[30] The distinction between City and West End was well established – cartage firms in the 1840s drew the line somewhere through the centre of Holborn and past Temple Bar[31] – and the autonomy of the south is a well-known fact. The fundamental reason for the maintenance of these frontiers may not be simply tradition and transport, but the very real division between the working-class areas of the city. The river was and is an unmistakable barrier, and north of it there was a wide wedge of business districts – the City and Holborn – and the belt of open spaces and middle- or upper-class residential areas which stretches from the heights of Hampstead and Highgate down to beyond Regent's Park. Thus the London Union of Printers' Pressmen could plausibly defend its sub-divisions by the argument: 'From the East End, as a matter of course, it would take a long while for a man to walk to the West.'[32] The centres of working-class life in the west – Westminster and Chelsea, Marylebone and Paddington – were hardl' n the same city as those in the Tower Hamlets and Shoreditch. As for the south, it has always lived its own life. It had its specialized activities – engineering, the special types of docking done on the Surrey side – and it is not surprising to find that in 1889 two quite separate general labour unions developed on the two sides of the river: the Dockers' Union in the north, the Labour Protection League in the south.

Of these regions the south was by far the most clearly defined. It was that part of London which conformed most closely to the general pattern of the provincial town, though it lacked a real town centre, for neither the Borough Road, which used to function as such, nor the Elephant and Castle, which tends to occupy this position today, were and are really suitable.[33] At all events the area enclosed by the big bend of the Thames between Vauxhall Bridge and the Surrey Commercial Docks formed a fairly compact whole. Eastwards it continued without a break into Bermondsey and Deptford, with an isolated outpost in Woolwich; in the west it came to possess a similar outpost in Battersea. Ideologically and politically its character was strongly marked. In a metropolis not much given to nonconformism, it contained a powerful body of lower-middle-class dissenters, whose spiritual headquarters was Spurgeon's Tabernacle in Newington, as Bradlaugh's Hall of Science in Old Street was that of the Painite Radicals in north-east London. Politically the area was strongly radical. In the LCC elections from 1889 to 1907, Walworth, Newington West, Bermondsey, Southwark West and Camberwell North voted Progressive without a break; Battersea, Peckham and Rotherhithe – on the outskirts of the area – Progressive all but once in seven elections; Deptford, Greenwich, Lambeth North and Kennington voted Progressive all but twice.*

So far as the working class went, the south contained by far the strongest concentration of trade unionists in the metropolis, and before 1889 probably the only real concentration. It is no accident that it was the headquarters of mid-Victorian union leaders, for Robert Applegarth, a Lambeth vestryman, lived there, and William Allan of the Amalgamated Engineers operated from his room at the Rising Sun, south of Blackfriars Bridge.[34] Since the South Side was an important centre of engineering work, one might perhaps have expected it to contain the greatest number of organized engineers – 60 per cent or so in 1865–71 (excluding Woolwich).[35] But it was less natural that by far the smallest of the three London regions† should contain twice as many organized bricklayers as west London, and much more than north and east London; or that in 1871 seven of the bricklayers' sixteen branches with just under half their London membership should be in the south. The carpen-

---

*The political implications of armaments gave Woolwich a somewhat different electoral history.

†In 1851 the approximate population of each region was (in thousands): 860 for the north and west, 950 for the north and east, 550 for the south.

ters, as Appendix I shows, had a marked connection with west London, but even they had slightly under a third of their members in the south. Most of the stone building of mid-Victorian London was certainly north of the river; but two south London branches of the stonemasons provided 633 out of 1,562 metropolitan members. Even more marked was the trade-union concentration in certain large branches in the nucleus of south London, Southwark and Lambeth. Among the bricklayers (1871), the Lambeth and Borough branches alone accounted for more than a third of their London members. The average branch membership of the carpenters was 58: their three Lambeth branches totalled almost 300. Southwark and Lambeth contained more than a quarter of all organized engineers in London. And so on.[36] It is evident that the south formed a peculiar sub-area of the London labour market.

No other region of London was equally clearly defined, because none had equally clear geographical boundaries and compactness. In west London the stretch of riverside which runs from Westminster to Fulham may perhaps be regarded as a comparable zone, but its working-class centres were much more tenuously connected with one another, as were the more northerly nuclei of Marylebone, Paddington and Kensington. North-west London voted overwhelmingly Moderate in the LCC elections of 1889–1907, with the exception of Chelsea - whose ancient radicalism still survived - and North and West St Pancras - which belonged socially with their eastern neighbours. But even these voted Moderate in two elections. Western working-class London was therefore little more than a geographical category.

The great north and east London working-class area stretched in a large curved band from Camden Town in the west through Islington, Shoreditch and Bethnal Green, to Stepney and the riverside. Economically and socially it had three possible foci: the area of small craft production north and east of the City (Clerkenwell and Finsbury, Shoreditch, Bethnal Green), the riverside from the Tower to opposite Woolwich, and the railway works at Stratford, which formed the centre of a highly individual working-class community, a sort of northern analogue to Woolwich.[37] In fact, it had no common centre, being a congeries of small and often very localized communities.[38] This lack of definition emerged both from its political and its trade-unionist complexion. The only areas which voted solidly Progressive in 1889–1907 were the two divisions of

Bethnal Green and Hackney South. On the other hand, St George's, Stepney and Whitechapel had no overwhelmingly dominant political allegiance at all. As for the trade unions, the number of organized engineers in the whole of this vast area was only two-thirds of that in the south in 1865, and one-third in 1871; the corresponding number of organized bricklayers was a little more than half in 1865, one-third in 1871; that of the organized carpenters, a little more than half in 1865, not much more than a quarter in 1871.[39] In fact, east London was a trade-unionist desert, an amorphous zone of weak and fluctuating organization united only by its general poverty.

It will be clear that the 'regions' were not simply areas of economic specialization, even though certain industries were virtually confined to, or absent from, a region.[40] In the 1890s the main centres of cabinet-making were all in the north and east (Bethnal Green, Shoreditch, Hackney, Stepney, St Pancras), and so were the main centres of boot- and shoemaking (Bethnal Green, Shoreditch, Stepney, Hackney). There was very little tailoring in south London. Few trades had a distribution which quite cut across the three sectors, as did printing, which was concentrated in a central strip running from north to south, or upholstery which ran east-west from Bethnal Green to Paddington. The point was that, whether or not an industry was localized in a region, each region remained surprisingly autonomous. The river, for instance, was a rather effective barrier. In the 1830s even the City, which relied on daily in- and out-flows much greater than any other area, had not more than about 28,000 daily in-migrants who crossed the Thames, and in the early 1900s it was still observed that 'on the whole the passage from one side of the river to the other (for work) is very small', in spite of the Blackwall Tunnel.[41] Consequently, even where unions or trades operated theoretically all over London, we find traces of 'regionalism'. The stonemasons had continuously functioning branches throughout the 1860s in the south and west, but not in the north and east; the carpenters at the outset showed a similar pattern, while the engineers tended to be in the south, the north and east, but not the west. The Amalgamated Painters in 1880 and the Metropolitan Operative French Polishers in 1867, operated virtually only in the west, while the Amalgamated Cordwainers in 1871 had no branches at all in the south.[42] However, while these had branches in the City and north-east as well as in the west, the two sectors were specialized and tended to quarrel, since they had totally different union policies.[43] John O'Neil, whose autobiography has already been quoted, only left his original home base in the City when work fell off as a result of the great strike of 1811 ('in the time of the great comet' as he says, to indicate the catastrophic nature of the event), and even then he only 'went away to work in the West End' just beyond what is now Kingsway.[44]

Nevertheless, though the distinction between the three regions was persistent and obvious – so obvious indeed, that the London County Council Planning Department was sub-divided to fit in with them after World War II – there is no strong evidence that each region developed its own wage level or standard of hours. There were indeed marked variations in these within London, but on the whole they seem to have been over rather smaller areas than the entire regions. Thus the *Return of Hours of Work 1850–1890* quotes three different areas for London builders' hours (South-east, South-west, North-west); for cabinet-makers (East, East Central, North-west); for the cigar and tobacco trade (South-east, West Central, East Central); for engineering (South-east, South-west, East); for printing (South-east, West Central, East Central); and four areas for tailoring (West, South-west, West Central, East Central).[45] Some, but not all these areas coincide with the triple regional division. The most persistent sub-area was in the south-east, which as has been suggested above, normally had somewhat lower wages and longer hours than the rest. A slighter tendency for parts of the East End (but not the entire north and east area) to enjoy less favourable labour conditions will be less surprising. On the whole, however, occupations spread all over London would most likely be aware less of these, than of even more localized and apparently capricious variations, such as are recorded in the monthly reports of the 'state of trade' of the carpenters, which every London branch prepared separately, and which, while sometimes reflecting a general metropolitan *Konjunktur*, at other times present a totally incoherent picture.[46]

III

We have briefly surveyed the metropolis as a single labour market and its internal sub-divisions. It remains to say something about

London's relations with its environs and with the rest of the country, from whose other urban and industrial areas it was separated by large stretches of agricultural land, but with which it was linked by the sea.

One would expect the striking, high wage rate of London to have had a measurable influence on the wages, hours and conditions of the home counties; and possibly also certain currents of rural immigration to have had a converse influence on parts of London. Ideally it ought to be possible to construct a sort of relief map by plotting the various local standard rates of wages and hours in places round London, a map which might be expected to slope downwards from the peak of London wages, or upwards from the valley of London hours. Unfortunately, such a relief map cannot yet be constructed, partly because our information is not always complete or comparable, even in the period when the government had begun to collect statistics, and partly because the number of places for which we possess such figures in the area round London is simply not large enough to provide enough reference points for our purpose. The following observations, though based on representative data,[47] are, therefore, correct in outline rather than detail.

The sector of the home counties whose links with the London labour market were most patent and striking was Kent. The mere fact that every union which collected material about local conditions found out relatively much more about Kent than about any other neighbouring area speaks for itself. The carpenters in 1876-7 got information about fifteen places in that county, as against four in Surrey, one in Hertfordshire and one in Essex; the bricklayers in 1890-1 about fourteen Kentish places, as against three in Surrey, two in Hertfordshire and five in Essex.[48] It is equally significant that, when the London Dockers Union (which organized all workers within reach) expanded after the 1889 strike, the only area adjoining the metropolis in which it made immediate and massive headway was that along the line of Watling Street and up the Medway Valley. Within six months of the strike the union had fifteen branches with 3,500 members in a special Medway district; three months later it had 5,000 members in the Medway and Northfleet districts, and branches in Dartford and Sheerness. By the end of 1890 the union had reached Maidstone, though it spread no farther.[49] There is no sign of its expansion into contiguous areas in any other direction out of London. On the relief map the effect

of the metropolitan high wages would be most obvious and extensive in the same area, both in builders' and farm labourers' wage
rates.* It is reasonable to suppose that the markedly lower wage
rates which long made south-east London into a bridge between
Kent and the metropolis reflect these strong links with Kent, that
is, presumably the known tendency to draw on Kentish immigration for the London labour market.

South of London the active expansion of suburbia and the presence of Croydon, which was assimilated to the London wage-level
in the 1870s (at least among the carpenters), pushed a tongue of
London influence into the country. Caterham, Redhill and Reigate,
and to a smaller extent Dorking, show it, though not as markedly
as the Kentish places.† This influence seems to have been distinct
from that experienced by the Kentish neighbour, for the Amalgamated House Decorators, whose expansion in 1873–81 was demon-
strably from Surrey outwards, expanded only very little into Kent,
but very much into the area west of a line from London to
Hastings.[50] However, this markedly southern and south-western
orientation, which is somewhat anomalous, may be connected with
the well-known seasonal movement of house painters between London and the south coast resorts.

North-eastwards there seems to have been a similar tongue of
London influence licking outwards towards Epping and Romford.
But in general, in that quarter, farming wage rates seem to have
declined steeply towards the wage levels of Essex, and were much
lower than those of any other area adjoining London. What little
we know of builders' wages in that area – the unions' information
about it was fragmentary and geographically somewhat capricious
– makes a similar impression.‡ North and westwards of London
the slope of wage rates seems also to have been somewhat steeper
than in Kent; the London influence was less marked. The main
impression is one of gradual encroachment by the suburban belt,
with its attendant high wages, upon the generally flat plain of
low-wage localities. For the bricklayers in the 1870s the rather

---

* Thus the London hourly rate for bricklayers in 1906 was 10½d. It was 10d as
far away as Dartford and Swanley, 9d as far away as Rochester–Chatham and
Tonbridge.

† Bricklayers' rates in 1906: Caterham 9d; Reigate, Redhill 8½d.

‡ In 1876 the bricklayers reported only from Saffron Walden; in 1890, also from
Colchester, Halstead, Grays and Brentwood.

sharp border between the two zones ran between Twickenham and Egham; for the better organized carpenters farther out. The absence of trade-union wage data from the Surrey–Hampshire border – except for Guildford and Aldershot – probably also suggests little contact in that quarter. North of London there is an equal dearth of information. Watford, St Albans and Hertford seem to be the only places within the ken of the London unions, and of these only Watford, and possibly St Albans, reflected the influence of London in slightly higher wage rates, but only at a rather late date. It is perhaps worth noting the feeble tendency of unions to expand westwards, or northwards, as witness the house decorators, and especially the carpenters, even though their initial strongholds were very strikingly in west and north-west London.

Beyond this somewhat eccentric area immediately affected by the general London wage level (or rather by the level of unskilled and building wages), there stretched the tentacles which linked London labour with the remoter parts of the country. Except in special or highly migratory trades, we should not expect such links to be reflected in the crude mirror of wage rates and hours: even quite large and steady streams of migration in or out of London, such as those of many groups of artisans, were hardly ever large enough to affect its wage levels in the short run.[51] Nevertheless, more delicate indicators can bring out, as it were, the pattern of London radiation. The most useful of these is the pattern of expansion of trade unions which grew out of local movements.

The most obvious of London's long-distance links was the sea, which linked it to other ports and provided cheap and traditional transport for migrants such as the Cornishman Lovett. The pattern of expansion which brought the typical west-country sect of Bible Christians from Devon and Cornwall to Kent and London without apparent intermediate stops, is typically sea-borne.[52] Another traditional maritime link of London no doubt brought colonies of at least one Tyneside union into the metropolis.* Naturally the London influence outside was normally much stronger than the provincial influence on London. And its limits are graphically shown by the expansion of the London-based unions among the waterside workers elsewhere. The area in which these unions

---

*The National Amalgamated Union of Labour (subsequently merged in the National Union of General and Municipal Workers).

(chiefly the Dockers' Union, now the Transport and General Workers) became the chief or only organizers of waterside labour stretched from Tees-side up north, round the east and south coasts and the Bristol Channel, to the borders of South Wales, though there (as on the east coast northwards from the Humber) the London unions shared the field with regionally based organizations of the same kind.[53] The London influence, as is clear from the records of the Dockers' expansion, did not spread simply along the coasts, but jumped to major centres, the intermediate areas being organized later, sometimes from the original colonies.[54]

Overland, similar links are more tenuous. There is, as we have seen, evidence of expansion westwards along the south coast by the Painters' Union, though their case was probably untypical. There is also evidence of some links with the eastern counties, which will not surprise students of the patterns of migration into and out of London. The Navvies' Union, which was composed of migratory workers, had fifty-one branches in Greater London, and twelve outside: three in East Anglia, one in Bedfordshire, one in Hertfordshire, six in Northamptonshire (Northampton contained an abnormally high percentage of London-born inhabitants), one elsewhere. The 'new' union of unskilled railway workers, the General Railway Workers' Union, had a markedly eastern orientation, perhaps because many London railwaymen were East Anglians. Thus in 1891 it had ten branches in East Anglia as against four on the Great Western line, and a scattering elsewhere.[55] However, until the subject has been much more fully studied, it is perhaps best not to read too much into such fragmentary data.

The picture of the London labour market which I have attempted to draw will not be unfamiliar to students of nineteenth-century London. Indeed, the lack of homogeneity in the great metropolis has often been used to explain the weakness or ineffectiveness of London's popular movements in the earlier parts of the century, and, since London was essential to the success of national movements, the ease with which the British ruling classes, secure in their capital city, fended off agitation outside.[56] There was no chance that London would imitate Paris. As Francis Place explained to Richard Cobden in 1840:

London differs very widely from Manchester, and, indeed, from every other place on the face of the earth. It has no local or particular interest as a town, not even as to politics. Its several boroughs in this respect are like so many very populous places at a distance from one another, and the inhabitants of any of them know nothing, or next to nothing, of the proceedings in any other, and not much indeed of those of their own. London in my time, and that is half a century, has never moved. A few of the people in different parts have moved, and these, whenever they come together, make a considerable number – still, a very small number indeed when compared with the whole number.[57]

Time and again the card of London disunity has been played in the political game, when London unity appeared to work in favour of the radicalism which was to be expected in vast accumulations of labouring people. The London boroughs were created in the 1890s to weaken the new London County Council, which had fallen under the control of the left. Their position was reinforced against the new Greater London Council, formed in the belief – which proved mistaken in the 1970s – that the inclusion of the outer suburbs would weaken the hold of Labour on the metropolis. The Conservative government of 1979 opted for the extreme solution of fragmenting London, thus depriving it, alone among the capital cities of the world – and at the cost of extreme administrative confusion and prospective expense – of any form of unified municipal existence.

Yet, if we turn it upside down, the question of the London labour market has a wider significance, for it illustrates the obstacles which faced the formation of a single British working class with a single unified movement. Historians are often tempted to take its existence, or its inevitable emergence, for granted. Yet, as we have seen, that is not what things looked like on the ground, even within the confines of a single built-up area, geographically not very large, and which was actually seen in some sense as constituting a unity, distinct from its surroundings. The metropolitan labour force was and remained fragmented and localized, its links with the rest of the country uneven and variable. The forces making for greater size and homogeneity – at least for particular occupations and strata – were not negligible, but their net effect for most of the nineteenth century was not dramatic, And still, as a subsequent chapter tries to show, some time between 1870 and 1914, or perhaps even later, the complex set of pieces of the jig-saw puzzle of the Victorian labouring classes came to be fitted together into something like the recognizable, and recognized, picture of a single national class and movement. How a single class and movement was formed out of a pile of largely disconnected potential components, remains one of the major problems for research in the history of British labour. Its investigation, which takes us beyond the study of labour markets and work into the history of politics and institutions, culture and ideas, has a long way to go.

(1964)

## Appendix I

**Trade unionists' London**

The following table summarizes the local distribution of the branches of nine trade unions in London, 1850–92.

1. *Friendly Society of Operative Stonemasons*, 1859–71.
2. *Operative Bricklayers' Society*, 1850–92.
3. *Amalgamated Society of Carpenters and Joiners*, 1860–76.
4. *Friendly Society of Ironfounders*, 1859–71.
5. *Amalgamated Society of Engineers*, 1851, 1860, 1868–71.
6. *Amalgamated Society of Cordwainers*, 1871.
7. *Amalgamated Society of Tailors*, 1877.
8. *Amalgamated Society of House Decorators and Painters*, 1880.
9. *United Operative Society of Plumbers*, 1892.

Most of these unions contain one or two branches whose location cannot be identified, either because they are merely described as 'London' or because they are named after public houses or parishes which may be situated in two or more divisions of the metropolis.

|  | 1. | 2. | 3. | 4. | 5. | 6. | 7. | 8. | 9. |
|---|---|---|---|---|---|---|---|---|---|
| (*West*) | | | | | | | | | |
| West London | x | | | | x* | | | | |
| Chelsea | x | x* | x | x | | x | | x | x |
| Pimlico/West- | | | | | | | | | |
| minster | x | x | x | | | | | | |
| Kensington | | x* | x | | | x | | x | x |
| Notting Hill | | | x | | | | | x | x |
| Paddington | | x | x | | | | | x | |
| Marylebone | | | x | | x | | x | | |
| Hammersmith | | x | x | | | | | | |
| Fulham | | | x | | | | | | x |
| | | | | | | | | | |
| (*South*) | | | | | | | | | |
| South London | x | | | x | x | | x | x | |
| Lambeth | | x* | x | | x* | | | | |
| Southwark | x | x* | x | | x* | | | | |
| Greenwich | x | x | x | x | x* | | x | | |
| Woolwich | x | x* | x | x | x* | | x | | |
| Deptford | | | | | x* | | | | |

| | 1. | 2. | 3. | 4. | 5. | 6. | 7. | 8. | 9. |
|---|---|---|---|---|---|---|---|---|---|
| (*South cont.*) | | | | | | | | | |
| Bermondsey | | | | x | x | | | | |
| Battersea | | x | x | | x | | | | x |
| Camberwell | | x | x | | | | | x | x |
| | | | | | | | | | |
| (*East*) | | | | | | | | | |
| East London | | | | x | x* | | x | | x |
| Stepney/Tower | | | | | | | | | |
| Hamlets | | | x | | x* | x | x | | |
| Shoreditch | x | x | x | | | | | | |
| Poplar | | x | x | | x | | | | |
| Hackney | | | x | | | | | | |
| Stratford | | | x | | x | | | | |
| West Ham | x | x | x | | | | | | |
| | | | | | | | | | |
| (*North*) | | | | | | | | | |
| North London | x | | | x | x* | | | | |
| King's Cross | | x* | x | | x | | | | |
| Camden Town | | | x | | | | | | |
| Kentish Town | | x | x | | | | | | |

*indicates branches of over 100 members.

The following branches were not included in the 'London district':
*Stonemasons:*
Croydon, Ealing, Isleworth, Plumstead, Richmond, West Ham, Woolwich.
*Bricklayers:*
1876–7: Belvedere, Bromley, Croydon, Hounslow, Tottenham, Twickenham, Woolwich.
1890–1: Brentford, Bromley, Croydon, Ealing, Edmonton, Penge, Richmond, Tooting, Tottenham, Twickenham, Wimbledon, Woolwich.
*Carpenters:*
1860: Richmond.
1866: Barnet, Brentford, Croydon, Ealing, Greenwich, Richmond, Southall, Surbiton, Twickenham, Wimbledon, Wood Green, Woolwich.
1872–3: *Suburbs on, above or below London standard weekly rate:*
*On or above:* Norwood, Poplar.
*1s. 8d. below:* Barnet, Bromley, Chislehurst, Forest Hill, Greenwich, Penge, Tottenham, Woolwich.
*4s. below:* Croydon, Twickenham, Wimbledon.
*More than 4s. below:* Brentford, Kingston, Richmond, Southall.
1876–7: *Suburbs on, above or below London standard weekly rate:*
*On or above:* Barnet, Bromley, Chislehurst, Croydon, Deptford, Ealing, Forest Hill, Greenwich, Norwood, Penge, Poplar, Putney, South Norwood, Tottenham, Wimbledon, Woolwich.
*1s. 8d. below:* Brentford, Kingston, Richmond, Southall, Twickenham.
*More than 1s. 8d. below:* Harrow.
*Tailors:*
Brentford, Bromley, Croydon, Greenwich, Kingston, Woolwich.

## Appendix II

**London 'regions' and 'districts' as indicated by the title of local newspapers**

Source: May's *British and Irish Press Guide*, 1880.

1. Papers existing before 1860.

| | |
|---|---|
| South: | *South London Journal* |
| | *South London Gazette* |
| North and West: | *West London Observer* |
| | *Chelsea News* |
| | *Marylebone Mercury* |
| | *Paddington Times* |

North and East:
*East End News*
*East London Observer*
*Hackney Express*
*Islington Gazette*
*Stratford (& Bow) Times*

2. Total of local newspapers existing 1880:

South:
*'South London' papers*   6
*Bermondsey & Rotherhithe*   1
*Camberwell*   1
*Greenwich & Deptford*   2
*Southwark*   1
*Wandsworth & Battersea*   2
*Woolwich*   2
*Norwood*   1
*Sydenham*   3

North and West:
*'West London' papers*   2
*Bayswater*   1
*Chelsea*   1
*Hampstead & Highgate*   1
*Kensington & Hammersmith*   2
*Marylebone*   1
*Paddington*   1
*St Pancras*   2
*Acton*   1
*Kilburn & Willesden*   2
*Hendon & Finchley*   3

North and East:
*'East London' papers*   3
*Clerkenwell*   1
*Hackney*   4
*Holborn*   1
*Holloway*   1
*Islington*   2
*Seven Sisters & Finsbury Park*   1
*Shoreditch*   1
*Tower Hamlets*   1
*Stratford*   2
*Wanstead*   1
*Leyton*   1
*Tottenham*   2
*Walthamstow*   1
*Woodford*   1

# 9: The 'New Unionism' in Perspective

As applied to its period of origin, the 1880s and early 1890s, the term 'new unionism' suggests three things to a British labour historian. It suggests, first, a new set of strategies, policies and forms of organization for unions, as opposed to those associated with an already existing 'old' trade unionism. It suggests, in the second place, a more radical social and political stance of unions in the context of the rise of a socialist labour movement; and in the third place, the creation of new unions of hitherto unorganized or unorganizable workers, as well as the transformation of old unions along the lines suggested by the innovators. Consequently it also suggests an explosive growth of trade-union organization and membership. The dock strike of 1889 and its aftermath illustrate all these aspects of the 'new unionism', and it therefore provides the most popular image of the entire phenomenon. It is interesting that the very similar union upsurge and transformation of 1911–13 has never generated any similar label, though it was quite as innovative and much more radical. This suggests that even at the time it was regarded as a continuation, or a second instalment, of the process initiated in 1889. I believe that this is in fact the best way to see it.[1]

A comparative study of 'new unionism' in various countries during the period 1890–1914 implies that there were comparable trade-union developments in them. Now the British case was at this time unique in Europe in one respect. Here alone do we find an already established and significant 'old' unionism, rooted in the country's basic industries, to combat, transform and expand. This was notably not the case in the other country of old industrialism, Belgium. In Germany the Free Trade Unions, though they had multiplied their membership almost fourfold since 1889, had by 1900 just about reached a numerical strength comparable to the 'old unions' of Britain in 1887 (680,000 as against 674,000). In short, the continental 'new unionism' of the late nineteenth century was new chiefly inasmuch as it established trade unions as a serious force, which they had not hitherto been outside some localities and the occasional craft trade, such as printing and cigar-making. To this extent the 'new unionism' of Britain is *sui generis*.

Thus, on the continent, unionism developed simultaneously with the mass political labour movement and its parties, and largely under their impulsion. Its major problems arose when it became sufficiently massive to discover that the policies of trade-union leaders, however socialist, could not be entirely congruent with the policies of the political leadership of socialist parties. Union membership probably grew faster than party membership and eventually exceeded it in size, except in such countries as Bohemia and Finland where the party consistently had more members than the unions, presumably because of the local impact of national sentiment. However, the party *electorate* greatly outnumbered union membership, except in Denmark up to 1913.[2] On the other hand in Britain, as we know, the Labour Party was itself a creation of the unions, and before 1914 the total vote for *all* labour and socialist candidates, whatever their affiliations, never amounted to more than perhaps 20 per cent of union membership,[3] while in Germany, even after the unions had grown to a larger size (and, according to some, density of organization) than in Britain, the Social-Democratic vote was about double the membership of *all* unionists of whatever ideological persuasion, omitting only the organizations of salaried employees.[4]

In certain crucial respects the 'new unionism' of Britain and continental countries are therefore not comparable. However, there are analogies between the British and continental cases, insofar as the mass extension of unionism raised problems of strategy and organization which had not previously arisen. Moreover, in some respects all trade-union movements experimented with the same solutions to these problems, though the British pattern, which was eventually to supplement a broadened 'craft' unionism primarily by 'general unions' was not paralleled on the same scale in continental Europe. Conversely neither the policy of forming the union movement into a relatively small number of comprehensive organizations covering entire industries ('industrial unionism'), nor the formation of local inter-occupational bodies such as *Bourses du Travail* or *Camere del Lavoro* was notably successful in Britain.

Britain and the continent are also directly comparable, insofar as initiative and ideas in the union movement came largely from the radical, and indeed theoretically revolutionary, left, though naturally in Britain the bulk of the leadership in older unions were not socialists and still less revolutionaries. Still it is important to insist against sceptics like Clegg, Fox and Thompson[5] on the disproportionately large role of the numerically small socialist movement in the British unions, particularly from the middle 1890s. The total membership of all socialist organizations in the middle of that decade may be generously estimated at not more than 20,000, and their paid-up membership at the time of the foundation of the Labour Representation Committee cannot have been more than perhaps 10,000, since they themselves only claimed 23,000.[6]

Some of this British left – the Marxists and later the syndicalists – were undoubtedly guided by international ideologies and strategies and, conversely, British trade-union experience was taken note of on the continent. That movements in one industrial country thus claimed to be influenced by the experience, the ideologies and strategies of others, is itself evidence for some comparability, even though it may be doubted whether British union history would have been significantly different if nobody in Britain had heard of revolutionary syndicalism, or continental union history would have been notably different if nobody in France or Germany had been acquainted with the British term 'ca'canny' (go-slow).[7] However, such foreign or international models were not always mere colourful labels which national activists stuck on bottles containing strictly native beverages. The international Marxism of the 1880s had little to say about trade unions, except to demand comprehensive class organization and warn against craft exclusiveness, but from about 1906 the British objective of rationalizing trade-union structure along the lines of 'industrial unionism' was certainly derived from ideas and experiences drawn from, or acquired, abroad. In any case the fact that union leadership and activism in this period were so widely identified with social-revolutionary movements, and that trade unionism also came to develop its own international organizations, is itself significant.* It must affect our assessment of certain novel forms of action, occurring internationally and much debated, such as general strikes.

The most easily comparable aspect of 'new unionism' is the general pattern of trade-union growth through discontinuous 'leaps' or explosions.[8] Such leaps occurred in most European trade-union movements during our period, though not necessarily at the same time. If Britain and Germany both experienced such a leap in 1889-90 – both movements increased by about 90 per cent during this brief period, though the British movement from a base five times as large as the German – there is no British equivalent to the major continental leaps of 1903-4 (Norway, Sweden, Switzerland and The Netherlands) or of 1905 (Austria). Neither is there a real continental equivalent to the great British explosion of 1911-13. This should warn us against too close a correlation between trade-union expansion and cyclical economic fluctuations, national or international.

However, we may well ask ourselves whether there is much point in stressing the obvious, namely that trade-union growth at a certain stage must everywhere be discontinuous. Only when unionism in a country has been recognized and institutionalized, or when it has reached a density, by voluntary recruitment or compulsory membership, which only leaves room for marginal growth or expansion and contraction in line with the changing size of the labour force, can we expect the curve of union growth to be smooth and gentle. In no country and no industry (with rare exceptions such as British coalmining just before 1914) had this stage been reached in 1880-1914. Growth must be discontinuous under these circumstances, because if unions are to be effective they must mobilize, and therefore seek to recruit, not numbers of individuals but groups of workers sufficiently large for collective bargaining. They must recruit in lumps.

---

* International conferences attended by secretaries of national union federations occur from 1901, an international secretariat existed from 1903, an International Federation of Trade Unions from 1913. By 1912 we have records of thirty-two international trade secretariats for particular branches of unionism. However, such forms of international trade union coordination were not of much practical importance.

II

Let us leave international comparisons aside for the moment and consider the British phenomenon of 'new unionism'. 1889 unquestionably marks a qualitative transformation of the British labour movement and its industrial relations. Between the great dock strike and World War I we observe the appearance of effective and permanent employers' organizations on a national scale, such as the Shipping Federation, the Engineering Employers' Federation and the Newspaper Publishers' Association. We encounter the first genuinely nationwide and national industrial disputes and collective bargains, the first interventions of central government in labour disputes, and indeed the creation of government offices designed to take care of the now constant interest of government in these matters. For during this period we also observe the first expressions of political concern about the possible effects of strikes and unions on the competitive position of the British economy. The appearance of a national Labour Party consisting essentially of trade-union affiliates, and the welfare legislation of the years before 1914, are familiar to all.

So far as the unions themselves are concerned, the most striking difference lies not so much in the increased size and changed composition of the movement, but probably in its economic effects. Broadly speaking, before about 1900 trade unionism served, if anything, to widen wage differentials between different groups of workers. After 1900, and especially after 1911, it contributed to the progressive narrowing of differentials.[9] Nevertheless, the actual innovations in trade-union structure and industrial or occupational distribution, are not to be overlooked. If we compare the list of the largest unions in 1885 with that in 1963 (as recorded by the Royal Commission of Trade Unions and Employers' Associations of 1965-8), we see (Table I) that only one of the ten largest unions of 1885 was still in the list eighty years later – the Amalgamated Engineers. Conversely seven of the ten largest unions of 1963 were founded, or are the lineal descendants of new unions founded, during the period 1880-1914: the ancestors of the Transport and General Workers, General and Municipal Workers, National Union of Mineworkers and Electrical Trades Union were born in 1888-9, of the Shop, Distributive and Allied Workers in 1891, one of the predecessors of the National Union of Railwaymen (itself born in 1913) in 1889, and the National Association of Local Government Officers in the 1900s.

**Table 1: Ranking List of the ten largest unions: 1885 and 1963**

| 1885 | 1963 |
| --- | --- |
| Amalgamated Engineers | Transport & G. Workers |
| Durham Miners | Engineering Workers |
| United Boilermakers | General & Municipal Workers |
| Amal. Carpenters and Joiners | Mineworkers |
| Amal. Cotton Spinners | Shop, Distrib. & Allied Workers |
| Amal. Tailors | Local Govt. Officers |
| Northumberland Miners | N.U. Railwaymen |
| Amal. Ironfounders | Electrical T.U. |
| Oper. Stonemasons | N.U. of Teachers |
| Boot and Shoe Operatives | N.U. Public Employees |

A new era in labour relations (or class conflict) was clearly opening. The shock of 1889 was temporary, but it precipitated permanent changes in attitude not only among unions but among employers, politicians and government administrators, and it encouraged or even compelled them all to recognize the existence of transformations which had already taken place below the horizon of collective visibility. To this extent the shock of 1889 was probably more effective than the much larger and more lasting explosion of 1911-13. That upheaval added one and a half million members (or 66 per cent) to the forces of unionism and was accompanied by 3,165 strikes totalling sixty million man-days lost in three years: a far greater concentration of industrial conflicts than in any previous period of the same length. The absence of adequate statistics before 1892 makes it impossible to measure the impact of the years 1889-90, but the membership of the TUC increased by 650,000 (80 per cent) between 1888 and the peak year of 1890, with about 2,400 stoppages and eleven million man-days lost in 1889 and 1890.[10] However, unlike the membership acquired in 1911-13, more than a third of the new membership of 1888-90 had been lost by 1893, largely by the collapse of most of the 'new unions' of 1889. Their relative weight in the organized labour movement – impossible to estimate precisely given the absence of reliable official membership figures before 1892 and indeed the unreliability of the new unions' own statistics – was pretty certainly rather larger for a moment in 1889-90 than in 1911-13, but the mean size of strikes was at most a quarter of that in 1911-13, though the number of strikes per year was substantially larger. Many small strikes in 1888-90 were not recorded at all.

The size and impact of the 1889 shock was unexpected, but not in retrospect surprising. When industrial discontents have, for one reason or another, accumulated without being able to unload their charge of tension, the consequent outburst is almost inevitably large and dramatic, all the more so because in such situations the demonstration effect of the initial struggles is spectacular, especially if they are successful. The outbreak of mass unionism in Brazil and Poland in recent years illustrates this effect. On the whole the strikes of 1889 were extremely successful: of 1,051 whose outcome is known only 20 per cent were lost, 45 per cent were victorious, the rest settled by compromise.[11] This was partly because the moment of the trade cycle was well chosen for union demands, partly because in the pace-setting industries of the 1889 outburst, water-side labour and the gas industry, the mechanism which accumulated tension also created, or coincided with, unusual bargaining strength among the workers. For the gas industry the arguments put forward several years ago still stand.[12] As for water transport, 1889 was a record year both for outward and homeward freight rates, which explains why this was a good year for the young seamen's union to launch its national attack on a highly competitive industry. It was only defeated in Liverpool by the common front of the sixteen Atlantic liner companies, sufficiently small in number to concert their action.[13] As for the dockers, Lovell has demonstrated how inflammable was the combination in London of a rapidly growing traffic, essentially loaded and unloaded by speeding up labour which operated by primitive manual methods, with pressure on the dock companies' profits which made them attempt actually to cut labour costs.[14] We may take it that the first of these two factors applied to most British ports. In short, employers had for many years relied on squeezing workers, who now found themselves both relatively more indispensable and confronting employers who could not afford to face the cost of lengthy disputes.

John Mavor, who analysed the Scottish railway strike of 1890, summarizes the position. 'The strike', he thought, 'is best described as a revolt of labourers against the inefficient organization of their industry.' The Scots railways had grown too rapidly, without either adapting their structure or modernizing their equipment, meanwhile indulging in cut-throat competition between their two main lines. Mavor observed:

There is not an unlimited number of highly skilled artizans from which efficient workers may be promptly drawn. The artizan class has come to consist of a great number of strata, skill being specialized highly, and even localised on each plane. This gives an increasing amount of power to certain strata of artizans ... The widely extended paralysis caused by a strike of at most 9,000 men was a significant and serious circumstance.

In fact, though the companies fought the dispute to a finish and destroyed the union, they could not afford to sack the strikers en masse: only a little over 500 men of all grades in three railway companies were victimized.[15]

Such was the situation in established industries and occupations. Insofar as the 'new unionism' was the organization of unions in *new* industries and occupations, it was as yet largely symbolic. It symbolized the future, the shape of things to come. In this sense the beginnings of white-collar, distributive trades' and public service unionism or the foundation of the Electrical Trades Union are significant. In the short run such unions, if they survived, were as yet neither large nor successful.

Two conclusions can be drawn from this brief analysis. First, that the unions and strikes may have been 'new', but they were provoked by the fact that industry was the opposite of new. It had, by and large, kept pace with expansion not by modernization and rationalization, but by increasing the exploitation of its labour force in the old way. Rationalization was sometimes the response to the shock of 1889–90, not the other way round. No doubt the pressure on prices and profits during the long years of the 'Great Depression' encouraged such a policy, while at the same time depression made organized labour disinclined to offensive action, and postponed any revival of unionism in industries which had been briefly organized during the great boom of the early 1870s, but had been unable to maintain organization. The first battles of the future 'new unionists' in the middle 1880s had been precisely against this defensiveness of the old unions. As Tom Mann said in 1886, 'the true Unionist policy of *aggression* seems entirely lost sight of'.[16] And when the moment for successful aggression came, the example of success, or even the sight of hitherto inactive and demoralized workers going on strike, had a snowball effect.

However, there is a second conclusion. The lasting success of new unions or of union expansion depended on the readiness of employers to accept them. As it happened, British employers were quite prepared in principle to do so. Of the employers' suggestions for preventing or settling disputes which the Board of Trade collected in 1889-90, only 20 per cent were hostile to unions or intransigent, and this percentage did not change, on average, over the next six years. (See Table 2.) The attitude of the civil service was, as we know, favourable to a strong but moderate trade unionism. Large employers, or those capable of coordinated action, were in a position to counter-attack or resist old or new unions if these went beyond what they thought they could tolerate or afford. While a balance was normally recognized by both sides, a major explosion of trade unionism inevitably disturbed this in four ways.

**Table 2: Percentage of Employers' Responses Hostile to Trade Unions 1889-1895\***

| Year | (N) | % hostile |
|------|-----|-----------|
| 1889 | 214 | 20 |
| 1890 | 341 | 24.6 |
| 1891 | 244 | 23 |
| 1892 | 230 | 16.5 |
| 1893 | 270 | 10.7 |
| 1894 | 286 | 27.6 |
| 1895 | 194 | 18 |

\* Responses counted as 'hostile' include demands for restricting agitators, legal banning of agitators, restriction of 'outsiders', measures to prevent picketing and intimidation, the legal prohibition of unions, protection of capitalists and manufacturers against them, and the exclusion of unionists from employment.

Sources: Calculated from PP LXVIII, 1890, p 445; LXXVIII, 1890-1, pp 689 ff; LXXXIII/I, 1893-4, pp 461 ff; LXXXI/I, 1894, pp 1 ff; LXXXI/I, 1894, pp 409 ff; XCII, 1895, pp 211 ff; LXXXI/I, 1896, pp 441 ff.

First, it extended unionism to industries or types of workers to which or whom the old and essentially localized and sectional form of collective bargaining, hitherto dominant, was inapplicable. Thus on the docks unions had either to be mass closed shops or confined to small bodies of specialists, while on the railways the unit of negotiation was normally neither a single plant nor a locality but, ideally, the entire rail system of a company. Second, sudden and uncontrolled unionization could affect the labour process, either by lowering productivity or by cutting into managerial functions. Old unionists might intensify restrictive practices, inexperienced and undisciplined new unionists might simply work less hard – a very real problem in the London docks of 1890. Third, a vast extension of unionism brought to the fore issues which were by definition *national*, such as the Eight Hour Day or the principle of mechanization. Such issues were seen to require coordinated action by both sides as soon as unions were sufficiently widespread and extensively organized. Thus by 1893 even a simple wage reduction in the coalmines implied a simultaneous nationwide dispute, since the major coalfields (outside Wales, Scotland and the northeast) were now coordinated in the new Miners' Federation of Great Britain. Fourth, the sheer scale of such disputes had no precedent. Thus *The Times* commented, in 1890, *à propos* of a brief and successful wage strike by the Miners' Federation that 'twenty or even ten years ago it would have been out of the question for 300,000 workmen to combine so perfectly as to stop work at one moment and to resume it at another'.[17]

A counter-attack, spearheaded by large or newly federated employers, was therefore bound to develop, and it did so from 1890. It wiped out most of the 'new' unionism, and made a second and delayed instalment of the expansion inevitable. It was, after all, hardly conceivable that an industry like the railways would permanently remain without effective unions, except perhaps those of engine-drivers. For two reasons that second instalment largely took the form of a revival or expansion of the 'new' unionism of 1889, or of others formed along similar lines from time to time thereafter. First, because few attempts were made to eliminate unions altogether or to deny their right to exist. Nobody negotiated with the Amalgamated Society of Railway Servants and still less with the enfeebled General Railway Workers' Union, but they were not banned, and therefore capable of rapid expansion when occasion arose. They could therefore grow slowly, occasionally expanding and relapsing, as in 1897 when the so-called 'all-grades movement' briefly doubled their numbers. Second, because of the discovery of the device of the 'general union' which established its capacity to survive, not as an all-embracing union of unspecialized labourers, but as a changing conglomerate of miscellaneous local and regional groups of workers in particular industries, occupations and plants.[18]

However, the second instalment differed significantly from the first. In the first place, it organized not only the empty spaces in the existing Victorian industries, but also new, technically and or-ganizationally transformed industries. This is very clear in the metal sector. Of the million members added to the TUC between 1910 and 1914, about 200,000 were in the Amalgamated Engineers and in the Workers' Union which, as Hyman has shown, was primarily a body of semi-skilled engineering workers.[19] Even without count-ing this union, the numbers in the metal, engineering and ship-building unions rose by 50 per cent between 1910 and 1913. In the second place, the economic and political setting of unionism had meanwhile changed fundamentally. Bargaining was increasingly industry-wide and industrial conflicts interlocked, not only because employers drew together when faced with coordinated unions, but because industry itself, and indeed all sectors of the industrial econ-omy, were increasingly seen as strategically interlocked. Without entering into the debate on how far Lenin's analysis of monopoly capitalism applied to pre-1914 Britain, it is hard to deny that British capitalism between 1890 and 1910 grew in scale, and became more tightly structured in its organization than it had been in the 1880s. In short, while the outbreak of 1889 had consisted largely of a wave of local and generally not very large strikes propagated by chain reaction, the 1911 outburst was dominated by national confrontations, or battles deliberately engaged by national armies, as Askwith's Memoirs vividly demonstrate.[20] The cotton industry, stronghold of the old localism and individualism, illustrates this transformation very clearly.

The sensitiveness of government to labour disputes underlined and intensified this national and organized dimension of industrial conflict. Quite apart from the fact that employees in the rapidly growing public sector – as yet in local rather than central govern-ment employment – had become increasingly involved in trade unionism since 1889*, public authorities had three reasons for in-tervening in, and therefore shaping, the pattern of trade unionism. They now operated under a largely working-class electorate, whose pressures and demands they had to take account of, if only in order to prevent the class polarization of British politics. They had for

---

* The fashion for municipalizing public utilities and services swelled the number of publicly employed manual workers in this period.

the first time to confront the problem of how to meet a *general* disruption of the economy or of national life by national disputes in particular industries, and especially in transport and coal. And from the 1890s on they were increasingly aware of the relative vulnerability of the British economy to foreign competition. British labour and industrial relations began to be seen as a relevant aspect of British 'national efficiency'. This had not been so before 1880.[21] From 1893 on, and especially after 1906, central government intervention in large disputes became a regular incident in the industrial drama, and since its major objective was rapid settlement, its net effect was to strengthen trade unionism, if only by providing it with official recognition. One might add that the government's wider social programme had the incidental effect of providing new or weak unions with the means of surviving defeat. The National Insurance Act allowed them to acquire the advantages of Friendly Societies without high subscriptions, and therefore provided workers with a reason for maintaining membership. The war made this integration of unions into the administrative system permanent. Trade unionism in agriculture had virtually been wiped out after the 1870s, and was again destroyed after the 1889 explosion. It was not very strong in 1914, but it has never disappeared from the scene since then.

The novelty of the new phase is reflected in the differences between the strategies of union reform in 1889 and 1911. In both cases the object of the reformers, largely drawn from the contemporary left or ultra-left, was to replace defensive by aggressive, sectional by class unionism. However, in the 1880s the alternative was extremely vague, as indeed was the strategy to achieve it; perhaps naturally so in view of the extreme paucity of socialist thinking about trade unionism. In retrospect we can see that the reforming programme consisted of three points. First, new unions were to be created for hitherto unorganized labour, either consisting of the generally unskilled, believed to be mobile and interchangeable, or the occupationally more specialized for whom suitable occupational unions might be found. Second, the membership of existing craft unions should be extended to embrace the less skilled grades and negotiate for all; and third, the struggles of different groups of workers should be coordinated locally through trades councils and nationally through a radicalized TUC as well as through political action in favour of uniform and generally applicable demands such

as the Eight Hour Day. The most significant result of this programme was the invention of the 'general union', but in a form
which had been neither intended nor predicted, and which did not
demonstrate its full potentialities until after 1911. By and large, the
attempts to broaden the old craft unions failed. The TUC did not
stay radicalized for long, and the Trades Councils, whose expulsion
from the TUC in 1895 marks the end of the radical phase, remained on the margins of trade unionism. Indeed, they probably
played a less active role in the second expansion than they had in
the first.

The second phase, on the other hand, was inseparably linked
with conscious and well-considered attempts to rationalize and reform trade-union structure and strategy, the former mainly by
amalgamation and federation ideally aiming at one union for each
industry. The attraction of industrial unionism for its main spokesmen, like that of general unionism in 1889, may initially have been
political. It could be seen as a version of class unionism against
sectionalism, or even as a preparation for the syndicalist society of
the future. However, the extent to which trade-union structure and
strategy were debated for the twenty years after 1906, the wave of
actual federations and amalgamations which took place, the ex-
periments in joint national union strategy and battle from the Triple Alliance of 1914 to the General Strike, suggests that the stimulus for reform was by no means only ideological. Old and new
unions now plainly felt the need to adapt themselves to conditions
of industrial action which they recognized as new. This did not
produce any significant general shift towards industrial unionism.
In spite of the enthusiastic and persistent advocacy of this pattern
of organization by the left, and even the occasional commitment
of the TUC to it (as at Hull in 1924), the reorganization of the
British union movement along industrial lines was and has remained an unrealistic aspiration. However, about the major advances of the reform movement after 1911 there can be no doubt
at all. The British trade unions were largely restructured, even
though some of the major amalgamations did not take place until
after the war, when the decline in union membership made rationalization more urgent.

III

At this point we return to comparative history. For the question of trade-union structure arose, and was hotly debated, in all countries, but solved in very different ways. One major division is between countries which firmly opted for an essentially national unionism, with whatever concessions to local autonomy were necessary, and those which opted for localism or federalism, except in industries like the railways where it made no sense at all. The local and federal option, which clearly prevailed in France and Italy, was based on anarchist and syndicalist ideology, but essentially it represented the apparent irrelevance of the national economy for collective bargaining, or conversely, the potential strength of a purely local unionism, which is not to be underestimated in certain circumstances. Thus, building unions in the United States have always flourished by establishing local craft monopolies, since the building and public works market of cities is largely autonomous. Again, economic general strikes or extensive local sympathy strikes with one occupational dispute, are most likely to occur in towns – most typically port towns – whose economy is, as it were, topographically determined. In the early 1900s we find such strikes typically in such cities as Trieste (1902), Marseille (1904), Genoa (1904), Barcelona (1902), Amsterdam (1903).[22] The relative insignificance of the national dimension in a country like France is shown by the fact that, according to CGT statutes, the minimum number of (local) unions needed to form a national federation was no more than three.[23] It is clear that in countries like Britain and Germany the local option took second place to the national or regional option, though the degree of centralization envisaged was variable, and that achieved was much smaller in practice than in theory.

The second major issue was between craft or occupational unionism and various forms of more comprehensive organization covering a number of crafts or grades of skill within one industry, or more generally. The ideological history of 'industrial unionism' remains to be written. We do not even as yet have an adequate history of the very concept of the specific 'industry', i.e. of what led socialists, no doubt following official statisticians and others, to draw up a list of unions each of which was to be ideally coextensive with the appropriate 'industry' all of whose workers it was designed to organize. What – to mention the most systematic effort of this kind – led the Austrian socialists to envisage just fifteen or sixteen unions, somewhat inconsistently selected?* So there is much we do not know.

What we do know is this. First, that the struggle for a more comprehensive union structure was universal and directed primarily against craft and other sectionalism and its 'trade consciousness'. Outside Britain this sectionalism was primarily confined to old handicraft occupations. To the extent that all unionism before, say, 1890 was 'old unionism', the problems faced in all countries were similar, though the solutions could be highly specific. In certain cases craft unionism could work successfully even in the most patently 'industrial' industries, as on the American railroads where a complex of thirty-two unions, fourteen of them of major significance, covered the industry in 1940. Conversely, under certain circumstances even a trade as enormously proud of craft status as the Amalgamated Society of Engineers could call for a more comprehensive recruitment of the occupational labour force – e.g. in Western Australia, as distinct from all other parts of the world.[24]

Second, while a more comprehensive unionism advanced everywhere, it did not entirely succeed anywhere. Neither craft unions nor their correlative, labourers' or general or indiscriminate 'factory workers' unions disappeared totally, even in countries with strong national trade union centres committed to industrial unionism. All union movements thus developed as a mixture of narrower or wider craft/occupational unions, of industrial unions coexisting with them or absorbing them, and of general unions – but in different combinations. In the British mix industrial unions were not important, except for mining and railways. In the Norwegian mix general unions were temporarily dominant, though eventually (1954) they were to cover no more than 5 to 6 per cent of union membership,[25] whereas in Britain they became increasingly important, especially when we consider that the recent tendency to form conglomerate unions (as by the merger of the engineering union

---

*They were, in alphabetical order as given in the *Handwörterbuch der Staatswissenschaften* (1902 edition), article 'Gewerkvereine': 1) Building, 2) Clothing, 3) Mining, 4) Chemical, 5) Iron and Metal, 6) Gas and Water, 7) Glass and Pottery, 8) Printing and Paper, 9) Commerce, 10) Wood, 11) Horn, Bone and Tortoiseshell, 12) Agriculture, 13) Food and Drink, 14) Textiles, 15) Transport, 16) Women's Industries.

with foundryworkers and draughtsmen, the electricians with the plumbers) is essentially similar to general unionism. In Austria general unions were absent. And so on.

Thus the Norwegian union movement, committed to industrial unionism since 1923, in 1954 consisted of forty-three unions some of which can only be described as craft societies (e.g. the Lithographic and Photo-engravers), the Locomotive men, organized separately from the railway workers, and the bricklayers, organized separately from the building workers), not to mention the Union of General Workers. Industrial unionism has met considerable resistance even within the metalworking industry, where the internal pressures to build industry-wide unions in the twentieth century have almost everywhere been stronger than in any other industry except railways, coalmining and government employment.[26] Most unionism has remained mixed. There is a certain parallelism in this way between the British and continental movements.

Thirdly, the most comprehensive industrial unions (if we leave aside mines, railways and the public sector) were those founded and structured from outside and above, in effect as frameworks for subsequent expansion – like the Metalworkers' Federation in Italy which, before 1914, was nationally negligible. Evidently this implied both an influential working-class party and absent or relatively weak trade unions. The formation of general textile workers' unions, such as were common elsewhere, could hardly have been envisaged in Britain, where cotton had long been organized on its own. The relative success of industrial unionism elsewhere and its failure in Britain are thus largely explained.

Fourthly, and for the same reason, general unions, though not absent in Europe, lacked the scope for development they had in Britain. Where most organizable workers could be fitted, if they wanted to, into some already notionally existing national union, there was room for genuinely unclassifiable labourers' unions (e.g. of the mobile navvies who formed the core of the Norwegian general union), or for workers in factories who could not be readily attached to some already classified union. Such bodies, as we know, existed in Germany, Sweden, Denmark and Norway, but unlike the British general unions they were residual. As soon as enough workers had been organized in the relevant branches of activity, separate industrial unions – e.g. of sawmill workers or paper and pulp workers could be hived off the general association. The strength of the British general unions lay in their ability to penetrate any and every industry, to the absence of any other kind of union which could fill the spaces deliberately left empty by the refusal of craft unions to fill them. Quite often they would generate *de facto* industrial unions, but there was no particular reason why these should separate from the general unions within which they formed separate sectors or trade groups, such as the dockers in the Transport and General Workers Union.

This still leaves us with the question why, unlike Britain, industrial unions progressed on the continent, in spite of the already observed reluctance of skilled and craft groups, which was very marked, especially in the 1890s. For these groups, after all, still formed the natural nucleus of unionization, and it was among them that the most rapid advances were usually apt to occur. One reason, it may be suggested, was that much apparent 'industrial unionism' or what turned into 'industrial unionism' on the continent, was really the analogue of the so-called 'new model' of the British unions in the 1850s and 1860s. It envisaged essentially the formation of nationwide, relatively centralized, amalgamations of fairly closely associated craft occupations. It is perhaps no accident that the two typical 'new model' unions of mid-Victorian Britain, the Amalgamated Society of Engineers and the Amalgamated Society of Carpenters and Joiners, had their equivalents in the German woodworkers and metalworkers, who were for most of the 1890s both the strongest unions in Germany, and the most strongly committed to industrial unionism. However, the case of the metalworkers, or more precisely the machine builders, suggests another possible reason.

Almost everywhere unions of such workers opted for industrial unionism; or rather the ones which chose this option eventually prevailed. This was because in metalworking the position of the skilled manual craftsman was increasingly vulnerable and, apart from a few protected enclaves, threatened by the advance of complex machine tools and mass production. Skilled metalworkers were powerful, but not secure. The war years were to demonstrate that in all belligerent countries the armaments (i.e. metalworking) industries formed the front line of the industrial class battle. They did so precisely because here mechanization encountered self-confident, combative, often politically conscious skilled men who resisted downgrading. But the fact that the line between the apprenticed skilled craftsman, the skilled worker who 'picked up the trade', and the new categories of the semi-skilled workers or those with only the narrowest range of skills, became increasingly hazy, made it advisable for unions of skilled metalworkers not only to defend craft exclusiveness, but also to seek to recruit the growing mass of production workers whom they could no longer hope effectively to exclude. The two policies were sometimes in conflict. In Britain rank-and-file resistance to broadening the Amalgamated Society of Engineers into something closer to an industrial union was strong, and a constant brake on the reforming policies of the union leaders.[27] Where craft privilege was less entrenched and powerful, the forces favouring the broadening of the unions were stronger, or rather those resisting it were weaker. The weakness of craft unionism in metals, and the foresight of the continental pioneers of industrial unionism, based on a combination of feeble unions and radical ideology, is demonstrated by the eventual success of continental metalworkers' unions (e.g. in France and Italy) in organizing the motor industry. In the United States this industry was to be organized in the 1930s by a special industrial union, the craft union of skilled 'machinists' having long been extruded from it. In Britain, the organization of the majority of automobile workers was in practice to be left to the general unions (mainly the Transport and General Workers Union), leaving the unions of skilled workers in a minority; though they had proved in the struggles of the 1890s and 1900s that they were too strong to be overridden. In Italy and France the choice was either between no union or the industrial union of metalworkers, and indeed in Turin the FIOM won its first major automobile contract in 1906, when it succeeded in organizing 40 percent of all metalworkers in the city.[28]

The new phase of capitalism thus implied a change in union structure, but also in the distribution of trade unionism. Here also a comparison between the British and continental cases is possible and useful. Where mass unionism established itself – as it had not yet done in France and Italy by 1914, except for the Italian agricultural workers who formed one-third of all trade unionists in 1910[29] – its distribution had by 1914 changed both geographically and industrially.

The general pattern of change shows a growth in the unions of transport workers, of factory workers (whether organized in general, industrial or 'factory workers' unions), the rise of the miners – where these were not already well organized – and the expansion of the metalworkers' unions. In Germany, for example, transport, metalworkers and factory workers formed 12 per cent of the membership of the Free Unions in 1896, but almost 39 per cent in 1913. The rise in Britain – from 33 to 39 per cent – was less marked, because metals had already been strongly organized and grew rather slowly (by a little more than 100 per cent between 1892 and 1913), thus concealing the quadrupling of the organized transport workers and the equivalent rise among general workers. In 1888, which is in many ways more comparable to the 1890s in Germany, transport and general workers had comprised perhaps 8 per cent of British unionists, as against about 25 per cent in 1913.[30]

As for the regional distribution, it is clear that the German unions in the early 1900s were weak in the major industrial area of Rhine–Westphalia, with the fluctuating exception of the miners, but that their penetration into this region accelerated notably after 1907.[31] In Britain the old trade unionism was deeply rooted in the major industrial areas of northern England, though not of Scotland. The only geographical analysis is still that made by the Webbs in 1892, who found (roughly speaking) at least twice the mean density of national unionization in Durham, Northumberland and Lancashire, from 20 per cent to 100 per cent above the mean in the counties of Derby, Gloucester, Leicester, the East and West Ridings of Yorkshire and South Wales, mean density (plus or minus 20 per cent) in Cheshire, Northampton, Stafford, Suffolk, Warwick and Scotland, and below the average everywhere else.[32] Whatever a comparable geographical study for 1913 would show, it seems clear that the union explosion of 1911–13 made disproportionate progress in some hitherto rather weak areas, such as the dynamic new engineering regions of the West Midlands. This area now contained 40 per cent of the strength of the Workers' Union, which now became one of the five or six largest unions in the country.[33]

One final question has already been answered incidentally in the course of this paper, but is worth elucidating clearly. What was the role of the ideologically committed leftists who played so large a part in the union expansions of all European countries during this period?

Four observations may be made about this question. *First*, it

must be repeated that neither Marx nor Marxist theory had anything very specific to say about trade-union structure and strategy,
as distinct from the workers' immediate economic and social demands. And this in spite of the fact that, as Haupt has shown, the
bulk of the continental socialist parties initially developed closer to
the British than to the German social-democratic model – or more
exactly closer to the Belgian model, in which the party consisted of
a combination of political groups, unions and other labour organizations such as cooperatives. Admittedly the Great Depression of
the 1870s and 1880s tended to shift the centre of gravity of most
such parties away from the enfeebled unions.[34] I have suggested
that union strategy derived from socialist theory a general hostility
to exclusive, craft or sectional unionism, but it also increasingly
(especially after 1900) derived strategic ideas from the Marxist
analysis of the concentration and mechanization of capitalist production.

*Second*, with the rise of both mass unionism and mass working-
class parties, socialists who were primarily active in unions became
increasingly distinct from socialists who were primarily active in
the political party. This was most dramatically evident in trade-
union movements which, like the French CGT, and anarchist or
revolutionary syndicalist bodies in general, specifically rejected political (i.e. largely electoral) action. It was almost equally evident,
however, in movements closely identified with the working-class
party, even though a union position was a very helpful springboard
for workers who wished to launch themselves into a political career
in markedly proletarian parties such as the SPD; and even though
unions might wish, by strengthening their direct representation in
parliamentary factions, to underline their dominant position within
the party (as in Britain),[35] or their increased independence within
it (as in Germany).[36]

This divergence, often accompanied by friction between party
and unions, arose chiefly from the functional socialization of both.
Whether the union's daily work was or was not conceived as the
overthrow of capitalism, it was not the same as the party's activity,
which could therefore be conceived, according to taste and situation, either as an excessively radical diversion from the unions'
bread-and-butter tasks (e.g. by calling for political strikes), or as
diversionary electoral activity distracting the workers from their
direct assault upon the system. But it also arose from the differ-

ences within unions, such as the tensions between rank-and-file or
local militancy and the increasingly assertive national organizations. Judged by revolutionary criteria, the leaders of national
unions or union federations were excessively reformist, as indeed
almost all were in theory or practice. This could apply even to
syndicalist unions in the eyes of pure anarchists, as witness the
struggles, during and after World War I, between these and the
leaders of the anarcho-syndicalist CNT. Leaders were less radical
than militants: Verzi, the founder of the Italian Metalworkers' Federation, was expelled from it in 1909 as a reformist, and Buozzi
who replaced him, though not the most extreme of moderates, was
decidedly no leftist, and was to be denounced by the young communists of *Ordine Nuovo*.[37]

In fact revolutionary slogans alone made sense chiefly where
unions were too weak to do more than organize the occasional
rebellions of the unorganized, or in the preparation of great industrial battles, or as a defence of rank-and-file autonomy, or of localized unionism against encroaching national bureaucracy and
centralized strategy. This could lead to paradoxical situations, as
in Britain, where the most socialist in origin of all unions, the
Gasworkers, had by 1914 become distinctly moderate, while the
rank-and-file of the far from revolutionary Amalgamated Society
of Engineers resisted its socialist general secretary, the ILPer
George Barnes, on the basis of the ideology of old craft exclusiveness, before discovering – during the war – a radical left-wing
justification for their defence of craft rights. Classifying unions as
right or left may make sense in terms of their support of, or opposition to, various political and party programmes and proposals, but,
as every student of British trade unionism today knows, things are
rather more complex in reality. All we can say in general is that in
the period 1880–1914 those unions which were associated with labour and socialist parties and movements, tended to maintain their
party identification, in spite of friction between union and party or
within unions.

*Third*, we may claim that on the continent the strength and
national presence of mass parties with mass electorates provided a
framework into which unions could grow, and thus helped to
rationalize union structure. To this extent the role of socialists
was indeed important and could be decisive.

Nevertheless, it can be said *fourthly*, that the development of

union structure and strategy were largely independent of the prevalent ideology, Marxist, anarcho-syndicalist or otherwise; except inasmuch as political consciousness provided trade-union agitators,
leaders and activists with confidence, persistence and dynamism.
Structure and strategy largely reflected the actual economic and
industrial situation in which workers had to organize, and the conditions – including those created by the past history and development of the working class – in which they did so. This is probably
the main reason why syndicalism, though its appeal to labour militants and radicals was large and international in the years before
1914, was never really an international movement, as distinct from
an internationally useful set of ideas. It naturally made a greater
appeal in countries of weak or unstable unionism such as Spain,
France and Italy – but also Scandinavia[38] – than in countries with
strong unionism and fairly steady growth such as Germany, Britain
and Denmark. It naturally appealed to boom-town industrialization reminiscent of the Wild West, as in the South Wales coalfields
or in provincial Norway, where masses of raw workers from the
countryside or abroad flooded into a new industry *which already
had a union framework* – unless these greenhorns were themselves
organized by bodies opposed to socialism. It probably had a special
appeal to workers whose essential frame of reference was the local
community as much as, or more than, their industry or occupation,
as in Spain, Italy or France. Nor should we forget those special
cases among local communities, the seaport towns: Marseille, Le
Havre, Nantes, Genoa, Livorno, Barcelona, Belfast, Liverpool.[39]
The varying appeal of syndicalist ideas can be explained, but it
remains true, as Shorter and Tilly have shown, that 'ideological
differences account for almost none of the differences in the propensity to strike or the forms of strike action' in the country they
have studied.[40]

So it seems best to distinguish the various union movements of
Europe not ideologically, but according to the phase and rate of
industrialization they represent. We may thus distinguish between
countries of weak or backward industrialization, such as France
and Italy, countries dominated by the first industrial revolution
(Belgium and Britain) and countries rapidly and massively industrializing along more modern lines (Germany, Scandinavia). None
of them, except the 'workshop of the world' had developed craft
or professional trade unionism which had succeeded in colonizing

the basic industries of the country; certainly not Belgium, which perhaps lacked the large skilled sector of Britain. In fact, through-out this period Belgian unions remained unusually weak, barely stronger in 1913 than those of the much less or more recently industrialized Netherlands. Hence none developed the British pat-tern.

The first group developed no mass unionism in this period, ex-cept in the public sector, perhaps in the mines and – a special Italian case – among agricultural workers. It developed fairly strong inter-union local centres of mobilization and cadres of craft workers capable of leading occasional battles. The third group ranged from countries suddenly plunged into a novel industrial development, like Norway, where modern industries were organ-ized by a general union which virtually dominated the entire move-ment in the 1900s with 50 per cent of total membership before spawning various industrial unions, to countries like Germany, where fairly strong craft-based unions extended their field, before other workers were organized in such unions as those of transport workers and factory workers. Once again, by 1913, this combina-tion of industrial and general unionism dominated the field. Never-theless, as already observed, in none of these countries was craft unionism eliminated. In the countries of groups two and three trade unionism had, by 1913, begun to take its modern shape, allowing for subsequent occupational changes. In none of them, however, had it succeeded (with rare exceptions) in recruiting the majority of workers in any industry as a national whole.

The trade-union density in Britain, Germany, Denmark and Norway at the end of World War I was to be between twice and three times the percentage of 1913, in Sweden and The Netherlands more than three times, in Belgium almost five times as high. One cannot conclude this survey without observing that in some cases – notably Britain and Germany – the strength of trade unions as a percentage of the labour force was higher than it has ever been since, in others – France, Denmark, perhaps Norway – it was not reached again before the middle or late 1930s. Ought we not to see the great leap forward of unionism during and after the first war as the logical continuation of the pattern of trade-union expansion in the period 1880–1914? To this extent the 'new unionism' of the period before 1914 reached its apogee in 1918–20. In this respect the British and western European movements are, once again, comparable. And the measure of this remarkable international growth – and temporary radicalization – is also a measure of the historical significance of the phase of union development which is discussed in this paper.

(1981)

# 10: The Formation of British Working-Class Culture

Those who use the written word professionally mostly come from, or join, the upper and middle classes of society. The literature about the lives of those classes in the nineteenth century is therefore ample and, since it is largely written from within those classes it illuminates aspects of their existence which it would be difficult to reconstruct from purely external documentation. We do not need to be historians to know a great deal about the culture and *moeurs* of the nineteenth-century bourgeoisie. This is as true of Britain as of France.

Compared with this knowledge, our information about the culture of the British working classes is fragmentary, uncertain and problematic. In a sense we know less about them even than about the rural labourers and the marginal groups which can still be described as 'peasants' in nineteenth-century Britain, for their modes of life were easily visible, their patterns of culture customary and often fixed in public forms – from proverbs to festivals – and anyone born and brought up in the countryside would have or could have a good deal of knowledge of them. Thomas Hardy, the novelist, moved far away from his roots in the Dorset* of the first half of the nineteenth century, but his novels about the common people of what he chose to call 'Wessex' mirror this traditional culture of the rural society and its new tensions admirably, even if he did not always understand what he saw and recorded.†

---

*This chapter was originally written for French publication.

†Thus the crucial incident in his *The Mayor of Casterbridge* (1886) is the sale of his wife by a farm-worker, Michael Henchard. But historians, notably E.P. Thompson, have now established that such 'sales of wives' were a form of marital separation far from uncommon in the eighteenth and even part of the nineteenth century, whether or not they traumatized the subsequent lives of the people involved in them, as they did Michael Henchard's.

But the new urban and industrial working classes lived in a socially, and sometimes topographically, separate world from the middle and upper classes. The 'two nations', as Benjamin Disraeli called them in the 1840s, were sharply distinct and had little human contact with each other. To cross from the life of one class into that of the other, even within the same medium-sized town, was to travel into a different and unknown country even in 1940, when the present writer found himself transferred from the status of student at Cambridge, to the status of soldier, billeted on a working-class family barely ten minutes' walk away from his college. Moreover, for the bulk of those who wrote and published, the major part of the male worker's life – his daily labour – was entirely unknown. Even novelists who deliberately wrote about the workers' lives – as Disraeli in *Sibyl* (1844), Mrs Gaskell in *Mary Barton* (1848) and *North and South* (1855), and Dickens in *Hard Times* (1854) – remain, horrified, outside the gates behind which the actual labour of the working classes took place.[1]

For the most part, therefore, we see the nineteenth-century working class from the outside, as a subject for debate, of social enquiry, of reportage and fictional documentation. The quantity of such writing is enormous, and the quality often very high, especially in the period when 'the social problem' attracted particular attention, as in the 1830s and 1840s, and from the 1880s to 1914; but its limitations are obvious. And when workers wrote publicly about themselves, in the pamphlets and periodicals of the labour movement and in relatively infrequent memoirs and autobiographies, they often spoke in untypical voices by virtue of the fact that they belonged to the anomalous minority which wrote for publication. Even when the sons of workers began to become professional writers themselves, in the early twentieth century, they remained untypical not merely by their social origin but in relation to their family environment. It would be unwise to generalize about the working class from the writings of the first major British novelist of proletarian origin, the miner's son D.H. Lawrence (1885–1930).

The image of nineteenth-century Britain derivable from the printed page is therefore profoundly uncharacteristic. For this was a country in which, even in the second half of that century, a large majority of the population consisted of non-agricultural manual workers: perhaps 70 per cent according to the estimate of the statistician Dudley Baxter in 1867. And very little was known about their lives by non-workers. When a substantial number of urban workers were given the parliamentary vote by the Reform Act of 1867, an enterprising working-class journalist named Thomas Wright offered the middle classes what were in effect a series of guide-books to this unknown majority under such titles as *Some Habits and Customs of the Working Classes* (1867) and *The Great Unwashed* (1868).

The historian must therefore reconstruct the culture of the majority of the British people by his researches. A great deal of this work has already been done, particularly since about 1960, and the process of exploration continues. Until the 1950s this process of exploration was delayed, because labour historians tended to concentrate on the study of the ideology, the programmes and organizations associated with the working-class movement, and on the history of its most visible struggles and mass activities – from the British Jacobins, Owenites and Chartists, to the new socialists of the late nineteenth and twentieth centuries, from the 'trade societies' of the eighteenth century through the strikes and trade unions of the nineteenth, to the General Strike of 1926. Yet (except at occasional moments) the world of the militants and the national ideologists and leaders was not the same as the world of the majority:

who take their lives muchas they find them ... ; of what some trade union leaders, when they are regretting a lack of interest in their movement, call 'the vast apathetic mass'; 'just plain folk'; of what the working classes themselves describe, more soberly, as 'the general run of people'.[2]

The writer of the passage just quoted, himself a member of the first generation which produced intellectuals of working-class origin in substantial numbers – that which reached adulthood in the 1930s and 1940s – is one of the pioneers of this relatively new enquiry into the lives of the working class, as distinct from the labour movement. Of course it should be clearly understood that the two were and are organically linked. Most workers might have been neither militants, nor even organized, but (especially from the late nineteenth century onwards) the world and culture of the working classes is incomprehensible without the labour movement, which for long periods was its core.

The term 'the working classes' or even 'the working class' appears in the political language of Britain in the years after the end of the Napoleonic Wars. The first great movements which can be properly described as 'labour movements', both by their sense of class consciousness and by their procedures and programmes (e.g. trade unions, and cooperative societies), also become important and prominent in the post-Napoleonic decades. Indeed, the Chartist movement (1838-48)[3], which was held together by powerful bonds of class consciousness as well as the demand for electoral democratization, may well have mobilized a larger proportion of the (non-agricultural) workers than any other movement before the end of World War I. To this extent E.P. Thompson was right to call his great book *The Making of the English Working Class*, even though it concludes in 1830. Yet, in fact, this uniquely early appearance of the 'working class' on the national scene reflected not an industrialized society, but a society in the first phase of the first of all 'industrial revolutions'. Even within the cotton industry, pioneer of the factory system, the mechanized loom was only just appearing in many towns during the 1830s and 1840s, while the handloom weavers, rapidly declining, had reached their numerical maximum – about a quarter of a million – as late as the 1820s. The factory itself was virtually confined to parts of the textile industry. The so-called 'Factory Acts', providing a minimum of protective legislation, were not extended beyond the range of this industry until 1867. Indeed, until the end of the 1840s the British population remained predominantly rural, though from 1851 there was a small, but rapidly rising urban majority.

Consequently industrial centres remained isolated, though regionally concentrated, and many of them – e.g. in the Midlands – in a pre-factory stage. Men and women adapted to their new conditions of life by modifying the traditional ways of village and pre-industrial town. Lancashire workers enforced the traditional holidays of their localities (the so-called 'wakes') by a massive absenteeism which obliged the masters to close their factories (characteristically called 'mills') and celebrated these holidays, until the 1840s, with the traditional religious rituals and fairs. Weavers, miners and seamen (probably the largest single group of British proletarians until the industrial revolution) invented traditional folksongs in the old style about their new lives. In the 1950s enthusiasts were to rediscover, collect and record what remained of these 'industrial folksongs'. It is also true that new modes of struggle and organization were adopted: the strike, the 'trade union', the society for mutual aid or 'friendly society', which also functioned as a centre of sociability. However, even these had a lengthy pre-industrial pedigree.

The 'trade society' of skilled workers, which became the trade union' of the nineteenth century, may or may not have descended directly from the old craft guilds, but its very vocabulary still reflects its pre-industrial origin. It organized the members of a 'trade' or 'craft'; its members described themselves as 'journeymen'; artisans and skilled still call themselves 'craftsmen'. To this day union members address each other not by some modern term but as 'brothers'. And it was this age-old experience of pre-industrial organization which provided much of the framework for the organization of the new proletariat, and the typical militants of the new movement were, with some exceptions, a pre-industrial or semi-industrial elite. Of the worker-members of the Manchester Mechanics Institution – in the very heart of the new industrial Britain – only about 15 per cent were textile workers, almost 60 per cent were from the handicrafts and building trades, and the rest were handicraftsmen who happened to build machines (figures are averages for 1835–38).[4]

Many elements of what were later to be the characteristic lifestyles, culture and movements of the working classes may be traced back to this first phase of the industrial revolution, particularly in the original factory and mining areas of North England, not least the very industrial landscape itself, as Frederick Engels described it unforgettably in his *Condition of the Working Class in England in 1844*. Some of it still survives. Much of it, whether built then or not much later, survived until the middle of the twentieth century: as late as 1939 four million families still lived in houses built before 1865. Industrial centres long remained communities, either because they never ceased to be villages (as in the case of most mining settlements) or because they retained the character of 'neighbourhoods' even when they grew into the typical industrial town, which was of medium size – say 50,000–80,000 – or even when these towns merged together into the vast built-up areas in which, even in 1881, 40 per cent of Englishmen and Welshmen lived: London, Lancashire (Manchester and its surrounding towns), the West Midlands (Birmingham and the so-called 'Black Country'), West Yorkshire (Leeds, Bradford, etc.), Merseyside (greater Liverpool) and Tyneside (centred on Newcastle). For the geographer these might form single 'conurbations', but even today the physically invisible distinction between Manchester and Salford is perfectly clear to their inhabitants. The history of the labour movement is full of modest militants whose entire life, apart from a spell of youthful wandering and visits to congresses, was passed in the place of their birth or some nearby township. Among the miners even some nationally known leaders remained rooted like trees in their native village.

It is not easy to trace the heritage of this early period of industrialization, though we can detect it here and there, as in the custom (rare in nineteenth-century Britain) for married women to work in the cotton-factories of Lancashire. However, one important element surviving from that era was to be the dissident Protestant sects ('non-conformists') whose most spectacular period of numerical growth coincided with the troubled decades between Trafalgar and 1848. Almost certainly these sects did not convert a majority of workers, except in Wales, where religious dissent functioned as a national symbol, as Roman Catholicism did among the Irish immigrant labourers. These national groups were consequently the only ones among the British working classes to show interest in religion *en masse*, for the relative religious indifferentism of 'the labouring classes' was already noted in the Religious Census of 1851. There were indeed sects, such as the Primitive Methodists, which clearly had a particularly strong appeal to workers, but their major success was in industrial villages, as among coal-miners.[5] However, religious dissent was strikingly important in the formation of working-class elites – at all events in the geographical regions where the sects were particularly strong. Sixty per cent of the first substantial group of Labour MPs in 1906 claimed to have come from a 'non-conformist' background, and even in 1962 50 per cent of Labour MPs came from the sects. (Except in some regions – notably London – active atheism was not of major significance even among the militants: the typical British anti-clerical of the nineteenth century was a non-conformist.)

Nevertheless it is impossible to trace the characteristic patterns of working-class culture as a whole back to the period before 1848. They emerged in the course of the next thirty years in whch industrial capitalism became the common and accepted way of life of the labouring classes and, in Maurice Dobb's words, 'the working class began to assume the homogeneous character of a factory proletariat'.[6] And it was not until the 1880s, or at the earliest the later 1870s, that these patterns took the permanent shape which they were to keep until the dramatic transformations of the 1950s and 1960s. The well-known discontinuity of the history of the British labour movement demonstrates this. The great political ferment of 1815-48, the vast mass mobilizations of the Chartist period in the 1840s, disappeared. The continuous development of the modern labour movement and Labour Party only began again with the rediscovery of socialism and the so-called 'new' trade unionism of the 1880s. The intervening decades were unlike either what went before or what came after.

They were, however, crucial for the formation of the later working-class culture in three respects. First, they taught workers that capitalism was both national and – at least for for the foreseeable future – permanent. It was neither a temporary historical catastrophe, like some foreign invasion or occupation, nor a coalition of local economic tempests from which escape into quieter regions was possible. Trade unions learned, in the 1840s and 1850s, that during depressions it was useless to send their unemployed members 'on tramp' to look for work in some city where prosperity reigned. The fluctuations and movements of the economy were national. Second, the pattern of industrial Britain – of the mechanized (but still normally quite small) factory, the mine, forge, shipyard and railway – became dominant, and not merely a regional anomaly of Lancashire. Several of the major industrial areas – the coalfields of Durham and South Wales, the shipbuilding centres of Scotland, and the northeast – had hardly been developed before 1850, while industrial revolution began to transform formerly artisan-dominated manufacturing centres. The factory came to Birmingham, the great steelworks to Sheffield.

Third, the characteristic stratification of the working class developed. It was the joint product of an archaic form of industrialization and of the value-system of a confident liberal bourgeoisie, which became dominant as counter-ideologies lost their hold among the working classes with the decline of the pre-1848 mass movements – and of economic expansion. At the top of the working-class hierarchy there was an 'aristocracy of labour' recognized and recognizing itself as a stratum superior to and to some extent separate from the rest. Its members saw themselves as distinguished by 'craft' – ideally learned in apprenticeship – and hence skill –

from 'the labourers', and even those who clearly possessed neither craft training nor craft skill, assimilated themselves to the 'craftsman' stereotype. Indeed both could do so because both had effective trade unions, and with some exceptions – of which cotton-spinning (a monopoly of males) was one, most unions in the 1870s rested on the irreplaceability of certain kinds of manual skill, acquired by long training and experience. (See chapters 12–14.)

The labour aristocracy was 'respectable' – a key term in the social vocabulary of nineteenth-century Britain. It was flattered by the ruling class as 'the intelligent artisans', and indeed, the feebleness of a petite-bourgeoisie of the continental type and the extraordinary lack of a stratum of white-collar workers and petty officials in Victorian Britain – in 1871 the business of the greatest trading nation in the world employed a mere 200,000 in 'commercial occupations' – made the 'artisans' the core of what was sometimes described as the 'lower middle class'. And yet, as recent research has shown once again, it saw itself as a working class, even in some respects as the spokesmen and leaders of the rest of the manual workers. And necessarily so, because its economic advantages and status depended on the capacity to organize – in trade unions, in consumer cooperative societies, in societies of mutual aid and insurance. By these means, and *only* by these means, could it maintain the relative exclusiveness which separated it from 'the labourers', and safeguard itself to some extent against insecurity. It was existentially linked to those below it, though it had to keep them at bay.

The 'labour aristocracy' provided the model for a rather larger stratum of workers, estimated by contemporary middle-class observers at anything up to half the manual working class (though probably somewhat smaller), of those with reasonably regular earnings and who formed in the words of Charles Booth 'the recognized field of all forms of cooperation and combination', i.e. of labour organization. However, it should be remembered that before the early twentieth century the actual percentage of workers in trade unions was, outside specific skilled occupations, regions and industries, not more than 10 to 15 per cent of the male workers (1901). The remainder ranged from those classified vaguely as 'unskilled labour' (but who included many groups such as most railwaymen, who could have been organized by forms of trade unionism other than the prevalent type of 'craft union') to the large marginal population and sub-proletariat of the big cities and those forced to shed all self-respect by accepting the only form of social security available, the penal 'poor law'. The autobiography of Charlie Chaplin gives a vivid picture of what being 'a pauper' meant.[7] Social enquiries at the end of the century revealed that something like 40 per cent of the working class lived on or below the so-called 'poverty line'.

Lastly, the decades after 1848 laid the foundations for the subsequent working-class culture, inasmuch as (with the exception of the Poor Law, some legal control of working hours and conditions and, after 1870, the provision of state elementary education) they left the provision of goods and services for the working class almost entirely to its own voluntary organizations and to the – generally small – entrepreneurs who could make a profit out of supplying the poor.

The working-class culture which became dominant in the 1880s reflected both the new and fully industrial economy, the growing size of the working class as a potential market, and the striking improvement in average real wages during the period of rapidly falling living costs (c. 1873–96). From about 1890 on it also increasingly reflected a growing class consciousness and the changed – and greatly increased – role of the state in national life. The growing size of the working class was the natural result of an economy still largely based on manual labour. Thus the rise in the output of coal – the overwhelmingly dominant source of energy – required a proportionate increase in the number of coalminers, so that by 1914 something like one and a quarter million men, plus their families, were required by the British economy for this purpose alone. The growing class consciousness was the result not only of the increased class tensions in the period of the so-called 'Great Depression' (1873–1896) and the period of rapid industrial change thereafter, but also of the dramatic rise in tertiary employment. A new 'lower middle class', essentially composed of white-collar workers, inserted itself between the old 'artisan' stratum and the middle class. Since its economic situation was not obviously superior, its main object was to segregate itself as sharply as possible from the working class, both in a lifestyle much more modelled on that of the middle class and by means of a militantly conservative, patriotic and even imperialist ideology. The 'labour aristocracy', while maintaining its economic advantages over the rest of the working class, found itself increasingly pressed into a common stratum with the rest. When its actual industrial privileges came under pressure from mechanization, several of the most characteristic 'labour-aristocratic' groups of the middle decades of the nineteenth century were, after 1914, to move sharply to the left in self-defence. They were, notably in the metal industries, to become the main base of left-wing movements.

The culture of the British proletariat which was then developed is the one made familiar by the writings of both sociologists and intellectuals emerging from working-class families around the period of World War II, and even more by the British mass media of the 1950s and 1960s, some of which – notably television – had a strong 'populist' bias. In fact, it probably did not change substantially until the transformation of the material life of the working classes by full employment, high wages and the new consumer society in the 1950s. It may be argued that the old culture probably reached its peak between 1945 and 1951, for this was the period when trade union membership (as a percentage of the labour force), the electoral strength of the Labour Party (both in absolute terms and as a percentage of the total electorate), attendance at football matches and cinemas, and perhaps also the mass circulation newspaper appealing specifically to a proletarian audience, were at their maximum. The term 'culture' is here used in the wider sense familiarized by social anthropologists, for 'culture' in the narrower middle-class sense (i.e. literature and the arts considered as a self-contained phenomenon) were part only of the lives of a section of the working class, generally (but not exclusively) the politically conscious and active and that part of the younger generation which completed a secondary education. For the British workers as a whole the word 'book' was a synonym for a magazine. 'Theatre' meant the cinema, though also still to some extent the music-hall. 'Pictures' meant the cinema.

This working-class culture was so firmly established that it is difficult to forget that it had specific chronological origins. Football as a mass proletarian sport – almost a lay religion – was the product of the 1880s, though northern newspapers began to notice even at the end of the 1870s that the football results they printed to fill up space, attracted readers. The game was professionalized in the middle 1880s, and in that decade it developed its pattern – the League matches, the knock-out competition for the Cup, the almost

complete domination of the game by players of proletarian origin
(paid a wage, like all workers, though a higher one than the rest),
the curious binary opposition which divided industrial cities above
a certain size into rival parties supporting rival teams: Sheffield
United against Sheffield Wednesday, Nottingham County against
Nottingham Forest, Liverpool against Everton, Glasgow Rangers
against Glasgow Celtic (with a strong note of Catholic against
Protestant, or Irish against non-Irish in nationally-divided cities),
etc. The typical seaside holiday of the working classes, the holiday
resorts specifically associated with them – notably Blackpool in
Lancashire – also took shape in the 1880s and 1890s. The famous
little flat peaked cap, which became the virtual uniform of the
British worker at leisure – it is still recorded in a comic-strip about
traditional male proletarian values in the northeast, 'Andy Capp'
– appears to have triumphed in the 1890s and 1900s. Even the
fish-and-chip shop, the universal provider of standard ready-
cooked food until the 1950s, was not invented before 1865 in Lancashire. Indeed, it is often forgotten that even the domestic
kitchen-range did not enter working-class homes to any extent before the 1860s.

Even the characteristic shape of the worker's week – characteristically known abroad as *la semaine anglaise* – did not fully triumph
until the 1870s, when the practice of paying weekly wages on Fri-
days made the weekend, or rather Saturday, into the main day for
leisure activities. (Puritanism excluded ungodly forms of entertainment on Sundays, though not the custom of many an adult male
worker staying in bed all morning reading the type of newspapers
that featured meticulously accurate reporting of crime, sexual as-
saults and all forms of sport.) 'Saint Monday' – the declaration of
independence of the pre-industrial worker and artisan – still flourished in the 1860s, when it was still the biggest day of the week for
galas, fêtes and anniversary demonstrations in Wolverhampton, for
rowing races on Tyneside and for foot races all over England.

It was not until the 1880s and 1890s that the 'High Street', the
main shopping street of working-class cities and districts, could
begin to take the shape it was to keep until the rise of the super-
markets. It was the product both of the discovery of a mass consumer market among the working class and of imperialism. The
first led to the factory production (from the 1870s) of shoes, sold
in branches of multiple shops, and, a little later, of men's clothing.

(Cheap women's wear and cosmetics did not become big business until between the wars.) It also led to the factory production of cheap jams, sauces and pickles, part of a major transformation of food patterns. The second factor, imperialism, produced 'chain stores' – national or regional firms with numerous branches – Liptons had 500 such shops by 1914 – selling groceries from overseas and cheap frozen meat from Argentina or the Antipodes. (The cooperative stores were reluctant to stock this, for the British artisan preferred good British meat – and could afford it.) The fortunes of these chain stores rested largely on the sale of Indian and Ceylonese tea, which was first packaged on a mass production basis in 1884. After 1900 even more exotic products such as the banana were seen in popular greengrocers and fruiterers. Colonial fats were the basis of the soap empire of Lever, colonial cocoa of the (mainly Quaker) entrepreneurs who supplied the unlimited appetite of the British and especially Scottish working-class child for mass-produced chocolates and sweets.

Clearly British workers did not lose their regional, even local, characteristics, as market-researchers know even today.[8] Indeed, unlike the British middle classes, British workers never completely abandoned local dialects for a standard English language, and even today one of the few groups of prominent citizens of Britain whose accent can be immediately localized is that of the trade union leaders.* Nevertheless, the pattern of working-class life and culture which emerged in the last decades of the nineteenth century was remarkably standardized.

Nor did it change fundamentally, though between the wars it was enriched by new consumer goods, better housing and new forms of leisure. After 1918 municipal housing, previously negligible, became common: in 1939 about 10 per cent of the almost thirteen million dwellings in Britain had been built by municipalities – almost all since World War I. At the same time the vast house-building boom of the 1930s introduced a substantially new element into urban housing: the owner-occupier. Between the wars about four million of them appeared, not quite half of them workers.[9] New 'council estates' and working-class suburbs with gardens,

---

* However, with very rare exceptions; such as the – now almost extinct – quarry workers in North Wales, all workers in all industrial areas of the United Kingdom by the early twentieth century spoke English.

often, as in London, remote from the centre, developed. The privatization of working-class life had begun.

Meanwhile the great cinemas rose, palaces of temporary dreams in which to forget the years of depression and unemployment. Their very names ('Granada', 'Odeon') suited their opulent décor, though the wonderful baroque variety theatres, which had reached their peak between 1890 and 1914, still held their own, at least in the city centres. Another dream world was provided for the working class when in 1919 the first of the so-called 'palais de danse' opened its doors. Both cinema and the jazz-influenced dance were cultural imports from the United States, as well as symptoms of the emancipation of working-class girls. For the 'palais' was where girls went to meet boys, and the 'picture palace' where they went together; as, increasingly, did husbands and wives. At the same time the football pools, which offered large prizes for the correct prediction of the results of the week's matches, added a new dimension to proletarian intellectual activities. Although the middle class condemned the universal passion of (male) British workers for betting as immoral and ruinous, for most workers (who rarely wagered more money than they could regularly afford), winning was merely a possible reward for the pleasure of passing hours – in the case of the pools mainly at home – 'studying form' and testing their powers of rational prediction. It was probably the only form of regular study of men who did not read books. Finally, there was radio: uncommercialized, paternalist, but unquestionably by the end of the 1930s the most universal medium for popular culture, because the most domestic.

Radio marked the beginning of the transformation of life for the most permanent victim of proletarian culture, and indeed industrial life, the married working-class woman. For most of them a narrow house in a narrow street was not merely the centre of their lives, but the setting of virtually all of it after marriage. Their social contacts, outside the household, were largely confined to neighbours, neighbourhood shopkeepers, kinsfolk who very often lived close by, and perhaps a few outsiders such as the rent-collector, or the 'insurance man' who called weekly to collect the small payment which would normally achieve no more than the cost of a 'good funeral' for the dead. In the house she would, unless the children were very small, pass much of the weekday alone, while the men were out at work and children at school or in the street. Her solitude might be relieved by an occasional gossip with neighbours or in the corner shop. She was still excluded from the new possibilities of work – in industry, shops and offices – and of leisure, which opened before the *unmarried* working-class girl from the 1880s on. Marriage ended them. In 1914 only 10 per cent of British married ried women worked for wages, and even in 1931 only 13 per cent.

In return, the working-class wife was the centre of the family, the focus of its emotional relationships, the crucial influence – as all autobiographies make clear – on her children. She spent the money the men earned. In some industries or regions (as among some groups of miners) the man would hand his wages to his wife on pay-day and she would return part of them to him as 'spending money' for himself. (More commonly he would give her a sum for the weekly housekeeping and leave her to manage as best she could.) She established the visible status of the family by the curtains and potted plant in the front window – in better-off families this was the 'parlour', never used except on special occasions – and by the never-ending battle to keep soot and grime at bay by scrubbing, polishing and colour. By thirty she would have lost most of her sexual attraction, and would have stopped trying. In classical proletarian areas like South Wales even in the 1960s 'spending on women's clothes is low in general and spending on cosmetics and millinery lower still'.[10] By forty 'she rapidly becomes the shapeless figure the family know as "our mam"' (R. Hoggart), by fifty she would probably be in persistently poor health, vainly kept at bay by patent medicines or 'a bottle of something' from the doctor (after 1911, when a rudimentary form of national health insurance was introduced). She had probably begun going out with boys at sixteen, been 'courting regular' at eighteen, reached the culmination of her life on the day of marriage. The rest of her existence was sacrifice.

Not that the working-class male was commonly in good physical shape. A century of primitive industrialization left him 'small and dark, lined and sallow about the face by the time he has passed thirty' (R. Hoggart). In the early twentieth century twelve-year-old boys at (middle-class and aristocratic) private schools were on average 12.5 cm taller than those in state schools. When conscription was introduced for the first time in 1917–18 only 36 per cent of the recruits could be classified as fit and healthy, while 41.5 per cent (in London 48.5 per cent) had 'marked disabilities' or signs of past disease: small wonder, since in the poorest areas of Leeds (1902) half the children had rickets and 60 per cent carious teeth.

Nevertheless, the life of the working-class man was more varied than the married woman's since much of it was spent in the sociable environments of work, and the even more overwhelmingly masculine leisure centres of the 'pub' and football match. The two institutions were closely linked, since sport, expertly discussed, was overwhelmingly the most usual subject of conversation at the pub. Male sociability was inseparable from alcohol – in England overwhelmingly beer, in Scotland also hard liquor (whisky) – though convention distinguished clearly between the social glass and festive or intoxicating drinking. In fact, between the early 1870s, when it reached a peak, and the 1960s, heavy drinking was clearly on the decline. The classic working-class pub was 'the local' where men would tend to drop in regularly, generally in ones or twos after work or after the (early) evening meal, for a longer or shorter respite from labour and domesticity. As alternative forms of leisure for the young increased, the working-class 'pub' became increasingly (once again until trends reversed in the 1960s), a fortress for men over thirty.

Where, in all this world of cramped, enduring, stoic and undemanding men and women, do we find class consciousness? Everywhere. The lives of British workers were so impregnated with it that almost every one of their actions testified to their sense of difference and conflict between 'us' and 'them'. 'They' were not clearly defined, except in workshop or factory, although the virtual fusion between landed aristocracy, capitalist and a new lower middle class into a united Conservative Party between 1886 and 1922 made exact definition unnecessary. After 1922 the Labour Party replaced the Liberal Party as its rival, though there were only two short-lived and powerless Labour governments before 1945. Britain was a two-class society with a two-party system which reflected it, and everyone knew it. Yet while the rise of an independent workers' party based – as its name shows – exclusively on class allegiance was a crucial development of the twentieth century, or more exactly of the interwar years, the class consciousness of British workers cannot be measured by the Labour Party vote alone, if only because it never – even at its peak in 1945–51 – won more than a bare majority of proletarian voters. There were no doubt areas in Britain – notably in the coalmining districts, or in industrially specialized provincial towns – where the working class and the organized labour movement were indeed almost identical, but they were not the norm.

Three things characterized the class consciousness of British workers: a profound sense of the separateness of manual labour, an unformulated but powerful moral code based on solidarity, 'fairness', mutual aid and cooperation, and the readiness to fight for just treatment. The historian A.J.P. Taylor has written of the General Strike of 1926:

The voluntary recruitment of the first World War and the strike of 1926 were acts of spontaneous generosity, without parallel in any other country ... Such nobility deserves more than a passing tribute. The strikers asked nothing for themselves. They did not seek to challenge the government, still less to overthrow the constitution. They merely wanted the miners to have a living wage ... They went once more into the trenches, without enthusiasm and with little hope.[11]

But 'generosity' is the wrong word. It was the moral conviction that people had the right to fair treatment, to a decent wage for a hard life, to 'fair shares' even of poverty, which dominated them. And it was the knowledge, acquired in a century of industrialization which turned Britain into a country of proletarians, that workers must help each other against 'them'.

In most cases that help was small, informal, often pitifully inadequate. The state, the law, the authorities belonged to 'them', except for local municipalities controlled by Labour. A vast amount of working-class life until 1914, and even until 1945, was lived in a network of mutual aid and trust largely independent of the law. In workshops men knew that even the infirm and elderly had a right to earn a living, and their 'mates' saw to it that they could. Neighbours helped each other. Complex systems of mutual trust operated smoothly without sanctions, as in the system of cash betting on horses outside race courses, which stretched into every factory or working-class street. Technically it was illegal, unlike the credit-betting of the rich, though generally tolerated by the police. Yet it functioned perfectly, and – what is more surprising – without any significant involvement of organized criminals. Like the more organized and political forms of working-class action, it symbolized a certain sense of class independence, but above all the creation of a social space outside the control of the powerful and rich. Its ambitions were small; but it knew how to set limits to 'their' power, through a mixture of formal struggle and informal non-coopera-tion. British workers may have not aimed to overthrow the wages system, but no other working class has achieved the degree of *de facto* 'workers' control' on the factory floor which became charac-teristic of so many large British factories.

The politically conscious elite of militants constantly regretted that the ambitions of the masses were not greater, their interest in ideology not more pronounced; even though the great mass of the militants themselves, the activists in union and Labour Party, were not revolutionary enough for a generally Marxist fringe which has, ever since the rediscovery of socialism in the 1880s, operated on its left; usually with greater influence in the trade unions than in elec-toral politics. The present chapter, I repeat, is not concerned with them, if only because their history and social composition has not yet been satisfactorily investigated. They were probably not very different from similar elites in other countries, even those which contained far more people calling themselves Marxists. They were overwhelmingly – until the 1950s – a proletarian elite, not only because relatively few middle-class intellectuals were socialists, and not only because the social and educational system kept intelligent young workers largely in manual labour, but also because leaving one's class even, sometimes, to become a foreman was a sort of betrayal. And, as elsewhere, the organized labour movement was not only a form of struggle, but also for so many of its militants a form of self-education. However, able and devoted though the mil-itants were, they were a minority – though between the wars when the Labour Party had perhaps a quarter of a million male members and almost 200,000 women members, a substantial minority.*

Such, then, was the culture of the British working class on the eve of its crisis and change. The 1950s and 1960s transformed it, though, by integrating it into the modern British consumer-culture they also transformed that culture itself. In the past twenty-five years the British working class itself has changed profoundly. Today less than half the British occupied population consists of manual workers, and with the exception of the great complex of

---

*The bulk of Labour Party members were affiliated to the Party through the trade unions; in many cases only a minority of trade unionists were thus affiliated. Individual membership did not exist before 1918. The numbers in the smaller left-wing organizations were far smaller.

metalworking and electrical industries, the ancient strongholds of working-class culture – coal, textiles, shipbuilding, the railways – are dying or much diminished. More than half of all married women work for wages today. The young working-class militants have gone to school and are now young professional militants: the most characteristic Labour Member of Parliament today is not a miner or railwayman, but a lecturer in some college aspiring to the status of a university. Not the windy beaches of Lancashire but the sunny coasts of Spain see the annual holiday mass migrations of the British proletariat. Fish-and-chip shops have given way to take-away food. In material terms the gain is enormous. Since the 1950s, for the first time in history, most workers in Britain have been able to live a life worthy of human beings. In non-material terms, a way of life is ending or has ended. And, like Britain itself, anchored in the nineteenth century, the British working class is in danger of losing its bearings. But its present situation and prospects are a subject for the reporter and the sociologist. They are not yet a subject for the historian.

(1979)

# *11:* The Making of the Working Class 1870–1914*

If I call this chapter 'The Making of the Working Class' it is not because I wish to imply that the formation of this or any other class is a once-for-all process like the building of a house. Classes are never made in the sense of being finished or having acquired their definitive shape. They keep on changing. However, since the working class was historically a new class – not recognized as a social or institutional collective by itself or others before a specifiable period – there is some point in tracing its emergence as such a social group during some period. That is what E.P. Thompson attempted to do in a book which instantly and rightly became a classic.[1] On the other hand the working class of the 1820s and 1830s – assuming the name is already applicable – was patently very different from the so-called 'traditional' working class about which cultural observers, sometimes of proletarian parentage like Richard Hoggart, began to write bitter-sweet elegies in the 1950s. The famous fustian jackets of Chartism were still a long way from Andy Capp. It is the emergence of the Andy Capp working-class which is my subject here: the British proletariat which came to be recognizable not only by its headgear, about which I shall have something to say, but by the physical environment in which they lived, by a style of life and leisure, by a certain class consciousness increasingly expressed in a secular tendency to join unions and to identify with a class party of Labour. It is the working class of cup-finals, fish-and-chip shops, palais-de-danse and Labour with a capital L. Since the 1950s this class has both contracted and changed, though the 1950 theorists of 'classlessness' and 'embourgeoisement' were wrong in predicting its dissolution. A lot of it is still there. The transformations since 1950 have been profound,

* This chapter was originally given as a Ford lecture at Oxford University.

nevertheless. However, these more recent developments of and within the working class are not my subject here. I have joined a number of people in the labour movement in discussing the nature and implications of these changes elsewhere.[2]

But my title is also both a tribute to and a critique of E.P. Thompson's remarkable book. In one sense Thompson was right to date the emergence of the working class in British society in the early nineteenth century, for by the time of Chartism the image of British society expressed in Asa Briggs' 'language of class' was already formulated, and it was formulated as a trinitarian image of landlords, bourgeoisie and labour. And this image already implies the conceptual absorption into the working-class of all sorts of social strata which still existed in fact, but had, as it were, become socially invisible. The considerable body of people who played so large, and often so conscious, a part on the social stage of other countries under such names as peasantry, petty-bourgeoisie, small craftsmen etc., appear to be absent in Britain. By the time of Chartism, such terms as 'artisan', 'journeyman', 'craftsman' or for that matter virtually all terms associated with the ancient world of independent small producers and their organizations, denote something like the skilled wage-worker rather than the independent producer, while, conversely, the term 'manufacturer', which previously referred vaguely to the labour force, came to be monopolized by the industrial employer. Polarization of terminology indicates economic transformation. If the words 'trade' and 'tradesman', when used by workers came to mean primarily industrial skill, the same terms in middle-and upper-class usage, came to denote exclusively the function of retailing. The classic *Handwerker*, *artisan* or *artigiano* who both made and sold, disappeared into the gap between.

But if the Thompson period is in this and some other ways crucial for the emergence, the 'making' of the English working class, Thompson seems to me to be wrong to suggest – for he does no more than this – that the labour classes of the period before, or even during, Chartism *were* the working class as it was to develop later. In spite of the striking, and by international standards, quite exceptional continuity of the trade-union movement with its pre-industrial artisan past, most of the work since Thompson has shown how dangerous it is to read the proletariat, the labour movements and the ideologies of our century back into the post-Napoleonic

decades. Indeed, the lack of continuity between the labour movements before and after Chartism, the generation gap between the
socialism of Owen and the socialist revival of the 1880s, is so
obvious, that attempts to explain it still keep historians busy. Some
of our organizations may be very old and the occasional bit of
folklore may have survived, but the truth is that the continuous
history of British labour movements, including their historic
memory, only begins long after the Chartists. If the living tradition
of the movement reaches back beyond this, it is because labour
historians have disinterred the remoter past and fed it into the
movement, where it has become part of the intellectual baggage of
the activists. Owenism, Chartism and the rest, and the working
classes of that early period, are of course the ancestors of the later
British working class and its movements, but they are in crucial
respects different phenomena. In this sense the working class is not
'made' until long after Thompson's book ends.


II

It is hardly surprising that the working class of the powerful and
broad-based late Victorian economy was very different from the
labouring classes of the period before the railway network had been
built. We need not waste time in establishing so obvious a point.
In 1851 there were more shoemakers than coalminers, two and a
half times as many tailors as railwaymen, and more silkworkers
than commercial clerks.[3] The workshop of the world was not yet
what Clapham called 'the industry state', either in scale, pattern or
technology and industrial organization. If Lancashire had found
its industrial pattern, Birmingham, Sheffield, Tyneside and South
Wales were only finding it or about to find it. The question is
rather how the development of the new and broadened industrial
economy affected the working class. It did so in a number of ways.

In the first place, it greatly increased in absolute size and concentration. If total percentage employed in manufacture, mining and
industry did not increase much between 1851 and 1911, and hardly
at all until the 1890s – but transport did – it now constituted a
much larger and more concentrated mass.[4] In 1911 there were
thirty-six cities of over 100,000 inhabitants in Britain, compared to
ten in 1851; and they contained 44 per cent of the total population
compared to 25 per cent. Between 1871 and 1911 Merseyside in-

creased by about three-quarters, and Tyneside almost trebled in population. The mean size of the establishments in which people worked also increased, though in industries which had established their pattern early, this may not have altered the general order of magnitude. Whether or not the 400 or so miners who formed the mean labour force in a Yorkshire and Glamorgan-Monmouth mine in 1912 were much bigger than before, pits of that size had long been familiar; and the 220 operatives in the average cottonmill of 1906, though larger by a quarter than in 1871, hardly transformed the character of such establishments.[5]

On the other hand we cannot but be struck by the rise of large industrial concentrations where none had existed before. There is nothing before the 1850s to compare with mid-Victorian Tyneside where we already find in the 1860s perhaps twelve shipyards employing a minimum of 1,500 men each; Armstrongs already had 6,000 to 7,000 in their Elswick works. But by 1914 it was to be 20,000, or about three times as many. Just so the Great Western Railway's works in Swindon trebled its 1875 labour force to reach 14,000 by 1914. There is a qualitative and not only a quantitative difference between Barrow-in-Furness in 1871-2, when the town's largest shipyard and engineering works employed 600 men each, and the Barrow of World War I, in which Vickers employed 27,000 engineers and 6,000 shipbuilders.[6]

In the second place the occupational composition of the working classes changed substantially, as witness the rise of the railwaymen from less than 100,000 in 1871 to 400,000 in 1911, and of miners from half a million to 1.2 millions in the same period, while the total male population of England, Wales and Scotland only increased by 60 per cent. And so, plainly, did its age- and sex-composition, with the decline of school-age employment from 30 per cent of all children in 1851 to 14 per cent in 1914[7] and the modest, but novel, penetration of women into factory industries other than textiles. The changes in the manual skills of workers are less plain, and still the subject of much debate. Yet it is undeniable that in 1875 the largest national trade unions by far were the Amalgamated Engineers and the Operative Stonemasons, followed, in that order, by the Boilermakers, Amalgamated Carpenters and Joiners, Amalgamated Tailors and the Cotton Spinners. After 1895 the TUC was notoriously dominated by the big battalions of coal – now nationally organized – and cotton, and by 1914 by the Triple

Alliance of Coal, Transport and Railways. Moreover, even the powerful groups of labour aristocrats relied increasingly, and necessarily, not on the indispensability of irreplaceable manual skills, but on job monopolies guaranteed by the strength of organizations which kept out others who might quite easily have done their work. Hence the crucial issue for labour during World War I was to be 'dilution'.

In the third place, the growing national integration and concentration of the national economy and its sectors, and the growing role of the state in both, transformed the conditions of industrial conflict. Let us merely remind ourselves that the industrial dispute as a *national* strike or lock-out, does not exist for practical purposes before the 1890s. Indeed, Cronin has shown that the strike itself only came into its own after 1870.[8] For that matter the negotiated *nationwide* collective agreement is absent before 1890, except in parts of the cotton industry where 'the nation' coincided with sections of Lancashire. By 1910, as Clegg, Fox and Thompson point out,[9] there were such agreements in engineering, shipbuilding, printing, iron and steel, and footwear, as well as equivalent mechanisms elsewhere. Moreover, the direct and urgent interest of government in industrial relations is shown not only by the establishment of the Labour Department of the Board of Trade (1893) and the growing scope of its activities, but by the direct intervention of senior politicians in labour disputes, Rosebery's incursion into the coal lock-out of 1893 being the first major example.[10]

In the fourth place – and here we leave economics for politics – there was the widening of the franchise and mass politics. What proletarian voters might think and want, was henceforth a major preoccupation of politicians, and conversely, what central government could be got to do was of much more practical concern to workers, even though they took a while to wake up to this fact. When politicians – I am quoting the Edwardian Churchill – thought that the main problem was how to stop party politics turning into class politics, workers were also more likely to be struck by the potential of national class politics. Belonging to 'Labour', i.e. to manual labour, took on a political dimension it had not had since Chartism.

These developments are important, because without them it is difficult to understand how that aggregate of microcosms which constituted the British world of labour, that collection of often strictly self-contained little worlds, could transform itself into a national phenomenon. Take a late and rather extreme example, that of W.P. Richardson (1873-1930). He was born and lived all his life in Usworth, County Durham, worked for thirty years in Usworth colliery, married a local miner's daughter, presided over Usworth parish council, directed the Usworth Colliery Primitive Methodist Chapel choir and wrote a column on poultry for the local paper. It is safe to say that if, say, Manchester had been wiped out by an earthquake, it would have made no practical difference to him. Yet this man, who was as rooted in his village as any Herefordshire milkmaid, helped to found the local ILP branch, joined the board of the *Daily Herald*, championed the nationalization of all mines and was to become the national treasurer of the Miners' Federation. This is by no means as natural a development as it may seem in retrospect. For miners of Richardson's generation it became both easier, and in many ways essential, to see Usworth not only as part of the Durham coalfield, but of a national coal industry, and that being a miner implied being a member of a national working class whose specific political and social aspirations were expressed in an independent party of Labour with its own newspapers and specific programmes. An older figure like Henry Rust (1831-1902) never really reconciled himself to the fact that the miners of West Bromwich and Darlaston had anything to gain from joining the rest of the Midland miners, let alone the national Miners' Federation.[11]

Given all this, we should expect the working class itself to change. But how and when? Let me take the simple and apparently frivolous case of Andy Capp. When did this particular headgear – the flat cap – become characteristic of the British proletarian? It was certainly not so in the 1870s in London, for Jules Vallès, the Communard refugee, specifically complained about the lack of the local workers' class consciousness, because they did not, unlike the Paris artisans, wear '*la blouse et la casquette*' when off work.[12] The illustrations and photographs of the 1870s and 1880s show a mixture of headgear and, incidentally, – as Keir Hardie's deerstalker demonstrates – even caps were not yet standardized. Yet by 1914 any picture of masses of British workers anywhere, on or off duty, reveals the familiar sea of flat peaked caps. The detailed chronology of this transformation awaits research on the rich iconographic material. But it is evident that within a matter of a couple of decades or so, the British male workers had taken to wearing a badge which immediately stamped them as members of a class. And moreover, they knew that it did. The argument of my paper is that the so-called 'traditional' working class with its specific patterns of life and views of life did not emerge much before the 1880s and took shape in the next couple of decades. I should perhaps also add that this was also the period of the emergence of the 'middle class' as we know it, which is very different indeed from its early and mid-Victorian predecessors and from the upper bourgeoisie of 'the Establishment'. The sudden rise of the cap is parallelled by the equally rapid rise of the old school tie[13] and the even more sudden rise of the golf club. Twenty-nine golf courses were laid out in Yorkshire in 1890–5: before 1890 there had been just two.[14] However, though the restructuring of each of the two main social strata of Britain is not separable from the other, this is not my subject here.

III

The 1880s are familiar to every labour historian as the decade of the so-called rebirth of socialism in Britain, but the phenomena I am here concerned with are statistically more significant than the ideological shifts among the few hundred people who, in the 1880s, constituted the British socialist organizations and their sympathizers. They are more massive even than the beginnings of the transformation of trade unionism in this decade, known as the 'new' unionism. I pick out the 1880s, because the substantial transformation of the material conditions of working-class life and of what might be called the social and institutional compass-bearings of the working-class course across the territory of national life, were hardly visible before then. I am not claiming that they were not present. It is easy to play the well-known historian's game of pushing origins backwards, especially into a period as curiously lacking a definable working-class profile as the decades after Chartism; a period when it is often still hard to decide whether time off for working men meant the weekend – the famous *semaine anglaise* of which continentals dreamed, or the traditional Saint Monday.[15] Thus, to take a familiar landmark in the map of the 'traditional' working class, the fish-and-chip shop originated, probably in Oldham, in the 1860s, and a local firm began to manufacture ranges exclusively for fish-frying in the first half of the 1870s. In 1876 this was still described as 'a petty trade', whereas by 1914 there were something like 25,000 fish-fryers.[16] Other innovations of the 1880s can be traced back to the 1870s. Football already had a modest subterranean life as a proletarian spectator sport in the later 70s.[7] Professional agents and national booking of music-hall *artistes* seems to have developed in that decade, which also saw the birth of a professional trade press for the pop music business.[18] It is not my intention to claim patent rights on the basis of priority for any decade, but simply to point out that, whatever may be the case in the 1870s, the new pattern emerged on the national scene in the 1880s and cannot any longer be overlooked, though both contemporary middle-class observers and subsequent historians have long succeeded in overlooking it.

Three factors affected the workers' material conditions of life after 1870: the dramatic fall of the cost of living during the so-called Great Depression of 1873-96, the discovery of the domestic mass market, including that of the well-paid or at least regularly employed workers for industrially produced or processed goods, and (after 1875) the so-called 'by-law housing' (under section 157 of the Public Health Act), which in fact created so much of the environment of working class life, the rows of terraced houses outside the old town centres. All imply or were based on, the modest, patchy, but plainly undeniable improvement in the standard of life of the bulk of British workers, which is not a matter of dispute even among historians. The crucial point about this improvement is not the mere rise in real incomes and consumer expenditures, but the structural changes which mediated them. These are most spectacular in distribution, i.e. in the relative decline of retail markets and small shops and the rise on the one hand of the Co-ops, whose membership increased from about half a million in the late 1870s to around one million around 1890, and three million in 1914, and, on the other, the rise of the multiple shops which were to give the British high streets their characteristic appearance between the 1890s and the rise of the modern supermarket since the 1950s.[19] Nor should we forget the rise and institutionalization of hire-purchase, which made possible the transformation of the working-class interior. Its history has been neglected, though work is in progress. Here again the 1880s and 1890s seem to have been crucial. The dates of the key cases which cleared up the legal and financial confusions surrounding this growing practice are 1893 and 1895.[20] But distribution and manufacture cannot be separated. The mass production of tea in standardized packets dates from 1884,[21] and the new jams and preserves which changed the working-class diet, were manufactured in those factories which are chiefly known to labour historians as the scene of the early struggles of women factory workers.

As for housing, the major development was not only that somewhat bigger and better houses were now built, but that there was growth of segregated working-class streets and quarters, and indeed, especially with the massive development of cheap public transport in the 1880s, even some segregated working-class suburbs – mainly inner suburbs. I shall say something about the effect of this growing residential segregation later. As for working-class suburbanization, we may as well note that it tended to fray or cut one of the strongest existential links of the working-class community, that between where people lived and worked, but probably only in London. By 1905 the LCC estimated that 820,000 workmen were making extensive journeys to work every day in London.

The most spectacular transformation, of course, was in the pattern of working-class leisure and holidays. I need hardly remind you today of the rise of football as a national, and increasingly proletarian, spectator sport and of the development of a male football culture, finally consecrated by the attendance of the king at the Cup Final from 1913. Nor that the emancipation of football from – or rather against – middle and upper class patronage took place in the 1880s, with the triumph of Blackburn against the Old Etonians, the open professionalization of the game in 1885, and the formation of the League in 1888, incidentally on the model of the system established earlier in the USA for professional baseball.[22] The 1880s are clearly equally crucial in the development of the working-class holiday. The first volume of Herapath's Railway Journal in which the index lists 'holiday traffic' as such is 1884, and the paper's comments deserve to be quoted:

Year by year the holiday traffic at Easter, Whitsun and August is growing in importance. Its dimensions have not yet swelled so far as seriously to affect dividends, but it is easy to foresee a time when this will be the case ... We may never turn Easter into a carnival, but our toiling masses seem determined to turn it to account as a substantial holiday.[23]

The growth of the links between the mill-towns and Blackpool can be traced through Bradshaw. In 1865 there were only two trains with third-class carriages daily between Bolton and Blackpool, in 1870 four, in 1875 twelve, in 1880 thirteen, in 1885 fourteen, but in 1890 twenty-three. But there is at least one more general and less labour-intensive way of estimating the growth of the holiday business, for an annual return by the Board of Trade under an Act of 1861 enables us to measure the amount of proposed investment in piers and harbourworks, many of which can be identified as pleasure or promenade piers, those characteristic structures of English seaside holidays.[24] The table (Table 1) breaks down the proposed investment into that destined for primarily middle-class and working-class resorts, omitting doubtful cases[25]:

**Table 1: Projected investment in Pleasure Piers 1863–1899**

| Period | Middle class | | Working class | |
|---|---|---|---|---|
| | total £000s | annual mean £000s | total £000s | annual mean £000s |
| 1863–5 | 78 | 26 | 30 | 10 |
| 1866–70 | 112.5 | 22.5 | 25 | 5 |
| 1871–75 | 98.5 | 19.7 | 30 | 6 |
| 1876–80 | 184.4 | 36.9 | 83.8 | 16.8 |
| 1881–85 | 292 | 58.4 | 70 | 14 |
| 1886–90 | 174.5 | 34.9 | 75.5 | 15.1 |
| 1891–95 | 172 | 34.4 | 291.5 | 58.3 |
| 1896–99 | 158 | 39.5 | 191.9 | 48 |

This necessarily crude index shows the rise of working-class resorts from the later 1870s, but above all the enormous spurt in proposed investment in the 1890s which, for the first time, pushed the plans for investment in working-class holiday entertainment massively above those for middle-class resorts.

We may illustrate this by the classic example of Blackpool, where the first real signs of action are in the 1860s, with the opening of the North Pier (it cost little more than half of what was spent on that of Ventnor, Isle of Wight) the second pier, and the first theatre. With the 1870s we are clearly getting into substantial business: the Winter Garden (which was to cost £107,000) was started in 1878. But the Blackpool we know best is that of the 1890s: that of the Tower, the Great Wheel, the Victoria Pier on the South Shore, the extended promenade, the Opera House (1889), the new market, free library, town hall and, for good measure, a special bench of magistrates and a coat-of-arms.

Now everyone knows that British workers, unlike the English middle class which developed a high degree of standardization in this period – notably in its speech – did not lose its regional or even local identity, its local pecularities, tastes and pride. And yet it is equally clear that the new pattern of life was more nationally homogeneous than anything before. At the coalface miners might insist on wearing the working-clothes of regional custom. Even in World War II, the Board of Trade's attempt to replace these by standard 'utility' garments caused a considerable uproar from the unions. Yet outside work, the miner, like most of the rest of male workers, wore the same clothes from Blyth to Midsummer Norton. The worker identified with his local team against the rest of the world – indeed in sufficiently large towns with one of the two moieties – City or United, Forest or County – which between them defined the citizen of Manchester or Nottingham or wherever. Yet the pattern of the football culture was the same everywhere – give or take an extra dose of emotion – and it was a *national* pattern – or to be more precise a pattern of the proletarian nation, since the map of the Football League was virtually identical with the map of industrial England. It was national even in the symbolic annual conquest of the public space of the national capital by the two local proletarian armies which invaded London for the cup final. Since the later 1860s there had been regional collective rituals of the same kind, notably the miners' annual demonstrations of which the Durham Miners' Gala has survived – perhaps just because, unlike the others, it had exactly this characteristic of a symbolic occupation of a local capital by the miners – but not yet national ones.

A single, fairly standardized, national pattern of working-class life: and at the same time one increasingly specific to the working class. It is the segregation of the British manual worker's world which is so striking.[26] In the first place it was a growing residential segregation, due both to the exodus of the middle and lower middle strata from formerly mixed areas – the process has been traced for the East End of London[27] – and to the construction of new, and de facto single-class urban quarters and suburbs. Some of these new quarters, buildings or estates were intended for the working class, such as the Queen's Park Estate in Paddington, most for the new 'suburbanites' who were, quite correctly, identified with the new white-collar lower middle class; and 'Villa Toryism': the sort of people who, as the *Cornhill Magazine* supposed in 1901, would naturally live, if they could, in one of the 'clerks' suburbs' of London – Clapham, Forest Gate, Wandsworth, Walthamstow or Kilburn.[27] Others would not be specifically designed for a social stratum and a class lifestyle, but would become so either because the rents precluded poorer tenants or, more likely, because in fact the life-styles of manual workers and black-coated employees of comparable income increasingly diverged. By the early 1900s the residential separation of the better-paid workers (the 'artisans') and the new lower middle class was by no means universal. The better type of popular dwellings – five- or six-room houses – were still reported as being inhabited indifferently by 'artisans, clerks, insurance agents, shopmen' and the like in Birkenhead, Bolton, Chester, Crewe, Croydon, Darlington, Derby, Hull, Newcastle, Oldham, Portsmouth, Preston, Sheffield, South Shields, and Wigan, but in a number of places the absence of workers from such accommodation is specifically noted, or it is described as being inhabited 'more frequently by clerks, shop-assistants and the like than by people of the kind usually included in the term "working classes" '.[28] These included Birmingham, Bradford, Bristol, Burton-on-Trent, Gateshead, Grimsby, Halifax, Hanley, Huddersfield, Kidderminster, Liverpool (or at least Bootle), Manchester, Middlesbrough, Northampton, Norwich, Nottingham, Plymouth, Reading, Southampton, Stoke on Trent, Walsall, Wolverhampton and most of outer London. Since the better housing was commonly the more recent housing, we may reasonably suppose that segregation was increasing.

So, of course, and for the same reason, was the segregation between the better-paid artisans and the lower-paid, even though their cohabitation is still noticed in several towns – Norwich, Nottingham, Preston and Stockport for instance – and though the concentration of the working class in the inner zone of cities and their reluctance to move too far away from work, which is noted in various towns – meant that the working-class belts, though residentially stratified, formed a coherent quarter. The Shaftesbury buildings in Battersea, which were a stronghold of artisans (and of Battersea socialism) were, after all, part of that area between Lavender Hill and the river in which 'the bulk of the working *class* ... are housed'.[29]

In the second place, workers were segregated by expectations. As Robert Roberts says, before 1914 'skilled workers generally did not strive to join a higher rank',[30] but in fact even the chance of improvement within the stratum below the accepted middle class was diminished by two developments: the increasing use of formal schooling as a class criterion, not to mention a way out of the manual working class, and the decline of the alternative way forward to self-respect and pride, the training and experience of the all-round craftsman. Workers were increasingly defined as those who had no education or got nothing out of it; and the contrast between those who left school and those who stayed, or those who got jobs on the strength of schooling and those to whom it was irrelevant – a contrast sometimes between fathers and sons, though not so much between mothers and sons (see D.H. Lawrence) – intensified the felt differences between manual and non-manual workers. On the other hand the fairly extensive de-skilling which took place in the last thirty years before 1914 created the frustration which Askwith, the government's chief industrial conciliator in those years, thought so important: The young worker:

... does not like to admit to himself that he is not being trained as an engineer or a shipbuilder or a housebuilder, but to become an operative. But in a brief time to the majority comes disillusionment; and when once a man is disillusioned, bitterness is a very natural result, and antagonism to the system which he deems to be the cause.[31]

The horizons of the skilled worker were thus increasingly bounded by the world of manual labour, and those of the less skilled even more so. In spite of their differences they were pressed into a single class by their exclusion from the rest of society.

In the third place, workers were segregated by the divergence of lifestyles, of 'what workers do' from those of other classes. Thus it seems clear that as football gained mass support, it became increasingly a proletarian activity, both for players and supporters. No doubt primarily an activity of the more skilled or respectable workers, but insofar as support for the team united all who lived in Blackburn or Bolton or Sunderland, and insofar as football became the main topic of social conversation in the public bar,[32] a sort of lingua franca of social intercourse among men, it was part of the world of *all* workers. Again, the peculiar working-class form of betting which plainly increased enormously from the 1880s on was spectacularly proletarian. It was, as McKibbin suggests, 'the most successful form of working-class self-help in the modern era':[33] an illegal, but almost totally honest network of financial transactions stretching into every proletarian street and every workshop. The same class distinction increasingly separated the Sunday paper (of which *The News of the World* became the ideal type, until the later rise of the proletarian daily) both from the quality press and from the new lower-middle class press pioneered by Northcliffe. And then, as I have already noticed, there is the cap.

And finally, the working class was not so much segregated as alienated from the ruling class by two developments which, together with the fall in real wages, Askwith made responsible for the labour unrest of 1910–14. These, he told the Cabinet confidentially, were the conspicuous display of luxury by the rich, especially demonstrated by the use of the motor-car, and the growth of the mass media, which made for greater national coordination of news – and activity.[34] I quote Askwith not as proof that the plutocracy – the phrase belongs to the Edwardian political vocabulary – flaunted itself any more in the *belle époque* than under Queen Victoria, though this is possible; but as evidence for the belief that the wealth of the rich was now more visible and more resented.

What all this amounts to is a growing sense of a single working class, bound together in a community of fate irrespective of its internal differences. A class in the social and not merely in the classificatory sense: a body within which it would be absurd any longer to speak of 'the class of miners' as distinct from 'the class of cotton-workers', as Keir Hardie had still done in the early 1880s.[35] And this indeed explains how a period which provided plenty of reasons for growing sectionalism and infighting among groups of workers – one thinks of the shipbuilding industry – could also be a period when workers increasingly saw themselves and acted as Labour, with a capital L. The history of that capital L remains to be written, like the history of the working class as a singular rather than a plural noun, but there is little doubt that the transformation becomes noticeable in the twenty-five years before 1914. And indeed, even in purely economic terms, from 1900, and even more from 1911, a convergence rather than a divergence between local, regional, skilled and unskilled wage-rates becomes observable. As Hunt has shown, until 1890 trade unions and the whole environment of industrial relations in Britain helped to sustain differentials, between 1890 and 1910 they exercised no clear influence in either direction, but by 1911 they were a force helping to reduce differentials.

Politicians were aware of this class consciousness – of what Chamberlain, in 1906, called 'the conviction, born for the first time in the working classes, that their social salvation is in their own hands.'[36] If party politics was not to be identified with class conflict, one now had to pay one's respects to the supremacy of class when appealing to workers on the grounds of party. The Rhondda, as both its MP, the Lib-Lab Mabon and the local paper, proclaimed, was 'Labour in every aspiration', but the point of this observation was of course to argue that it was not *only* Labour: 'Since men cannot live by bread alone, the Rhondda mining electors are Nationalists, they are Nonconformists', etc. Edwardian political rhetoric 'had to use a language, and in particular the word "Labour" to bind their supporters into the established pattern of politics',[37] from which they threatened to escape. Where, as in Ulster and in Salvidge's Liverpool, the appeal to religion and nationality was sufficient, class did not loom large – or to much effect – in the language of local politics.[38]

Paradoxically, class initially made its way into Labour politics by a back door. Insofar as a man was seen as 'a class representative' he was in fact seen as 'outside the arena of "party politics"', even though as an individual he might be Liberal, Tory or, more rarely Socialist.[39] This meant not merely that socialists and non-socialists could collaborate happily in the new Labour Party, or that the solidly Liberal miners could transfer to Labour without changing their views. It also meant that Tory workers who would not vote for Liberals, could vote for Labour men. This was commented on when Will Crooks won Woolwich in 1903, a seat so hopeless that the Liberals had not even fought it in 1900, and it was significant in Lancashire, where workers were politically divided, even though Joyce's 'factory politics' were already in rapid decline in the 1890s. It was the Lancashire coalfield which had much the largest majority for affiliation to Labour, and in 1913[40] the notoriously un-radical cotton unions voted in favour of the political levy by a substantial majority everywhere except in the Tory working-class stronghold of Oldham.[41]

Yet we must ask whether this could have happened if the common interests of workers as a class did not already seem, even in politics, *more* important, or at least more immediately relevant, than other loyalties; as they clearly were not in Liverpool and Belfast. Very soon a choice for Labour had to become a choice *against* other parties, not a way of by-passing party politics. It may well be that the stagnation of the Labour vote after 1906 reflects the difficulty of taking this next step. The 1914 war was to remove this difficulty.

For this step implied the socialists' view of the independent party of Labour, which was fundamentally different from the earlier struggle for independent labour representation in Parliament. This had essentially been a demand that there should be *some* workers in Parliament who could speak directly for the special interests of manual labour, as railway directors spoke for the railway interest or shipowners for shipping. The trouble with the Liberal Party was not that, as a national party, it opposed this – on the contrary – but it could not understand that the new concept of independent Labour implied more than a handful of authoritative workers or ex-worker MPs: a Joseph Arch, a Burt, even – why not? – a John Burns, who spoke for Labour as Cobden and Bright had spoken for Lancashire manufacturers. It implied that workers should *only* vote for class-representatives. As Ramsay Macdonald explained in 1903, 'so soon as there is a Labour movement in politics, the very meaning of Labour representation must change', for 'Labour politics was the expression of the needs of the working class'. *Not*, he added characteristically 'as a class, but as the chief constituent of the nation'.[42] But the class struggle could not be so easily eliminated from working-class politics, least of all at a time when it was conducted with growing acrimony on both sides.

This brings me to my last point: class consciousness. I have deliberately avoided identifying the sentiments and opinions of the mass of workers, so far as we know them, with those of the avantgarde of activists and militants, because the two were plainly not the same. Activists were imbued with the spirit of nonconformity at a time when dissent was on the decline. They actively disliked much of the new working-class way of life – notably the football culture. One could compile a large anthology from the writings of contemporary socialists expressing hatred, ridicule and contempt for the stupidity and sluggishness of the proletarian masses. Whatever the implications of class consciousness for the militants, the masses were not living up to their expectations. And yet it is equally wrong to see the working class simply as an apolitical stoic under-world, a ghetto comprising most of the nation, or at best as a force which could be mobilized in defence of their narrow economic interests as potential or actual trade unionists. They also acquired a consciousness of class. I do not want to make too much of the conversion of a smallish minority of workers to socialism, though this is not negligible; nor even of the astonishing success of this minority and its organizations in getting itself accepted as a cadre of leaders and a brains-trust from the 1890s on. Labour movements need leaders and leaders need training. Since the revival of social-ism, the organizations of the socialist left have provided by far the most effective mechanisms both for bringing together the self-selected elite of able, intelligent, dynamic and innovatory workers – mainly young workers – and by far the best schooling for them. In our period such people started their careers as SDFers or ILPers or Syndicalists, just as between the wars the future leaders of na-tional trade unionism started in the Communist Party. They were accepted as leaders by people who did not share their views, because they were the best and they had relevant as well as apparently irrelevant ideas. But there is clearly more to the political transformation of Labour than this. What we have to explain is the transformation of the miners from a body notoriously immune to the appeal of the socialists to what has been called 'the Praeto-rian guard of an explicitly socialist Labour Party'.[43] What we have to explain is not only why this happened in areas of embittered class battle like South Wales, but in areas of no notable industrial militancy like Yorkshire; not only in coalfields where miners were doing poorly, like Lancashire, but in some where they were doing well.

Unlike the progress of the trade-union movement in our period, which doubled in numbers and then, after a couple of decades, doubled again to reach over four million in 1914, the progress of class consciousness is almost impossible to chart. The rise of what is even by our standards mass unionism and – in 1910–14 mass militancy – certainly indicates some transformation, but its exact nature is unclear. Electoral indicators fail us, partly because other workers are not so identifiable as voters as the miners, but mainly because the statistics of the independent Labour vote are obscure before 1906 and not significant from then till 1914. It is only from 1918 on, when Labour suddenly appears with 24 per cent of the total votes cast, rising to 37.5 per cent in 1929, that voting Labour can reasonably be used as an index of political class consciousness. At that point it becomes possible to say that large and growing masses of British workers regard voting Labour as an automatic consequence of being workers. Before 1914 this is not yet so. In 1913 even 43 per cent of the miners still voted against paying the union's political levy to the Labour Party.[44]

Yet if the making of the working-class consciousness before 1914 cannot be quantified, it is still there. In 1915 Beatrice Webb could say: 'The power of the Movement lies in the massive obstinacy of the rank-and-file, every day more representative of the working class. Whenever this massive feeling can be directed for or against some particular measure, it becomes almost irresistible. Our English governing class would not dare overtly to defy it.'[45] In 1880 nobody could or would seriously have made such a statement. The two nations of Disraeli were now no longer the rich and the poor, but the middle class and the working class, a working class which, in its physical environment, its practices and reflexes, is recognizably, at least in the industrial areas, as Richard Hoggart describes it from interwar experience. Insofar as it was not deferential, apolitical and apathetic, its politics were no longer implicit in a general belief in the rights of man, workers being merely one large section of a comprehensive 'the people'. The politics of Chartism, whether as an independent mass movement or as part of Liberal-Radicalism, fade out. The last movement of this type was founded very nearly at the same moment as the Labour Representation Committee. It united the mid-Victorian left of *Reynolds News*, which inspired it, powerful Lib-Lab figures like Howell, Fenwick and Sam Woods, with New Unionists on the socialist left: Tom Mann, Bob Smillie. John Burns blessed it. Yet this National Democratic League disappears by 1906 after a few years of by no means negligible influence. I doubt whether any general history of Britain in this period so much as mentions its name. Even labour historians treat it as little more than a footnote. The future lay with the Labour Representation Committee, and the essence of its programme, whatever it was, was that it specifically served the demands and aspirations of the working class.

Let me conclude with yet another miner. I choose Herbert Smith,

1862–1938, because he was neither a chapel activist nor a man one would associate with ideology or, in spite of his enthusiasm for education, with much reading. He was probably as close to the average pitman as any leader, even among miners, even in South Yorkshire, has even been: a slow, hard, reliable man, keener on cricket and Barnsley Football Club whose matches he attended religiously, than on ideas; a man more inclined to ask opponents to step outside than to argue. Herbert Smith advanced steadily from checkweighman to the presidency of the Yorkshire miners and eventually, in the 1920s, the Miners' Federation. In 1897, at the age of thirty-five, he decided to support the ILP. It is the late age of this decision which makes his conversion significant. Henceforth he remained a socialist, and while in the 1920s he hammered the communists, by Edwardian standards he was a rather left-wing ILPer. It was clearly not ideology that attracted him. It was the experience of the miners' struggle, and that the socialists demanded what he thought the miners needed, a legal eight-hour day, a guaranteed minimum wage and better safety.

But his choice also expressed a visceral, a militant and profound class consciousness which found visible expression in his dress. Herbert Smith was famous for his cap. A biography of him has been written under the title _The Man in the Cap_.[46] He wore it like a flag. There is a photograph of him in old age, as mayor of Barnsley, with Lord Lascelles in the elongated elegance, bowler and furled umbrella of _his_ class and the Chief Constable in a frogged uniform. Herbert Smith, a stocky, rather fat old man, wore the Mayor's chain and insignia, but above them he wore his cap. One could say a lot about his career, not all of it complimentary, though I defy anyone to withhold all admiration from the man who, in 1926, sat at the negotiating table in his cap, minus his false teeth which he had put on the table for comfort, and said 'no' on behalf of the miners to the coal-owners, the government, and the world. All I want to say here is that Herbert Smith as a labour leader and his career would have been unthinkable in any earlier period of labour history – perhaps also in any later one. He was made by, and he helped to make, the new working class whose emergence in the decades before 1914 I have tried to sketch. Among the millions of men in caps he was certainly exceptional; but he was exceptional only as a particularly majestic tree is in a large forest. There were innumerable others, less prominent, less political, less active, who recognized themselves in his image, and we should recognize them also.

(1981)

# 12: Debating the Labour Aristocracy

In the 1970s a fairly intensive debate began, mainly among historians of the left, about the so-called 'aristocracy of labour'.[2] Since much of it refers back to my paper on this subject, first published in 1954,[3] which was in its time the most systematic attempt to survey the question, it is reasonable that the original author should comment on a discussion which, inevitably, often criticizes his work. However, the object of this chapter is not to defend the original essay against criticisms or to restate the old argument, although, as another chapter in this book shows, I stand by a good deal of it. But that is, as it were, almost a private matter. Any work written years ago must be well behind the times in some respects and, even insofar as it is not, the argument and its context are quite different from what they were in the cold war years of the early 1950s, or even in 1964, when the original paper was published in a book without raising excitement. Even if the paper were now quite out of date, it would have achieved its object. For the function of the historian is not to establish permanent truth (except about what the evidence can establish), but to advance a discussion which must, inevitably, sooner or later, make his or her work obsolete, except to students of intellectual history for whom it has become a source. The present chapter is therefore written rather from the commentator's box than in the role of player or fan. It can hardly be written from the position of an impartial referee.

The first point that should be made in any survey of the labour aristocracy debate is to stress its essentially political origin and character. In the past it has, I think invariably, been not about working-class stratification *per se*, but about the political or ideological implications of such stratification. The early examples of the paradoxical use of the actual term 'aristocracy' in connection with labour, cited e.g. by Shepherd and Baxter for the 1830s and 1840s[4] confirm the point. Let us note, by the way, that the question whether this precise term is used, is secondary, or rather, it is a different and somewhat narrower question from the one originally raised and considered again here. It suggests questions of historical semantics which have not always been adequately recognized, but which this is not the place to investigate, notably the use of the term 'aristocracy' in the political discourse of the left during a period when, following the tradition established by the French Revolution, and kept alive by the visible importance of royalty and nobility in the life of most European states, the chief political enemy of the common people seemed to be 'privilege' (i.e. characteristically 'aristocratic privilege') rather than, or in combination with, 'capitalist exploitation'. At all events, what is at issue is the existence of a superior stratum of the manual working classes, whether this was called a 'labour aristocracy', 'the artisans' or by some other name or names.

Before 1848, in mid-Victorian times, the debate on such a top stratum of workers was also primarily political. That is why it became particularly lively at the time of the arguments about the Second Reform Bill and the possible consequences of enfranchising sections of the working class. Radical liberals and others argued that 'the intelligent artisan' (or whatever the group was called) formed a body which was politically sound and a guarantee against revolutionary and anarchic tendencies. Somewhat later, Socialists and their like were to argue, in the manner of the Chartists cited by Baxter, that, on the contrary, they were narrow reformists or sectionalists who stood in the way of a wider and hopefully revolutionary movement of the working class. Both, in their different ways, singled it out because of its supposedly moderate political characteristics. Where no working-class stratum with such characteristics was identified – e.g. for most of the nineteenth century in France – there was no comparable discussion of a labour aristocracy in the nineteenth century, though towards the end of the century and since 1900 both socialists and anti-socialists took up a theme originally based primarily on the British experience, for their own programmatic or explanatory purposes.[5]

Politics has continued to shape the debate ever since. Broadly speaking, after 1917 it came to be dominated by the Leninist thesis that a 'labour aristocracy' explains the reformism of social-democratic movements, that is to say that it accounts for the failure of working classes in developed countries to be as revolutionary as Marxist theory expected them to be. We need not here analyse, even in outline, the development of the Marxist theory of the labour aristocracy from Engels onwards, or discuss the political context and nature of Lenin's own views,[6] their subsequent evolution or the use made of them by Marxist historians. It is enough to observe that the Marxist thesis, in what came to be regarded as the orthodox Leninist version, still haunts some of the current discussions.[7] About this aspect of the debate only two things need to be said. First, and contrary to what some have supposed, my own writings on the subject have never accepted the Leninist argument either as the main 'explanation' of the 'reformist' character of British Labour or, for the twentieth century, at all. What was defended in the paper from which much subsequent debate has sprung, was the classical, and by no means only Marxist, view that a labour aristocracy existed in nineteenth century Britain, and that it was politically moderate. While a labour aristocracy of this sort is plainly not irrelevant to the moderation of the British labour movement, I do not believe that the roots of British 'reformism' can be adequately explained in such terms. Second, few Marxist historians today, with the major exception of John Foster[8], try to maintain this explanation, and his views on this matter are not shared by most historians, Marxist or otherwise. This phase of the debate may therefore be regarded, at least for the time being, as exhausted.

The phase which began in the late 1960s has been dominated less by the argument for or against orthodox Leninism than by the arguments for or against the intellectual 'new left' of the period, and its prolongation into the field of trade unionism, in the shape of industrial militancy based on 'rank-and-file' action. The issue here is not so much whether or not a labour aristocracy explains the absence of a strong revolutionary movement in Britain at any period, but whether the conventional view on the left of the roots of twentieth-century industrial militancy is historically legitimate. There are younger historians on the left who consider it to be a piece of political mythology and who, in criticizing the various versions of Marxist-inspired analysis on which it rests, or purports to rest, also find themselves criticizing the concept of a labour aristocracy which is undeniably part of the traditional Marxist analysis of the structure and development of the British working class. All that need be said here about this most recent phase of the debate, which is not yet concluded, is that the questions at issue are very much wider than in the earlier phase; but also that the debate on the labour aristocracy is incidental, rather than central, to them.

It would follow that it is now time to divorce the historical investigation of the labour aristocracy in the nineteenth century from an old political setting which has lost its significance, and a contemporary one which has no specific relevance to it. This is now not only desirable, but also possible.

What, then, is at issue in the debate? One thing that is not, or ought not to be, is the belief in mid- and late-Victorian times in the existence of a 'labour aristocratic' stratum of the British working class, whatever exactly it was called. There is really too much contemporary evidence to the contrary. Indeed, without this massive body of contemporary evidence, the debate would hardly continue. Some historians deny that this proves the *existence* of such a stratum, and these arguments are considered at greater length elsewhere in this book. Here it is not necessary to do more than observe that those who argue against its existence, seem to assume that contemporary observers of all kinds were living a collective delusion. It is, of course, not impossible that the 'labour aristocracy' (under whatever name) was a Victorian equivalent of Unidentified Flying Objects, but it seems simpler to assume that we are dealing, somewhere inside the cloud of contemporary words, with an observable social phenomenon.

Its nature remains a subject for legitimate disagreement. Two questions about it are at issue: the size and the dating of the phenomenon. On the dating, many writers since 1954 – not least E. P. Thompson – have taken the view that I was mistaken in supposing that a labour aristocracy did not exist before the 1850s. They are obviously right, inasmuch as a superior stratum of artisans ('the trades') and perhaps others existed before the great mid-Victorian turn – as indeed was not denied – and it is also now clearly established that terms like 'an aristocracy of labour' were more frequently used before the 1850s than I had supposed. The relevance of this earlier upper stratum to the present debate will be considered below. As to whether we regard it as a labour aristocracy in the sense of the period 1850–1914, this is a question not so much of fact as of judgment. If we believe that the 'making of the working class' in the modern sense was more or less achieved by the 1830s, it is logical to project the later labour aristocracy backward into that period. My own view is that what Maurice Dobb called, perhaps with some oversimplification, a 'homogeneous industrial proletariat' did not emerge until the later Victorian period,[9] a view also taken by historians of rather different ideological sympathies such as Henry Pelling and John Vincent.[10] Following recent studies such as those of Lazonick,[11] one might also stress the substantial transformations even within the mechanized factory sector after the 1830s. The case need not be argued here. It may merely be pointed out that, as so often in history, the answer to an apparently factual question may differ if the general context of the question is not the same.

How large was the labour aristocracy? Here a more serious difficulty arises, which the 1954 paper did not recognize, and which others have not recognized either, though Pelling hints at it.[12] Marxist students have been inclined to apply the term to a more restricted stratum than many Victorian oberservers, i.e. to a group of workers estimated by contemporaries at 12 to 13 per cent of the workers and by myself at up to 15 per cent. Victorians writing about such a stratum sometimes thought of a much larger stratum, as did Edith Simcox (who actually used the term 'aristocracy of labour') in 1885, or Rowntree, whose 'class D' included all those with 'regular standard earnings' rather than only the most highly paid or favoured. The question of size does not seem to have bothered recent students: Crossick[13] does not even attempt a numerical estimate. Of course, if this larger stratum were not excessively large, and could be defined as a working-class stratum socially distinct from a working-class plebs, and not only statistically, a relatively larger size would not in itself affect the argument. In any case Booth himself regarded his 'class E' as a socially miscellaneous group and thought that 'only in a very general way of speaking do these people form one class'.[14] Still, the problem of the relation between the 10 to 15 per cent (an order of magnitude, broadly, like that of unionized British workers before the 'new unionism') and the larger group, whose upper limits correspond, perhaps, to the 40 per cent of workers who may have been members of friendly societies, remains to be clarified. If we are speaking about something closer to 40 per cent than to 10 per cent of the working classes, then the metaphor 'aristocracy' risks misleading the uninformed, and a different word might be more apposite.

A third, and connected, question in the debate concerns the nature and composition of the labour aristocracy. Is it to be defined functionally by its relation to the process of production, e.g. by skill? Or by its economically favoured position which may or may not reflect its functions? Or by its lifestyle and beliefs? Or by its relative position in the social hierarchy? Or by a mixture of all these, and if so by what mixture?

By the accepted social criteria of Victorian Britain it belonged to the 'respectable' as distinct from the 'rough' classes, but 'respectability', at least as an aspiration, extended much beyond its limits, as Roberts' *Classic Slum* shows.[15] Similarly it was regarded as part of a broad stratum of shopkeepers, small employers and, until the end of the century, office workers: the Victorian 'lower middle class'. Recent work as by Crossick and Gray has suggested that in Victorian Britain they formed the *core* of that class, given the small numbers of white-collar workers, the exiguousness of the central and local bureaucracy, and the absence of a self-conscious political stratum of independent handicraft masters. Indeed, a point I want to return to later, the absorption of the traditions and even the vocabulary of the old handicrafts into the skilled labour movement is characteristically British. Statistically the independent artisan-masters no doubt continued to exist: socially they become invisible, unlike, say in Germany. I suggested long ago that the emergence of a new and mainly white-collar lower middle class, which wedged itself into the intermediate position between the old labour aristocracy and the middle classes, is one main reason for the growing incorporation of the labour aristocracy into a wider proletarian culture and movement, and there is certainly evidence for this social relegation of the labour aristocracy by the Edwardian period, in spite of its continued economic advantages.

Was the criterion functional? Yes and no. The model or ideal type of the labour aristocrat, as the term 'artisan' indicates, was that of the pre-industrial skilled craftsman who had learned his trade by apprenticeship, as distinct from the 'labourer' who had neither trade nor training. How common the 'ideal-type' artisan actually was in Victorian Britain is an interesting question which remains to be answered concretely and quantitatively. However, two important points should be noted. First, as I already suggested, not all tradesmen were labour aristocrats. Second, any group of workers which could establish the economic advantages of the artisan, notably an institutionalized scarcity on the labour market and some control over its own work, was assimilated to artisan status. Cotton spinners established this position and status, not through any difficulty in acquiring their skills, but through the institutionalized exclusion of most piecers from the job. White has called them 'contrived aristocrats' as distinct from, say, the tapesizers, one of the groups in the cotton industry able to enforce a real apprenticeship system.[16] Lazonick[17] has lately argued, in my view convincingly, that mule-spinners, after the destruction of their original privileges in the 1830s, were re-aristocratized by the reluctance of the masters to develop a more costly system of direct workshop management, which therefore - and probably at considerable long-term cost to British capitalism - left certain groups of workers as a sort of sub-managers or supervisors or maintainers of factory floor discipline. If I understand him right he disagrees with Foster, inasmuch as he does not believe that this was deliberate policy. Reid and McLelland[18] argue that the position of the late-nineteenth-century shipyard platers was similar, though of course by traditional standards they would be genuine artisans whose skills had been simplified and narrowed to the point where they no longer had the natural protection of a genuine scarcity. One might go further and suggest that mechanization and the subdivision of processes which would (as J.W.F. Rowe pointed out long ago)[19] have reduced a lot of engineering fitters to little more than a labourers' rate, made an increasing number of even the genuinely apprenticed artisans depend on a contrived rather than a natural aristocracy of labour. They would, as a group, have been lost without powerful craft unions.

This brings me to a crucial division of opinion. As against several colleagues who have primarily stressed the cultural element in the labour aristocracy - its lifestyles, ideology, etc. - I remain sufficient of a traditionalist Marxist to stress its determination by the economic base. Of course, nobody would deny the autonomy of the cultural element, and I may well have pushed the economism a bit farther in 1954 than I would do today, but the basic argument stands. Only men who could expect a certain level of wages, which in the nineteenth century indicated relative scarcity in a free market, however this was obtained, could enjoy the life-styles and develop the tastes and characteristic activities of the labour aristocracy. For this you needed money, more than the usual safeguards against other than cyclical unemployment, more than the usual potential for saving. The nineteenth century knew that the correlation of class and money applied to all classes. Norman Gash has recently reminded us that in general men who were raised to the peerage had first to prove that they were rich enough to live like aristocrats.[20]

Now it may be held that voluntary collective organization and, above all, unions, were essential to the social existence of a labour aristocracy, because under nineteenth-century conditions their relative scarcity could only be maintained by collective action, or their capacity to save and their relative social security ensured by it. If unions, for whatever reason, were ineffective or only locally or intermittently effective – as perhaps in France – I doubt whether a permanent *proletarian* labour aristocracy could emerge, though islands of privilege could exist. If the way out of the working class was relatively open, as I think was the case for white Protestant nineteenth-century Americans, it would not need to develop. Now in Britain craft unionism – whatever the reasons for its unusual success – had three additional functions: it reinforced the collective consciousness of each skilled occupation by establishing a standard rate within it, irrespective of individual differences. It established a mechanism for fixing demands in the light of 'comparability' with other trades believed to be of equal or comparable status – even if they had as little in common as the mule-spinners and engineers of Oldham, both of whom expected the same sort of wage. Lastly, it served to establish, maintain and probably between 1850 and 1900 to increase, the differential between the aristocrats and the plebeians. It either excluded the plebeians or, if they had to be admitted, insisted on their getting aristocratic treatment.

But by this very fact it ensured that the aristocracy was a proletarian one, which could not but see itself as part of a wider working class; however much it was devoted to keeping the lower orders of the proletariat in their place.

I shall say nothing about the peculiarities of the life-styles and culture of the labour aristocracy, which have been excellently studied by Crossick and Gray.[21]

However, the question of life-styles and attitudes raises another controversial problem. Marxists have insisted on the respectability, political moderation and 'reformism' of the Victorian labour aristocracy. But it has often been pointed out, not least by Pelling[22]

that the skilled artisan was the core of organized labour movements, and to that extent might properly be considered more radical than the rest of the working classes, and not less so. This
applies not only to Britain, but perhaps even more so to countries
in which non-aristocratic sections of the working class such as
coalminers were less prominent in labour movements. It is now
accepted that the cadre of continental, and often frankly social-
revolutionary, mass movements, also consisted, as in Germany,
essentially of skilled and largely of apprenticed artisans such as
woodworkers, printers, cigar-makers and increasingly metalworkers. This is also notoriously true of many communist parties.

Here Marxists must practice some self-criticism. Starting with
Engels in the 1890s they long tended to counterpose 'the masses',
allegedly less corrupted and potentially more revolutionary, to the
reformist labour aristocrats, thus attempting to explain the failure
of the working class to be as subjectively revolutionary as they
expected it to be. (For an iconographic version of this view, see pp.
101–2 above.) This cannot be maintained. Without arguing the case
at length, it seems preferable to rely on three propositions. *First*,
that it is wrong to suppose that *any* particular class or social stratum
is subjectively and incorruptibly revolutionary *per se* – i.e. independently of the concrete historical situation in which it finds itself.
*Second*, it is wrong to suppose that subjective revolutionary attitudes are simply and directly correlated with poverty and oppression. *Third*, it is a fact that, broadly speaking, the unskilled proletarians, though probably more riotous, were in the nineteenth
century distinguished chiefly by being less politically conscious and
far less organizable than the skilled. Of course it is true that, insofar
as any workers in late Victorian Britain were revolutionary, it was
the overwhelmingly unskilled Irish. But they almost certainly sympathized with revolution not because they were labourers, but
because they were Irish, and they were apt to think in terms of
insurrection because a tradition of armed rebellion formed part of
the political experience of their country – as it did of some other
countries, but not, in any living sense, of Britain. It is therefore
wrong to contrast a reformist labour aristocracy with Engels' 'sons
of the Chartists' whose revolutionary instincts had somehow been
stifled or kept under control by labour aristocratic reformism.

However, having said this, there really is no denying that the
labour aristocrats, so long as their privileged position lasted, were

not aiming at the overthrow of capitalism, and were indeed both subjectively and objectively furthering the subaltern integration of the workers into the system. The fact that most proletarian socialists – some tens of thousands at most before 1914 – were labour aristocrats no more proves that the labour aristocracy as a whole was socialist than the fact that Oxbridge in the 1930s produced a fair number of communist intellectuals proves that Oxbridge students as a body were revolutionary, or the fact that 'Hampstead' became an epithet for Labour intellectuals between the wars proves that this most bourgeois of all London constituencies was Labour. In fact, it has only once in its history elected a Labour MP, or any non-conservative MP, and that was in the 1960s.

To identify the labour aristocracy in its period of glory with a moderate and reformist labour movement remains correct. Such strata could be politically or socially radicalized when their position was threatened or undermined. This is what has happened in the twentieth century, which is why the classic Marxist analysis of the labour aristocracy, whatever its relevance for the nineteenth century, plainly ceases to be useful after 1914, except, paradoxically, for the opposite purpose to the one for which it was originally devised. If it explains anything, it is how and why respectable skilled craft unionists defending their privileges found themselves, as Hinton showed,[23] turning into Bolsheviks.

As Prothero demonstrates,[24] the same was true of many old, unrevolutionary, pre-industrial artisans in the early nineteenth century, whose initial aspirations amounted to little more than to maintain or restore a social order which respected their trade, and the rights and expectations of the skilled and honourable journeymen within it. But here a significant difference between British and continental artisan strata of this kind should be noted. It seems that continental artisans, notably the French, turned to primitive mutualist or cooperative socialism much more massively than their British equivalents, though with similar ideological justifications. Moreover, it is common knowledge that producer cooperatives, which were the most concrete form of demonstrating that the capitalist was unnecessary to the process of production, flourished far better on the continent than in Britain. Successful cooperative production on the continent was familiar[25] – one has only to think of the 'red belt' of North-Central Italy – whereas in Britain it became a by-word for impracticability,[26] as is indeed easily explicable, since it was usually undertaken by groups of workers who had lost strikes or, as in recent times, where the enterprises in which they were employed had proved unprofitable.

It is not necessary to give reasons for this difference here, though one may suggest in passing that it reflects the much greater erosion, in Britain, of independent small-scale artisan production by the earliest of the great industrial transformations. But, whatever the reasons, the British artisans entered the mid-Victorian period very much less steeped in a tradition of artisan socialism than the French, and therefore with a much smaller built-in resistance to the political economy and ideology of liberal capitalism, so long as it did not challenge their existence as a favoured working-class stratum.

This brings us to a final observation. It is now widely accepted that the British labour aristocracy, and indeed all British labour organization was, until at least the 1880s, deeply marked by its pre-industrial heritage, and in particular by that of the pre-industrial elite of journeymen. A great deal of recent work converges on this conclusion. It penetrates Prothero's excellent work, is implicit in Raphael Samuel's reminder of the very incomplete mechanization of the first industrial economy (which, paradoxically, returns to a view expressed with different ideological perspectives by Clapham), and is supported by R.A. Leeson's persuasive case for the direct continuity between gilds and trade societies or unions.[27] This does not mean that the old elite of artisans and mechanics is identical with the labour aristocracy of 1850 to 1914, but the historical continuities are nevertheless fundamental. Until the 'revival of socialism' in the 1880s, and perhaps even long after, it is important to see what parts of the pre-industrial heritage survived among artisans, what parts they modified to adapt to their new situation, how they modified it, and at what point they reached the limits of modification and adaptation and found themselves obliged consciously to innovate. In short, the discussion of the labour aristocracy must be widened and chronologically extended into a more general study of the artisan heritage as a whole, and this is in fact now being done. Or, to put it differently, the junction must be made between the study of the labour aristocracy which has been essentially centred on the later nineteenth century, and the revived interest, among historians, in the early industrial and protoindustrial period.

At the same time the actual heritage of the labour-aristocratic period, i.e. of a uniquely strong labour movement in Victorian Britain established predominantly on a 'craft' basis, ought to be much more seriously analysed. After all, it has determined the shape and nature of British trade unionism to this day. For 'industrial unionism', which was the basic model of so many non-British labour movements, and long the preferred recipe of both Marxists and syndicalists in Britain, proved to be a historical dream in this country, with the exception of the mining industry. The basic British pattern of development has been a dual unionism. On the one hand craft unions amalgamated sideways with other crafts or so-called crafts, on the other a hold-all 'general unionism' developed for those who could not establish viable unions of the craft type on their own. As the distinction between the Victorian labour aristocrats and the rest was eroded, these differences have also diminished. Both former craft amalgamations and general unions have assimilated to a general pattern of conglomerate unionism, in which the most heterogeneous groups of workers are joined together – e.g. plumbers and electricians, boilermakers and municipal workers. But what is left is the coexistence of rival unions within the same industry and, indeed, enterprise and plant, and a tradition of embittered sectionalism, of job monopoly and (theoretical) inflexibility, of demarcation disputes and the struggle to maintain a group's position in the proletarian hierarchy. To what extent this pattern, and the adaptation of craft-union tactics to groups of workers remote even from the 'contrived aristocracies' of the nineteenth century, is, like so much else in Britain, determined by the peculiarities of our industrial past, is a question which must interest labour historians.

At this point these reflections on the labour aristocracy debate may be concluded – for the time being. To summarize, one might say that much of the revived debate on this subject is beside the point, since it polemicises against a quasi-Leninist view of the origins of British 'reformism' which is no longer tenable, and which some students of the labour aristocracy have never held. Some of it is part of a wider conceptual debate about the relation between (in Marxist terms) 'base' and 'superstructure', between economics and culture, between class and status. This is a very general complex of questions, and the labour aristocracy is merely one of many pegs on which it can be hung. By implication rather than explicitly, it is also a debate about the specific character of British industrial development, and therefore about the 'making' and the transformations of the working class within it. Perhaps this would benefit by being made more explicit.

Concretely, however, it has produced three interesting developments. *First*, it has contributed to a notable advance in our understanding of the notion of a labour elite in Victorian Britain, though the specific character of its life-styles and its independent but subaltern ideology, on which recent work has tended to concentrate, do not exhaust the subject. This understanding is limited by the continued fuzziness of the distinction between such elites and the rather larger bodies of 'respectable' and regularly employed workers. If the concept of a labour aristocracy is vulnerable, here is its Achilles heel. A very much fuller investigation of the contemporary vocabulary of social classification, and the models of society which lie behind them, is much needed. *Second*, it has produced some important work on exactly how developments in technology and management enabled some groups of workers to establish themselves as labour aristocrats, how these positions could be defended and how they were eventually undermined. *Lastly*, the study of the labour aristocracy has logically led historians back into the wider study of its evolution out of the pre-industrial 'artisans', and consequently into the long-neglected pre-history of industrial Britain and its working classes. The concept of a labour aristocracy remains controversial. It may or may not survive as a tool of analysis for Victorian Britain, though it is difficult to see how it can be entirely dispensed with.[28] But whatever its future, it has proved profitable for historians.

(1979)

# *13:* The Aristocracy of Labour Reconsidered

That Victorian observers in Britain believed in the existence of a superior stratum of manual labouring classes described in various ways, but also by such terms as 'an aristocracy of labour' or 'an aristocracy of the working classes',[1] is not in doubt. The superiority of this stratum or group was both economic (higher and more regular wages, greater chances of saving), social ('there is as great a social gulf fixed between some working class neighbourhoods in my parish and some others ... as between my own plane and what shall I say? the Duke of Devonshire's'[2]), political and cultural. Its members were 'respectable' ('the respectable artisan classes'[3]), or, as Victorians would have preferred to put it, moral. They were believed to shade over into, and indeed were sometimes classified as belonging with the 'lower middle classes' ('The artisan is really more connected in feeling with the small shopkeeper than with the unskilled workman'). However, though 'the rift on either side' of this stratum was 'deeper below than above'[4] this stratum was also, in its own and observers' minds, essentially associated with such organizations as trade unions, cooperatives and, of course, friendly societies. For the *Athenaeum* in 1866 the 'higher working class' whose admission to the franchise was suggested, consisted of trade unionists and cooperators.[5] They clearly belonged to the world of labour. As for social mobility between this elite and the lower strata, it was said no doubt with journalistic exaggeration that 'we have here two radically different classes living under wholly different conditions, which scarcely allow the individual to pass upwards from one to the other.'[6] At all events the physical differences between working-class strata struck both middle and working class contemporaries. The physical condition of children from the 'highest' class of labour in Rowntree's York was distinctly better than the rest – 61.2 per cent of boys and 65.2 per cent of girls (aged three to thirteen) were described as 'very good' and 'good' as against 27.5 per cent (28.7 per cent) from the 'middle' class of labour and 17.4 per cent (16.7) per cent from the poorest strata. The average difference in height for boys was $3\frac{1}{2}$ inches between the top and bottom strata, almost 1 inch between the top and middle, and in weight $5\frac{1}{2}$ pounds and $2\frac{3}{4}$ pounds respectively.[7] Small wonder that John Burns noted the difference in physical size between the 'old' and 'new' unionists at the 1890 TUC.[8] In short, contemporaries took the existence of such a stratum for granted, and so may we.

It has been so much taken for granted that a variety of theories have been developed about the political, and the wider historical, significance of its existence and its social, political and ideological attitudes. Indeed, its discussion as a special stratum of labour has constantly been mixed up with political debate. It first entered the public domain during the debates on the Second Reform Bill and its possible consequences. From the 1880s Marxists took it up – the term does not occur in Marx or in Engels before that decade. Broadly speaking, Liberals and Radicals congratulated themselves on the solid worth of this group and its immunity to social disorder and revolutionary appeals, while revolutionaries regretted these characteristics, and used the existence of a 'labour aristocracy' to explain the lack of appeal of their cause. The classical formulation of the thesis that the 'reformism' of the British (and by extension of other) labour movements and social-democratic parties was due to it, occurs in Lenin, who based himself on both Engels and the Webbs.[9] Neither the classic Liberal view of 'the intelligent artisan' nor the classic Leninist or quasi-Leninist explanation of the roots of British labour 'reformism' are today widely held. However, the politico-ideological element in historical debates on the labour aristocracy, the modern phase of which began during the cold war is obvious and persistent. Even though it is no longer, or ought not to be, important, it raises the question whether historians have not been discussing a question of working-class stratification in the nineteenth century in terms invented by outsiders for quite unhistorical purposes.

It may therefore be useful to begin by returning to the Victorians' own ways of classifying the 'working classes' or 'industrious classes', for even if their criteria of classification were (like our own) in some respects imposed on social reality *a priori*, they nevertheless attempted to reflect aspects of that reality. Unfortunately in

Britain, unlike France, there have been no systematic quantitative studies of political vocabulary, and we are in the dark even about such elementary data as how, when and by whom the distinction between 'the working classes' and the 'working class' was made, how the terms were used, and how their uses changed. Though several students have preferred to extend the concept of an 'aristocracy of labour' backwards beyond the 1840s the classifications here discussed are not so frequently found before the middle of the century as after. They are of two kinds. First, there is a broad 'moral' distinction between the 'respectable' and the 'rough' working classes. Though most members of the labour aristocracy would certainly – almost by definition – be 'respectable'[10] the group was evidently larger, both because it included most people between the upper working class and the aristocracy, and because it also included a section of 'the poor'. Second, there was a broad stratum which included the labour aristocracy, but also other sections such as shopkeepers, small employers, probably until the last decades of the century many white-collar workers and formed (as already pointed out in 1954) what was then called the 'lower middle class'. The 'industrious classes' were said to include not only the labourers but artizans, shopkeepers, employers of labour (using the term in a moderate sense), clerks'.[11] Whether shopkeepers were included in the 'artizan class' (as by witnesses in the RCFS) or – perhaps no longer accurately – with 'foremen, mechanics and clerks' by a colonel in the Royal Commission on Militia and Volunteers,[12] or artisans were subsumed under, or even identified with, the 'lower middle class', the distinction was shadowy and shifting. Recent work, however, has rightly argued that 'this lower middle class belonged ... to a social world whose centre of gravity lay in the "superior" artisan, rather than to a middle class world, into which the "superior" artisan aspired to ascend.'[13] The artisan who became a shopkeeper, or even the trade unionist who – as was quite possible[14] – 'set up for himself' did not change class and life-style, or even abandon his trade union, which provided for the contingency,[15] unless he ascended beyond the line which separated the lower middle from the middle class. Conversely, other members of this 'lower middle class' both shared the organizations of the 'artizans' (friendly societies, cooperatives) – except, omitting marginal cases, trade unions – and their characteristic activities such as the Volunteer movement (to which Gray rightly draws attention)[16].

The Oldham building societies in 1871 were composed of skilled men and managers – who were bracketed with them – in cotton and engineering, plus small shopkeepers.[17] The Volunteers in East Surrey contained 'a fair proportion of clerks, some small trades-men, a large proportion of artisans',[18] in East Yorkshire 'the ar-tisan and mechanical class and small shopkeepers', in the Gordon Highlanders '50 per cent artisans (carpenters, blacksmiths, tailors), 20 per cent farmers, 10 per cent clerks, schoolmasters, teachers'.[19] It may be noted in passing that Britain is probably the only nineteenth-century country in which the term 'middle class' was extended to include sections of the manual workers.[20]

The third set of criteria were more specifically designed to stratify the manual working classes. It may be noted, by the way, that the membership of these classes was by no means beyond dispute; if agricultural labourers were generally included, though as a rather separate group, domestic servants were omitted by Rowntree, as well as workers in public institutions (i.e. indoor paupers). The position of a substantial number of poor people was far from clear, though they could be subsumed under the partly overlapping, partly residual category of 'the poor'. It will be recalled that May-hew's 'cyclopaedia of those who work, those who cannot work and those who will not work' was called *London Labour and the London Poor*.[21] Still, those who were by common agreement within the 'working classes' were universally divided into two parts: the 'artis-ans' or skilled workers and the 'labourers' or unskilled. 'The work-ing classes', wrote the *Beehive* in 1864:

are divided into two sections, one comprising the skilled artisan and mech-anic and the other the labourer, costermonger, the men who find their daily living by means which they would find it difficult to describe, although yet honest withal, and the roughs of all descriptions.[22]

So far as possible all workers were assigned to one category or the other, though even in the mid-century there were groups which did not fit: the occupational classification of the Ancient Order of Foresters listed 'factory operatives' as a separate group, though 'spinners and weavers' were *not* included among them.[23] As the structure and mechanization of the industrial economy evolved, this binary classification became increasingly unreal, and by 1900 causes serious difficulties. It is 'no longer always possible to label a parti-cular man categorically as skilled or unskilled' wrote the statistician

A.L. Bowley.[24] The Salvationist Bramwell Booth spoke of 'mechanics, operatives and labourers'.[25] The 'semi-skilled' appear under this name, and as a special intermediate category, sometime before 1914.[26] Nevertheless, the artisan-labourer dichotomy survived as late as the 1936 Housing Act, taken over almost unchanged from a 1902 Select Committee which attempted to define what constituted the 'labouring class' (by 1936 'the working class'), which was said to include:

mechanics, artisans, labourers and others working for wages, hawkers, costermongers, persons not working for wages, but working at some trade or handicraft without employing others except members of their own family, and persons other than domestic servants, whose income does not exceed £3 a week, and the families of such persons who may be residing with them.[27]

In short, the *Beehive*'s classification had not become officially obsolete.

An interesting point should, however, be noted. While 'labourers' as a stratum – whether or not classified together with the unclassifiable poor – were rarely sub-divided into subgroups other than town and agricultural (but occasionally such sub-divisions are found[28]), artisans were essentially a set of distinct occupational groups generalized into a stratum. They consisted of 'every description of mechanic; men of every trade, working tradesmen'. However, it is not surprising that in this increasingly conventional dichotomy anyone who enjoyed the income, conditions and lifestyles of the upper working class, was assimilated to the conditions of the 'artisan', whether or not he was anything like the skilled tradesmen who originally formed the core of the 'artisan' group. Locomotive drivers, cotton-spinners and the later boiler-makers could thus be bracketed with joiners, patternmakers and shipwrights. However, coalminers or iron and steel workers (except for the known tradesmen such as iron-moulders) seem rarely if ever to have enjoyed this status: a miner who left the pit was, after all, likely to be eligible simply for a labouring job. In fact, miners readily interchanged with navvies or went out harvesting in the slack summer season,[30] whereas bricklayers, even in periods of bad unemployment, would not go into the gasworks, for when they came back, known to have done so ('and it is generally found out'), they would not be accepted by their mates. 'It would tell against him in this way: if he is a mechanic and went to work in the gasworks in winter ... they would say: "He is only a gas stoker. He is no mechanic." '[31]

It is evident that during the Edwardian period the unreality of this binary system had to be acknowledged. The Census of 1911 did so by introducing the familiar five-fold social classification, which divided the workers into three groups: skilled, partly skilled and unskilled. But it is equally evident that for most of the nineteenth century it was not regarded as raising major problems of classification, except in one respect: how to consider men who were unquestionably 'artisans' in the pre-industrial sense, but who clearly did not, or did not fully, belong to the favoured upper stratum of labour. The major problem, particularly striking in the first half of the century, was the growth of mass output in manual crafts not transformed by factory or mechanization, that is to say the division of an old 'trade' into a branch working for the high-class market and a larger group working the cheap end of trade, generally by the subdivision of the old all-round skill of the art into more specialized varieties of tradesmen trained only to undertake a limited range of processes or kinds of work: the 'honourable' and 'dishonourable' wings of the trade.[32]*

But it should be noticed that the subdivision of crafts only declassed an artisan where he was unable to maintain the wages and conditions of his status. Where he was, as in shipbuilding, which developed its production essentially through the multiplication of manual specialization, no difficulty arose. The other problem arose, because even untransformed trades, especially when entry into them could not be effectively controlled, were unable to maintain the conditions of labour aristocracy for more than a portion – generally a minority – of their members. The building trades were very much a case in point.

The Victorian classifications of the working classes were, like our own, conventions largely imposed on social reality *a priori*, or attempts to fit a changing reality into pre-industrial pigeon-holes ('artisans' and 'labourers'). Nevertheless, they attempted to describe aspects of that reality and, as we have seen, adjusted their descriptions – no doubt with the delays due to inertia, bias and

---

*'Instead of a man being competent to act as an artisan, (the cabinet maker) ... was often only able to produce one particular article of furniture, and sometimes only a portion of the article was committed to him'.[33]

ideology – as they were proved to be strikingly inadequate. And about the reality of the division of the workers into a more favoured stratum and the rest, whatever its exact name, there seems to have been little contemporary doubt. Most later historians have taken it for granted on the same grounds.

Naturally the favoured stratum consisted, like the rest, of manual wage-earners possessing the common stigmata of proletarian existence: insecurity, uncertainty, and the risk of poverty. But this is not incompatible with stratification.[34] Nobody was likely to claim that skilled engineers and shipbuilders were not better off or enjoyed higher status than, say, railway guards, though the ones were disproportionately subject to cyclical unemployment, and the others might enjoy both regularity and security. Again, workers both flowed into and out of the favoured stratum. Entry could rarely be controlled institutionally (e.g. by apprenticeship), and indeed the sheer numerical expansion of the labour force would have made such restriction quite impracticable. It is inconceivable that the skilled part of the male workforce in the manufacture of metals, machines, implements and vehicles etc, which doubled between 1851 and 1891, could have been recruited exclusively by formal apprenticeship. During a period of secular economic growth exit from higher- to lower-paid occupations was perhaps less likely, except by technological replacement of manual skill, but clearly every skilled or favoured occupation contained a mass of marginal men, engaged in a sort of Brownean movement up and down, and some might well sink so low as to enter that bottom stratum of the casualised poor, the 'residuum', from which escape was virtually impossible. Yet even among the more marginal in a badly hit trade, the difference between those of skilled status and the rest was normally marked. The number of builders' labourers applying to the West Ham Distress Committee in 1905-16 was double that of tradesmen, though the proportion of skilled in the industry was, if anything, larger than that of labourers, and most in some obscure way managed to keep above the danger-line.[35] Moreover, there was always a stratum of 'the best men' who could always get work.[36]

Again, it is undeniable that in a market economy what determined the wage-rate and all that went with it was demand and supply rather than some objective characteristic of labour such as skill, in the sense of a qualification for work which could only be acquired by relatively long training. But in the nineteenth-century economy, that 'juxtaposition of hand- and steam-powered technology',[37] skill implied a degree of real scarcity which could be artificially reinforced. Even in the 1960s the Donovan Commission on Trade Unions still noted that 'the difficulty of acquiring their expertise protects (the most highly skilled)'.[38] It was probably the most reliable, or rather, manipulable, way of establishing bargaining strength, as is obvious when formerly skilled occupations transformed into semi-skilled ones, managed to maintain their status.

In any case, to use the uncertainties and mobilities within the working class as an argument against the existence of a labour aristocracy is to misunderstand the nature of such an elite. Its primary concern had to be the protection of the advantages enjoyed by its *actual* members, never mind where they came from or might go. Restrictionism or control of entry, insofar as it operated, was not an end in itself but overwhelmingly one of the instruments to achieve this protection. Craftsmen who insisted that no labourer must be allowed to 'take up the tools' of the trade knew perfectly well that many of themselves had learned their trade in just such an 'illegitimate' way. The effective test of their status was that they had proved their ability to earn a tradesman's rate, that they could get away with refusing to work below the rate, and could, as a group, insist on their due status and conditions which included refusing to work with people who might be paid less, or indeed more for the job. Skill, in the sense of 'the difficulty of acquiring their expertise'[39] except by relatively long training was doubtless the best way of establishing and reinforcing scarcity in the market in the nineteenth-century economy. Moreover, a nucleus of skilled workers, excessively expensive to replace or declass en masse, provided the best weapon by which an occupation could maintain its skilled status even when industrial change transformed it into semi-skilled labour. It was not necessarily the only one. The test was the ability to exclude, never mind how. And even mid-Victorian unions of *bona fide* craftsmen had no hesitation in excluding the weaker bargainers or more doubtful actuarial risks among otherwise eligible workers, so long as elite status could be maintained for the pick of the trade.

The cotton spinners are an extreme case in point. Their actual work was at best semi-skilled, and little different from that of their assistants, the 'big piecers' from whose ranks all spinners were recruited. A spinner normally worked with two or three assistants,

pretty well all of whom knew how to do a spinner's job. All spinners thus began their career as 'plebeians' and not 'aristocrats',
their aristocratic standing depending entirely on defending a limited
number of strategic positions in the work-process which enjoyed
some bargaining-strength, against the potential competition of a
larger number of men quite capable of replacing them. The vulnerability of their position is shown by the fact that a 'minder' who
had to give up his job through sickness or injury might well, on
recovering, have to revert to piecing until a vacancy occurred at a
mule, and even then he might have to take his place in the queue
of piecers eligible for promotion by seniority.[40] But so long as the
line between those who succeeded in becoming minders and those
who did not was sharply drawn, spinners as a group *were* labour
aristocrats, their position ratified by the level of their earnings and
the differential separating them from piecers. In Oldham spinners
earned 41s 10d, big piecers 19s 4d, in Bolton 45s 9d and 15s 9d respectively (1914).

Could a labour aristocracy be said to exist where this line was
hazy or absent, i.e. where the strategies of craft unionism were
inapplicable? Probably not, insofar as the criterion of such a group
was economic, but the question must remain open. This does not
mean that there could not be non-aristocratic groups in the top
wage-brackets, or indeed enjoying certain advantages over others
in their occupation. But one would hesitate to class coal-hewers as
labour aristocrats, if only because no case is known in that century
where this grade of miners attempted to form or succeeded in
forming a separate hewers' union, as distinct from forming the core
of unions of all miners. Conversely, the only groups on the railways
which tended to form separate craft unions were the footplate men
whose road to promotion was quite separate, once the boy's initial
step on the road to the footplate had been taken. Lateral transfer
from other grades to locomotives does not seem to have occurred.*
An interesting and ambiguous case is that of foremen, or similar
supervisory workers. While management fairly consistently and in
the end successfully attempted to separate them out as a group
from the rest[14] in skilled trades, the tradesmen among whom they

---

* Less successful tendencies to separate organization occurred among signalmen,
and - especially in rural areas - these certainly show some symptoms of labour
aristocratic status. Their numbers were limited, their work highly responsible, and
they must certainly have felt themselves to be a group selected for special steadiness
and reliability.

were recruited continued, so far as possible,· to regard them as members, and indeed as representatives of 'the trade'.[42]

Yet the labour aristocracy, natural or 'contrived' was not merely a matter of higher wages and status. The very fact that these men felt themselves to be a select minority – selected by the employers – gave them a feeling of *personal* superiority. Spinners, in the words of their union's secretary, James Mawdsley, belonged to the 'giants ... in working capacity', picked out from among the mass of the 'slow and unsteady ones'.[43] Mawdsley looked down on those who could not make it, and had to leave the industry when not promoted, for some unskilled job ('as labourers ... hawking ... portering ... in the coal trade') or who 'remained piecers all their lives with an occasional attempt at spinning in the case of the sickness of the spinner'.[44] Artisans, recalls Robert Roberts, 'considered themselves culturally and socially superior beings'.[45] And indeed, their superiority could even be maintained by the Darwinian arguments so congenial to late Victorians:

'The progressive raising of the Common Rule', argued the Webbs, by constantly promoting the 'Selection of the Fittest', causes an increasing specialisation of function, creating a distinct group, having a Standard of Life and corporate traditions of their own which each recruit is glad enough to fall in with.[46]

The attempts to deny the *existence* of a labour aristocracy, are thus unconvincing, though of course there can be legitimate disagreement about its size, composition, characteristics, social and political significance and other matters.[47] It is not even seriously undermined by pointing to the undeniable sectionalism of British trade unions, for the existence of vertical divisions within the working class does not prove that they are more significant than horizontal ones. Sectional struggles, such as the shipyard demarcation disputes which form the background to Reid's critique, were disputes for monopoly rights, i.e. for artisans defending their status or those with chances of acquiring it, for recognition as members of a superior stratum. For non-artisans there were fights for monopoly rights at their more modest levels. They challenged the existence of hierarchy no more than the establishment of a monopoly of graduates in university typing pools would necessarily challenge the difference in professional status and prospects between secretaries and university teachers. Under Victorian conditions – in this respect fundamentally different from those of the late twentieth century – not all groups of workers were in a position to use the methods of craft union exclusiveness with equal effect: the difference between compositors and what would still have been called 'printers' labourers' had not yet been eroded, or even challenged, even in Fleet Street.

Moreover, if lesser groups could rarely shift their hierarchial position as groups, individuals seeking to do so relied precisely on the strength of hierarchy. The best chance of improvement for the Victorian labourer in a segregated occupation was to disapppear from sight and turn up somewhere else claiming the status of artisan and proving it by his ability to earn the artisan rate. His next-best chance was to attach himself, by a conventional 'differential' fixed from above, to a more favoured elite trade: say, in the building trades, to plasterers and plumbers, rather than bricklayers or painters. It was certainly not to challenge the privileges of the elite as a group.

However, the argument from sectionalism can be used, not to challenge the existence of stratification but the subjective coherence of a 'labour aristocracy' so patently composed of men of varying and sometimes not comparable skills or of no real skill, and sometimes of groups in visible competition and conflict with each other. And indeed nobody can possibly deny the existence of such conflicts, or of the much-observed pecking order within the upper stratum. Yet an apparently heterogeneous collection of occupations *were* habitually classed together: as an 'elite of the working class' which includes 'engineers, masons, carpenters, compositors etc';[48] as members of certain organizations such as the Hearts of Oak Friendly Society, where 'we have carpenters, joiners ... we have mechanics and engineers (both stationary and engine drivers), firemen, small shopkeepers, clerks, chemists'[49] who, the witness agreed, could be classed as 'artizans, and those artizans taken from carefully selected trades'. Moreover, as a good deal of recent research has stressed, there was a difference in life-styles, ranging from housing and clothing – sometimes, as with tradesmen who insisted on wearing stiff collars in the workshop, even of working clothes[50] – to sociability and leisure activities.[51] And, whatever the sectional differences between individual groups claiming 'artisan' or equivalent standing, or the pecking order within the stratum, any member would take it for granted that he had more in common with artisans than with non-artisans, and most would consider themselves to be, but for personal misfortunes, superior to the plebeians. When asked why unemployed bricklayers did not want their wives to work, a building foreman said: 'I think they have a little more of what they term "pride".' When asked why they avoided the Poor Law at all costs, he said simply: 'They would lose their votes. They are English you see.'[52]

What united artisans into a single labour-aristocratic stratum? Recent work in social history has insisted, rightly, on attitudes and life-styles rather than mere income-levels, and, more doubtfully, on a degree of control over a man's own work, and the absence of direct supervision. Labour aristocrats, and especially tradesmen, would certainly expect to enjoy a degree of independence, and a good deal of control over their actual jobs, but it is now clear that they were by no means the only kinds of worker to enjoy such autonomy, if only because a great many jobs in the Victorian economy were simply neither routinized nor easily supervisable. The example of the coalminers has often been quoted.[53] The artisan's job control distinguished him, not so much from any non-artisan workers, but from the particular non-artisans with whom they worked under their direction. Yet the growing interest in working-class culture, life-styles and the nature of the actual work on the job, should not lead us to underestimate the actual level and predictability of the labour aristocrat's income, which was originally used as the main criterion of its membership.[54]

Wages were crucial to the labour aristocrat's status in three respects. First, his rate and income indicated the relative scarcity of supply, or the strategic bargaining situation, which enabled him to establish his economic superiority in an uncontrolled economy of free enterprise. It also enabled him to make some provision (individual and collective) against economic insecurity, and thus to maintain some bargaining power. Booth's 'class F' 'live better, but beyond this they save more. The risk of loss of work through bad trade does not usually affect them.' Second, it measured the 'differential' which separated the 'artisan' from the 'labourer' in his own occupation, and thereby the relative strength of his position as a labour aristocrat. Third, it provided the concrete expression of the comparability of otherwise incommensurable groups, and hence a convenient way of indicating their common membership of the same stratum. Subject to historical and customary factors, which may themselves have tended to impose a certain general wage-level among occupations of comparable status, the 'artisan' in one occupation was likely to fix his demands by what 'artisans' in other local occupations demanded or enjoyed. If in Oldham the cotton-spinners and engineers who were the pillars of the local building societies both 'will get 30s' in 1871,[56] it was presumably for this reason.

The labour aristocrat's life-style, his 'pride' like his choice of job in times of difficulty, was largely a function of this economic strength or aspiration. Hence London bricklayers, in spite of the inability of their union to give out-of-work pay, would not let their wives go out to work, or apply to the Poor Law, which declassed them. Hence the stigma of being known to go to the pawnshop, unless a catastrophe affecting the entire group legitimized it – as during the engineering lock-out of 1897–8 in Newcastle.[57] Hence, conversely, the importance of publicly demonstrating one's capacity to save and buy status symbols, and even in tight times 'to keep intact the "front room", hardly ever used, but conferring somehow through its shiny furniture a feeling of independence and status to them.'[58] Hence, in short, the link between labour aristocracy and 'respectability', to which many others also aspired, but which was most easily achieved by those who could rely on the labour aristocrat's income.

Yet, since individual resources were too exiguous for personal 'self-help', the labour aristocrat inevitably relied on collective methods – friendly societies, cooperatives, but above all trade unions which, in most cases, he alone was able to maintain before the end of the nineteenth century. Hence the familiar habit of virtually equating the nineteenth-century labour aristocracy with the unionized sector of workers, as with Schulze-Gaevernitz[59] who identifies the upper stratum of the workers with the main body of cooperators, of trade unionists, of members of sporting clubs and of numerous religious sects. In itself unionism is not a conclusive indication of labour aristocracy, even in craft trades, partly because its strength fluctuated, partly because most unions carried a body of weaker brothers who hung on to their status barely, if at all, by virtue of their union card, partly because some of the advantages of formal unions could also be achieved by the informal consensus of workers on the job. Organized or unorganized, the tradesmen on London building sites insisted on the same time-rate for all men doing the same work, irrespective of individual productivity. 'It is a building trade rule rather than a trade union rule, I should say.'[60] Moreover, starting in mid-Victorian times with coal-miners and cotton-operatives, effective unionism began to extend to non-artisans. Nevertheless, other things being equal, unions were a favoured elite even within the crafts, as Mayhew's discussion of the difference between the 10 per cent of 'society men' in the London trades and the rest, makes clear.[61] Their ability to improve their members' wages and conditions and the general superiority of both to non-unionists in the same trades, is not in serious doubt. Unionism also reinforced the collective consciousness of the artisan stratum, both by establishing standard rates within each trade, irrespective of differences between individuals, and a mechanism for fixing demands in the light of 'comparability' with others of a similar status. Craft unionism rested on a wage-differential over the less favoured, and indeed sometimes set out specifically to maximise it, as with the cotton-spinners, who insisted – against the employers – on working with four times as many 'piecers' than management considered necessary, on the grounds that only this arrangement guaranteed them the highest wage.[62] And indeed the spinners tended to earn from about two to four times as much as even their senior piecers,[63] relying entirely on strength of their union exclusiveness. In the second half of the nineteenth century it is almost certain that trade unionism served to maintain or even increase wage-differentials over the less favoured, though from 1900 – or more precisely after 1911 – mass unionization began to have the opposite effect.[64] In short, whatever its intentions, minority unionism functioned as a mechanism for establishing exclusiveness and superiority.

Recent work has stressed the differences in habits, life-styles, life-expectations and living conditions of the favoured labour stratum. It is unnecessary here to summarize the various studies in this field. It has benefited not only from the growing interest in debates about the labour aristocracy, but also from the development of research into working-class housing,[65] leisure and sports[66] and the large field of demographic or family history. With the development of housing for the 'artisan' market and the journey to work by public transport[67] it is likely that their residential segregation increased.[68] This is not only because the larger dwellings in more favoured, and less central, areas were likely to be out of reach of all but the 'well-do-do artisan' or the 'better class artisans'[69] but also because others who reached the required income through high family earnings, might fail 'to penetrate into these more favoured districts, preferring to live with classes "B" and "C", among whom they felt most at home'.[70] Work on patterns of intermarriages is recent and patchy[71] and biased by the tendency of some occupations, artisan or not, to be largely endogamous, but undoubtedly shows, as one might expect, a distinct reluctance of artisans' children to marry those of labourers. Differences in the artisan attitude to the schooling of their children has also been noted,[72] as has the familiar difference in career expectations for the children.[73] For the politically conscious, the invaluable *Dictionary of Labour Biography* now provides material about their reading,[74] and a useful content analysis of mass circulation weeklies *c.* 1850–1890 now exists.[75]

Such differences in life-style, though evidently dependent on a higher or more regular income, were not simply a function of better wages. If the Edwardian cooperative stores did not sell much imported meat, because, as in Sheffield, 'the artisan class strongly favours a good-quality British meat',[76] it was presumably not wholly on gastronomic grounds. It is evident that 'the extraordinary piano mania of later Victorian society', exceeded only by that of the United States, which provided something like one piano for every five to ten British citizens,[77] was not primarily musical. It symbolized respectability, achievement and status. As a Yorkshire miners' leader stated in 1873: 'We have got more pianos and perambulators, but the piano is a cut above the perambulator.'[78] The point to note is that the new availability, after 1880, of what, in spite of the spread of instalment buying, remained expensive goods beyond the range of the poor, was likely to increase the overt signs of status differentiation of those who could afford them. The 'seven or eight pianos a week, unless there are labour troubles', which traders could hope to sell in the boom year of 1911 in 'a Northern manufacturing town'[79] clearly helped to distinguish the minority who could afford them from the majority who could not.*

It is not for nothing that Rowntree describes the typical front room of the 'well-to-do artisan' in York as used, besides formal receptions for visitors, 'by the husband, when he has writing to do

---

* A mean sale of four pianos a week (allowing for slumps, 'labour troubles' and a rising trend of sales reaching its peak in 1913) would, in the course of fifteen years, put a piano into about 16 per cent of the houses of a town of roughly 100,000 inhabitants; a mean sale of five a week, into about 20 per cent.

in connection with friendly or other societies, or by the children, when practising music.'[80] Such activities did not merely mark differences in material life-styles, but they were, by the criteria of Samual Smiles' Self-Help and Victorian middle-class ideals, in themselves means of distinguishing, because means of creating, elites within the lower orders. They symbolized effort, intelligence and education, in short 'improvement'. But of course for the labour aristocracy, unlike the aspiring lower middle classes, 'improvement' was not only individual but collective.

For recent studies of the concept of 'respectability'[81] have confirmed that, though the hunger for 'respectability' united the upper working-class strata with the remainder of the 'lower middle class' and struggling sections of 'the poor', it did not imply (though it did not exclude) a simple ideological *embourgeoisement*. In the first place, the labour aristocracy unquestionably regarded itself as a part of the 'working classes', and indeed eventually of 'the working class', and, where organized, as in some sense a spokesman for all of it, including even the 'labourers'[82] – certainly the agricultural labourers. It is, of course, likely that there were people or groups so impoverished, marginal or 'rough' as to be considered outside the scope and range of the 'working classes' and 'the labour movement', but unfortunately this has been hardly investigated. There was no doubt an element of self-defence in this class identification. Even if artisans had wanted to barricade themselves off against the rest of the labouring classes permanently, they could not have done so, for reasons considered above. Their fortunes and 'differentials' were bound up with those of the less skilled occupations or the masses from among whom they could be recruited and replaced, or into which, as any glance at marginal members of their stratum showed, they could easily sink. They knew themselves to be part of a working class from which, economically, they could not isolate themselves.[83] But it is also evident that the bulk of the more favoured workers did not want to give up working for wages, while they could, and accepted the proletarian status as a lifetime destiny. In this respect they almost certainly differed from American workers, for many of whom wage-work was (at least hopefully) a temporary stage in the life-cycle.

Second, it is therefore clear that their 'respectability' was not identical with that of the middle classes, however much the two ideals had in common. It could not be, for too wide an income gap separated the top of the unquestionable 'working class' from the bottom of the unquestionable 'middle class'.[84] Moreover, the very process of 'bettering oneself' by personal effort and self-help, to which both classes subscribed, had to produce such a divergence, inasmuch as for the one group self-help could not become real without collective institutions (friendly societies, cooperatives, etc.). Insofar as they were wage-earners, trade unionism which was indispensable to them as a group, actually implied the opposite of the middle class ideal, namely social levelling within the organized group: that 'most erroneous and mischievous purpose of seeking an *uniform rate of wages without regard to differences* of skill, knowledge, industry and character'.[85] In crucial respects labour aristocrats, however 'respectable' could not behave like members of the middle class, even if they wanted to. If they did, as might happen with former trade unionists who became masters or managers – but not necessarily with those who moved sideways into 'penny capitalism' or other petty enterprise – they had to change roles. Even the cotton spinners, who identified their interests with the prosperity of their masters and invested their funds in cotton-mills, knew that this must not affect their policy *as a union.*[86]

Moreover, though the actual symbols and indicators of 'respectability' were often modified copies of middle-class prototypes, the concept itself was not borrowed. Something of puritan virtues and efforts are also necessary for the collective improvement of a class, though if practised by revolutionaries, for example, they are unlikely to be regarded as 'respectable' by the middle class. In any case working-class respectability in Victorian times included activities (mainly connected with public houses) of which the middle classes disapproved. There is no evidence that the 200 Oldham Friendly Societies who met in pubs in 1874 were by working-class standards less respectable than the twenty-six who met in schools.

'Respectable', 'superior' and yet members of the 'working classes': the combination raises the much-debated question of the labour aristocracy's political attitudes, or more precisely, of their moderation. As we have seen this was asserted both by radical Victorian Liberals and by Marxists, and has been consequently challenged by their critics, on the ground that the bulk of organized working class activism in the later Victorian and Edwardian periods, leaving aside special cases like mining, came from among this stratum. If anything, the labour aristocracy was therefore the nursery of the left.* It is undoubtedly both true and natural that labour activists came disproportionately from within the 'artisan class'. The stratum itself could not have existed as such without some organized collective activity, and what is more the gap between the Victorian stratum which included the 'artisans', and the 'middle class', kept the upper ranks of manual workers full of 'men and women of personality, character and high intelligence' whom a more meritocratic or upwardly mobile society might have drained away.[9] What proportion of this upper working class was in any sense activist, we do not know, though the question is not beyond research – e.g. into the rate of participation in trade-union votes and elections. The highly politicized election of the general secretary of the ASE in 1892 did not attract much over 50 per cent of votes.[90] At a guess, activity was greater in small and local organizations, though much of it cannot always be distinguished from formal or informal sociability. Thus three-quarters of the members of the numerous Oldham building societies in 1871 (their membership ranged from fifty to 150) attended meetings, for – it was claimed – 'the working classes generally take an interest in attending the meeting for conversation and to see what is going on.'[91] And there can be no doubt that working-class activists were more likely than not to stand somewhere left of whatever was the contemporary political centre.

Yet, taking them as a whole, there can be no serious doubt that, in Robert Roberts' words, 'until 1914 the members of this elite generally, as far as class values were concerned, stayed almost as conformist and establishment-minded as their Tory counterparts. Together they stood, the great bulwark against revolution of any kind.'[92]

But this does not mean that some other section of the working class was politically more advanced or revolutionary.† The 'labourers' and the unorganized 'poor' were potentially more riotous. They may have distrusted what came to them from their rulers more than the artisans, since they remained outside the range of organization and politics, even largely of voting.[93] They lacked the ability of the superior stratum to win sectional improvements

---

* This raises some difficulties for critics who wish to maintain *both* that no labour aristocracy existed *and* that it was radical rather than moderate.[88]

† I was careful not to suggest this in the original essay on the labour aristocracy.

by collective action. They had obviously more cause for discontent. However, it cannot be seriously suggested that the lower strata of the British working classes in the nineteenth century (with the possible exception of the Fenian-influenced Irish in Britain) were in any realistic sense of the word politicized, let alone revolutionary.

There is thus no good reason to eliminate the aristocracy of labour, as traditionally envisaged, from the history of the nineteenth-century working classes. Nevertheless some questions about it remain in legitimate dispute. The most important of these is what stratum precisely we are talking about. Modern (largely Marxist or left-wing) students have been inclined, sometimes without noticing it, to apply the term to a much more restricted stratum than many Victorian observers. They have thought rather in terms of a group which corresponds to the 12 per cent of Rowntree's 'well-to-do artisans', the 12.4 per cent of the population in Booth's East End or the 13 per cent of the working class in Webb's estimate of 1912.[94] Of course such strata have some significance. They would hardly have been singled out otherwise by competent social enquirers. On the other hand such enquirers also applied terms like 'the well-to-do class of operatives' or 'the prosperous aristocracy of the working classes' to a larger group – say 25 per cent of the total of urban and rural working classes and the poor,[95] or even more, as in Rowntree's 'Class D' and Booth's 'Class E'. And certainly for some the class primarily identified as 'the recognized field of all forms of cooperation and combination' were those with 'regular standard earnings' rather than only the most highly paid. It is evident that while we can reasonably speak of a minority of 10 to 15 per cent as an 'aristocracy', such a term becomes unrealistic and misleading when applied to, say, 40 per cent of the labouring classes.

There are two difficulties here. First, we know too little about what united or divided the smaller group of 10 to 15 per cent and the larger strata below them, often composed of essentially similar workers. Thus in Booth's London one third of his 'artisans' (and Booth naturally uses the Victorian dichotomy*) belonged to the

---

* Booth's occupational classification (vol. 1, p. 34) distinguishes between 'different classes of labour, lowest class, casual, regular etc' (groups 1–6) and 'different classes of artisan' (groups 7–12). The remaining groups, apart from, presumably, many of the 'female heads of families, etc', clearly do not belong to the working classes.

relatively and absolutely poor, and only 19 per cent of the top stratum of builders, furniture and woodworkers, metalworkers and 'sundry artisans' of 'Classes E and F' to the 'best-paid of the artisans'.[96] It is equally clear that many of these less favoured artisans had the same aspirations as the most favoured, and tried to pursue them, evidently with less success, by the same methods. To this extent the continuum of artisan values must have stretched well beyond the labour aristocracy in the narrow sense. Indeed, almost the only groups which could draw sharp frontiers separating the strata, were what has been called 'contrived' labour aristocrats such as cotton spinners and boilermakers, consisting of members who, but for their unions, would have clearly not have been classified as 'artisans'. On the other hand, as the tendency of so many London crafts in the early nineteenth century to divide into 'honourable' and 'dishonourable', 'fair' and 'foul' sectors shows, there were limits to the sense of common trade membership, essentially determined by the determination of those who could organize (i.e. maintain their 'honourable' status), to concentrate on their own affairs. The aristocratic tailors, even when accepting the desirability of a general union, confined the more marginal members of the trade to an inferior branch of the organization. The carpenters who succeeded in remaining in unions after 1834, regarded the defeat of that year as 'the separation of the good from the bad'.[97] Once the attempt to establish universal organization in the trades ('general union') had been *de facto* abandoned, it became clear that the strength of the mid-Victorian craft unions was based on recruiting an elite within the trade, capable of maintaining the high benefits which in turn attracted such men. That, if anything, was the real 'new model' which distinguished the unions of the 1830s and 1840s from those of subsequent decades. When Applegarth proudly told the Royal Commission on Trade Unions that foremen from all parts of the country applied to his branch secretaries for spare men, knowing they would be 'good workmen and of good moral character',[98] he was not merely making a point which would appeal to middle-class commissioners. He was stressing what distinguished members of the Amalgamated Carpenters and Joiners from the unorganized, and what gave his union its power. Certainly among the artisans there was 'no hard-and-fast line between society and non-society men'. But it could be taken for granted that 'the trades unionist is better off than the outside workman; his wages not infrequently average a shilling or so higher, he has more facilities for obtaining work, and usually receives both sick and out-of-work pay'.[99] And plainly, in permanently organized societies, he knew it.

The second difficulty is that we do not know whether, or how far, the attitudes of the top stratum differed from those of the larger stratum, e.g. in politics, or indeed whether, en masse, they had any specific political attitudes. Until the decline of Chartism it is reasonable to assume that most politically conscious workers would have been drawn to a broadly radical and Chartist position, always excepting the Irish, who were primarily open to the appeal of their national cause and church. From the 1880s on class consciousness, though in itself regarded as quite separate from party loyalty, increasingly acquired a political dimension which eventually produced a class party of Labour. Here, certainly, the role of the self-confident organized sector of the class, in which 'artisans' were prominent, was notable in some regions. Thus in London 'the intelligent portion of Socialism' in Battersea was, according to Booth, chiefly to be found among the 'superior artisans' of the Shaftesbury Estate.[100]

But in the intervening period it would certainly seem, in the light of Joyce's important work[101] that the workers were depoliticized *as a class*, choosing their political loyalties according to religion, the commitment of their employers, local tradition, community loyalties or in other ways: roughly as they might later choose rival football teams to support. As we know, during this period even unions formerly associated with radicalism liked to stress their avoidance of 'political' debates.[102] The Liverpool Trades Council's rules proscribed 'party or political matters unless bearing upon labour questions'.[103] Admittedly even in this period the 'labour interest' remained democratic-radical, even in Lancashire where Tory working class activism was stronger than elsewhere. It was a minority, but, perhaps because the earlier radical-Chartist ideology had been particularly attractive to artisans, a minority whose strength lay largely among men of artisan tradition. It was in the factories, including the factory 'labour aristocracy' such as the cotton spinners, that its hold was weak.

This suggests that, insofar as the labour aristocracy can be identified with the sector organized by craft unionism, there may have been some differences between its political engagement and that of those immediately below it. The question must remain open. However, in the 'classic' period of labour aristocracy – from the mid-Victorians to the Edwardians – these differences were so overlaid by the regional, local or confessional colouring of politics that they were often difficult to discern. Where Toryism was strong, as in Lancashire, the Liberal-Radicalism of artisan activists was more visible – but typically among such 'crafts' as the 'tailors, shoemakers, building craftsmen and metal-workers of various kinds' who were Vincent's typical 'working class Liberals'.[104] On the other hand where the local or regional tradition was solidly Liberal as in the northeast, they were not. 'Everyone' was for Gladstone. Of course, given the width of the gap between class identification and political identification in the years between Chartism and the rise of a *political* class party of Labour, the search for national generalizations about Victorian working class attitudes may not be a very profitable branch of research.

All the same, these observations raise real difficulties for historians interested in the labour aristocracy. If, in much of the period regarded as its heyday, the differences in its attitudes from those of the bulk of the 'respectable' and more or less regularly employed workers were marginal, or overlaid by local and regional patterns, then what exactly do we hope to achieve by investigating it? Can the study of this stratum survive the extinction of the political debate which gave rise to so much of it, i.e. the thesis that its specific 'moderation' was responsible for the immunity of the British proletariat to the appeal of revolution?

Since the present writer never subscribed to this thesis, readers will expect the answer 'yes'. Study of the labour aristocracy would be pointless only if we regarded it as a pure ideological construct. But, as I argued in my original study and have tried to re-affirm in the present chapter, 'so far as nineteenth century Britain is concerned, it rests upon solid foundations of economic and political reality'.[105] Social realities are there to be investigated, even if some of the theories propounded about them from time to time are wrong. At the very least, the labour aristocracy illuminates the structure and stratification of the working class in the first industrial nation, and the 'making' of that class. Indeed, these things are incomprehensible without it. It can also illuminate – though there is not much research in this field – the specific differences between the British working class and those of other industrializing nations, in which contemporary analysis did not discern a similar stratum of comparable significance though later Marxist theory mistakenly tried to introduce the concept.*

On the other hand one substantial point of the classic argument about the Victorian labour aristocracy remains intact: it *was* politically and socially moderate. At about the same time as Thomas Wright produced his guide-book for armchair tourists in the country of the working classes[106] a French author – also with experience of manual labour in engineering workshops, and the equivalent of a Liberal-Radical in Britain – produced a very similar guide to the world of the Parisian workers, and in particular the skilled artisans.[107] In the first place, though clearly describing the same group as Thomas Wright (i.e. skilled metal-workers) Denis Poulot hardly refers to the distinction between 'artisans' and 'labourers', which is central to Thomas Wright. Labourers are mentioned only in passing as being more biddable from the employer's point of view than the skilled. (Poulot himself was an employer who had graduated from the shop-floor.) In the second place, the sort of non-political craft unionism so characteristic of Britain, and which he considers admirable while regretting its weakness in France, is constantly contrasted with class-imbued revolutionary politics, which he deplores. In the third place the most desirable type of skilled engineer from the employer's point of view (the 'true worker'), and who conforms to the 'intelligent artisan' of contemporary British debate, constitutes a small minority of the total work-force (10 per cent is the author's estimate), and *less than a third* of the workers con-

---

*It may be convenient to summarize what the present author has previously written on this matter. 1) The 'Leninist thesis' is clearly rejected for the period since the formation of the Labour Party, though with a polite nod towards orthodox phraseology, the original papers having been written in 1949 and 1954. (*Labouring Men*, chapters 15, 16.) 2) The emergence of a labour aristocracy, based on a century of British economic world supremacy, was included among the 'roots of British reformism' in the period since 1850, but only as one among five factors, of which the other four have no specific relation to it. (*ibid.* p. 341) My texts, I believe, have carefully avoided any commitment to the exclusive or primary explanation of 'reformism', even in 1850-1914, by the existence of a labour aristocracy. 3) The ambiguities of Lenin's own views about the labour aristocracy are analysed in a paper republished in *Revolutionaries* (London, 1973, pp. 121-29). 4) The author's disagreement with the 'Leninist thesis' was not expressed as clearly, or even polemically, as it might have been, both because he was, for reasons which seemed good at the times of writing, reluctant to stress views which were then heterodox among Marxists, and because he preferred to engage in polemics against those who, on anti-Marxist grounds, denied the existence or analytical value of the concept of a labour aristocracy in nineteenth-century Britain.

sidered the most skilled, reliable and capable of responsible and supervisory work.[108] Even these admirable workhorses are, of course, highly politicized in the spirit of the French Revolution, though devoted to parliamentarism and opposed to violence. Conversely, and fourth, the impassioned social revolutionaries are estimated at 23 per cent of the workforce, and clearly seen as the major influence on a further 45 per cent,[109], the remainder being occasionally political or socially marginal. Poulot's estimates, made on the eve of the Paris Commune, seem realistic enough, for metal-workers were to provide the largest contingent (13.2 per cent) of those arrested for active participation in the Commune and the second-largest group of those sentenced.[110] There could hardly be a more striking contrast than that between contemporary British and French 'journeyman engineers'. The contrast is underlined by the evident similarities in the labour process and in the workshop behaviour and practices of the two groups.

In short, the French metal-workers of 1869 suggested to observers neither an aristocracy of labour nor political moderation, whereas the English ones did. Is there a connexion between these two aspects of their image? It is not unreasonable to suggest that there is. Thus the weakness of effective trade unionism among French engineers clearly lent more weight to politics as a method of asserting class interests. In France the political tradition happened to be one of revolution, interspersed with much stronger elements of utopian communism (i.e. the ideal of a world of producers' cooperatives) than in pre-1848 Britain. However, the inverse correlation between union strength and political radicalism has been noted in Britain too by historians of the ILP.[11] Strong unions were certainly favoured by the employer Poulot as a potentially moderating influence, and – logically, but somewhat unexpectedly – he strongly defended the First International for this reason in France against those who accused it of subversion.[112] Conversely, it is certain that in Britain the 'old' unionism was hostile to political ultras, so long as capitalism both seemed a going concern and was disposed to accept the status and demands of its members. But, as has been suggested, effective formal or informal unionism of the predominant craft type was essentially exclusive in practice. Indeed, the less workers could rely on the natural monopoly of their skills and experience, the more it functioned as a mechanism for separating the superior ins from the inferior outs.

From the 1890s on this situation changed. (The change is discussed elsewhere in this book.) A labour aristocracy threatened by technological and managerial innovation, increasingly pushed out of the old 'lower middle class' by the rise of a new white-collar stratum which was apt to push all but the foremen out of the formerly socially mixed 'better' districts of 'lower middle class' housing, found itself both pressed into a common and apparently inescapable working-class universe, and potentially radicalized in defence of its own privileges. Whatever the implications of a labour aristocracy, insofar as this continued to exist, they obviously were no longer those of the Victorian period. But that is not a new observation, nor, today, a controversial one. It was already made in the original paper of 1954, which is the starting-point of most of the current debate of the subject.

(1978)

# 14: Artisans and Labour Aristocrats?

This chapter is not intended as a continuation of the debate on the labour aristocracy, which has been gathering pace and impetus in recent years. In this sense the question-mark at the end of the title is deceptive: there will be no direct answer to the question whether the concept of a labour aristocracy is useful, what this stratum consisted of, or how it developed. Of course such an answer is unnecessary for the group on which I want to concentrate, namely the skilled workers usually known in the nineteenth century as 'artisans', since as a group they, or certainly their organized sector, would certainly have considered themselves a privileged stratum or aristocracy of labour. Conversely, insofar as there was a model of the 'labour aristocrat' in the minds of the many who used this term, or equivalent terms, in the nineteenth century, it was almost certainly that of the skilled artisan, separated by an abyss from the 'labourer'. Whatever may have been the case elsewhere, in the world of the tradesman 'according to workshop etiquette – and nowhere is professional etiquette more sternly insisted upon than among the handicrafts – all who are not mechanics are labourers'.[2] However, while I believe that my observations have some bearing on the debate about a labour aristocracy, my argument does not depend on any particular position in that debate.

It is essentially an argument about the fortunes and transformations of the skilled manual wage-worker in the first industrial nation. His characteristics, values, interests and, indeed, protective devices, had their roots deep in the pre-industrial past of the 'crafts' which provided the model even for skilled trades which could not have existed before the industrial revolution, such as the Journeymen Steam Engine Makers. Skilled labour continued to bear the marks of this past until well into the twentieth century; in some respects it survived strongly until World War II. It is now generally accepted that the British industrial economy in its prime, relied extensively, and often fundamentally, on skilled hand-labour with or without the aid of powered machinery. It did so for reasons of technology – insofar as manual skill could not yet be dispensed with; for reasons of productive organization – because skilled labour supplemented and partly replaced design, technological expertise and management; and, more fundamentally, for reasons of business rationality. So long as it did not stand in the way of making satisfactory profits, the heavy costs of replacing it, or incidental to its replacement, did not seem to be justified by the prospects of the profits to be made without it. This applied not only to special cases like Fleet Street. Sir Andrew Noble of Armstrong's argued, no doubt correctly, that there was more money to be made from building one river boat than from producing 6,000 cars.[3] Unlike the United States, skilled manual labour was not in short supply. And the major incentive to replace it, namely the mass production of standardized goods, was unusually weak or patchy in the British home market until the last decades of the century, while the commanding position of British goods on the world market, or more precisely in the markets of what today would be called the 'Third World' and the white empire, kept old methods of production viable. Moreover, it may be suggested that, in terms of money wages, British skilled labour was probably not expensive. It may well have charged less than the traffic could have borne.

The British skilled worker thus occupied a crucial position of considerable strength, and the longer he occupied and exploited it, the more troublesome and expensive it would be to dislodge him. Skill could indeed have been toppled. Skilled men were defeated in pitched and apparently decisive battles between the early 1830s and the 1850s – even the powerful engineers. Yet what followed in the 1850s and 1860s was, in most industries, a tacit system of arrangements and accommodations between masters and skilled labour, which satisfied both sides. The position of the skilled men was reinforced to such an extent that the much more systematic later attempt to displace them by a new and more sophisticated mechanization and 'scientific management' also largely failed. The nineteenth-century artisan was indeed doomed. Except in some small if crucial patches of the industrial economy, and in the undergrowth of the black economy, he – for even in our days it is very rarely a she – no longer counts for much. But then, neither does British industry.

The history of the artisan is thus a drama in five acts: the first sets him in his pre-industrial heritage, the second deals with his struggles in the early industrial period, the third with his mid-Victorian glories, the fourth with his successful resistance to renewed attack. The last finally, sees his gradual but far from smooth decline and fall since the end of the first postwar boom.

I shall begin with a simple observation. In most European languages the word *artisan* or its equivalent, used without qualification, is automatically taken to mean something like an independent craftsman or small master, or someone who hopes to become one. In nineteenth-century Britain it is equally automatically taken to refer to a skilled wage-worker, or indeed sometimes initially (as in Gaskell's *Artisans and Machinery*) to any wage-worker. In short, artisan traditions and values in this country became proletarianized, as nowhere else. The term *artisan* itself is perhaps misleading. It belongs largely to the world of nineteenth-century social and political discourse, probably entering the public vocabulary in the course of the ill-fated campaigns, almost the last collective endeavours of both craft masters and journeymen – the latter already vastly predominating – for putting life back into the Elizabethan labour code at the end of the Napoleonic wars. The term seems rarely to be used for social description or classification in the eighteenth century. The actual word almost universally used in working-class circles is 'tradesman'. While in nineteenth-century middle-class usage it came to mean almost without exception a, generally small, retailer (a man who was 'in trade'), in working-class usage it retained, and perhaps among older men still retains, the ancient craft usage of the man who 'has a trade': here language and the differentiation of the estate of artificers into those who make and those who sell, go together. We may note in passing that while 'being in trade' develops connotations of contempt or deference, 'having a trade', at least for those who have it or compare themselves to its possessors, maintains its connotations of self-satisfaction and pride.

As the word 'master' shows an analogous development, becoming in nineteenth-century usage a synonym for 'employer', so conversely 'journeyman' becomes synonymous with a wage-working tradesman. Indeed, in the dawn of industrialization it is sometimes used for any wage-worker. Trade societies and trade unions, in which the name of the old artisanate survives, are now not only bodies of traditional crafts like hatters or brushmakers, but unprecedented ones like journeymen steam engine makers and boilermakers. While unions gradually dropped the word 'journeyman' from their titles, the word itself continued as a description of the skilled man, no longer in contrast to the 'masters' in his trade, but rather in contrast to the apprentices whose numbers he sought to control, and especially the 'labourers' or 'handymen' against whom he defended his job monopoly. Nineteenth-century class differentiation and stratification is thus deeply rooted in the vocabulary, and hence the congealed memories, of the pre-industrial craft world.

What is more, the term 'the trade' becomes essentially identified with the skilled workers who practise it. 'The men of every trade speak of their trade among themselves as "the trade"'.[4] 'In connexion with labour affairs', says an early twentieth-century labour dictionary, 'this term denotes either 1) a specific craft or occupation in the field of manual employment, or 2) the collective body of workers engaged at a single specific craft or occupation.'[5] Indeed 'the trade' may actually become a synonym for the union. Thus as late as World War II we find a cooper's apprentice, outraged by seeing a labourer doing skilled work, successfully threatening the boss to bring the matter to the attention of 'the trade', if he is not told to stop.[6]

I do not wish to labour the linguistic point, though the question of language is significant and would repay systematic research. At all events, it is clear that not only the vocabulary and institutions of pre-industrial craft organization passed over to the working class almost *en bloc*, but the basic Victorian classificatory distinction within the working classes also derived from craft tradition. It is common ground that the Victorian division of workers into either 'artisans' (or some similar term such as 'mechanics') and 'labourers' was unrealistic, and had always been descriptively inadequate. Yet it was very generally accepted, and not only by skilled workers, as representing a real dichotomy, which caused no major classificatory problems until the expansion of groups which could not be realistically fitted into either pigeon-hole, or neglected, and who, from the 1890s, came to be known vaguely as 'semi-skilled'.[7] From the masters' point of view it represented the difference between all other labour and skilled labour, i.e. 'all such as requires a long period of service, whether under a definite contract or agreement, and in a single firm, or with no such agreement, the learner moving about from firm to firm.'[8] This was also essentially the men's definition.[9]

From the men's point of view it represented the *qualitative* superiority of the skill so learned – the professionalism of craftsmanship – and simultaneously of its status and rewards. The apprenticed journeyman was the ideal type of labour aristocrat, not only because his work called for skill and judgment, but because a 'trade' provided a formal, ideally an institutionalized, line of demarcation separating the privileged from the unprivileged. It did not much matter that formal apprenticeship was, almost certainly, not the most important gateway to many trades. George Howell estimated in 1877 that less than 10 per cent of union members were properly apprenticed.[10] They included so firm a pillar of the crafts as Robert Applegarth, secretary of the ASCJ. The basic fact was that good fitters – even good carpenters and bricklayers, who were much more vulnerable to interloping – were not made in a day or a month. So long as genuine skill was indispensable, artisans – the kind who would never be out of a job if jobs were going – were less insecure than has been sometimes suggested. What they had to protect themselves against was not so much labourers or even handymen who could immediately take over their jobs, but a long-term over-supply of trained tradesmen – and of course the insecurity of both trade cycle and life cycle. In many trades – e.g. in engineering – the risk of an uncontrolled generation of a reserve army of tradesmen were small, though in some of the building trades, with their large influx of country-trained men, it was significant.

Such, then, were the artisans we are dealing with. I may note in passing that they are not to be confused with the so-called 'intelligent artisan' of the mid-Victorian debates on parliamentary reform, or of Thomas Wright, that 'hero of a thousand footnotes', to quote Alastair Reid. Artisans were indeed apt to be more adequately schooled than most non-artisans and, as the history of most labour movements shows, far more apt than the rest to occupy responsible and leading positions. Even in the 1950s skilled workers provided the same proportion of full-time union officials – about 95 per cent – in former craft unions with a heavy admixture of the semi-skilled, as in unions still described as skilled unions.[11] Yet, as Thomas Wright correctly observed, the reading artisans with intellectual interests – at least in England – were a minority among their mates whose tastes did not differ notably from the rest of the proletariat.[12] An analysis of a sample of what might be considered 'intelligent artisans' by definition confirms the point. In the first three years' intake of the London Mechanics Institution such groups as, say, hatters, coopers and shipwrights were grossly under-represented, though they would scarcely have considered themselves less skilled, or lower in the artisanal pecking-order, than, say the somewhat over-represented woodworking trades.[13] The truth, confirmed by later attendance statistics at evening schools,[14] is that some trades found it professionally more useful to make written calculations and use or produce designs than others, and therefore tended to be more studious. We may therefore safely leave the 'intelligent artisan' to one side.

What did they derive from their pre-industrial craft heritage? Academics should have no difficulty in grasping the assumptions behind the thinking and action of corporate crafts, since we largely continue to act upon those assumptions ourselves. A craft consisted of all those who had acquired the peculiar skills of a more or less difficult trade, by means of a specific process of education, completed by tests and assessments guaranteeing adequate knowledge and performance of the trade. In return such persons expected the right to conduct their trade and to make what they considered a decent living corresponding to its value to society and to their social status. It is quite easy to translate this last requirement into the terms of market economics, and indeed much of what the crafts did served to restrict entry to the trade, to exclude competition by outsiders (possessing their own trade or not) and to restrict output and labour supply in such a manner as to keep the average income at the required level. In our days market economics have indeed taken over, but the basic assumptions of crafts had only a peripheral relation to the discourse of business schools. They spoke the ancient language of a properly structured social order, or in E.P. Thompson's terms, a 'moral economy':

The obvious intention of our ancestors in enacting the Statute (of Artificers) ... was to produce a competent number and perpetual succession of masters and journeymen, of practical experience, to promote, secure and render permanent the prosperity of the national arts and manufactures, *honestly wrought by their ability and talents* [my italics, EJH], inculcated by a mechanical education.

And this in turn meant that they had 'an unquestionable right ... (to) the quiet and exclusive enjoyment of their several and respective arts and trades which the law has already conferred upon them as a property.'[15] That labour was the working man's 'property' and to be treated as such, was, of course, a commonplace of contemporary radical political debate.

Conversely, the duty to work properly was assumed and accepted: the London Operative Tinplate Workers who left their job, were obliged to return to complete any unfinished work, or to pay for it to be completed, on pain of fine by their Society.[16] In short, the trade was not so much a way of making money, but rather the income it provided was the recognition by society and its constituted authorities of the value of decent work decently done by bodies of respectable men properly skilled in the tasks which society needed. The ideal, and indeed the expected, situation was one in which the authorities left or conferred these rights on the body of the trade, but in which the trade collectively ensured the best ways in which they were carried out and safeguarded.

In the classical, or if you prefer the ideal-typical corporate crafts of the pre-industrial period, this regulation and safeguarding was essentially in the hands of the craft masters, whose enterprises formed the basic units of the collectivity, as well as of its educational and reproductive system. It is clear that artisan interests represented essentially by hired workers would be formulated rather differently. It is less evident that a 'trade' so identified would not be the same as a self-contained stratum of craft journeymen within a craft economy, even when organized in specific journeymen's gilds, brotherhoods or other associations. The difference between the latter type of organization and the British 'trade society' which developed directly into the craft union deserves more analysis than it has received, though some recent work has advanced it significantly. It has been suggested that such forms of collective journeyman action tended to stress 'honour' and the social prestige of the journeymen *outside*, and often at the expense of, their economic interests, often by a sort of hypertrophy of symbolic practices such as the well-known journeymen rituals, fights and riots.[17] All we need note here is that this road of journeyman development – which has no British parallel, so far as I know – could not easily lead directly into trade unionism.

The economic interests of wage-workers were clearly fundamental in British journeyman trades organizations even before the industrial revolution. That is to say, they were designed to safeguard them against the primary life risks to manual workers, namely accident, sickness and old age, loss of time, underemployment, periodic unemployment and competition from a labour surplus.[18] Whereas the core of German or French journeyman collectivity was to be found outside the workshop – in the institutionalized period of travel, the journeymen's hostel or lodging-house where the rituals of initiation took place, the essential locus of the British apprentice's socialization into the ways of the journeyman was patently the workplace. There he was 'taught both by the precept and the example of his mates, that he must respect the trade and its written and unwritten laws, and that in any matter affecting the trade generally he must sacrifice personal interest, or private opinion, to what the trade has rightly or wrongly ruled for the general good'.[19] There was thus no clear distinction between the 'custom of the trade' as tradition or ritualized practice, and as the rationale of collective action of workers on the job or the sanction of concessions won by it. Thus some formalized rituals could be allowed to atrophy without weakening the force of the 'custom of the trade'.

The basic journeyman institutions, as Prothero's *Artisan Politics* shows, were the friendly benefit society, the house of call, the tramping system – which gave artisans a nation-wide dimension – and apprenticeship. To these research has rightly insisted we must add the unorganized, yet by no means totally informal, work group in the shop or on the site.[20]

They protected the interests of hired men – yet it must never be forgotten that this was seen to be 'the trade', composed essentially of hired men, that is to say a specific body of respectable and honourable men defending their 'craft', i.e. their right to independence, respect and a decent livelihood which society owed them in return for the proper performance of socially essential tasks which required their education in skill and experience. The 'right to a trade' in the original constitution of the ASE was compared to the right belonging to the holder of a doctor's diploma.[21] The qualification for the job was identical with the right to exercise it.

The artisan's sense of independence was, of course, based on more than a moral imperative. It was based on the justified belief that his skill was indispensable to production; indeed on the belief that it was the *only* indispensable factor of production. Hence the artisan's objection to the capitalism which, in the early nineteenth century, increasingly denied the moral economy which gave the trades their modest but respected place, was not so much to working masters, whom they had long known, or to machinery as such, which could be seen as an extension of hand tools, but to the capitalist seen as an unproductive and parasitic middleman. Masters who belonged to the 'useful classes' both insofar as – to quote Hodgskin – 'they are *labourers* as well as their journeymen' and insofar as they were needed 'to direct and superintend labour, and to distribute its produce'[22] were fine: only, unfortunately, 'they are also' – Hodgskin again – 'capitalists or agents of capitalists, and in this respect their interest is decidedly opposed to the interests of their workmen.' Small masters raised no problem at all, and indeed could often be, or remain, members of unions. The theoretical foundations of early socialism, misnamed 'utopian', are to be found in this attitude. Essentially it envisaged the elimination of competition and the capitalist by means of cooperative production by artisans. Prothero has shown how artisans who began simply by trying to defend or re-restablish the old 'moral economy' could find themselves driven, under the pressure of the economic transformations of the early nineteenth century, to envisage a new and revolutionary way of re-establishing the moral social order as they saw it, and in so doing to become social innovators and revolutionaries. And Prothero has also, rightly, drawn attention to the fact that in this respect the evolution of the British journeyman artisan runs parallel with that of the continental, or rather French, ones.[23] Both tended to become politically active as artisans and in doing so to transform themselves into the 'working classes' or essential sectors of these.

Yet there is a vital difference. Utopian socialism, or rather mutualism and producers' cooperation, became and long remained the core of French socialism. But in Britain, in spite of occasional surges of popularity and an attraction for journeymen cadres, cooperative socialism was always a peripheral phenomenon, on the way to oblivion even as Chartism swept the country, the first mass working-class movement, in which journeymen artisans, like all

others under economic pressure, took their share. Socialism declined in the Britain of the 1840s, as it rose on the continent.
Whatever the reasons for this difference – and they remain to be
fully explained – they will probably have to be sought partly in the
political conditions of the country, but chiefly in the very advance
of the British capitalist economy over the rest, which already made
an economy of small commodity producers, individual or collective, somewhat implausible or economically marginal. Journeymen
were workers. They lived in a world of employers. Characteristically, the only form of cooperation which proved to have genuine
appeal from the start was that which sought to replace an economic
sector of small independents, namely the coop shop.

Thus the tradesman had no difficulty in coming to terms with an
economy of industrial capitalism, once that economy decided to
accept his modest claims to skill, respect and relative privilege, and
plainly offered expanding opportunities and material improvement.
And this clearly came to be the case in the 1850s and 1860s. Their
position may be symbolized in the anniversary dinner of the Cardiff
branch of the Amalgamated Society of Carpenters and Joiners in
1867, in the Masons Arms, 'nicely decorated with evergreens etc.
and over the head of the president's chair was a design portraying
the friendship existing between employer and workman, by their
cordially shaking hands'.[24] This iconographic theme appears frequently at the time.[25] 'In the background was represented the commerce of all nations and in the corner were busts of ancient philosophers etc. This design bore the following inscription: "Success to
honourable competition" and "the prosperity and wealth of nations are due to science, industry and a just balance of all interests".' It would be an error to suppose that such sentiments were
incompatible with going on strike.

It may be worth noting, as Richard Price reminds us, that if the
artisan certainly required collective organization, his collective
force is normally not yet to be measured by the membership of
trade unions. The general assumption, by Mayhew and others, was
that 'society men' represented perhaps 10 per cent of all but exceptional trades. Powerful bodies like the masons had perhaps 15
per cent of the trade organized in 1871, the carpenters and joiners
perhaps 11 to 12 per cent, the plasterers under 10 per cent.[26] The
Amalgamated Engineers with perhaps 40 per cent in 1861 were quite
exceptional.[27] Whether or when society men in unorganized trades

acted as pace-makers of economic advance, is today a re-opened question. At all events, in wage and hours movements there was no sharp distinction between the organized and the unorganized, inasmuch as both had the same interest in restriction against non-tradesmen. Thus among the bricklayers of poorly organized Portsmouth, where there were no indentured apprentices and 70 per cent of the men had just 'picked up' the trade, there was nevertheless no piece-work, and the advancement of labourers, once frequent, had become rare.[28] In Glasgow, where the Webbs found poor relations with employers, no working rules, no limit on apprentices and far from dominant unions, there was no piece-work, and labourers did not 'encroach'.[29] The truth is that craftsmanship was not only the criterion of a man's identity and self-respect, but the guarantee of his income. The best men, said a student of unemployment in the London building trade, always get work.[30] In the Amalgamated Carpenters and Joiners it was taken for granted that 'the success of the society depends on the members being invariably competent workmen',[31] and they were recruited accordingly, and indeed kept up to the mark. 'If a man's not worth 36 shillings a week', said the ASE *Monthly Record* proudly, though perhaps in 1911 no longer with total sincerity, 'the union has rules to deal with incompetence.'[32] Just so James Hopkinson had observed in the 1830s: 'Our shop was a strong union shop and the leading workmen in the town worked there.'[33] The small-arms fire with which the artisans fought the big guns of the employers derived its effectiveness from the ramparts of skill which protected it as well as the solidarity of the marksmen.

The skill, and the artisan's independence, were symbolized by the possession of personal tools,[34] those small but vital means of production, which enabled him to work anywhere at his trade. Broadhurst, the union leader and Lib-Lab MP, kept his mason's tools packed and ready throughout his time of political eminence: they were his insurance.[35] Many years later, in 1939, when the boiler-maker Harry Pollitt was deposed from his post in the Communist Party, his mother proudly wrote: 'Your marking-off tools are here, and I have kept them in vaseline, ready for use at any time.'[36] At a more modest level, when Jess Oakroyd, in J.B. Priestley's *Good Companions*, lost his job and went on tramp, the most important thing he took with him was his bag of tools.

The highest skills did not necessarily require the most expensive or elaborate tool-kit, though proud tradesmen – notably in wood-working – spent heavily on tools and luxury containers as status symbols. The ASCJ in 1886 limited benefit for the loss of a tool-chest, on the grounds that 'if a member takes a more valuable chest to work (i.e. than is necessary) he should do so at his own risk'.[37] Tool insurance by the union was usual among wood-workers, though less so among metal-workers, presumably because their personal tools were ancillary to shop equipment.[38] The 'tool bene-fit' of the ASCJ was clearly intended as a major selling-point for the union – it insured against theft, and not only against fire and shipwreck – and its importance is indicated by the frequency of branch resolutions and notices on the subject.[39] Indeed, in their first thirty years the amount of tool benefit paid per member was roughly comparable to accident benefit, and amounted to about 55 per cent of funeral benefit.[40]

Yet the value of implements was secondary to their symbolic importance. London shipwrights, than whom few were more skilled, owned perhaps 50 shillings' worth in 1849, according to Mayhew,[41] and in the 1880s the union paid 50 per cent of replace-ment costs up to a maximum of £5.[42] Mayhew estimated cabinet makers' tools at £30 to £40, joiners' tools at up to £30, coopers' at £12. These figures, except for carpenters and joiners, are rather higher than those quoted in the Royal Commission on Labour or derivable from the lists of stolen tools in the carpenters' reports; and according to both Mayhew and probability, tools were bought piecemeal in a man's last years of apprenticeship, and usually secondhand to begin with.[43] But they symbolized independence. Hence the disputes about 'grinding-time'. Since the tradesman brought to the job his skill and his tools, both must be absolutely ready for action. He and only he must sharpen them – at a weekly expense which was not negligible.[44] Logically the moment for this was at the end of the last job, and in the employer's time, which (or money in lieu) was expected to be made available.[45] Even today, as Beynon shows for Ford's, tools still imply some indepen-dence for tradesmen as against production workers.[46]

But if personal tools symbolized independence for the artis-ans, conversely control of the tools symbolized the superiority of management. We know that management was about to transform its plant organization, where emery wheels were taken from the shop and workers were no longer allowed to sharpen tools in their

own way and to their own specifications, but must have this done
to angles determined by others in a special tool-room.[47] And
characteristically, the tool-room was to remain the last stronghold
of the craftsman in the semi-skilled mass production engineering
works of the twentieth century. Even in the non-union motor industry between the wars, management would be careful of the
susceptibilities of the tool-room and turn a blind eye to the unionism of toolmakers. In the nineteenth century such control was most
visible in the giant railway companies, enterprises which employed
and trained numerous artisans and, though recognizing that their
foremen were essentially drawn from among them, and hence were
likely to have the artisan view,[48] saw no need for a symbiosis with
partly autonomous labour. Thus the Great Western and the Great
Eastern turned craftsman's pride into an obligation, by *obliging*
workmen, in the unilaterally imposed Working Rules, to buy and
insure their personal tools. Foremen in Stratford were to examine
the men's tool-chests before they were taken out of the works, and
in Derby they needed a special pass to do so.[49] The labour policies
of the railway companies, which deserve more study than they have
so far received in Britain, sometimes look as though they had been
specifically designed to replace craft autonomy and exclusive control by managerial control of hiring, training, promotion to higher
grades of skill and workshop operations.

For tools symbolized not merely the relative independence of the
artisan from management, but, even more clearly, his monopoly of
skilled work. The standard expression for what the unskilled or the
not specifically trained men must be prevented from doing at all
costs, i.e. 'encroaching' or 'following the trade', is some variant of
the phrase 'taking up the tools', or 'working tradesmen's tools' or
'getting hold of the tools for himself'.[50] Bricklayers' labourers, in
more than one set of working rules, are prohibited specifically from
the 'use of the trowel'.[51] Coopers' labourers were only allowed to
use some specified coopers' tools such as hammers.[52] Conversely,
artisans recognized each other's status by lending each other
tools.[53] In short, they may be defined essentially as tool-using and
tool-monopolizing animals.

The right to a trade was not only a right of the duly qualified
tradesman, but also a family heritage.[54] Tradesmen's sons and
relations did not only become tradesmen because, as among the
professional middle classes, their chances of doing so were notably

superior to the rest, but also, because they wanted nothing better for their sons, and fathers insisted on privileged access for them. Free apprenticeship for at least one son was provided for in many a set of Builders' Working Rules.[55] The formidable Boilermakers Society was largely recruited from sons and kin,[56] and in Edwardian London hereditary succession was considered usual among boiler-makers and engineers, in some printing trades, though among the builders only for the favoured masons, plasterers and perhaps plumbers. Here it was also pointed out that the attractions of office jobs for tradesmen's sons were small.[57] This is confirmed by the analysis of some 200 biographies from the *Dictionary of Labour Biography*[58] (mainly of those born between 1850 and 1900) which shows that, though the number of sons of non-tradesmen was only about 75 per cent of that of tradesmen, the number of tradesmen's sons who went into white-collar or similar jobs was not much more than half of that of non-tradesmen's sons. In short, for the Victorian artisan workshop education rather than schooling was what still counted, and a trade was at least as desirable or better than anything else effectively on offer. Indeed, the largest single group in the *Dictionary* sample (from which I have excluded the overwhelmingly self-reproduced miners) consisted of about seventy sons of tradesmen who took up trades, in about half the cases, their father's. And we know that in Crossick's *Kentish London* (1873–5) 43 per cent of the sons of engineering craftsmen were sons of men in these crafts, and 64 per cent came from skilled fathers in general; 64 per cent and 76 per cent of shipbuilding craftsmen came from shipbuilding and skilled families respectively; as did 46 per cent and 69 per cent respectively of building tradesmen. I leave open the question whether, as Crossick suggests, the links binding artisans together and separating them from the unskilled, actually tightened during the mid-Victorian period.[59]

This does not mean that entry into the trades was closed. It could hardly be, considering the rate of growth in the labour force, not to mention powerful enterprises like the railways, which deliberately saw to the training and promotion of unskilled labour, and provided a significant road for its upgrading; in the *Dictionary* sample this is very noticeable. What it does suggest is the relative advantage the stratum of tradesmen had in reproducing itself, and the significance within the skilled labour force of this block of self-reproducing artisans; and not least their capacity to assimilate the non-artisans who succeeded in joining their ranks, so long as artisan status meant a special and lengthy education in skill, essentially conducted by artisans in the workshop. And in 1906, according to an estimate, about 18 per cent of occupied males between the ages of fifteen and nineteen were still classified as apprentices and learners.[60] In industries and regions dominated by artisans – the northeast coast immediately comes to mind – their ability to assimilate new entrants was clearly enormous. One recalls that even in 1914, in spite of considerable efforts, 60 per cent of the workforce of the Engineering Employers' Federation were still classified as skilled.[61] Under these circumstances the artisans, or the bulk of them, were both privileged and relatively secure.

The crux of their position lay in the economy's reliance on *manual* skills, i.e. skills exercised by blue-collar workers. The real crisis of the artisan set in as soon as tradesmen became replaceable by semi-skilled machine operators or by some other division of labour into specialized and rapidly learned tasks, i.e. broadly speaking in the last two decades of the nineteenth century. This phase of artisan history has been fairly intensively investigated, at least for some industries,[62] and it is at this point that the main attack on the concept of an 'aristocracy of labour' has concentrated. Apart from a diminishing minority, the craftsman's position was no longer protected by the length of training and practice, by skill and the willing toleration of employers. It was protected primarily by job monopoly secured by trade unions and by workshop control. Yet the jobs now monopolized and protected were no longer skilled jobs in the old sense, though those who were best at protecting them were usually formerly skilled trades, like compositors and boiler-makers, which insisted on their members' monopolizing the new de-skilled jobs. But even this undermined the special position of the artisan. For, as we all now know from the Fleet Street printing trade, when skill and privilege or high wages are no longer correlated, artisans are merely one set of workers among many others who might, given the right circumstances – generally the occupation of a strategic bottleneck – establish such strong bargaining positions.

Speaking generally, at the end of the nineteenth century the trades found themselves, for the first time since the 1830s and 1840s, threatened by industrial capitalism as such but without the hope of bypassing it. Their existence as a privileged stratum was at stake. Moreover, the employers' *main* attack was now against their craft privileges. Hence, for the first time, their key sectors turned against capitalism. Thus unlike some of the traditional trades, the new metal-working crafts of the industrial economy had not been given to breeding political activists. There are few if any engineers and metal shipbuilders among the nationally prominent LibLab politicians before the 1890s. Yet almost from the start, engineers were prominent among the socialists. At the ASE's Delegate Meeting in 1912 more than half the delegates present appear to have been advocates of 'collectivism' to be achieved by class war.[63] The small argumentative Marxist sects like the SLP were full of them. Engineering shop stewards and revolutionary radicalism in World War I went together like cheese and pickles, and metalworkers – generally highly skilled men – later came proverbially to dominate the proletarian component of the Communist Party, to be followed a long way after by builders and miners.[64] The left attracted them for two reasons. In the first place a class-struggle analysis made sense to men engaged in battle with organized employers on what seemed to be the crucial sector of the front of class conflict; and by the same token the belief that capitalism wanted 'a just balance of all interests', was plainly no longer tenable. In the second place, the radical left in the unions, ever since the 1880s, specialized in devising strategies and tactics designed to meet precisely those situations which appeared to find traditional craft methods wanting.

I do not wish to underestimate this shift to the left, which now gave to the British labour movement a political outlook fundamentally different from that of Chartist democracy, which still prevailed amid the sober suits of Liberal Radicalism – a new political outlook which, some might argue, was *de facto* more radical than many continental socialist movements. At the same time this shift should not be identified with the various brands of socialist ideology which now sprang up, and, naturally, attracted young artisans conscious of their new predicament: in the 1880s men in their mid- to late twenties, from Edwardian times perhaps men in their late 'teens. For most tradesmen the shift to anti-capitalism simply began as an extension of their trade experience. It meant doing what they had always done: defending their rights, their wages and their now threatened conditions, stopping management from telling the lads how to do their job, and relying on the democracy of the workplace rank-and-file and against the world, which, if need be, included their unions' leaders. Only now they had to fight management all the time, because management was permanently threatening to reduce them to 'labourers', and now had the technical means to do so.

They were far from revolutionaries, but how did this constant confrontation differ from the class struggle which the revolutionaries preached? If the masters no longer recognized the interests of the skilled men, why should the men recognize those of the masters? I do not believe that many tradesmen were as yet affected by the drastic renunciation of old craft assumptions suggested by some of the ultra-left, who recommended fighting capitalism with its own market principles, by working as little or even as badly as possible for as much money as the traffic would bear. Such ideas were put forward in the syndicalist period. However, at this stage there is no evidence that tradesmen – still often suspicious of payment by results, though increasingly pushed into it – thought in such terms which, as the Webbs pointed out, undermined their basic principle of pride in work, rewarded by a wage which recognized their standing.

Yet the period from 1889 to 1914 introduces us to an artisan predicament which is similar to that of the British economy as a whole, because it is one aspect of it. Just as there were men in business who recognized that fundamental modernization was needed in the British productive system, but failed to mobilize sufficient support to achieve it, so also in the field of labour. The left, including the artisan left, knew that craft unionism of the high Victorian kind was doomed. It was the target of all critics. The mass of proposals for trade union reform between 1889 and 1927, ranging from federation and amalgamation to a complete restyling of the union movement along industrial lines,[65] were all directed against a position which was barely defended in theory even among the leaders of old-style craft unions. Yet no systematic general union reform was achieved, though craft unions recognized some need to expand, federate and amalgamate, and also accepted that elite organization must henceforth be part of the mass unionization of all workers, and that in such mass unionism the craft societies would inevitably be less dominant, either numerically or strategically. Yet attempts at general reform failed so clearly, that after 1926 they were *de facto* abandoned.

Railways and engineering are obvious examples of this failure. The new National Union of Railwaymen, designed as the model of a comprehensive industrial union, never succeeded in integrating most of the skilled footplate men, and the engineers did not even try, though their left-wing leadership time and again committed them to broaden their recruitment: in 1892, in 1901 and again in 1926. But as late as 1931 the Amalgamated Engineering Union told the Transport and General Workers:

With regard to the organizing activities of the AEU, whilst it was true that the constitution of the union was amended to permit of all grades of workers being organized within the union, this had not been operated, the AEU confining its organizing activities strictly to those sections of the industry which it had always organized. It was not the intention of the AEU to depart from this policy.[66]

For, just as the British industrial economy appeared to enjoy its Edwardian Indian summer, so did the artisans. Did they need to reform themselves out of existence? Sheer bloody-minded shop-floor resistance reversed the total victory won by the Engineering Employers' Federation in the 1897–8 lock-out, incidentally driving the union's socialist general secretary George Barnes into the wilderness.[67] It had so far restored the position that buying off the craftsmen became the major task of the 1914 war economy. Their position had actually been strengthened, because the system of payment by results, which employers preferred to Taylorist and Fordist strategies, laid the base for endless shop-floor conflicts and, in consequence, shop-steward power. Moreover, during the war the industry was flooded, not with promotable semi-skilled machine men, but with 650,000 women, virtually all of whom rapidly disappeared from the labour market after 1919. The union had to be defeated once again in frontal battle in 1922. After that unions were virtually driven out of such new sectors of the industry as motors and electrical goods, even though once again employers in general found the costs of systematic plant rationalization too high, and the foreseeable profits insufficiently attractive to justify such heavy outlays.

Once again the artisans therefore had their chance in the 1930s, as recovery, rearmament and war made times more propitious for labour organization. This was the last triumph of the Victorian trades. The men who brought the waters of unionism back into the desert of non-union shops were largely, perhaps mainly, craftsmen, like the toolmakers and the men who built the aircraft of the 1930s and 1940s, and whose role in the growth of mass metals unionism was crucial. They were the first nucleus of the revived shop-stewards' movement. These men were craftsmen, or at least, even when engaged on what was in effect semi-skilled work, craftsmen by background and training. They were now also largely communists, or became communists.[68]

Yet, whether they wanted to or not, they were initiating their own liquidation as a special stratum of the working class. This was largely because the mechanized engineering industries they organized no longer rested on artisan skill, though they still needed it. But it was also partly because the left no longer had a coherent union policy. Given the failure of general union reform, it lacked a practicable 'new model' of union organization. It benefited from a government policy, particularly from 1940 when Ernest Bevin took over the Ministry of Labour, which favoured unionism; but it neither controlled, nor often understood or usually even approved it. Its major weapon (leaving aside the production-oriented unionism of the communists in 1941-5) was much the same as in 1889-1921: sheer blinkered, dour, stubborn, defence of 'the custom of the trade' in the shops. It is irrelevant that some of the left may have identified this in some way with the road to revolution or at least to political radicalization. *De facto*, the left had no specific union strategy, but merely pursued the old tactics with intelligence, dynamism and efficiency – in a situation quite unlike that of 1889-1921.

What they achieved, was the generalization of the old craft-monopoly methods to all sectors of the trade union movement, and in industries where tradesmen formed a diminishing minority among the mass of semi-skilled operatives. And in doing so the artisans became merely one set of workers among many others who were in a position to apply such methods, and not necessarily the ones who could strike the best bargains. In the Fleet Street of the late twentieth century, not only has the qualitative difference between compositors and 'printers' labourers' disappeared, but the chapel of the National Graphical Association is not necessarily a more powerful bargainer than that of SOGAT '82. There is no longer anything special about being a tradesman.

Some are clearly on the way out, like the locomotive drivers of the old craft union ASLEF. Some survive, but in a world they no longer quite understand. It works for as much money as it can get, and nothing more.[69] This is a fundamental break in craft tradition, which, as has been argued, aimed at an income corresponding to the craftsman's status as a group, as professors still do.[70] Hence the persistent historical distrust of piece-rates. A communist engineer, interviewed by a researcher, recalls his amazement when he discovered during the war in Coventry that workers not merely could, but were *expected* to push their earnings into what seemed the stratosphere. And, indeed, the famous Coventry Toolroom Agreement of 1941 reflected this curious intermingling of old and new principles, until its breakdown in the 1970s. Whereas in the past the toolmakers' earnings had provided the measuring-rod of their 'differential' over and above less favoured groups, this differential was henceforth fixed against the entirely undetermined level of what non-toolmakers on piece-work could earn. Craftsmanship, *good work*, was no longer the essential foundation of good earnings. If anything, it was now a liability, since it stood in the way of the sky-high wages which could be earned by the men who deliberately and consciously put speed and skimping before sound work. Financially, the 'cowboy' – the term is of uncertain origin, but seems to emerge in the building trade during the hey-day of 'the lump' in the 1960s – could do better than the good tradesman.

Finally, the possibility of training as a craftsman grew less. In 1966 the number of apprentices was only about three-quarters of what it had been sixty years earlier, or indeed in 1925, and by 1973 it had plummeted to 25 per cent of the 1966 figure.[71] And so did the incentive to follow one's father into a proper trade. Book education and not skill is now the road to status and, with diminishing exceptions, even skill has moved into the world of diplomas. And, of course, the road into that world has broadened. There was a time when miners might want their sons out of the pit at all costs, but engineers were content to offer their sons a presumably improving version of their own prospects. How many of the sons of toolmakers today are content to become toolmakers?

The artisans no longer reproduce themselves or their kind. The generation of men who grew up with artisan experience and artisan values in the 1930s and 1940s, still survives, but is growing old. When the last men who have driven and cared for steam locomotives retire – it will not be long now – and when engine-drivers will be little different from tram-drivers, and sometimes quite super-fluous, what will happen? What will our society be like without that large body of men who, in one way or another, had a sense of the dignity and the self-respect of difficult, good, and socially useful manual work, which is also a sense of a society not governed by market-pricing and money: a society other than ours and poten-tially better? What will a country be like without the road to self-respect which skill with hand, eye and brain provide for men – and, one might add women – who happen not to be good at passing examinations? Tawney would have asked such questions and I can do no better than to conclude by leaving them with you.

(1983)

# 15: The 1970s: Syndicalism without Syndicalists?

Syndicalism in the literal sense was a philosophy and style of quasi-revolutionary trade-union action that first took shape in the French unions a little before 1900 and played a part of varying importance in the labour movements of a number of industrial countries for about twenty years. In Britain its influence was almost certainly much smaller than enthusiastic historians of the left have sometimes supposed. In any case, in this literal sense it is now dead and gone. However, the word has also been used metaphorically and polemically for other phenomena which have nothing to do with the original meaning of the word, such as 'the abuse of bargaining power by labour and other sectional interests at the expense of the general interest'. These metaphors do not concern us. But there is also a third sense, in which 'syndicalism' can stand for certain characteristics of labour movements which happen to have been particularly visible during the classical years of syndicalist agitation and ideology, but still survive – if in a truncated and peculiar fashion. This is why the subject is not of purely historical interest. The present paper looks at the industrial agitations of the 1970s in this light.

The original syndicalism consisted of four things: an attitude, a technique, a strategy and a hope. The attitude included hostility not only to the capitalist boss but to any bureaucracy, public, private or trade unionist, the belief (in G.D.H. Cole's words) that 'the producer should have the fullest possible share in the control of the conditions under which he works'[1] and a wish to substitute direct industrial action for politics, unions for parties. The technique relied on preferably spontaneous militancy in direct industrial action, a fight with the gloves off. Any means of effective pressure, i.e. of hurting where it hurt the adversary most, must be used: even sabotage, though this was more talked about than applied. This was rationalized into the thesis that workers must turn the capitalist's methods against them. The implications of this transfer of capitalist values to labour caused some uneasiness even then. Not only anti-syndicalists like Jaurès and the Webbs argued that this risked undermining the workers' pride and self-respect as workers, but so did Georges Sorel, the most formidable theorist of syndicalism.[2]

The strategy was of two kinds. In general it sought to raise class consciousness by multiplying militant strikes, any one of which might, with luck, precipitate the supreme form of class action, the revolutionary general strike, which (unlike the action of socialist parties) would overthrow capitalism. More specifically, syndicalists tried to reconstruct the union movement on democratic as against bureaucratic lines, as a class rather than sectional movement. This was sometimes conceived in the form of the 'one big union' consisting of industry-wide groupings ('industrial unionism') as against sectional or craft unions. The hope was that, after the revolution, the unions would turn into the basic organizations for production and distribution in a socialist society. This would therefore rest not on the oppressive centralized state but on functional self-governing producers' groups.

Both syndicalism in this specific historical and in the broader sense are rooted in two ancient and probably permanent characteristics of labour movements. The first is the tension between the 'political' and the 'industrial' aspects of labour movements, to use the familiar British terminology. The two have almost always been linked in some ways, even when the movement itself has not taken the political form of a party or parties specifically based on the working class and/or dedicated to the socialist transformation of society. A completely apolitical trade unionism hardly makes sense, and would today be about as unrealistic as a motor industry which claimed to have nothing to do with roads. At the same time there have always been tensions and divergences between the political and the industrial aspects of the movement.

This has been so from the early nineteenth century, though it was not very noticeable until both sides of labour came to be organized in what was supposed to be a single consolidated and coordinated movement. They became obvious even when the unions were *de facto* created by the socialist party, as often happened on the continent in the later nineteenth century, or when the party was designed as the political arm of the unions, as in Britain.

Sometimes, as in the German Social-Democratic Party before 1914, the unions were distinctly on the right wing of the party. Sometimes, as in France, they claimed to be so much to the left of it as to reject it and any politics as incurably opportunist. 'Syndicalism' as a concept and policy arose out of this rejection. But what is important is not the political topography of unions or parties at any given time, but the fact that both, though claiming to march arm in arm towards the common goal, were rarely in step for more than a brief period, unless one or the other or both were too weak to make more than public gestures.

The most obvious reason is that the daily work of any effective union, the defence and improvement of its members' (or potential members') conditions, insofar as this depends on collective bargaining, goes on under any government, and cannot but be concerned primarily with improvements *now*, whatever its hopes for the future, or its political sympathies and commitments. As we know, this may bring British unions into conflict even with Labour governments which they certainly much prefer to any available alternative, though in the days when all governments were 'bourgeois', things looked simpler. But in any case the most impassioned revolutionary Marxist union activist or leader – and there have been and are plenty – must spend most of his or her time on activities which could equally well be conducted in theory by someone uninterested in replacing capitalism.

In practice revolutionaries have made a disproportionately large contribution to trade unionism because, paradoxically, a lack of commitment to the *status quo* (including that in 'moderate' unions) has made them (in their industrial capacity) better at winning concessions. It has made them ready to pioneer new methods of union struggle, organization, strategy and tactics, and thus in Britain the extreme left – Marxist, syndicalist or whatever – has functioned not only as a training school for cadres but as a vanguard and brains trust of the movement ever since the 1880s. They also tend, at any rate in the early parts of their careers, to be less tempted by the fleshpots of capitalism and (even when not excluded from them by their allegiances) by the alternative careers open to them, e.g. in politics. Still, the fact remains that effective and militant unionism is not the same as making revolution. The syndicalists, who tried to get round the difficulty by claiming that it was, were proved wrong.

This preoccupation of unions with the present rather than the future reorganization of society and with their own narrow activities, has long caused much head-shaking in the movement. Pure anarchists worried about anarcho-syndicalists, and socialists or communists have rarely ceased complaining about 'economism' or 'corporativism'. Marxist theory before 1914 went so far as to argue (with Kautsky, followed by Lenin) that the workers themselves were capable of developing only a 'trade-unionist' class consciousness, leaving 'socialist consciousness' to be imported into the movement from outside. This desperate analysis is historically mistaken, but not irrelevant.

In fact, the original form of working-class socialism was entirely home-grown. Groups of workers envisaged the abolition of capitalism by means of a network of producers' cooperatives, since (with some justification) they could not see that the capitalist employers of the early nineteenth century fulfilled any technical or managerial functions which could not be just as well carried out by the people who actually did, and largely also organized, production. This ideal of 'mutualism' or a 'cooperative commonwealth' is often confused with the contemporary forms of what Marx called 'utopian socialism', and was sometimes, as in the case of Owenism, mixed up with it. Nevertheless it is best regarded as an independent form of artisan or semi-industrial workers' socialism.

We can now see, as Marx did, that this early industrial equivalent of the Russian *narodniks* or Spanish village anarchists, misunderstood both the nature and complexity of the modern economy and the extraordinary transformation of production and society which capitalism was even then beginning to bring about. It may have seemed plausible then to think of socialism as what was left when the superstructure of landlord and capitalist was stripped away, and competition was replaced by cooperation, though the problems of a national cooperative economy raised a few question-marks even then. It plainly became increasingly less plausible. Indeed, even in countries where producers' cooperation remained far stronger as an ideal and a limited reality than in Britain, where it rapidly dropped out of sight, the 'mutualist' perspective of socialism faded away. Syndicalism attempted to revive it but, except perhaps among Spanish anarchists, the actual ideas on how an economy run not by a collectivist state but by autonomous units of producers ought to operate, recognized complexities beyond the range of artisan cooperatives. Of course for most syndicalists (and to be fair, most other socialists) these were remote problems which would only arise after the revolution and would then somehow solve themselves economically. Unlike mutualist socialism, syndicalism was in practice a slogan of the struggle and not a programme for social transformation.

Where such mutualism or proto-syndicalism was strong, it left behind a strong distrust of 'politics' and an increasingly vague hope of social revolution by escalating direct industrial action into a revolutionary general strike. Everywhere it left behind a strong tradition of union democracy, of rank-and-file initiative and direct action, a belief that workers should be in charge of the actual labour process and a strong dislike of management interference on the shop-floor. The increasing scale, hierarchization and bureaucratization of production and management have reinforced these sentiments. But all this implied an instinctive restriction of rank-and-file workers' perspective to their particular group or place of work. The real unit of experience and action was and still is, let us say, Longbridge or Halewood (or even some part of these plants) and not British Leyland or Ford, let alone 'the motor industry' or 'the national economy'. This is natural enough. Even in the Russian revolution of 1917 it has been observed that the great street demonstrations contained relatively few workers: after the first few days they were holding meetings in their factories.

This built-in localism and sectionalism can be offset, or at least obscured, in various ways, quite apart from the reflex of class solidarity and mutual aid. Grass-roots movements tend to cluster at times of general working-class ferment and are easily propagated during such 'labour explosions' or revolutionary and other mobilizations. They are also unified by politics. Indeed, most (but not all) grass-roots 'labour explosions' have tended to be sparked off by events in the wider world of politics rather than internal developments in industrial relations, as in France in 1936 and 1968. Kautsky and Lenin were right to argue that the effective consciousness binding together all sections of workers as a class required something more than trade-union consciousness. It has been achieved by parties, often symbolized by individual leaders, but rarely if ever (without the help of parties) by national trade-union movements, which have usually been federations coordinating autonomous unions by means of grey and tactful functionaries. The great personalities of British unionism belong to and represent particular unions rather than the TUC: Arthur Horner and Jack Jones rather than Woodcock or Murray.

National trade-union organizations have always been aware of the need to weld such piles of localized and sectionalized action into a general movement and policy. And here lies the second root of 'syndicalism' in the wider sense. There is a permanent potential or actual tension between rank-and-file and leadership in unions. For, as the Webbs showed long ago, in spite of the deep-rooted union passion for direct local democracy, which still survives in the practice of decisions by mass meetings, an effective movement could not develop without national organization, discipline, leadership and full-time functionaries. The unions of classical syndicalism were mostly too ineffective for more than the occasional battle.

The question is one of balance. If it is tilted exclusively on the side of the rank-and-file, national unions might disintegrate, as sometimes happened in the nineteenth century, or become incapable of conducting a coherent policy for all their members. That danger is particularly great where, as often in Britain, they include a variety of groups or industries with divergent and sometimes conflicting interests. If it favours the leadership exclusively, as has been much more common (e.g. in the 1950s), the union risks losing contact with its members. British unions have striven in various ways, and with varying success, to combine or make allowance for both democracy and national leadership, but the balance is not often permanently stabilized.

It becomes particularly unstable, not only at times when the leadership wishes to impose unacceptable policies on the rank-and-file, but also when the basic pattern of industrial relations changes and established methods of organization, negotiation and struggle become irrelevant, ineffective and obsolescent. In the 1960s the Royal Commission on Trade Unions noted such a change: the shift of the centre of gravity in collective bargaining from broad and increasingly vague national agreements to plant negotiation, and with it the increasing role of shop-floor and plant leaders. At present the balance has therefore tilted towards the rank-and-file, with national leaderships falling into line. The situation is complicated by the changeover in the leadership of crucial national unions, by internal and inter-union rivalries, by technical and other changes, and above all by the conflict between the national economic policies of even Labour governments and the perfectly rational interest of unions in making the best bargain for their members.

How far is the 1970s British labour militancy comparable to classical syndicalism? Of the four main components of this now forgotten movement it has lost the strategy and most of the hope and retained some of the attitudes, but above all the technique. It is not directly concerned with restructuring society, and not so much an alternative to politics as unconcerned with them. Little is now heard about the systematic reconstruction of the union movement, let alone the syndicalist ideal of social transformation through unions, as it were, becoming the basic organs of society. In 1979 'The Miners' Next Step' (to quote the title of a famous syndicalist pamphlet of 1912) was to ask for a 40 per cent wagerise. In any case today those militants who hope that the industrial struggles will bring socialism closer, a matter which does not appear to concern most of the strikers, are not syndicalists. So far as one can tell, their hope lies in the *political* radicalization of the working class as a whole, precipitated by industrial struggles directly or indirectly. The evidence that this is happening is slim.

There remain the attitude and the technique. Both of them have something in common with classical syndicalism, though without the strategy and the hope they are impoverished. True, 'the fullest possible share in the control of the conditions under which (the producer) works' is once again a live issue, and, under such general labels as 'workers' control' and 'participation', has become part of the thinking of Marxists and others who did not, until the 1960s, pay much attention to it. To this extent demands pioneered by syndicalism have been revived – but mainly on the *political* left. Neither the practice nor the rhetoric of the actual industrial militancy of the 1970s reflect this preoccupation significantly. In fact, and in contrast to both the classical syndicalist era and the general tendency of strikes for a good deal of this century, the great strike movements of the 1970s are overwhelmingly economic in the narrowest sense.

So what we are left with is an essentially rank-and-file based, particularly militant and effective technique of strike action, of which the old syndicalists would certainly have approved, even though its aims are narrowly 'economist' and sectional: to raise wages, to hold or change the place of a group of workers in the pecking order of the pay envelopes, to protect jobs against redundancy, mechanization or other competing groups of workers. This has wider implications, including political ones, only insofar as the movement treats its demands as an inflexible first charge upon the economy, and refuses to consider their wider economic consequences. One hundred and fifty years of experience have made rank-and-file unionists sceptical of the argument that winning wage-rises produces economic catastrophe. That the situation may not look quite so simple when seen by governments or even at a national level of union leadership, is another matter.

The technique is effective because, unlike before 1914, complex, highly integrated societies can today be disrupted at very short notice by strategically placed groups of workers – and many more groups than ever before (but by no means all) are now strategically placed. It is all the more effective because one restraint of classical syndicalism has been tacitly dropped. Even Pouget, the champion of the extreme tactic of sabotage, made it quite clear – at least in public – that militancy was directed 'only against capital; against the bank-account'. 'The consumer must not suffer in this war waged against the exploiter.'[3] But the strength of strikes today, particularly in the public sector where the market and profits are not the determinants, rests largely on the ability to put political pressure on the government by the ability to make life difficult for the public, including all non-striking workers. It is pointless to pretend otherwise. Naturally they may think the inconvenience tolerable in a good cause and (if strong bargainers) look forward to using the same methods when their turn comes.

All this is inevitably a long way from syndicalism. If we forget the political cheers and hisses, the ideological commentaries and the wishful (or fearful) thinking, what we see today is a set of effective rank-and-file strike tactics being militantly applied by one group of workers after another, for objects which, even by the criteria of 'trade union consciousness' are rather narrow. At present union action is not only like what R.H. Tawney and Hugh Clegg (with differing sentiments) called 'an opposition that never becomes a government' but, to the disappointment of socialists and such syndicalists as may survive, it does not seem bothered about it. The sectionalism of industrial action imposes great and silent strains on class solidarity, strong though this is; for much of the militancy aims to increase inequalities within the working class and much has this effect without the intention. Striking workers are often uneasily aware of isolation. In spite of the hopes and efforts of the left, the militancy is largely apolitical. Indeed the gap between a militant and strong union movement and an organizationally enfeebled Labour Party, whose political support has long been eroding, is dangerously wide.

And yet, this militancy unquestionably reflects a striking assertion of class consciousness and class power: a combination of mass discontent with the discovery that a generation of unnoticed changes has given direct action a new effectiveness. The history of labour movements is punctuated by such moments of discovery or rediscovery at intervals of a few decades. France in 1968 and Italy in 1969 are recent examples. The present British wave of industrial militancy seems to lack the sense of hope and liberation, the almost holiday feeling of earlier 'labour explosions' – e.g. in 1889 or 1911. It is surrounded by doubt, uncertainty and bad temper. Nevertheless, it is a genuine class movement growing upwards from the grass roots, against which governments and even union leaderships are relatively powerless.

And in spite of the fact that our generations have been brainwashed by capitalism into the belief that life is what money can buy, there is more to this movement than asking for wage-rises. There is more even than despair about a society incapable of giving its members what they need, and forcing each individual or group to look after themselves, and never mind the rest. It has been said: 'Inside every worker there is a human being trying to get out.' In the history of the British working class there have been better and more hopeful attempts by the human beings to get out. But this *is* such an attempt. It will not do to dismiss it, damn it, and even less to wish it away. Attention must be paid. But it will not do either to overlook its limitations.

(1979)

# *16:* Should Poor People Organize?

Once upon a time, say from the middle of the nineteenth century to the middle of the twentieth, the movements of the left - whether they called themselves socialist, communist, or syndicalist - like everybody else who believed in progress, knew just where they wanted to go and just what, with the help of history, strategy, and effort, they ought or needed to do to get there. Now they no longer do. In this respect they do not, of course, stand alone. Capitalists are just as much at a loss as socialists to understand their future, and just as puzzled by the failure of their theorists and prophets. Liberals incline toward apocalyptic forecasts. The Catholic Church, which held the nineteenth century at bay with surprising success, is visibly succumbing to the late twentieth. At the end of the most extraordinary period of transformation in human affairs, old landmarks have disappeared, new ones are not yet recognized as such, and intellectual navigation across the suddenly estranged landscapes of human society becomes unusually puzzling for everybody.

Neither the practice nor the theory of the left, the latter pouring out in a record-breaking flow of print, can be properly understood without an appreciation of this secular crisis, which, more often than not, is reflected only obliquely in recent commentary: through the discussion of theories and strategies in general, rather than of the changes in reality which have thrown doubt on both. Piven and Cloward's remarkably interesting book,[1] which belongs firmly in the left-wing tradition, is almost exclusively concerned with the strategies of 'poor people's movements'. It makes a general analysis of such movements and considers the experience of four of them in the United States during the 1930s and 1960s: that of the unemployed workers during the Depression years; of the industrial workers who formed the CIO; of the civil rights activists centred around Martin Luther King; and of those who made up the Na-

tional Welfare Rights Organization in the 1960s. Piven and Cloward argue that all leaders of such movements have been on the
wrong track throughout, in trying to organize them. Building an
organization is not merely futile but dangerous:

> During those brief periods in which people are roused to indignation, when
> they are prepared to defy the authorities to whom they ordinarily defer
> ... those who call themselves leaders do not usually escalate the momen-
> tum of the people's protests. They do not because they are preoccupied
> with trying to build and sustain embryonic formal organizations in the
> sure conviction that these organizations will enlarge and become powerful.

This proposition could be discussed on its merits, and indeed has
to be. Yet it cannot be adequately discussed, or indeed even understood outside the historical context which encourages the
authors to formulate it. For whatever their theory, virtually all who
have had anything to do with modern labour and socialist movements (except the anarchists) have hitherto taken it for granted
that the way to the future, whatever it might be, led through *organization:* through associations, leagues, unions, and parties, the
more comprehensive the better.

That this must be the case seemed so evident and so clearly
proved in practice that the belief itself was hardly ever investigated
seriously. Historically, for instance, the debate on organization
within the labour movement has been primarily about its scale,
pausing only occasionally to consider problems of flexibility, and
internal democracy. The left stood for national unions against local
or regional ones; for industrial against craft associations, for big
against little unions – perhaps even for the One Big Union which
was, for the syndicalists, the estuary through which the river of the
movement reached the sea of socialism. The working ideal of the
labour movement has been a disciplined and mobile army, though
a civilian and democratic one; as witness the widespread unconscious, and insufficiently investigated popularity of military metaphors in its language. 'The ever-expanding union of the workers'
of the *Communist Manifesto,* which could 'centralize the numerous
local struggles into one national struggle between classes', implied
organization. What is more, the purely pragmatic arguments for
organization have appeared so convincing that the organizers have
overwhelmingly prevailed over the anti-organizers for the past century and a half.

It is true that opponents of organization, in one form or another, have surfaced from time to time. Generally this has occurred in one of three situations: when the movement has been broken and weak; when it was becalmed; or - a somewhat different situation - in pre-industrial communities. In the first case occasional mass mobilization by small groups of activists, or comparable techniques, were not adopted as an alternative to organization but as a poor substitute for it. If the Lawrence, Massachusetts, textile workers could have been organized during 1912 by an effective union, as Lancashire cotton operatives were, they would not have had to rely on heroic raids by the IWW. The third case does not concern us here. For what made modern mass organization apparently irrelevant to, say, Andalusian anarchist *pueblos* or highly skilled pre-industrial craftsmen was the informally or traditionally structured cohesion of their communities or occupations, and their (increasingly unreal) belief that the decisions which determined their lives were either cosmic or purely local. The former being a matter for hope or millennial convulsion, only the latter were of practical everyday concern.

The second case is the one which has traditionally stimulated a systematic *critique* of organization, because it seemed that radical movements which were not getting anywhere tended to substitute their organizational growth for real achievement, and, conversely, that the concentration on the organization and its activities as such made them into participants in the system, led them to miss - or even worse to dismiss - various opportunities for struggle, and produced various kinds of bureaucratic and oligarchic ossification. The mass socialist parties before 1914, especially the German Social-Democratic Party (SPD), were rightly criticized on those grounds by a variety of rebels, revolutionaries and militants as well as by disappointed intellectuals (e.g., Robert Michels). The 1960s stimulated analogous criticisms of established mass labour and socialist organizations in another period of apparently stable and flourishing capitalism. Piven and Cloward are part of such a wave critical of organization, though, unlike most familiar critics of this kind - anarchists, followers of Rosa Luxemburg, etc. - they are not primarily concerned with the long-term dangers of bureaucratic or totalitarian transformations of organization but almost entirely with its inadequacies as a means of mobilizing mass movements here and now.

The periodic fashions for anti-organization did not and could not last. Either they collapsed more or less rapidly, like the student movements of the 1960s, or they themselves tried, often rather ineffectively, to transform themselves into something like permanent mass organizations, as the 'anarcho-syndicalism' of the CNT in Spain tried to substitute itself for pure anarchism. The heirs of the pre-1914 anti-organizational rebels were to be the super-organizations of the communist parties. The vast transfer of formerly anarchist support in Barcelona to the communists is a belated example of this phenomenon. What else could be expected? In the broadest and most general sense, to quote Robert Michels (no friendly witness), 'democracy is unthinkable without organization. Only organization gives consistency to the masses.' In the narrower sense it pays off in everyday experience. If industrial workers have the choice between even a corrupt and racketeering union and no union at all, few would hesitate before making their choice.

The situation which encourages a policy opposed to organization is thus historically specific; which does not, of course, necessarily invalidate the criticisms of organization. They reflect a sense of failure, and perhaps even more, a crisis of confidence. In Piven and Cloward's case, part of this disappointment derives from the particular experiences of the left in the US during the 1960s, the specific problems of trying to mobilize extremely unstructured groups of 'the poor' (e.g., blacks on relief), and the disillusion of the authors with the campaigns with which they have been actively associated, and on which they speak with first-hand authority, such as the 'welfare rights' movements of the 1960s.

Whatever the gains of the black movements of the 1960s, which Piven and Cloward are far from denying, one of the most obvious results has been to absorb 'much of the leadership of the black movement ... into electoral politics, into government bureaucracy, into the universities, and into business and industry', leaving the masses as leaderless as before; perhaps, for the time being, more so than before. However, both their argument and their air of disenchantment with the established model of past movements are more general. Of the four movements they have chosen, two are indeed marginal. The object of the unemployed in the 1930s and the welfare rights protests of the 1960s was relief. But the other two were central. Unionization in the 1930s and the civil rights movements in the 1960s were not only intended to change the situation of *all*

workers and blacks (and not only a section of the working population), but capable of doing so; and they were able as well to
change the structure of industrial relations and national politics.

The lengthy and well-documented chapters on these four movements may be read simply as fascinating and intelligent analytical
surveys of chapters in recent American history; but for the authors
they are primarily illustrations of their central thesis. The curve of
all of them, as Piven and Cloward see it, was similar, though the
incubating period of the civil rights movement was both longer and
less dramatically sudden than that of the other three: the Great
Slump and the political events of the 1960s, including the civil
rights breakthrough. A phase of unarticulated discontent ('Folks
are restless' as a senator they quote put it) is followed by a cluster
of local eruptions, led (if at all) by relatively tiny cadre-groups.
Conflicts escalate in a political situation which has become uncertain. The authorities make concessions – and the activist movements stop the pace of disruption and choose instead to exercise
further pressure through mass organization and to use both the
new machinery for concession and the apparently promising and
welcoming old machinery of established politics, with varying
results.

And so, as Piven and Cloward see it, the unemployed groups of
the 1930s 'had become entangled in bureaucratic procedures and
were declining'. The industrial unions 'had become over time less
and less dependent on the workers and more and more dependent
on the regular relations established with management'. As for black
leaders, most 'depend on the Democratic Party and its continued
ability to command a majority of the electorate', which is not
black. The National Welfare Rights Organization 'had relatively
little influence in the lobbying process' to which it progressively
devoted its (therefore) inevitably declining years. After the bang,
the whimper.

The air of pessimism which pervades *Poor People's Movements*
thus expresses more than the disappointment of the hopes of the
1960s. The fundamental proposition on which Piven and Cloward
build their strategic recommendations is the impotence of the poor.
'The poor can create crises but cannot control the response to
them.' They can merely get a slightly better or a slightly worse deal
within quite narrow margins, largely predetermined. 'Protestors
win, if at all, what historic circumstance has already made ready to

be conceded.' Even if the workers in the 1930s 'had demanded public ownership of factories, they would probably have still gotten unionism, if they got anything at all; and if impoverished southern blacks had demanded land reform, they would probably still have gotten the vote'. It is not negligible, but it is not what we wanted, and neither are the results. Capitalism inevitably reintegrated poor people's protests.

What lies behind this sense of disenchantment? Not the failure to achieve any results, which has dogged some movements of the left, such as the anarchists, since the movements Piven and Cloward discuss had distinct successes, even disproportionate ones, considering their actual strength. Certainly what disorients the left is not that the case against capitalism seems less convincing than it used to, or less easy to make (unless we insist on denying that capitalism has changed since the days of Marx and Lenin). Indeed, it is rather easier today to predict a dark future for humanity under capitalism that it has been for a generation. Admittedly the experience of both Western industrial societies and socialist regimes has shown the inadequacy of the traditional conception of socialism, which was usually, and simply, defined by its opposite; or defined even more naïvely as what capitalism at any given time did not provide.

The realization that the critique of capitalism does not automatically tell us much about socialism has certainly been traumatic. It is now clear that the 'expropriation of the expropriators' by itself may produce a noncapitalist society, but not necessarily a desirable one. It is also clear that capitalist evolution has provided much that older socialists thought impossible, and that this foretaste of what used to be utopia is not very desirable either. We now have much of what a Spanish anarchist congress in 1898 forecast as the glorious future of man after the revolution, namely a world of high-rise buildings full of elevators, electricity, and automatic rubbish disposal, and inhabited by supervisors of automated machinery. This, as we know, is as far from utopia as the abolition of the distinction between town and country by means of radio, television, and the internal combustion engine. Still, if the left may have to think more seriously about the new society, that does not make it any the less desirable or necessary, or the case against the present one any less compelling.

But what radicals and socialists no longer know is how to get from the old to the new. Neither capitalism nor its designated gravediggers are any longer what they were in 1914 or even in 1939. The historical forces and mechanisms on which socialists relied to produce an increasingly militant proletariat and increasingly vulnerable capitalist ruling class are not working as they were supposed to. The great armies of labour are no longer marching forward, as they once seemed to, growing, increasingly united, and carrying the future with them. It is significant that Piven and Cloward's social movements are, as the title of their book indicates, not 'the workers' (whose disintegration as a class or 'balkanization' they note in passing) but 'poor people', a heterogeneous body whose sections have nothing in common but relative poverty and the fact of discontent. The content of their movements, as shown by the title of their first chapter, is merely 'protest'.

The strategists of the left are at a loss. How much more modest are the actual aspirations of the great socialist mass-parties (where they still exist in Europe) than in the days of Bebel, Adler, and Jaurès, as well as the hopes – and this at a time of global capitalist crisis – of the communist parties than when their leaders were young. Few who lead substantial and politically effective parties of the left in the Western world any longer believe in victory by frontal offensive, whether peaceful or not. But neither are they at all clear about the alternative prospect of the Gramscian 'war of position' in which they are involved, or even about precisely who this war is against. A cautious and complex strategy may eventually transform capitalism into socialism, but it is fair to say that at present nobody has a clear idea how, let alone when.

Emotionally, the responses to this frustration may range from the rejection of the reality that has not lived up to the theory, to the rejection of the gods and theories that have failed – often, as with the current ex-Maoist, anti-Marxist 'new philosophers' of Paris, by the same people. Intellectually, the range of choices is considerably wider and its results more interesting. They include systematic efforts to rethink both the theories and traditions of socialism and the history of popular and labour movements; for it is characteristic of the present crisis that it has not, on the whole, produced a contraction, but a striking expansion of the European intellectual left, though of a rather puzzled left. Politically, the choices have become increasingly restricted by the dramatic failures and disappointments of the 1960s and 1970s.

Yet one modest and uncontroversial task remains unaffected by failures: getting the best deal for the poor here and now. New societies may not be on the immediate agenda, but getting more people jobs, or on relief, is. The poor can't achieve much anyway, and they can't control their destiny. Let them at least bargain from strength on the rare occasions when they have some strength to bargain with. This is the task on which Piven and Cloward concentrate, and it is perhaps natural that a book such as theirs should come out of the problem-solving United States, in which the prospect of a fundamental social transformation never looked particularly imminent.

Their analysis therefore deliberately keeps its nose to the ground. It rests on the correct assumption that poor people do not usually find ways of expressing their discontents effectively or at all, mainly because a stable social order makes them docile and keeps them so by the knowledge of their political weakness. They are only likely to 'break the bonds of conformity enforced by work, by family, by community, by every strand of institutional life', and by the moral hold ('legitimacy') which people at the top usually exercise over people at the bottom, during periodic dislocations of the social order.

The Great Slump was plainly such a dislocation. In the relations between white and black, the 1960s saw the accumulated tensions arising out of the transformation of the South and the emigration to the Northern ghettoes reach their breaking-point. Piven and Cloward argue that the part of the structure of rule most sensitive to pressure at such moments in the United States was politics. For it is during such dislocations that people in a voting society show signs of 'a sharp shift in traditional voting patterns', which is thus 'one of the first signs of popular discontent'. The shift toward the Democrats in the 1930s, the shift away from the Democrats in the South and the competition for what (they argue) was regarded as a potentially movable black vote in the 1950s and 1960s were thus not only signs of crisis, and recognized as such, but also means for disposing politicians to make concessions.

Thus such dislocations will disorient or divide the elites – some of whom may actually appeal to the poor at such times – while simultaneously weakening the structure of power, which thus becomes more vulnerable than usual to pressures from those it can normally neglect. This analysis is similar to the classic one of 'revolutionary situations', though Piven and Cloward are interested in less spectacular crises.

We are not here concerned with the authors' specific analysis of the 'dislocations' of the 1930s and 1960s, which may be less comparable than they suggest. In spite of the significance of FDR's Wagner Act, it seems likely that the black movements of the 1960s were much less the power which forced the government's hand, and much more the – unpredictably escalating – response to what looked like encouragement from above, than had been the case in the 1930s. The major point of Piven and Cloward, I take it, is to identify situations which make the system sensitive to pressure from below.

However, the pressure of 'the poor' itself is institutionally determined by what the system establishes as legitimate protest (for instance, in parliamentary-democratic states, voting) and, when it goes outside the permitted forms, by what the actual situation of the protesters urges and permits them to do. What it urges them to do is to aim protests about specific grievances at specific targets. Piven and Cloward have clearly grasped a point which often eludes ideological analysts, namely that workers 'do not experience monopoly capitalism' but the factory, the assembly line, the foreman, the pay packet, and the employer; and people on relief 'do not experience American welfare policy' but shabby waiting rooms, overseers, case workers, and the dole.

On the other hand, what the situation permits protesters to do depends on how the protesting groups have organized everyday lives and their labour. Most of the protesting poor, unlike factory workers, are relatively unstructured. Nevertheless, what they can always do, if there is any possibility of action at all, is to rebel 'against the rules and authorities associated with their everyday activities', i.e., to withdraw collaboration. The most original contribution of Piven and Cloward to the subject is their argument that this local rebellion is actually the most effective form of action open to them. If protesters did anything else they would be less effective, since 'people cannot defy institutions to which they have no access, and to which they make no contribution' – such as Congress. A crowd of welfare clients outside a state capitol or in Washington is more easily ignored than the same crowd breaking up a relief office, especially if a lot of crowds break up such offices. Similarly, Piven and Cloward argue, the anti-Vietnam students were strategically right to demonstrate *in the universities*, though administrators and faculty probably shared their views of the war.

In short, for Piven and Cloward there are times when the man who has been robbed by a big man and beats up a little one instead, because it is easier, can make a rational political case for himself.

What the poor can do is to disrupt and *rely on the political reverberations of their disruption*, which will be considerable in times when the social and political system is dislocated, which are precisely the times when the poor can be moved to disruption. This does not give them much leverage, and their action cannot be effectively planned or its results controlled. The results will be controlled by those who make concessions from above, but concessions will be made. At such times 'a defiant poor may make gains'. Yet the very process of concession from above which gives them these gains is also one which attempts to reintegrate protest into 'more legitimate and less disruptive forms of political behaviour', e.g., by coopting its leaders. When protest is thus swallowed by the institutions, the poor give up the one thing which actually extorts improvements: their refusal to play the established game. They are once again disarmed. But a movement which instead of escalating disruption concentrates on transforming it into permanent organization helps to reinstitutionalize and therefore to dismantle it. The poor, even if they do not lose all their gains, are once again forced to wait for the next crisis.

This argument is unsatisfactory, but its main point is not to be dismissed. For 'organization' undoubtedly needs to be realistically analyzed. It can readily be shown that the immediate successes of popular movements are not proportionate to their degree of organization. Mass union organization, in the US of the 1930s as in all analogous 'explosions' of labour unionism with which I am familiar, was the *result* of worker mobilization and not its cause. Such mobilization requires stimulation and leadership, but it is an error to suppose that these are inseparable from mass organization. In the extreme case of revolution the divergence is even more spectacular. As distinct from coups, launched from positions of established power, successful revolutions are hardly ever planned, in spite of the efforts to do so. They happen, sometimes, though today not usually, in the actual absence of organized revolutionaries.

It is equally evident that the attempts to build permanent mass organizations out of unorganized constituencies ('the unemployed', draft resisters, consumers, or even such more existentially cohesive groups like blacks and women) have almost universally failed. Such organizations, generally feeble and fluctuating, are either groups of leaders whose aim is to mobilize essentially unorganized masses for action, or more likely stage armies marching about making a noise like real armies and, with luck, being accepted as the representatives and interlocutors of their constituencies, because under certain circumstances the institutional system requires someone to fill this role. But, as Piven and Cloward clearly recognize, the strength of such stage armies depends not on the few people they can actually put into uniform, but on the need to consider the unorganized masses off stage. The National Welfare Rights Organization, with a few thousand dues-paying members, gained money and official recognition because it 'could present itself as the representative of the welfare poor'. And since the 'political influence of the poor is mobilized, not organized', organization which gets in the way of mobilization is self-defeating.

Thirdly, it is sometimes even true that firmly structured and organized movements are less effective at mobilizing mass discontent than loose and unstructured ones. These may not last, but while they do they can be unusually formidable, precisely by virtue of their capacity to catch and propagate a mood at a crucial moment to discover and secure that spontaneous consensus among militants and masses which produces massive action. The student movements of the 1960s are textbook illustrations of this. Nobody could have planned them. Nobody will underestimate their scale, scope, and impact at the time. But it must be admitted their limitations were equally spectacular.

Piven and Cloward's powerful contribution to the cause of realism is therefore welcome. They may (as they themselves recognize) no longer surprise many historians of social movements, but their book will clear the minds of politicians, for a lot of politics still takes place in those thick clouds of ideological myth, traditional folk wisdom, and self-delusion which this activity generates around itself, especially when nobody quite knows what is happening. Moreover, it is important to demystify specific concepts such as 'mass movement' and 'mass organization' and to see what precisely they mean in practice. For these reasons their book is enormously instructive.

However, it is also inadequate, because its field of vision is excessively restricted. Or rather, the authors take too much for granted. Thus in the narrowest sense their criticism of organization in specific movements assumes the existence of organization as an essential factor in situations where such 'protests' arise. Any historian of past social movements is familiar with episodes which conform exactly to the Piven–Cloward formula of escalated defiance winning concessions undisturbed by the desire to collect dues, draft constitutions, and organize congresses. But *only* historians are familiar with them, since, in the absence of organization, they disappear rapidly, leaving nothing behind. What the mobilization of American workers in the 1930s won was not entirely lost because it produced permanent mass unionism; but the labourers' insurrection in the Peruvian highlands which briefly forced collective contracts on the great estates in 1948 came, went, and was forgotten.

In a wider sense 'the poor', or indeed any subaltern group, become a subject rather than an object of history only through formalized collectivities, however structured. Everybody always has families, social relations, attitudes toward sexuality, childhood, and death, and all the other things that keep social historians usefully employed. But, until the past two centuries, as traditional historiography shows, 'the poor' could be neglected most of the time by their 'betters', and therefore remained largely invisible to them, precisely because their active impact on events was occasionsal, scattered, and impermanent. If this has not been so since the end of the eighteenth century, it is because they have become an institutionally organized force. Even the most dictatorial regimes today learn sooner or later what ancient rulers knew, how to make concessions to unorganized and spontaneous pressure from the masses, if necessary underlining their continued authority by face-saving punishment for 'agitators'. It is *organized* popular action they seek to prevent. What is lacking in Brazil today is not popular unrest but organizations that could mobilize that unrest.

Of course this poses a double dilemma for populists, democrats, and the left in general. Organizations, which give reality to 'the people', class or group, are by definition superimposed on them, and tend to substitute themselves for their members and constituents, subject to various limitations, generally inadequate. More to Piven and Cloward's point, their very strength – permanence, planning, long-term perspectives – may get in the way on days of battle. Militants blamed the French Communist Party on these grounds both in 1936 and 1968. For paradoxically, even if they are devoted to revolution, revolt is not the forte of organizations.

Non-revolutionary grass-roots insurrections, which are what Piven and Cloward write about, do not find organizations at their best. It is not on the first day of battle that organizations come into their own but from the second day on.

But then they become indispensable, even – perhaps especially – for movements which conform to the Piven–Cloward formula, which is 'to escalate the momentum and impact of disruptive protest at each stage of its emergence and evolution'. For the authors are not blind utopian sluggers, for whom escalation is an end in itself (*'soyons réalistes, demandons l'impossible!'*), but are concerned about what more could have been got for the poor out of the New Deal and the 'Great Society'. But to call for escalation in itself is merely to press for as much as possible, without any mechanism for deciding not only *how much* is possible, but how much of *what*. If no one else formulates the content of the concession, it can only be done by the ruling elites themselves, to suit themselves. The movement remains, in the authors' own words, one of 'protest', which is by definition the reaction of the subalterns. The organizations of the left may at such times be blamed for recommending the wrong policies, but right or wrong they are the only bodies which can formulate *policies* for the poor and, with luck, make them effective. They are essential for those who want to improve society, because for them the problem is not to get more or less of the same, but something different.

Of course, Piven and Cloward are pessimistic about the chances of achieving such results. The poor, they say, can only 'create crises'. They 'cannot control the response to them'. Yet the pessimism which overshadows such books as theirs should be evenly distributed. The other face of the disorientation of the left today is the disorientation of capitalism. Non-socialists are also rudderless, in spite of a large expenditure on futurology, a pseudo discipline invented for this reason. Quite apart from the present global economic crisis, the foundations on which the stability and progress of 'bourgeois society' were built are also visibly crumbling: the work ethic, the family, established relations between sexes and age groups, the acceptance of social norms ('law and order'), even the long-accepted framework and function of its basic political unit, the medium-sized or large nation state. Moreover, 'the system' cannot always absorb or even afford the concessions – quantitative or qualitative – forced upon it from below. There are countries, such as Britain and Italy, in which this poses major economic and political problems at this moment.

In fact, the mid-nineteenth-century liberals' suspicion that democracy would prove incompatible with a market economy may well prove as justified in the late twentieth century as some other long-dismissed predictions of the time, such as the disappearance of the peasantry. In short, if the masses are incapable of controlling, or even predicting, their destiny, neither at present are the elites. A lot of *them* would pay good money to know whom, if anybody, the mechanisms of history are working for as the year 2000 approaches.

That is why the Piven–Cloward formula for action, which is to wait for a propitious moment, push hard, and see what happens, is a peculiarly uncertain as well as limited guide. It assumes that the qualitative response to 'protest' is already structured. The political system will always know what to concede, though it can always afford, if pressed, to give a little more. Its concessions will bring 'the poor' some gains, but at the price of reabsorbing protest into the system, until the cycle is broken by another crisis permitting another mobilization of mass discontent, which will have the same results.

But this is no longer so. The role of 'poor people's movements' is no longer simply to push and receive, for its demands, which can no longer be necessarily integrated into the operations of the system, help to change and shape it. It is characteristic of the present state of the world that nobody can be quite sure 'what historical circumstance has made ready to be conceded', or what the consequences of concessions will be for the poor or for the system. The only thing certain is that, short perhaps of military dictatorship and terror, nobody controls the response to crises unilaterally, and even dictatorship cannot control their consequences. In short, what 'the poor' do matters. They need, more than ever, not only a strategy of effective pressure but policies – and bodies capable of carrying out policies. They are not outside the system, battering, but inside, potentially able to transform it.

Here lies the essential weakness of the strategies of blind militancy of which Piven and Cloward provide us with one version. It is not enough to push and see what will happen. The apparently dramatic changes in the university system made as a concession to the European and American student insurrections neither achieved what the students wanted (if they knew), nor have they worked to the evident advantage of either students or the system. It is not enough to tell them (or any other body of potential insurrection-aries) that, next time they have the opportunity, they can get more.

(1977)

# *17:* Labour and Human Rights*

Philosophers have argued about the nature of rights with greater zeal and competence than historians; not least American philosophers, and not least today. I do not want to venture into the minefield of such discussions, but the least even a historian can do is to say clearly in what sense he uses the word 'rights'. Here I shall use it to mean simply any form of entitlement which a person or a group of people can claim under some positive law which, at least in principle, penalizes the refusal to grant this entitlement. I also use it for entitlements which they believe they can claim on grounds of a widely acccepted set of beliefs about what such entitlements should be, even if it is not expressed in any actual legally enforceable law, but based on some moral or ideological belief. This may, of course, be formulated in quasi-legal terms such as those which claim 'natural rights' under 'natural law' against the existing law, or the superiority of custom to government law. Such a set of beliefs must be widely accepted, though it often happens that several such sets of beliefs about rights coexist in a society, and may be in conflict. Rights which are not based on such a consensus cannot be distinguished easily, or at all, from subjective desires. A 'right' is something which must be recognized as such by other people. A man who feels he needs my money badly enough and has a knife may mug me, and may even privately think he is justified in doing so. But whether he has a right to do so, depends on what others think, not he alone.

I also want to make two supplementary points. We can only talk realistically of 'rights' where they can be secured by human action. Farmers may assert legal or other rights to irrigation, but none of

---

*This chapter was originally given as a lecture at Emory University, Atlanta, Georgia, in 1982.

them are fools enough to assert a right to rain. And, from a historian's point of view, rights don't exist in the abstract, but only where people demand them or may be assumed to be aware of their lack. We may, on philosophical grounds, think that all people ought to have the right to choose whether to eat ham or not, but it would be quite anachronistic and unreal to accuse, say, Jewish communities in the sixteenth century of violating the human rights of their members by not giving this option. A right is what is recognized as such.

Now the main connection between the history of labour movements, which are a historically fairly modern phenomenon, and human rights, is that labour movements are by and large composed of people who are in F.D. Roosevelt's phrase 'under-privileged', and are concerned with their problems. That is to say they are concerned with people who, by the definitions of their times, have no such rights or less rights than other people and groups. Now people rarely demand rights, fight for them, or are worried about them, unless they do not enjoy them in sufficient measure or at all, or if they do enjoy them, unless they feel that these rights are insecure. Nobody has ever started a movement for the right to walk, because all of us take it for granted that we can when we want to, and are unlikely to be stopped. On the other hand there have been agitations for the right to walk for certain purposes – for instance in public demonstrations – or in certain places – for instance along public rights-of-way closed by private landowners – or at certain times. And, of course, the right not to be arbitrarily jailed (which would interfere with walking) forms part of most Declarations of Human Rights. Special groups of people who expect to enjoy certain entitlements rarely bother to demand what they already have. The rich do not have to bother about the right to free or cheap medical treatment. It is the poor who have to. Labour movements are concerned with people who have cause to demand a lot of rights, and that is why, irrespective of their philosophical attitude to 'natural law', political theory, or the legal theory of justice and rights, they have played a very large role in the development of human rights. And, it might be argued, that is really all that needs to be said about the subject of this paper.

However, the historian cannot be content with this obvious observation. For European labour movements came into existence, and consequently began to influence the struggle for human rights and their definition, at a time when the concept of such rights itself was undergoing rather profound changes. In fact, at that time a variety of *types* of 'rights' coexisted, each influencing and being influenced by the special characteristics and requirements of labour movements, and by developments arising out of their existence.

For 'rights', whatever some philosophers say, are not abstract, universal and unchanging. They exist as parts of particular sets of beliefs in the minds of men and women about the nature of human society and the ordering of relations between human beings within it: a model of the social and political order, a model of morality and justice. It is possible that, as Barrington Moore has argued,[1] there is a general conception of what is just or unjust which holds good for all societies at all times, but in practice the concrete set of beliefs about rights is not the same for all societies, places and periods. But what is certainly true is that, to my knowledge, there is no society which does not recognize some rights, for at least some of its members, and rejects claims to others. It is doubtful whether any society could exist which fails to establish such distinctions.

Certainly the common labouring people of most of pre-industrial Europe believed they had or could claim some rights. What is more, even when these rights were not recognized as legally enforceable before the courts of the governing authorities, which they might or might not be, certain such entitlements were morally accepted even by governments and ruling classes. Thus the preamble to the Elizabethan Statute of Artificers of 1563 plainly regarded it as the state's duty to 'banish idleness, advance husbandry and yield unto the hired person both in the time of scarcity and the time of plenty a convenient proportion of wages'.[2]

This was part of that 'moral economy' which E.P. Thompson has discussed so well.[3] It was based on a general view of what constituted a just social order, and we know that it not only appeared to legitimize certain demands or expectations of poor labouring people, but also, insofar as this moral entitlement was infringed, their rebellions against it. Thus in the 1790s the noblemen and gentlemen landowners who monopolized the soil of England did their best to guarantee the rural poor a minimum income or social security by modifying the Poor Law, when the amount of rural pauperism seemed to increase beyond all precedent and reason. (I am not here discussing the effects of their initiative, but their intentions.) Again, when the unemployed and pauperized labourers took to destroying the threshing machines which deprived them of their main winter employment, many of the gentry not only sympathized with them: Sir B. Bunbury, Bart. actually circularized his East Anglian tenant farmers in 1822 asking them not to employ such machinery, and he was not alone. They also, insofar as they tried machinebreaking cases as magistrates, treated the accused with notable indulgence. George Rudé and I have discussed this matter in our monograph on the 1830 rising.[4] Conversely, when the British gentry established a class privilege which was believed contrary to the moral consensus, their constitutional right to do so was sharply distinguished from moral legitimacy. The Game Law of 1674 gave the monopoly of killing game (in the rather specialized legal sense of the word) to people owning or renting land above a certain, for the time, quite enormous value or to the sons and heirs of noblemen and gentlemen. This was not only rejected by all countrymen on the grounds that God gave every man the right to take wild creatures if he could – hence poaching, widely indulged in, was not seen as a crime, though it was a legal offence. The same view in principle was taken by the great guru of the Common Law, whose views in the eighteenth century – as Americans will know – carried vast authority, namely Blackstone.[5]

However, the system of 'rights' prevailing in most European pre-industrial societies differed from subsequent conceptions of rights in three ways. In the *first* place, it accepted inegalitarianism, though the Game Law case I have just quoted demonstrates that elements of equality and universalism may be found in it. That poor people had a right to earn a modest livelihood did not imply that they had the right to the same livelihood as lords. Rights depended on rank, hierarchical or personal status and situation, and could not necessarily be generalized. In the *second* place rights implied duties and the other way round. Protest and rebellion were legitimate insofar as those whose duty it was to guarantee that poor people could earn a living or buy bread at reasonable prices, failed in that duty. Conversely, as my quote from the Elizabethan statute showed, the right to a 'convenient proportion of wages' was inseparable from the duty to labour, i.e. to avoid 'idleness'. Indeed, it may sometimes be misleading and anachronistic to separate rights and duties even to this extent, since in many cases rights *were* obligatory and not optional. For instance, in certain kinds of popular jurisprudence, the right to take blood-vengeance upon an offender was at the same time the duty to do so. It was a right (in our sense) since some kinds of homicide were always considered wrong; but at the same time the man who exercised this exceptional freedom to kill, also *had* to 'take blood'.[6] Walter Scott's marvellous story, 'The Two Drovers', brings this out extremely vividly. In the *third* place, these rights were rarely specified rigidly in law or at all, except in terms of precedent and consensus, which were of course much the same. In this sense, for instance, the modern conception of equality before the law is difficult to apply, even to people of essentially the same social status. At most, in legalistic societies, there was equality in the sense that all were subject to the same mandatory due process of law, so that any infringement of its formalities and rituals, however insubstantial, invalidated an accusation or verdict. Beyond this, we can say broadly that what was judged was the person and the circumstances in the light of the values of those who judged. A man known in his village as a ne'er-do-well would be less likely to get away with an action than an honest and hard-working citizen; though of course there might be differences of opinion about his character between the gentry and his co-villagers. But both official rulers and public opinion would apply flexibility. Conversely, the history of trial by jury in Britain shows that juries were frequently prepared to acquit in the teeth of the evidence when they felt that a wider issue of justice or freedom was at stake.

I do not want to go further into the traditionalist concept of how a society should properly operate, and what its rulers and communities must do to ensure this, or what common people were entitled to do about it themselves, or under what circumstances they intervened to do it. All I want to say here is that 'rights' in this sense formed a powerful component of the moral philosophy and – if the phrase is the right one – the political experience, of the men and women who emerged from their own past to form the novel phenomenon of labour movements. It is not possible to generalize further about them. Some such assumptions led directly into labour movements, for instance those of corporately organized craftsmen, and especially craft journeymen, which were transformed both into political ideologies and the labour unionism of skilled workers, at least in Britain. This process has been traced in the career of a single such activist, the shipwright John Gast in the

early nineteenth century.[7] Some such assumptions were not directly
compatible with later forms of labour movement. For instance, it
is likely that many Russian factory workers at the end of the nineteenth century, or for that matter many Victorian English workers
saw employers in a paternalist manner, i.e. essentially as people
whose duty it was to provide them with work. *Some* could spark
off revolution in the context of situations in which the traditional
'moral economy' broke down. In effect, the Tsar fell in February
1917 because the Petrograd poor exercised their right to ask for
bread, and the bulk of the troops ordered to disperse them, being
farmers' boys themselves who were also convinced that it was legitimate to ask for bread, and that circumstances justified their doing
so, refused to fire upon them.

In the course of the later eighteenth century a *second* type of
'rights' was partly combined with these, partly superimposed on
them. These were what may be called the 'Rights of Man', which
still provide the basic model for programmatic Declarations of
Human Rights. Such lists of basic rights are no doubt implicit in
earlier legal and political documents, but in fact were not specifically formulated until the American and especially the French Revolution with its Declaration of the Rights of Man and Citizens.
They are not to be confused with such documents of revolution as
the seventeenth-century British Petition of Right of 1628 or the Bill
of Rights in 1689, which were petitions against specific grievances
rather than formulations of universally applicable human rights. I
do not want to call this set of rights exclusively 'bourgeois' or
embodying 'bourgeois revolution', though in fact they can be seen
as one aspect of the system of beliefs about human nature and
human society which finds another form of expression in the political economy of Adam Smith and his successors. I shall not treat
them only as 'bourgeois' rights, both because they were plainly
influential far beyond the range of supporters of bourgeois liberalism – Tom Paine's *Rights of Man* is a case in point – but also
because many of the Rights formulated in the late eighteenth century context still correspond to what most people in modern
societies want and need.

The new 'Rights of Man' type of human rights was novel and
peculiar in three ways. *First*, such rights belong to individuals,
conceived as such in the abstract, and not in the traditional manner
as persons inseparable from their community or other social con-

text. This was historically somewhat novel. They were, of course, the rights of men within organized 'political associations', from family or tribe to cities and states, but as the very term 'association' (which I have taken from the 1789 Declaration) implies, these collective entities are conceived of as bodies of persons who enter into association and can, as it were, be imagined outside them. The 'political associations' have the duty, or are set up to, protect the individual's rights against them (e.g. the state) as well as against other persons. Hence their power must be limited in scope and means, their agents must be held to account, and the rights of individuals must be guaranteed against them. We now take this approach for granted in constitutional societies, but it belongs to a specific historical view of human relations.

*Second*, and in consequence, these rights are theoretically universal and equal, since individuals conceived in isolation, can only have equal claims as such, even though as persons they are quite different. There can be no reason why, as abstract individuals, lords should have greater claims than peasants, rich men than poor men, Christians than Jews (or the other way round). They are regarded, as it were, like people who have bought a ticket at a standard price to a movie: never mind who they are, they have the same right to a seat. Hence Declarations of Rights have been, in theory, universally applicable. In fact their most powerful appeal has been that they provide *groups* who claim a better condition for themselves on *special* grounds – for instance as women or blacks or workers – with a *universal* justification for doing so, which makes it difficult for other people who accept the idea of such rights to resist the claim in principle. Jefferson knew what he was doing when he proposed that the colonists demand independence not just because they had particular grievances against King George, but because the inalienable rights of all men, to secure which governments had been instituted, were being violated by King George. The relevance of this to labour movements is obvious.

*Thirdly*, and also in consequence of what has been said above, these rights were essentially political or *politico-legal*: since the whole point about proclaiming them was to provide institutional guarantees to human beings and citizens. The right to free speech in this sense must imply ways of protecting free speech, as Russian dissidents know well. Rights of the 'Rights of Man' type therefore implied political programmes and political action, insofar as these rights were not already effectively guaranteed by constitution and law. And of course in practice that was precisely the reason for drawing up Declarations of the Rights of Man.

But they did *not* imply a social and economic programme, because the freedoms guaranteed by such rights were negative: not to be interfered with. In Anatole France's famous phrase, 'the law in its majestic equality gives every man an equal right to sleep under a bridge or eat at the Ritz'. This was their *fourth* characteristic. Bourgeois-liberals welcomed this, since they argued that maximum economic welfare would be achieved by the untrammelled private enterprise of individuals. The bulk of modest farmers, small producers and traders did not want to be interfered with either by government or law, though they reserved the right to call on government to help them when times were bad: they were both for and against the unrestricted rights of property, which created intellectual problems that seldom troubled them but have troubled interpreters of Rousseau and Tom Paine. Yet, as Adam Smith knew well, for certain purposes a declaration of rights to negative freedom was not enough. And among those for whom it was quite evidently not enough, were the future constituency of labour movements, whose primary claim was to work at a decent wage, to social security which they certainly would need at some time in their lives, to benefits which poverty prevented their purchasing – such as health care and education – and to political rights not covered by the classical Declarations which would make it easier for them to fight for these, e.g. to form labour unions and strike.

How to combine the 'Rights of Man' rights with these other demands? Later socialists and labour militants have been puzzled by such movements as Chartism in Britain, which was undoubtedly a working-class mobilization – probably the greatest in British history relative to the size of the population – but whose demands were exclusively for the democratization of elections. They have argued that political democracy was seen instrumentally. Chartism was, as a widely quoted speaker said, 'a knife-and-fork question'. Democracy was necessary because, once the poor majority was politically decisive, it could pass the laws which would realize its social programme. That is not completely untrue, but recent research has shown that early radicals and political labour militants saw the achievement of political democracy as an end rather than just a means.[8] In fact there is little doubt that, in terms of their

politics, radical and labour movements before the rise of socialist
political parties were indistinguishable from non-socialist and
non-working-class democrats. We may say – this is certainly the
case in nineteenth-century Britain, but not only there – that until
the rise of mass labour and socialist parties, or, ideologically, of
Marxism, labour and socialist movements were not political as
such, though their potential members as individuals often were.
They operated outside politics by means of various collective ini-
tiatives such as unions, cooperative societies and communities or
utopian colonies, though naturally they needed to acquire the legal/
political rights to do so, which classical Declarations of Right did
not include, and sometimes excluded. They might even, as in the
case of the later anarchist and syndicalist traditions, specifically
reject political action. The essential difference between Marxists and
anarchists was precisely that the ones insisted on *political* action
and the others refused it. In politics pre-socialist labour militants
were democrats. What exactly they expected from the triumph of
political (i.e. electoral) democracy and why they thought it would
solve their problems, are questions which historians are now investigating, but from our point of view it is sufficient to observe that
in general they did not look beyond the achievement of political
democracy. Chartism may or may not have implied a social programme in the minds of its labouring supporters, but it certainly
did not, as a movement, have such a programme. Now socialist
labour parties, especially the Marxist ones, obviously had such a
programme and, apart from its intrinsic attractions, saw political
democracy chiefly as a way of creating the conditions for achieving
it. But, of course, since there were very few political democracies
in Europe before the very late nineteenth century, the fight to
establish or make effective democratic political rights remained primary. By far the most powerful mobilizations of labour on the
continent, e.g. general strikes, were for electoral reform, as in Belgium and Sweden. The first labour movement in Europe which gave
a systematic priority in its politics to social reforms and specific
labour demands over general democratic and republican political
demands, was probably the British at the very end of the century.

Hence, insofar as they were politically active as movements, most
nineteenth-century labour movements still operated in the framework of the American and French revolutions and their type of
the Rights of Man. In other words, they fought for the rights of

workers to be full citizens, even if they hoped to go on to fight for something more. They gave a special edge to the fight for these citizen rights, because they consisted largely of people who did not enjoy them, and because even those legal rights and civil liberties which were accepted in theory, were challenged in practice by the adversaries of labour. Nobody in Britain doubted the right to free speech, a free press and public demonstration, even though there was no clause in any legal document guaranteeing them. Yet, as we know, the effective right of free speech and assembly (e.g. on Trafalgar Square and in the royal parks of London) had to be fought for in a series of 'free speech fights' or mass demonstrations, and the effective right to a popular or radical free press had to be fought for similarly. The major nineteenth-century contribution of labour movements to human rights was to demonstrate that they required a lot of extension and that they had to be effective in practice as well as available on paper. This was, of course, a major and quite crucial contribution.

But it still left a number of potential human rights covered by neither of the two major families of rights which were the heritage of labour from the past. To be more precise, even when such rights had been formulated in theory or practice in the pre-industrial past, the situation of nineteenth-century bourgeois, capitalist and industrializing societies was so different from that past, that the old formulations simply could no longer serve.

The first group of such rights were the political and legal ones essential for the operation of any labour movement – for instance the right to strike and collective organization. I need hardly remind you that some of these were specifically excluded from the liberal-radical Declarations of the Rights of Man, or law-codes or constitutions, e.g. in France legally between 1791 and 1884. To this extent the era of classical bourgeois liberalism actually cut down the rights of corporate organization and action which pre-industrial societies had not only recognized in practice, but actually regarded as key institutions in the structuring of society. So these rights, and various consequential rights, had to be re-established and re-defined in terms of the nineteenth-century economy. The history of labour unions and struggles in all countries illustrates the chief field for the development of such human rights, and there is no need to pursue it in detail. Still, these were and are *instrumental* rights, by which I mean that the right to strike or form a union is significant not usually for itself, but essentially for what strikes and unions can get for workers. In this respect they are not ends in themselves but means.

This is not true of the second group of neglected rights, of which the classical formulation is Roosevelt's 'freedom from want'. As I argued at the outset of this paper, pre-industrial societies recognized that people had a legitimate moral claim to certain basic essentials of life. They recognized a basic obligation for the social community of which men and women formed part to ensure these, so far as was humanly possible, and rulers or political authorities who failed to do so, lost some or all of their legitimacy. For instance paupers or those who could not yet or no longer maintain themselves – orphans, widows, the old – had to be given succour. In Britain there actually existed a national legal obligation to do so since Elizabeth I, the Poor Law. Society and its political organizations had positive duties towards its members.

Now the dramatic, and indeed for most people the diabolical, innovation of bourgeois society and its capitalist economy was that it had no place for these positive rights and duties, and indeed tried to abolish them. To quote a nineteenth century folksong:

If life was a thing that money could buy
The rich might live and the poor might die.

And often it was: and the poor were left to die, as in the great Irish famine. The point was not that liberal economics did not mind if people died, let alone wanted them to. On the contrary, it argued with great force that the mechanisms of profit-making enterprise operating through the market would make most people better off than ever before. The point is that it could not, and did not want to, express this aspiration in the form of *rights*. There could be no place for, say, a right to employment or a right to earn a living wage in its system. Yet most people felt and still feel that they have such rights, or at least that they ought to have.

But for the great mass of the population who felt that way in the early nineteenth century – and, I repeat, they included not only the poor but also many of their traditional superiors and rulers, who thought in terms of some kind of paternalism – for all these the appeal to the numerous old institutions designed to ensure these rights, was increasingly barred. Thus the first instinct of the trade societies in Napoleonic England, was to appeal against the new capitalist market economy to the Elizabethan labour code (from which I have already quoted), which, for instance, gave the Justices of the Peace the authority to fix wages. They tried to put life into the old system. They failed. More than this: the old laws which provided for these rights were abolished. We find a similar struggle – which was also lost – over the Poor Law between 1795 and 1834. And so on. Hence, while the infant labour movements were morally certain of these rights, and inspired by the memory that they had once actually been recognized, they could no longer directly appeal to them. And, of course, even if they could have done so, the old methods of ensuring them were no longer literally applicable in an industrializing society: to this extent the Elizabethan Statute of Apprentices *had* to be repealed. Furthermore, an industrial society created the need for new rights which had not previously been required, for instance the right to be protected at work against hazards which previously did not exist or could be regarded as negligible. In a word, under the new capitalist society the ancient human rights to life and livelihood *had* to be thought out afresh in theory and practice.

For obvious reasons no body of people was more acutely interested in this than the emerging working class and its movements. They were, after all, a historically new social and economic class, operating largely in novel, indeed sometimes unprecedented conditions, and above all they had, by definition, no significant independent access to the means of production, but depended on the sale of their labour-power for wages. A lot of peasants might still escape from the universal market into a sort of hill-billy existence of self-sufficiency and localized barter. Small crafts and their like needed a market, but not necessarily the capitalist one. Until the factories and modern distribution pushed them to the wall, they could rely on the basic needs of their locality: someone, after all, had to repair its boots and shoes. But hired men and women who had no resources except their wages, could encounter the denial of the right to survive at any moment, and might certainly come up against it at certain stages of their life-cycle – for instance as married couples with small children, and above all in old age. What is more, as we have seen, traditional provisions designed to protect it, broke down spectacularly in their case. In agricultural village communities it might still be possible to leave the relief of the poor to neighbours or community assistance. In Manchester or London this was no longer a realistic option. Thus for obvious reasons the pressure to introduce protective legislation, and modern systems of social welfare and security came primarily from the existence and demand of the working classes. Old age pensions, probably the earliest such provision to be widely introduced, are a case in point.

But just at this point we meet a paradox. There is absolutely no doubt that the poor, the working people and the potential or actual members of labour movements spoke the language of *rights* (and still do), if only because this is the natural language of anyone who sets up a model of morality and justice (of 'what is right' in the convenient vocabulary of Germanic languages) and makes claims in the light of this model.* It is also the natural language of politics, since it provides a built-in moral backing for any demand or action. British politicians defending some debatable decision invariably claim that 'we have thought it right' to do this or that or not to. When British labour movements demanded 'a living wage' or 'that wages should be the first charge on industry', they were patently speaking this language: whatever the market decided, people had a *right* to what Elizabeth I called a 'convenient proportion of wages'. The Right to Work, the Right to the Whole Product of Labour and similar phrases instinctively rose to the lips of social and socialist agitation in the nineteenth century.

On the other hand the theorists of labour movements did not universally talk the language of rights, at least after the early or middle decades of the century. The Right to Work mobilized people, but not the Right to Socialism, even though most political parties of labour in Europe were, in theory at least, profoundly committed to this aspiration. There are two main reasons for this.

The first, and less significant, is that the most influential socialist theory by far, Marxism, specifically rejected the language of human rights for various reasons, which are not directly germane to the subject of this paper. Insofar as Marxism claimed to be an analysis of the operations of society, past, present and future, rather than a programme, that language was, of course, irrelevant to it, as indeed it was or is to Ricardo and Paul Samuelson. 'Rights' are

---

*In English and German the identification is linguistically clear. It is right to demand my rights, because they are themselves right. In German *Recht* may mean both law and entitlement and (as an adjective) the rightness of the claim.

not an analytical concept in science, any more than 'law' is, in the sense of something which *ought* to happen. A scientific 'law', if we choose to use the term, implies no claims or entitlements whatever. However, Marx was not merely indifferent to 'rights of man' but strongly opposed to them, since they are essentially individualistic, belonging to 'egoistic man ... separated from other men and from the community'.* In this sense Marx still speaks an ancient social language. This fundamental incompatibility of Marx' ideas with classical liberal theory has had far-reaching consequences for the position of individual citizens in states established on the Bolshevik model since 1917, though it is quite wrong to deduce from this incompatibility in theory a permanent incompatibility of Marxist regimes with legal and constitutional guarantees of citizen rights, either formally or in practice; any more than it is legitimate to suppose that no state based on the classical liberal rights of man can be a police state. The objection to the 1936 Soviet Constitution is not, as a reading of critics like Kolakowski might suggest,[9] that its drafters failed to understand that, as Marxists, they could not draw up such a list of rights, but that the Soviet state paid not the slightest attention to it. However, the justified critique of the deficiencies (including legal, constitutional and political ones) of *states* claiming inspiration from Marx, has no bearing on the problem of the historical connections between *labour movements* (which are not to be identified with states even when states claim such identification) and human rights.

But the second, and much more significant reason is that rights in the sense of wide-ranging claims to a good or tolerable life, are not ends in themselves, but broad aspirations which can be realized only through complex and changing social strategies, on which they throw no specific light. It is possible, as Jefferson saw, to make 'the pursuit of happiness' into a 'natural right' - we may, of course, prefer to think of it simply as a psychological generalization, true or false, about the behaviour of individuals - insofar as we can

* 'None of the supposed rights of man, therefore, go beyond the egoistic man ... that is, an individual separated from the community, withdrawn into himself, wholly preoccupied with his private interest and acting in accordance with his private caprice. Man is far from being considered, in the rights of man, as a species-being; on the contrary, species-life itself - society - appears as a system which is external to the individual and a limitation of his original independence.' 'On the Jewish Question', cited in T. Bottomore, ed. , *Karl Marx, Early Writings* (London, 1963), p. 26.

define certain immediately removable situations which inhibit this pursuit. If we suppose that being a slave inhibits it, then the elimination of slavery helps to secure this right. But it is not possible to formulate a right to *be* happy in the same sense, since only advertising agencies would argue that there is a readily definable programme - e.g. drinking Coca Cola or smoking dope - which could guarantee happiness, which could thus be assured by a law to supply all citizens with the requisite quantities of the magic ingredient. So a declaration of the Right to Live a Good Life is either a rhetorical flourish, as it is in most cases, or a sort of declaration of intent.

To say that human beings have the right to freedom from want is merely another way of saying that public policy or private behaviour or both ought to be dedicated to this broad purpose. Such a declaration tells us nothing at all in itself about how this end is to be achieved in practice. There is no way it could do so. Some people might try to achieve it by a social revolution introducing a centrally planned socialist economy; others by a Reaganite trickledown effect from unrestricted private enterprise in a market society; yet others by means of Scandinavian social-democratic strategies. We may legitimately discuss which of these and other possible strategies is more effective, and under what circumstances - providing we define the meaning of 'freedom from want' adequately. However, this is not an argument about the purpose, but about the means of achieving it. We may also question whether some of these strategies are really devoted to this purpose as distinct from paying their tribute to the values of public opinion. One may well ask how far some believers in supply-side economics *really* believe in the right of every last man, woman and child in the world to a decent life. But of course, today no politician in a democratic country will say flatly 'to hell with the poor', unless they are a negligible minority of his or her constituents: and if some of them are lying through their teeth, others may be entirely sincere in believing that freedom from want is achievable by giving J.R. more in *Dallas*.

So the language of human rights was and is unsuited (except rhetorically and agitationally) to the struggle for the achievement of the economic and social changes to which labour movements were dedicated: whether reforms within existing society or gradual changes, or revolutionary transformations of the social and economic order. In short, it is possible to translate the Rights of Man of the classical Declarations, which are essentially concerned with individuals, into laws which specifically guarantee them, even though the guarantees may be neither invariable nor unconditional, and even though experience shows that they do not guarantee them as simply and automatically as one might hope: as witness the right to equality irrespective of race and sex. But it is not possible to give the rights to a decent human life equal expression in law. They are not rights of individuals in the same sense, but programmes for society and social action. Everything depends on the strategies and mechanisms for achieving them, not to mention situations beyond legal control which may affect them.

So this is the paradox. More than any other force, the labour movement helped to unlock the politico-legal, individualist strait-jacket which confined human rights of the type of the French Declaration and the American Constitution. Compare the UN's Universal Declaration of Human Rights, which is, I suppose, the currently standard document of this kind, with the American Bill of Rights. If the UN Declaration includes economic, social and educational rights, – and in doing so is closer to Tom Paine than to Madison – it is primarily due to the historical intervention of labour movements. At the same time labour movements demonstrated the limitations of a 'human rights' approach to politics. Madisonian rights can be made operational to some extent by laws and constitutions. Such concepts as the right to live a decent life can become operational only in a society so constructed as to make them possible, and can be approached only indirectly through *policies* and ongoing institutional changes. This is clear even in the famous fifth chapter of the second part of Paine's *Rights of Man*. The crux of this chapter is not that men have economic and social rights, but in the *policies* of taxing the rich to create a fund for paying the poor, the unemployed and old as well as the cost of popular education. Without such policies, these human rights are entirely ineffective.

Now in pursuit of such policies, conflicts between the individual and the social rights inevitably develop. Almost any attempt to change society or to improve it in the interests of the poor in our century, has been shown to mean more public interference with the freedom of the individual than is provided for in the literal meaning of the American Bill of Rights: hence the exegetical contortions of the US Supreme Court in this century. The classical Rights (or rather freedoms from interference) have not only tended to be of little operational use to people trying to improve social arrangements. They have readily served the propaganda of their adversaries. The right to work at a decent wage, as seen by labour movements (i.e. to quote an early Jacobin-communist Declaration of Rights, society's 'duty of providing for the sustenance of all its members'[10] is opposed by the Right to Work laws of American state legislatures, which are a charter for scabs and sweaters, and implicitly deny any claim to social rights. You will recall that British Conservatives thought Lloyd George's National Insurance Act opened the way to state slavery ('the servile state') because it forced ladies to buy insurance stamps for their maids, and perhaps even personally to lick them in order to stick them on insurance cards. It is the paradox of liberty that it became the slogan of those who needed it least and wanted to deny it to those who needed it most: of the Liberty and Property Defence League which opposed socialism in Britain in the 1880s, of the Liberty League which fought the New Deal, or for that matter of General Pinochet, who used coercion and torture to persuade Chileans of the virtues of the free market economy, as understood by the disciples of Professor Milton Friedman, whom there is no reason to think of as other than sincerely devoted to libertarian ideals.

This observation is not to be understood as a criticism of liberty in the old-fashioned individualist sense of the French revolutionary Declarations of the Rights of Man. The theorist may regard this concept of freedom as inadequate, unsatisfactory and analytically feeble, but it is an empirically verifiable fact that for most human beings in the twentieth-century freedom from being told by outside (secular) authorities what to do and what not to do – beyond a varying minimum accepted as legitimate in the interests of society and its members – is a crucial component of what they consider liberty. No modern political order is likely to be considered satisfactory by its members which overlooks people's dislike of being coerced.

This needs to be said, for the other paradox of freedom is that those who want to change society in order to create the conditions for the free development of all individuals, of which Marx dreamed, have tended to put the rights of the individual against state and society on the back burner, when they have been in a position to proceed to a reconstruction of society. In extreme cases, such as the Soviet Union under Stalin, they have taken them off the burner altogether. An entire polemical literature has therefore grown up, especially since 1945, which seeks but fails to demonstrate that this is the fundamental characteristic of revolutionary, socialist, or sometimes of all labour movements.

As against this it must be said that, historically, labour movements and the associated movements for social reform and social transformation have been movements for the Rights of Man in the individual as well as in the social sense; and their contribution to establishing and extending these rights has been capital. This is partly due to the fact that their most influential ideologies belong firmly to the family of what Bernard Shaw once called: those who believe in the great sentimental verities of Jefferson, Life, Liberty and the Pursuit of Happiness. They are children of the rationalist eighteenth-century Enlightenment, and unlike the traditionalist right, Fascism or most ideologies of nationalism, they have never rejected or abandoned its hope and aspirations. But it has been mostly due to the fact that, as already observed, the constituency of these movements is one of people who are short of rights, who need them and demand them. Where labour and socialist movements have become powerful, they have naturally gathered in their neighbourhood protesters, defenders of civil liberties, champions of the rights of minorities and the rightless of all kinds – slaves, blacks, women, homosexuals or whoever – as well as libertarian believers in individual development and a new society, counter-culturists and new lifers of various sorts, who in turn demand their rights – from vegetarians to those who refuse compulsory vaccination.

Socialist movements of the late nineteenth and twentieth centuries – particularly in the early days – thus provided one of the few environments in which, say, emancipated women, Jews, and people with coloured skins could expect to be accepted on their merits as human beings and not suffer formal discrimination; perhaps the only such environments for those who had neither a great deal of money nor family connections. Perhaps they did not give the rights of such groups as exclusive a priority as their supporters might have wished, but they not only defended them, but actively campaigned for them, as part of the general championship of Liberty, Equality and Fraternity – slogans which early labour and socialist movements took over from the French Revolution – and of human emancipation. The struggle against social oppression implied the struggle for liberty.

What makes this libertariansim more impressive is that we know that most rank-and-file workers in these movements were – to take some examples – strong male chauvinists, and the instincts of many of them were both conventional and xenophobic. We even know of leading figures in such movements – not on their Marxist wing – who themselves propagated anti-semitism and the inferiority of women, like Proudhon, one of the gurus of libertarian anarchism. It was the historical descent of labour and socialist movements from the eighteenth-century tradition of rationalist enlightenment which kept such instincts under control. Without it they would neither have tried nor succeeded in becoming the focus for universal and equal rights and universal human emancipation. For not all movements of those who demand rights had either this intention or this capacity. Roman Catholic minorities in the nineteenth century were often discriminated against, and therefore found themselves campaigning against discrimination, supported by, and sometimes supporting, those who were hostile to any discrimination. But, unlike the movements of the poor, Catholic agitation did not normally become the rallying-ground for the struggle for human rights in general.

Is all this still true? Probably only to a limited extent. The language of human rights is still spoken, but in a different setting from the nineteenth and early twentieth centuries. The fight for human rights is still seen in many countries as part of a general programme for the progress of mankind, individually and collectively, towards a better and more genuinely human future. But in even more countries human rights are today chiefly used in defence against the re-emergence of a barbarism, which has been encroaching on human society since World War I. Who would have thought in the days of John Stuart Mill and Karl Marx, that in the 1980s one of the primary human rights to fight for in most parts of the world would be the right not to be tortured, or for civilians not to be massacred in wars of which they have become the main targets? In both capitalist and socialist societies and in what is called the 'Third World', people are fighting for the good, just and human societies which were never achieved, but also for the maintenance of, or the return to, the rights and liberties which were at least partly achieved during the 150 years when, on balance, the world was advancing, however unevenly, towards a greater state of civility as well as prosperity: the era of hope for and belief in progress. What the future will be, we do not know. But we can say that one of the main forces which helped civility to progress in the century and a half between the American Revolution and World War I when it clearly did, was that which found its organized expression in the labour and socialist movements of the western world.

(1982)

# Notes

## Chapter 1: Labour History and Ideology

1. Paolo Spriano, *Storia del Partito Comunista Italiano*, 5 vols (Turin, 1967-75).
2. Claude Willard, *Le mouvement socialiste en France, 1893-1905. Les Guesdistes.* (Paris, 1965).
3. Studs Terkel, *Hard Times. An Oral History of the Great Depression.* (New York, 1970).
4. London, 1973.
5. Georges Haupt, *La Deuxième Internationale 1889-1914. Étude critique des sources.* (Paris-Hague, 1964).
6. 'The Possibility of Radicalism in the Early 1930s: The Case of Steel'. (*Radical America* 6/6 Nov.-Dec. 1972).
7. J.P. Nettl, *Rosa Luxemburg*, 2 vols (Oxford, 1966); Royden Harrison, *Before the Socialists: studies in labour and politics 1861-1881* (London, 1964); J.F.C. Harrison, *Robert Owen and the Owenites in Britain and America* (London, 1969).
8. Rolande Trempé, *Les mineurs de Carmaux 1848-1914.* 2 vols (Paris, 1971).

## Chapter 2: Notes on Class Consciousness

1. *Geschichte und Klassenbewusstsein*, Berlin, 1923, p. 62. All my references are to this original edition.
2. *loc. cit.*, p. 62.
3. *loc. cit.*, p. 67.
4. The relevant passage from *Eighteenth Brumaire*, VII, is famous, but will not be harmed by yet another quotation:
   'The small peasants form a vast mass, the members of which live in similar conditions, but without entering into manifold relations with one another. Their mode of production isolates them from one another, instead of bringing them into mutual intercourse. . . . Their field of production, the small holding, admits of no division of labour in its cultivation, no application of science and, therefore, no multiplicity of development, no diversity of talents, no wealth of social relationships. Each individual peasant family is almost self-sufficient; it itself directly produces the major part of its consumption and thus acquires its means of life more through exchange with nature than in intercourse with society. The small holding, the peasant and his family; alongside them another small holding, another peasant and another family. A few score of these make up a village, and a few score

villages make up a Department. In this way the great mass of the French nation is formed by simple addition of homologous magnitudes, much as potatoes in a sack form a sackful of potatoes. Insofar as millions of families live under economic conditions of existence that divide their mode of life, their interests and their culture from those of other classes, and put them in hostile contrast to the latter, they form a class. Insofar as there is merely a local interconnection among these small peasants, and the identity of their interests begets no unity, no national union and no political organization, they do not form a class.'

5. 'The Peasantry as a political factor' (*Sociol. Rev.* XIV, 1, 1966), pp. 5–27.
6. e.g. *loc. cit.*, p. 70.
7. 'On Peasant Rebellions' (*New Society*, 4.9.1969).

### Chapter 3: Religion and the Rise of Socialism

1. Karl Marx-Friedrich Engels, *Werke* (Berlin, 1956 ff.) VII, 565.
2. E.J. Hobsbawm, *Primitive Rebels* (Manchester, 1959), ch. VIII.
3. E.H. Carr, *History of Soviet Russia 1926–1929* (Penguin ed., Harmondsworth, 1974), II, 407–408.
4. Gaetano Cingari, *Brigantaggio, proprietari e contadini nel Sud (1799–1900)* (Reggio Calabria, 1976), pp. 54, 38.
5. Maxime Rodinson, *Marxisme et Monde Musulman* (Paris, 1972), pp. 165–166; cf. Irene Gendzier, *Frantz Fanon, A Critical Study* (N.Y., 1973), p. 259.
6. Olive Anderson, 'The Incidence of Civil Marriage in Victorian England and Wales', *Past and Present* 69 (1975), 50–87; R. Floud and P. Thane, *Past and Present*, *ibid.*, 84 (1979), pp. 146–54.
7. P-J. Proudhon, *Oeuvres Completes* II, 458, quoted in Gabriel Le Bras, *Études de Sociologie Religieuse* (2 vols; Paris, 1955–1956), I, 261.
8. Heiner Grote, *Sozialdemokratie und Religion. Eine Dokumentation für die Jahre 1860 bis 1875* (Tubingen, 1968), p. 134. *The British Dictionary of Labour Biography* (ed. Bellamy and Saville) provides some data about the cremation of labour militants.
9. M. Agulhon, *La République au Village* (Paris, 1970), pp. 181 ff.
10. cf. Patrick Hutton, *The Cult of the Revolutionary Tradition: The Blanquists in French Politics, 1864–1893* (Berkeley, 1981), pp. 53–8.
11. Heiner Grote, *Sozialdemokratie und Religion*, pp. 139–50, for tendencies to transform Easter and Whitsun in ways prefiguring the later 'May Day' ceremonies, for which cf. M. Dommanget, *Histoire du Premier Mai* (Paris, 1953), e.g., p. 343. For Christmas, cf. G. Luscher, V. Stoltetteiskanen, C. Ward, 'Family Ritual and Secularization (a cross-national study ...)' *Social Compass* XIX (1972), pp. 519 ff.
12. J. Obelkevich, *Religion and Rural Society: South Lindsay 1825–1875* (Oxford, 1976); M. Vovelle, *Pieté Baroque et dé-christianisation* (Paris, 1973); M. Vovelle, 'Les attitudes devant la mort: problèmes de methode, approches et lectures differentes', *Annales E.S.C.* XXXI (1976), pp. 120–132; J. Delumeau, 'A propos de la dechristianisation', *Rev. d'Hist. Mod. et Contemp.*, XXII (1975), pp. 52–60; Agulhon, *République*, pp. 238–9.
13. For such recoveries in religious vocations cf., for Spain, R. Duocastella, 'Géographie de la pratique religieuse en Espagne,' *Social Compass* XII (1965), p. 262, and, for parts of North Italy, M. Toscani, 'Ordinazione e clero nella diocesi di Lodi 1775–1900. Alcuni aspetti storico-sociologici', *Rivista di Storia della Chiesa in Italia*, XXVIII (1974), pp. 183 ff.

14. A.D. Gilbert, *Religion and Society in Industrial England: Church, Chapel and Social Change 1740–1914* (London, 1976), ch. 2.
15. F. Boulard, 'La déchristianisation de Paris. L'évolution historique du nonconformisme', *Archives Sociol. Relig.*, XXXI (1971), pp. 69–98.
16. Attendance at mass among men in the two most pious divisions of the Angers diocese dropped from 96.2 and 91% in 1898 to 74.6% and 49.2% in 1960. F. Boulard, 'La pratique religieuse en France, 1802–1939: les pays de Loire', *Annales E.S.C.* XXXI (1976), 768. For the dramatic decline in vocations in the mid-twentieth century. see André Tihon, 'Les Religieuses en Belgique du XVIIIe au XXe siecles: approche statisque', *Belgisch Tijdschrift voor nieuwste Geschiedenis: Rev. Belg. d'Hist. Contemp.* VII (1976), pp. 1–54.
17. L. Bedeschi, 'Il comportamento religioso in Emilia-Romagna', *Studi Storici*, IX (1969), pp. 387 ff; D. Goldschmidt, F. Greiner, H. Schelsky ed., *Soziologie der Kirchengemeinde* (Stuttgart 1960), pp. 199–200, 38–9.
18. For The Netherlands and Friesland, Jakob P. Kruijt, *De onkerkelikheid en Nederland: haar verbreiding en oorzaken* (Groningen–Batavia, 1932); for the Alemtejo cf. A. Querido, 'Elements pour une sociologie du conformisme catholique au Portugal', *Arch. Soc. Relig.*, VII (1959), 144–152; *L'ateismo contemporaneo. A cura della Fac. Filos. della Pontificia Universita Salesiana di Roma*, (Torino 1967) I, 88; for Andalusia, R. Duocastella, 'Geographie de la pratique religieuse en Espagne', *Social Compass*, XII (1965), 253–302, esp. 282.
19. Aldo Leoni, *Sociologia e geografia religiosa di una Diocesi: saggio sulla pratica religiosa nella Diocesi di Mantova* (Rome 1952), pp. 179–80; for other religious but 'red' areas, cf. Erich Bodzenta, *Die Katholiken in Oesterreich* (Vienna, 1962), pp. 75–6.
20. *Annuaire International de Statistique* (The Hague, 1916), pp. 146 ff. The Italian figures are arrived at by adding the persons declaring themselves 'of no religion' and the unusually large number of those who refused or failed to answer the question. The percentage of actual atheists rose from 0.11 to 2.52.
21. Something like 40% of those without religion in the Italian and Dutch censuses of 1910 were women. cf. also, S. Bonnet, C. Santini, H. Barthelemy, 'Appartenance politique et attitude religieuse dans l'immigration italienne en Lorraine siderurgique', *Arch. Soc. Relig.*, XIII (1962), pp. 45–72.
22. For a particularly clear correlation – the Strasbourg diocese – cf., Le Bras, *Études* I, 184.
23. Hugh McLeod, 'Class, community and religion: the religious geography of nineteenth-century England', *Sociol. Yearbook of Religion*, VI (1973), p. 47. For a more qualified judgment see F. Isambert, *Christianisme et classe ouvrière* (Paris, 1961).
24. M. Argyle, *Religious Behaviour* (London, 1958) and 'Religious Observance' in *International Encyclopedia of the Social Sciences* XIII; Duocastella, *Social Compass*, XII (1965), 253–302.
25. Y.M. Hilaire, 'Les missions interieures face à la déchristianisation pendant la deuxieme moitié du XIX siecle dans la région du Nord' (*Revue du Nord* 46/ 1964, p. 65).
26. Bodzenta, *Katholiken*, p. 77 discusses the survival of an increasingly eroding tradition of peasant religiosity, whose weakness is revealed by 'the sudden decline in church attendance as soon as contact with industry or the city is made'.
27. P. Allum, *Politics and Society in Post-war Naples* (Cambridge, 1973), pp. 58 ff.
28. Claude Willard, *Les Guesdistes* (Paris, 1964), p. 237 n.

29. Le Bras, *Études*, I, p. 135. For possible explanations, T. Zeldin, *France 1848–1945* (Oxford, 1973), pp. 168–69.
30. A.D. Gilbert, *Religion and Society*, pp. 107–9.
31. Jean Maitron, *Le mouvement anarchiste en France* (Paris, 1975), I, p. 131.
32. Maitron, *La mouvement anarchiste*, I, p. 21.
33. Thomas Paine, *The Age of Reason* (N.Y., 1945), I, pp. 1–2.
34. Ernesto Ragionieri, *Un comune socialista: Sesto Fiorentino* (Rome, 1953), pp. 153–59.
35. Le Bras, *Études*, I, 71; C. Marcilhacy, *La Diocese d'Orleans sous l'episcopat de Mgr Dupanloup, 1849–1878* (Paris, 1962).
36. Le Bras, *Études*, I, p. 150.
37. E.J. Hobsbawm, *The Age of Capital 1848–1875* (London, 1975), ch. 5.
38. R. Mandrou, *De la culture populaire en France au XVIIe et XVIIIe siècles, la Bibliothèque bleue de Troyes* (Paris, 1964).
39. Carlo Ginzburg, *Il formaggio e i vermi: il cosmo di un mugnaio del '500* (Turin, 1976), pp. xxiv–xxv.
40. On Deubler, see Arnold Dodel-Port, *Konrad Deubler* (2 vols., Leipzig, 1886) and Gernart Baron, *Der Beginn: Die Anfänge der Arbeiterbildungsvereine in Oberösterreich* (Linz, 1971), pp. 53–100, *passim*.
41. Agulhon, *République*, p. 474.
42. For the 'male chauvinism' of the quintessentially 'freethinking' and anticlerical Radicals in France, see Jean Touchard, *La gauche en France depuis 1900* (Paris, 1977), p. 113.
43. Le Bras, *Études*, I, 163; Nimes diocese.
44. G. Duveau, *Les Instituteurs* (Paris, 1957), p. 122; cf. also, the extracts from the 'Contre-Catechisme Elementaire', cited by J. Touchard, La Gauche, p. 76 from R. Remond, *L'anticlericalisme en France de 1815 à nos jours* (Paris, 1976).
45. Hugh Thomas, *The Spanish Civil War* (1977 ed.), p. 62.
46. Andrew D. White, *The Warfare of Science with Theology* (N.Y., 1896).
47. H-J. Steinberg, *Sozialismus und deutsche Sozialdemokratie: zur Ideologie der Partei vor dem ersten Weltkrieg* (Hanover, 1967), pp. 43–50, 129–139; W. Emmerich ed., *Proletarische Lebenslaufe* I: Anfange bis 1914 (Reinbek, 1974), pp. 284–5, 287, 294.
48. Agulhon, *République*, pp. 321–9.
49. L. Lavandeyra, 'St. Maur-des-Fosses' in P. George ed. *Etudes sur la Banlieue de Paris* (Paris, 1950), p. 109; Paul Bois, *Paysans de l'Ouest* (Paris, 1971), pp. 71–2. Between 1929 and 1955 non-baptism in the three most anticlerical cantons of the Sarthe department dropped from 34, 25 and 41% to 8, 11 and 10% respectively.
50. E. Poulat, 'Socialisme et anti-cléricalisme: une enquete socialiste internationale', *Arch. Soc. Relig.* 10 (1960), pp. 109–32.
51. The religious development of the typical labourers of the 'proto-industrialization' period (for the concept of which see F. Mendels, 'Proto-industrialization: The First Phase of the Industrialization Process', *Journ. Econ. Hist.* XXXII (1972), pp. 241–61 and especially Hans Medick, 'The proto-industrial family economy: the structural function of household and family during the transition from peasant society to industrial capitalism', *Social History*, I (1976), pp. 291–315 requires investigation, and cannot be dealt with here.
52. cf. F. Boulard, loc. cit., 87–8, who shows that the de-Christianized population of Paris consisted both of locals and of a constant inflow of migrants who rapidly assimilated to the local pattern. For doubts

about 'culture shock', McLeod, *Sociol. Yearbook of Religion*, VI (1973), p. 47.

53. A. Gramsci, *Il Materialismo Storico* (Turin, 1949), pp. 87–8. For this substratum see Obelkevich, *Religion and Rural Society*, ch. V.

54. The modern electoral map often registers ancient divisions, as between Catholics and Huguenots, acceptance or rejection of the French Revolution, or between Austrian North Italy in which priests stood for Italianness, and Papal North Italy, where they stood for Roman rule – i.e., between the Christian Democracy of the Veneto and the Communism of Emilia-Romagna. cf. G. Braga, *Il Comunismo fra gli Italiani* (Milan, 1956), pp. 56–7. M. Lagree 'La structure perenne: evénement et histoire en Bretagne orientale XVI–XX siècles', *Rev. Hist. Mod. & Contemp.*, XXIII (1976), pp. 395–407 traces the right/left (religious/secular) division in one region back to the 1580s.

55. E. Caranti, 'Sociologia e statistics delle elezioni italiane nel dopoguerra' (Rome, 1954), 142; Bois, *Paysans*, pp. 25–6, 63–4, taking up again questions raised in A. Siegfried, *Tableau Politique de la France de l'Ouest* (Paris, 1965).

56. Carlo Ginzburg, 'Folklore, magia e religione' in *Storia d'Italia* I: *I caratteri originali* (Turin, 1972), p. 670.

57. It might be possible to construct a political ideology out of the bible-saturated statements of Primitive Methodist rural trade unionists (cf. *Bull. Soc. Stud. Labour History*, XXXIII (1976), p. 6, and E.J. Hobsbawm, *Primitive Rebels* (1971 edn.), pp. 190–91, but the main bond for the sect was the maintenance of its rules of behaviour, e.g. abstention from alcohol.

58. Isambert (1958), 21. cf. Giorgio Spini, 'Movimenti evangelici nel Italia Contemporanea', *Riv. Stor. Ital.* LXXX (1968), pp. 463–98, for its relation to the rise of socialist movements in Italy.

59. This is well brought out for Lincolnshire in Obelkevich, *Religion and Rural Society*, chs. II, VII.

60. E. Schwiedland, *Kleingewerbe und Hausindustrie in Oesterreich* (Leipzig, 1894) II, 264–65: 'Those among them who do not simply describe this change ... as progress, explain the prevailing indifference toward religious matters, sometimes not without some bitterness, as a result of the profoundly unchristian behaviour of the ruling and possessing classes towards the proletariat, which makes the State's action in favour of religion among the poor and oppressed, appear as a device by the essentially unchristian upper classes to protect their class interests'.

61. This is suggested by Bois, *Paysans*, p. 64, in line with Siegfried: 'ce serait l'anticléricalisme plutot que le cléricalisme qui constituerait le facteur decisif dans une prise de position'.

62. Susan Budd, *Varieties of Disbelief. Atheists and Agnostics in English Society 1850–1960* (London, 1977). E. Royle, *The Infidel Tradition from Paine to Bradlaugh* (London, 1976); *Radicals, Secularists and Republicans: Popular Freethought in Britain, 1866–1915* (Manchester, 1980).

63. cf. e.g., Paul Friedrich, *Agrarian Revolt in a Mexican Village* (Englewood Cliffs, 1970), pp. 60–64, 89–90, 120–23.

## Chapter 5: The Transformation of Labour Rituals

1. R.A. Leeson, *United We Stand: an illustrated account of trade union emblems* (London, 1971); J. Gorman, *Banner Bright: an illustrated history of the*

*banners of the British Trade Union Movement* (London, 1973); W.A. Moyes, *Banner Parade: a selection of lodge banners of the Durham Miners' Association on exhibition at the D.L.I. Museum and Arts Centre, January/ February 1973* (Newcastle-upon-Tyne, 1973); W. Moyes, *The Banner Book* (Gateshead, 1974); J. Smethurst, 'The Manchester Banner Makers' in *North West Group for the Study of Labour History Bulletin*, 1976.

2. Sidney and Beatrice Webb, *History of Trade Unionism* (London, 1911), I, p. 1 ff.

3. R.A. Leeson, *Travelling Brothers. The six centuries' road from craft fellowship to trade unionism* (London, 1979); Iorwerth Prothero, *Artisans & Politics in Early Nineteenth-century London: John Gast and his Times* (London, 1981); William H. Sewell Jr, *Work and Revolution in France: The Language of Labor from the Old Regime to 1848* (also bibliography), (Cambridge, 1980); Christopher H Johnson, *Utopian Communism in France, Cabet and the Icarians 1839–1851*, (Ithaca, New York, London, 1974); Cynthia M. Truant, 'Solidarity and Symbolism among Journeymen Artisans: The Case of Compagnonnage', *Comparative Studies in Society and History* 21, April, 1979. pp. 214–26; Joan W Scott, *The Glassworkers of Carmaux. French Craftsmen and Political Action in a Nineteenth-Century City*, (Cambridge, Mass., 1974); Bernard H Moss: *The Origins of the French Labor Movement: The Socialism of Skilled Workers 1830–1914* (Berkeley, London, 1976).

4. Wilhelm Matull, *Ostdeutschlands Arbeiterbewegung. Abriss ihrer Geschichte, Leistung und Opfer* (Würzburg, 1973), pp. 33–4.

5. Marx-Engels, *Werke*, XXIV (Berlin, 1956), p. 308 ff.

6. cf. E.J.Hobsbawm and T. Ranger ed., *The Invention of Tradition* (Cambridge, 1983).

7. J.E. Williams, *The Derbyshire Miners. A Study in Industrial and Social History* (London, 1962), p. 885.

8. On 'Red Vienna', see D. Langewiesche, 'Arbeiterkultur in Österreich: Aspekte, Tendenzen u. Thesen' in G.A. Ritter ed. *Arbeiterkultur* (Königstein, 1979); the same, *Zur Freizeit des Arbeiters. Bildungsbestrebungen und Freizeitgestaltung österreichische Arbeiter im Kaiserreich und in der ersten Republik* (Stuttgart, 1979); *Mit uns zieht die neue Zeit: Arbeiterkultur in Österreich 1918–1934. Eine Ausstellung der Österreichischen Gesellschaft für Kulturpolitik und des Meidlinger Kulturkreises*, 23 Jan–30 Aug, 1981 (catalogue, Vienna, 1981); Roberto Cazzola, 'Die proletarischen Feste', *Wiener Tagebuch*, April 1981, pp. 18–20.

9. John Dunlop, *Artificial Drinking Usages of North Britain* (Greenock, 1836) and various edns. Brian Harrison, *Drink & the Victorians. The Temperance Question in England 1815–1872* (London, 1971), pp. 95, 149, 309, 359; William Lovett in SCHC on Public Libraries, Parliamentary Papers, 1849 (548), XVII, Q 2783.

10. Bob Gilding, 'The Journeyman Coopers of London', *History Workshop Pamphlet 4* (Oxford, 1971), p. 13.

11. Hywel Francis, 'The Secret World of the South Wales Miners' in David Smith ed. *A People and a Proletariat* (London, 1980), p. 174.

12. Michelle Perrot, *Les ouvriers en grève. France 1871–1890* (Paris, 1974), p. 380; Sewell, *op. cit.*, pp. 166, 186–7; Truant, *op. cit.*, pp. 215, 224; Moss, *op. cit.*, pp. 31–2.

13. German Communist Party leaders with this background include Wilhelm Pieck (joiner) and Walter Ulbricht (joiner), both of whom had done their journeyman travel. cf. Hermann Weber, *Die Wandlung des deutschen Kommunismus* (Frankfurt, 1969), vol. 2; August Sander, *Menschen des Zwanzigsten Jahrhunderts: Porträtphotographien 1892–1952* (Munich, 1980),

plates 103, 104 for pictures of German travelling journeymen of the 1920s in traditional costume.

14. See Ellic Howe, *The London Compositor* (London, 1947), introduction, pp. 22–32; Thomas Ford, *Compositors' Handbook*, 1854; C.H. Timperley, *Encyclopaedia of Literary and Typographical Anecdotes* (London, 1842); Charles Manby Smith, *The Working Man's Way in the World* (London, 1854). More recently: J.M. Sykes, 'Trade Union Workshop Organization in the Printing Industry – the Chapel', *Human Relations* 13, 1 Feb 1960, pp. 9 ff.; Cynthia Cockburn, *Brothers. Male Dominance and Technological Change* (London, 1983), pp. 16–19.

15. cf. Heiner Grote, *Sozialdemokratie und Religion: Eine Dokumentation für die Jahre 1863 bis 1875* (Tübingen, 1968). A point to note, especially on the continent, is the association of 'class conscious' movements with cremation, on the ground of its greater affinity to science and progress: 'since the new system of cremation does not derive from obsolete religious views, but is rather ... the necessary consequence of the progressive understanding of Nature' (Grote, p. 134). Or, in the words of the motto of the Workers' Funeral Association 'The Flame' (Austria): 'Proletarian in life, proletarian in death, and buried in the spirit of cultural progress' (Langewiesche, *Zur Freizeit*, p. 387). See also Patrick H Hutton, *The Cult of the Revolutionary Tradition, The Blanquists in French Politics 1864–1893* (Berkeley, 1981), pp. 53–8 and chapter 4.

16. F. Machin, *The Yorkshire Miners. A History* (Barnsley, 1958), p. 162.

17. Williams, *op. cit.*, pp. 258–9.

18. K. Tenfelde, 'Bergarbeiterkultur in Deutschland: ein Überblick', *Geschichte und Gesellschaft*, V/1, 1979, pp. 12–53.

19. R.W. Postgate, *The Builders' History* (London, 1923), p. 63.

20. P.H.J.S. Gosden, *The Friendly Societies in England 1800–75* (Manchester, 1961), p. 127.

21. Christian Müller, *James Sharples und das Zertifikat der Amalgamated Society of Engineers. Studien zur Bildkultur Britischer Gewerkschaften* (Hamburg, 1978).

22. J.H. Treble, 'The Attitude of the Roman Catholic Church towards Trade Unionism in the North of England, 1833–1842', *Northern History*, vol V, 1970, p. 93–113.

23. 'The Reminiscences of Thomas Dunning (1813–1894) and the Nantwich Shoemakers' Case of 1834', ed. W.H. Chaloner, *Trans. Lancs. and Cheshire Antiq. Soc.*, lix, 1947, p. 98.

24. cf. the administrative decision in the Münster district of Prussia, 1885: 'Funerals with a demonstratively social-democratic tendency are to be counted as public demonstrations and to be treated under paragraph 9 of the (Anti-Socialist) law, K. Tenfelde, *Sozialgeschichte der Bergarbeiterschaft an der Ruhr im 19. Jahrhundert* (Bonn-Bad Godesberg, 1977), p. 392. For the politico-ritual significance of funerals, see also Hutton, *op. cit.*, pp. 53–8, 61–2, and note 13, and chapter 6.

25. Machin, *op. cit.*, p. 162. For the encouragement of miners' banners in Germany by state and management after 1815, see Tenfelde, *op. cit.*, pp. 97–8.

26. Machin, *op. cit.*, p. 162; Williams, *op. cit.*, p. 145.

27. Williams, *ibid.*

28. Müller, *op. cit.*, pp. 139–40.

29. *ibid.*, p. 141.

30. Leeson, *United We Stand;* Müller, *op. cit.*

31. Centro Studi Piero Gobetti, Istituto Storico della Resistenza in Piemonte, _Un'altra Italia nelle bandiere dei lavoratori: Simboli e cultura dall'unità dell'Italia all'avvento del fascismo_ (exhibition catalogue, Turin, 1980).
32. For the most widely reproduced of these socialist iconographers, cf. O.v.Schleinitz, _Walter Crane_ (Bielefeld, 1902). For the diffusion of his work, cf. U. Achten ed. _Zum Lichte Empor_ (Berlin–Bonn, 1980), pp. 30, 110 (May Day journals of German Social Democracy 1891, 1901).
33. Machin, _op. cit._, p. 162.
34. Williams, _op. cit._, p. 143 ff.
35. M Agulhon, 'La Statuomanie et l'Histoire', _Ethnologie Française_, nos. 3–4 (1978), pp. 3–4. See also Eric Hobsbawm and Terence Ranger eds, _The Invention of Tradition_ (Cambridge, 1983), especially chapter 7, pp. 263–307.
36. Müller, _op. cit._, p. 232.
37. J.P.H. Carter, 'Contributions, Badges and the Liverpool Carters', _Northwestern Labour History Bulletin 2_, (1975), pp. 17–21.
38. cf. R.A. Leeson, _United We Stand_, e.g., p. 49.
39. For an erudite discussion of the evolution of this symbolism, see _Un'altra Italia nelle bandiere_, pp. 12–48 (S. Pettenati, 'Note sulla tradizione iconografica delle bandiere'; P. Alessandrone, 'Una lettura delle bandiere operaie', and the _Schede storiche_, pp. 143–270).
40. Müller, _James Sharples_, pp. 24–38; Gorman, _Banner Bright_, p. 55.
41. Peter Flora, _State, Economy and Society in Western Europe 1815–1975: A Data Handbook_ vol I: _The Growth of Mass Democracies and Welfare States_ (Frankfurt–London–Chicago, 1983), ch. 3.
42. Tenfelde, _Sozialgeschichte_, p. 595.
43. G. Cyriax and R. Oakeshott, _The Bargainers. A survey of modern trade unionism_ (London, 1960), p. 15.
44. A.R. Griffin, _Miners of Nottinghamshire 1914–1944, A history of the Nottinghamshire Miners' Union_ (London, 1962), p. 63 ff.
45. Perrot, _op. cit._, pp. 558–9.
46. Gabriel Perreux, (Paris, 1932), pp. 50–51. M. Dommanget, _Le drapeau rouge et la révolution de 1848_ (Paris, 1948).
47. Perrot, _op. cit._, p. 567.
48. Sir Walter Citrine, _ABC of Chairmanship_ (London, 1939), p. 3.
49. Perrot, _op. cit._, p. 592.
50. Citrine, _op. cit._, p. 162.
51. Perrot, _op. cit._, p. 595.
52. Citrine, _op. cit._, p. 20.
53. For the history of May Day, see F. Giovanoli, _Die Maifeierbewegung, Ihre wirtschaftlichen und soziologischen Ursprünge u.Wirkungen_ (Karlsruhe, 1925); M. Dommanget, _Histoire du Premier Mai_ (Paris, 1953); G. Haupt, _La Deuxième Internationale, 1889–1914: Etude critique des sources_ (Hague, 1964); André Rossel, _Premier Mai. 90 ans de lutte populaire dans le monde_ (Paris, 1977); M. Massara, C. Schirinzi, M. Sioli, _Storia del Primo Maggio_ (Milan, 1978); Udo Achten, _Illustrierte Geschichte des Ersten Mai_ (Oberhausen, 1979); D. Fricke, _Kleine Geschichte des Ersten Mai_ (Frankfurt, 1980).
54. For such a 'trade-union festival' replacing the socialist May Day under conditions of political constraint, see K-E. Moring, _Die Sozialdemokratische Partei in Bremen 1890–1914_ (Hanover, 1968), pp. 25–27. The occasion was enormously successful, no doubt because it included not only national political speakers but the usual fairground paraphernalia – carousels, marquees for dancing, stalls – of popular festivity. Thirty-five unions, twenty

choral societies and several bands took part in 1890. The authorities in 1894 banned a formal march of participants to the scene, or informal processions accompanied by music, singing, the carrying of flags *and the participation of women* (*ibid.* p. 27).

55. John Wilson, *History of the Durham Miners' Association, 1870-1904* (Durham, 1907), pp. 59-61; Gorman, *op. cit.*, p. 36.

56. Wilson, *ibid.*, p. 34.

57. F. Engels to Sorge 17 May 1893 (Marx-Engels, *Werke* vol 39); see also Victor Adler, *Aufsätze, Reden und Briefe* (Vienna, 1922) I, p. 69.

58. A. Van Gennep, *Manuel de Folklore Français* I, iv: Les cérémonies périodiques et saisonnières 2: cycle de Mai (Paris, 1949), p. 1719.

59. Dommanget, *op. cit.*, p. 343.

60. Ettore Ciccotti, *La psicologia del movimento socialista* (Bari, 1903), pp. 112-13.

61. Maxime Leroy, *La coutûme ouvrière* (Paris, 1913) vol I, p. 246.

62. *Un'altra Italia*, p. 278.

63. Helmut Hartwig, 'Plaketten zum 1.Mai 1934-39', *Aesthetik und Kommunikation*, vii, no. 26 (1976), pp. 56-9.

64. On the functions of 'Zahlabende' (dues-collecting) see W.L. Guttsman, *The German Social Democratic Party, 1875-1933: from ghetto to government* (London, c. 1981), p. 170.

65. *Un'altra Italia*, p. 33.

66. Dommanget, *Eugène Pottier, Membre de la Commune et Chantre de l'Internationale* (Paris, 1971), ch. 3.

67. *Un'altra Italia*, p. 277.

68. Matull, *op. cit.*, p. 34.

69. Guttsman, *op. cit.*, p. 169. For the membership of similar bodies in Austria, see Langewiesche, *op. cit.*

70. Stephan Hermlin, *Abendlicht* (Leipzig, 1979), pp. 35-6.

## Chapter 6: Man and Woman: Images on the Left

1. This paper grew out of a conversation with Peter Hának of the Hungarian Academy of Sciences, Institute of History, about a paper by Efim Etkind (formerly of Leningrad, now of Nanterre) on '1830 in European Poetry'. On the art-historical side I have since had essential help from Georg Eisler, Francis and Larissa Haskell, and Nick Penny. In a sense this is therefore a cooperative work, though the interpretations and errors are all my own.

2. cf. the catalogue of the exhibition *La Liberté guidant le peuple de Delacroix*, catalogue établi et redigé par Helène Toussaint, Etude au laboratoire de la recherche des musées de France par Lola Faillant-Dumas et Jean-Paul Rioux (Paris, 1982) for a full discussion and bibliography, to which should be added H. Lüdecke, *Eugène Delacroix und die Pariser Julirevolution* (Berlin, 1965), and Efim Etkind, '1830 in der europäischen Dichtung' in R. Urbach ed. *Wien und Europa zwischen den Revolutionen* (1789-1848) (Vienna-Munich, 1978).

3. T.J. Clark, *The Absolute Bourgeois* (London, 1973), p. 19.

4. Etkind, *op. cit.*, pp. 150-1.

5. Heinrich Heine, *Gesammelte Werke*, vol. IV, (Berlin, 1956-7), p. 19.

6. E. Ramiro, *Félicien Rops* (Paris, 1905), pp. 80-1.

7. Eduard Fuchs, *Die Frau in der Karikatur* (Munich, *op. cit.*, 1906, p. 484.) Fuchs described *Peuple* not implausibly as 'Megäre Volk' or 'The People as

Virago'; Ramiro, *op. cit.*, p. 188. A less explicit version of the same figure, because omitting the lower half of the woman's body, is on an unpaginated plate of Franz Blei, *Félicien Rops* (Berlin, 1921).

8. M. Agulhon, 'Esquisse pour une archéologie de la République: L'allégorie civique féminine', *Annales* 28, 1973, pp. 5–34. A non-revolutionary heroine is almost simultaneously presented in the opposite manner to Delacroix in David Wilkie's *Defence of Saragossa*, 1828 (Wilkie Exhibition, Royal Academy, 1958). The real Spanish heroine is shown fully dressed but in allegorical pose, while a male partisan crouches beside her, nude to the waist. (I owe this reference to Dr N. Penny.) Byron, who discusses the role of the Spanish female freedom-fighters and the Maid of Saragossa at length, and admiringly (*Childe Harold* 1, 54 ff.) stresses the apparently unfeminine heroism: 'Her lover sinks – she sheds no ill-timed tear;/Her chief is slain – she fills his fatal post;/Her fellows flee – she checks their base career;/The foe retires – she heads the sallying host.' But he also stresses that she remains within the range of what male superiority regards as desirable in women: 'Yet are Spain's maids no race of Amazons,/But formed for all the witching arts of love.' In fact, theirs – unlike Liberty's – is 'the fierceness of the dove'.

9. See Jean Duché, *1760–1960 Deux siècles d'histoire de France par la caricature* (Paris, 1961), pp. 142, 143, 145.

10. J. Bruhat, Jean Dautry, Emile Tersen, *La Commune de 1871* (Paris, 1971), p. 190 – an English picture.

11. Jean Grand-Carteret, *L'Affaire Dreyfus et l'Image* (Paris, 1898), p. 150.

12. *ibid.*, pls. 61, 67, 106, 251.

13. R.A. Leeson, *United We Stand: an illustrated account of trade union emblems* (London, 1971), p. 26.

14. Lucien Christophe, *Constantin Meunier*, pls. 6, 7, 8, 9, 21 (Antwerp, 1947).

15. Frans Masereel, *Die Stadt* (Munich, 1925).

16. John Gorman, *Banner Bright: an illustrated history of the banners of the British Trade Union movement* (London, 1973), p. 126.

17. Leeson, *op. cit.*, pp. 60–70.

18. Gorman, *op. cit.*, pp. 122–3.

19. W. Crane, *Cartoons for the Cause: A Souvenir of the International Socialist Workers and Trade Union Congress 1886–96* (London, 1896).

20. From the collection of Dr Herbert Steiner of Vienna. For the survival of the triple slogan of the French Revolution, see U. Achten ed., *Zum Lichte Empor: Mai-Festzeitungen der Sozialdemokratie 1891–1914* (Berlin–Bonn 1980), pp. 12–14, D. Fricke, *Kleine Geschichte des Ersten Mai* (Frankfurt, 1980), p. 61.

21. Joseph Edwards (ed.), *Labour Annual 1895*, Manchester.

22. Christophe, *op. cit.*, pl. 12.

23. See E. and M. Dixmier, *L'Assiette au Beurre*, pl. ix (Paris, 1974).

24. The replacement of the female allegory by the naked male figure in German socialist iconography round 1900 has been independently noted by Detlev Hoffman, Ursula Schmidt-Linsenhoff, *Unsere Welt trotz alledem* (Frankfurt, 1978), p. 375.

25. 'To draw a peasant's figure in action, I repeat, that's what an essentially modern figure is, the very core of modern art, which neither the Greeks nor the Renaissance nor the old Dutch have done ... People like Daumier – we must respect them for they are among the pioneers. The simple nude but modern figure, as Hennor and Lefèvre have renewed it, ranks high ... But peasants and labourers are not nude, after all, and it is not necessary to imagine them in the nude. The more painters begin to paint workmen's and

peasants' figures, the better I shall like it . . .' Vincent van Gogh, *The Complete Letters of Vincent van Gogh*, vol. 11 (London, 1958), pp. 400, 402. (I owe the reference to Francis Haskell.)

26. F.D. Klingender, *Art and the Industrial Revolution* (London, 1947), pls. 10, 47, 57, 90, 92, 103; Paul Brandt, *Schaffende Arbeit und bildende Kunst*, vol. 11 (Leipzig, 1927–8), pp. 240 ff.

27. Brandt, *op. cit.*, p. 243, pl. 314.

28. Leeson, *op. cit.*, p. 23.

29. Nicholas Penny, *Church Monuments in Romantic England* (New Haven & London, 1977), pl. 138.

30. Brandt, *op. cit.*, p. 270.

31. I.E. Grabar, V.N. Lazarev, F.S. Kamenov, *Istoriya Russkogo Isskusstva*, vol. XI, (Moscow, 1957), pp. 33, 83, 359, 381, 431.

32. Tsigal, Burganov, Svetlov, Chernòv (eds), *Sovietskaya Skulptura 74* (Moscow, 1976), p. 52.

33. Grabar *et al.*, *op. cit.*, p. 150.

34. In a work celebrating the fifteenth anniversary of the October Revolution, the first photo of this kind ('Socialist man and his enthusiasm are the motor of construction') only occurs in the year 1932. *Fünfzehn Eiserne Schritte, Ein Buch der Tatsachen aus der Sowjetunion* (Berlin, 1932).

35. Klingender, *op. cit.*, pl. XV.

36. 'An injury to one is an injury to all', 'We will fight and may die, but we will never surrender', 'This is a holy war/and we will not cease/until all destitution/prostitution and exploitation/is swept away.' Gorman, *op. cit.*, p. 130.

37. Grabar *et al.*, *op. cit.*, pl. XI, p. 431.

38. Peter Kriedte, Hans Medick, Jürgen Schlumbohm, *Industrialisierung vor der Industrialiserung* (Göttingen, 1977), chapters 2–3.

39. Thus in France 56% of all women employed in industry in 1906 worked in clothing, which also employed 50% of those in Belgian industry (1890), 25% of those in German (1907), and 36% of those in British industry (1891). Peter N. Stearns, *Lives of Labour: Work in a Maturing Industrial Society* (London, 1975), Appendix III, p. 365.

40. D.C. Marsh, *The Changing Social Structure of England and Wales 1871– 1961*, Revised edition (London, 1965), p. 129.

41. W. Woytinsky, *Die Welt in Zahlen*, Vol. II, Berlin, 1926, p. 76; Gertraud Wolf, *Der Frauenerwerb in den Hauptkulturstaaten* (Munich, 1916), p. 251.

42. Peter N. Stearns in Martha J. Vicinus (ed.), *Suffer and Be Still: Women in the Victorian Age* (Bloomington & London, 1973), p. 118.

43. Marsh, *op. cit.*, p. 129.

44. The problem here hinted at has been admirably presented in Louise A. Tilly and Joan W. Scott, *Women, Work and Family*, New York, 1978, esp. chapter 8 and pp. 228–9. This excellent discussion confirms the present analysis especially insofar as it situates the rise of that phase of the economy when 'the new organization of manufacturing required an adult male labor force primarily' and when 'during most of her married life a woman served as a specialist in child rearing and consumer activities for her family' precisely in the period when the mass labour movement emerged in the industrially advanced countries.

45. E.P. Thompson, 'The Moral Economy of the English Crowd in the Eighteenth Century', *Past and Present*, 50 (1971).

46. L. Levi Accati, 'Vive le roi sans taille et sans gabelle: una discussione sulle rivolte contadine', *Quaderni Storici*, September–December 1972, p. 1078;

Heine's comment on Delacroix reflects the role of the market women ('fishwife').

47. H.A. Clegg, Alan Fox and A.F. Thompson, *A History of British Trade Unions since 1889*, vol. I, (Oxford, 1964), pp. 469–70.
48. S. and B. Webb, *Industrial Democracy* (London, 1897), p. 496.
49. *ibid.*, p. 497.
50. *ibid.*, pp. 496–7.
51. *ibid.*, p. 497.
52. See Jean Touchard, *La Gauche en France depuis 1900* (Paris, 1977), p. 113.
53. Bebel's feminism may not be unconnected with his enthusiasm for Fourier, about whom he also wrote a book. Frederick Engels' influential *Origin of the Family* should also be mentioned.
54. Eugène Pottier, *Oeuvres Complètes*, ed. Pierre Brochon (Paris, 1966).
55. Gorman, *op. cit.*, p. 126.
56. The image of utopia increasingly shifted from one based on natural fertility to one based on technological and scientific productivity. Both were clearly present in utopian socialism – see Pottier's poem *L'Age d'Or*, quoted above: 'Oh nations, plus de torpeur./Mille réseaux vous ont nouées./L'électricité, la vapeur/sont vos servants dévoués' etc. (Oh nations awake! You are linked to a thousand networks. Electricity and steam are your faithful servants.) However iconographically nature/fertility prevailed over technology, certainly until 1917.
57. J.F.C. Harrison, *Robert Owen and the Owenites in Britain and America: the quest for the new moral world* (London, 1969), pp. 58–62.
58. *ibid.*, pp. 60–61.
59. *ibid.*, pp. 98, 102, 121 for frequency of female messiahs in this period.
60. Brandt, *op. cit.*, p. 269.

**Chapter 7: Political Shoemakers**

1. *A Village Politician: The Life-Story of John Buckley*, ed. J.C. Buckmaster (London, 1897), p. 41.
2. M. Sensfelder, *Histoire de la cordonnerie* (Paris, 1856), quoted in Joseph Barberet, *Le travail en France: monographies professionnelles*, 7 vols. (Paris, 1886–90), v, pp. 63–4.
3. Rudolf Stadelmann, 'Soziale Ursachen der Revolution von 1848', in Hans-Ulrich Wehler (ed.), *Moderne deutsche Sozialgeschichte* (Berlin, 1970), p. 140; E.J. Hobsbawm and George Rudé, *Captain Swing* (London, 1969), p. 181; Jacques Rougerie, 'Composition d'une population insurgée: l'exemple de la Commune', *Le mouvement social*, no. 48 (1964), p. 42; Theodore Zeldin, *France, 1848–1945*, 2 vols. (Oxford, 1973), i, p. 214.
4. Jean-Pierre Aguet, *Les grèves sous la monarchie de Juillet, 1830–1847* (Geneva, 1954); David Pinkney, 'The Crowd in the French Revolution of 1830', *Amer. Hist. Rev.*, lxx (1964), pp. 1–17; David Jones, *Chartism and the Chartists* (London, 1975), pp. 30–2; D.J. Goodway, 'Chartism in London' (London Univ. Ph.D. thesis, 1979), pp. 37–9, shows their proportional participation in London Chartism to be higher than any other large occupation (over three thousand members) except stone-masons; George Rudé, *The Crowd in the French Revolution* (Oxford, 1959), appendix 4.
5. Georges Duveau, *La vie ouvrière en France sous le Second Empire*, 7th edn. (Paris, 1946), p. 75.
6. Jacques Rougerie, *Paris libre* (Paris, 1971), p. 263.

7. Reinhold Reith, *Zur biographischen Dimension von 'Hochverrath und Aufruhr': Versuch einer historischen Protestanalyse am Beispiel des Aprilaufstandes 1848 in Konstanz*, pp. 33 ff. 44 ff. (master's thesis, Univ. Konstanz, 1981).

8. Edgar Rodrigues, *Socialismo e sindicalismo no Brasil, 1675-1913* (Rio de Janeiro, 1969), pp. 73, 223.

9. R. Hoppe and J. Kuczynski, '*Eine Berufs bzw. auch Klassen- und Schichtenanalyse der Märzgefallenen 1848 in Berlin.*' (*Jahrb. f. Wirtschaftsgesch.* 1964/IV, pp. 200-76).

10. Yves Lequin, *Les ouvriers de la région lyonnaise, 1848-1914*, 2 vols. (Lyon, 1977), ii, p. 281.

11. Karl Obermann, *Zur Geschichte des Bundes der Kommunisten* (East Berlin, 1955), p. 28.

12. Paul Voigt, 'Das deutsche Handwerk nach den Berufszählungen von 1882 und 1895', in *Untersuchungen über die Lage des Handwerks in Deutschland*, ix (Schriften des Vereins für Socialpolitik, lxx, Leipzig, 1897); J.H. Clapham, *Economic History of Modern Britain*, 3 vols. (Cambridge, 1952), ii, p. 43.

13. Hobsbawm and Rudé, *Captain Swing*, pp. 181-2.

14. *ibid.*, pp. 218, 246.

15. Keith Brooker, 'The Northampton Shoemakers' Reaction to Industrialisation: Some Thoughts', *Northamptonshire Past and Present*, vi (1980), p. 155.

16. Sample taken from Librairie A. Faure, 15 rue du Val du Grace, catalogue 5, Livres anciens et modernes, items 262-324; checked in Jean Maitron (ed.), *Dictionaire biographique du mouvement ouvrier français, Pt. 1, 1789-1864*, 3 vols. (Paris, 1964-6).

17. David M. Gordon, 'Merchants and Capitalism: Industrialization and Provincial Politics at Reims and St. Etienne under the Second Republic and Second Empire' (Brown Univ. Ph.D. thesis, 1978), p. 67.

18. William Sewell Jr., 'The Structure of the Working Class of Marseille in the Middle of the Nineteenth Century' (Univ. of California, Berkeley, Ph.D. thesis, 1971), p. 299.

19. 'De l'association des ouvriers de tous les corps d'état', repr. in Alain Faure and Jacques Rancière (eds.), *La parole ouvrière, 1830-1851* (Paris, 1976), pp. 159-68.

20. Gian Maria Bravo, *Les socialistes avant Marx*, 2 vols. (Paris, 1970), ii, p. 221.

21. Alfred F. Young, 'George Robert Twelves Hewes, 1742-1840: A Boston Shoemaker and the Memory of the American Revolution' (forthcoming in *William and Mary Quart.*).

22. Maurice Garden, *Lyon et les Lyonnais au XVIII^e siècle* (Paris, 1970), pp. 244 ff. Above-average literacy is noted for rural cordwainers in David Cressy, *Literacy and the Social Order: Reading and Writing in Tudor and Stuart England* (Cambridge, 1981), pp. 130-6, but average or sub-average literacy for the lower classification of 'shoemakers' both in London and countryside. For various reasons Cressy's London figures are more problematic than his rural ones.

23. Emmanuel Le Roy Ladurie, *Les paysans de Languedoc*, 2 vols. (Paris, 1966), i, pp. 349-51.

24. Peter Burke, *Popular Culture in Early Modern Europe* (London, 1978), pp. 38-9.

25. Jean Maitron, *Le mouvement anarchiste en France*, 2 vols. (Paris, 1975), i, p. 131.

26. For example, Anon., *Crispin Anecdotes: Comprising Interesting Notices of Shoemakers, who have been Distinguished for Genius, Enterprise or Eccentricity* (Sheffield and London, 1827); John Prince, *Wreath for St. Crispin: Being Sketches of Eminent Shoemakers* (Boston, Mass., 1848); Anon., *Crispin: The Delightful, Princely and Entertaining History of the Gentle Craft* (London, 1750); William Edward Winks, *Lives of Illustrious Shoemakers* (London, 1883); Thomas Wright, *The Romance of the Shoe* (London, 1922); Anon., *Lives of Distinguished Shoemakers* (Portland, Me., 1849); Joseph Sparkes Hall, *The Book of the Feet* (New York, 1847).

27. 'Bei leisten, drät und pech der Schumacher sol bleiben und die gelehrten leut lassen die bücher schreiben', 'predigender Schuster macht schlechte Schuhe': *Deutsches Sprichwörter-Lexikon*, 5 vols. (Aalen, 1963), iv, cols. 398–9. The injustice of such proverbs so outraged the nineteenth-century compilers of this encyclopaedia that they added a footnote citing two highly intellectual shoemakers who also produced excellent shoes (col. 399).

28. Charles Bradlaugh, the champion of atheism, was elected M.P. for Northampton, a shoemaking constituency. For the 'Schusterkomplott' of Vienna shoemakers accused of atheism in 1794, see E. Wangermann, 'Josephinismus und katholischer Glaube' in E. Kovacs ed. *Katholische Aufklärung und Josephinismus* (Vienna, 1979), pp. 339–340. One of the accused, inspired by the sermons of a reform-Catholic preacher, in typical cobbler style 'bought an old Bible, had it read out to me, compared the ... passages cited in Wiser's sermons ... with the Bible text itself, whereby I became doubtful in my religion.'

29. Karl Flanner, *Die Revolution von 1848 in Wiener Neustadt* (Vienna, 1978), p. 181.

30. Eugenia W. Herbert, *The Artist and Social Reform: France and Belgium, 1885–1898* (New Haven, Conn., 1961), pp. 14 ff.; for the shoemaker's revenge on Apelles, who originally invited him to stick to his last and abstain from art criticism, cf. the enormous influence (through Grave) of anarchism on post-Impressionist painters, see *ibid.*, pp. 184 ff.

31. Samuel Smiles, *Men of Invention and Industry* (London, 1884), ch. 12.

32. See *Crispin Anecdotes*, p. 144; cf. also Hobsbawm and Rudé, *Captain Swing*, pp. 63, 70.

33. *Crispin Anecdotes*, p. 45; Winks, *Lives of Illustrious Shoemakers*, p. 232.

34. John Brown, *Sixty Years' Gleanings from Life's Harvest: A Genuine Autobiography* (Cambridge, 1858), p. 239, cited in Nicholas Mansfield, 'John Brown: A Shoemaker's Place in London', *History Workshop*, viii (1979), p. 135.

35. Barberet, *Le travail en France*, v, pp. 62–3.

36. Wright, *Romance of the Shoe*, p. 218.

37. *Ibid.*, p. 307.

38. Paul Lacroix, Alphonse Duchesne and Ferdinand Seré, *Histoire des cordonniers et des artisans dont la profession se rattache à la cordonnerie* (Paris, 1852), pp. 116–17.

39. Shakespeare, *Julius Caesar*, I, i; Dekker, *The Shoemaker's Holiday*, iv, 48–76. The quotation is from the Cerne Abbas Inquiry of 1594 (Brit. Lib., Harleian MS. 6849, fos. 183–90), in *Willobie His Avisa*, ed. G.B. Harrison (London, 1926), appendix 3, p. 264. We are obliged to Michael Hunter for this early example of English radical shoemakers.

40. *Crispin Anecdotes*, p. 150.

41. Wright, *Romance of the Shoe*, p. 109.

42. *ibid.*, p. 4.

43. E.P. Thompson, *The Making of the English Working Class* (London, 1963), pp. 183–4.
44. *Crispin Anecdotes*, p. 126.
45. Lacroix, Duchesne and Seré, *Histoire des cordonniers*, pp. 206–7.
46. *ibid.*, p. 188.
47. Barberet, *Le travail en France*, v, pp. 64–5.
48. Wright, *Romance of the Shoe*, p. 46; Hall, *Book of the Feet*, pp. 196–7. Despite the suggestion of these authors no association between shoemaking and bookbinding has been established. In London sons of shoemakers are probably under-represented in the trade between 1600 and 1815. While bookbinding was not infrequently combined with some other occupation such as merchant-tailor, draper, barber, mason, glazier, weaver, dyer, needle-maker and wheelwright, in *no* case was it combined with shoemaking. Calculated from Ellic Howe, *A List of London Bookbinders, 1648–1815* (London, 1950).
49. cf. the role of one Hans von Sagan in the traditions of German shoemakers. He gained the emperor's favour and the craft the right to include the imperial eagle in its coat of arms, by intervening in a fourteenth-century battle. The relative scarcity of formalized custom in the trade has been noted in Rudolf Wissell, *Des alten Handwerks Recht und Gewohnheit*, ed. Konrad Hahm, 2 vols. (Berlin, 1929), ii, p. 91; Andreas Griessinger, *Das symbolische Kapital der Ehre: Streikbewegungen und kollektives Bewusstsein deutscher Handwerksgesellen im 18. Jahrhundert* (Frankfurt, Berlin and Vienna, 1981). We are very grateful to Andreas Griessinger of the University of Konstanz for making the manuscript of his book available to us prior to its publication.
50. *The Unknown Mayhew*, ed. Eileen Yeo and E.P. Thompson (London, 1971), p. 279. See also 'Mental Character of the Cobblers', cited in *The Man*, 9 April 1834 (New York), p. 168: 'Seated all day on a low seat, pressing obdurate last and leather ... or hammering heels and toes with much monotony – the cobbler's mind, regardless of the proverb, wanders into regions metaphysical, political, and theological; and from men thus employed have sprung many founders of sects, religious reformers, gloomy politicians, 'bards, sophists, statesmen' and other 'unquiet things', including a countless host of hypochondriacs. The dark and pensive aspect of shoemakers in general is a matter of common observation. It is but justice to them, however, to say that their acquisition of knowledge and their habits of reflection, are often such as to command admiration.'
51. Richard Watteroth, 'Die Erfurter Schuharbeiterschaft', in *Auslese und Anpassung der Arbeiterschaft in der Schuhindustrie und einem oberschleisischen Walzwerke* (Schriften des Vereins für Sozialpolitik, cliii, Munich and Leipzig, 1915), p. 6.
52. Calculated from Joseph Belli, *Die Rote Feldpost unterm Sozialistengesetz* (Bonn, 1978 edn.), pp. 54–94. We are obliged to Rainer Wirtz for this reference. Julius Pierstorff, 'Drei Jenaer Handwerke', in *Untersuchungen über die Lage des Handwerks in Deutschland*, ix (Schriften des Vereins für Sozialpolitik, lxx, Leipzig, 1897), p. 36, notes that journeymen stayed a maximum of six months in the same shop.
53. Griessinger, *Das symbolische Kapital der Ehre*, pp. 102–7, describes these rituals excellently for eighteenth-century Germany.
54. Burke, *Popular Culture in Early Modern Europe*, pp. 38–9.
55. Robert Chambers, *The Book of Days*, 2 vols. (London and Edinburgh, 1862–4), ii, p. 492; A.R. Wright, *British Calendar Customs: England*, ed. T.E. Lones, 3 vols. (Folk-Lore Soc., xcvii, cii, cvi, London and Glasgow, 1936–

40), iii, pp. 102–4. In England (but not in Scotland) it may have been aided by the association of St Crispin's Day with nationalism, for this was, as readers of Shakespeare's *Henry V* will recall, the date of the battle of Agincourt against the French.

56. As surveyed in Griessinger, *Das symbolische Kapital der Ehre*, pp. 130–3.

57. Brooker, 'The Northampton Shoemakers' Reaction to Industrialisation', *passim*, on conflicts arising out of this during industrialization. See also Mansfield, 'John Brown: A Shoemaker's Place in London', *passim*.

58. *Allgemeine Deutsche Biographie*, iii, entry for Jakob Böhme.

59. *Dictionary of National Biography*, v.

60. Winks, *Lives of Illustrious Shoemakers*, pp. 81, 180.

61. Brian Dobbs, *The Last Shall Be First: The Colourful Story of John Lobb, the St. James's Bootmaker* (London, 1972), pp. 27–8.

62. B. Aebert, 'Die Schuhmacherei in Loitz', in *Untersuchungen über die Lage des Handwerks in Deutschland*, i (Schriften des Vereins für Socialpolitik, lxii, Leipzig, 1895), pp. 39, 49; Siegfried Heckscher, 'Über die Lage des Schuhmachergewerbes in Altona, Elmshorn, Heide, Preetz und Barmstedt', in *ibid.*, p. 2.

63. US National Archives RG 217, Fourth Auditor Accounts, Numerical Series, 1141. We owe this reference to Christopher McKee.

64. Bernardino Ramazzini, *Health Preserved, in Two Treatises*, 2nd edn. (London, 1750), p. 215.

65. John Thomas Arlidge, *The Hygiene, Diseases and Mortality of Occupations* (London, 1892), p. 216, quoting William Farr's data of 1875 – below-average mortality at all ages except 20–25 as against the very high mortality of tailors – and Ratcliffe, an analyst of the mortality of members of Friendly Societies, who considered their 'vitality' inferior only to that of farm-labourers and carpenters.

66. *Crispin Anecdotes*, p. 126.

67. 'The frequency of the development of literary talent among shoemakers has often been remarked. Their occupation, being a sedentary and comparatively noiseless one, may be considered as more favorable than some others to meditation; but perhaps its literary productiveness has arisen quite as much from the circumstance of its being a trade of light labor, and therefore resorted to, in preference to most others, by persons in the humble life who are conscious of more mental talent than bodily strength': Hall, *Book of the Feet*, p. 4. In spite of the fact that the hammering of leather caused shoemaking sometimes to be excluded from certain quarters as a 'noisy craft' (lärmendes Handwerk) – cf. W.J. Schröder, *Arbeitergeschichte und Arbeiterbewegung: Industriearbeit und Organisationsverhalten in 19. und frühen 20. Jahrhundert* (Frankfurt–New York, 1978), p. 91 – noise is rarely noted in the literature about shoemaker-intellectuals.

68. Aebert, 'Die Schuhmacherei in Loitz', p. 38.

69. Nicolaus Geissenberger, 'Die Schuhmacherei in Leipzig und Umgegend', in *Untersuchungen über die Lage des Handwerks in Deutschland*, ii (Schriften des Vereins für Socialpolitik, lxiii, Leipzig, 1895), p. 169.

70. Pauly-Wissowa, *Real-encyclopädie der classischen Alterthumswissenschaft*, 2nd ser., iv (1), cols. 989–94, under 'sutor'. The low status of the trade is demonstrated in the language as well. In France *savetier* was a term of derision; in England a cobbler also meant a 'botcher' or unskilled workman. See Lacroix, Duchesne and Seré, *Histoire des cordonniers*, p. 179.

71. Arlidge, *Hygiene, Diseases and Mortality of Occupations*, p. 216.

72. W.H. Schröder, *Arbeitergeschichte*, p. 93.

73. On these references to shoemakers, see *Crispin Anecdotes*, p. 102; *Deutsches Sprichwörter-Lexikon*, iv, cols. 398-401; *English Dialect Dictionary*, i, under 'cobbler', 'Cobbler's dinner – bread and bread to it'. The popular impression from colonial America to Europe held that, whatever else he was, a shoemaker was rarely prosperous. Poverty and a propensity for philosophizing were not at all contradictory; indeed they may help to explain the long-standing reputation of shoemakers as radicals. Thinking men among the poor were very likely to become political or ideological radicals. John Brown's memory of 'the great orators of the craft' described 'men in ragged habiliments and of squalid looks' who 'pour forth in touching and eloquent language their appeals': Mansfield, 'John Brown: A Shoemaker's Place in London', p. 131.

74. Max von Tayenthal, 'Die Schuhwarenindustrie Österreichs', *Sociale Rundschau* [Arbeitsstatistisches Amt im k. u.k. Handelsministerium], ii pt. 1 (1901), p. 764.

75. George Unwin, *The Gilds and Companies of London* (London, 1908), p. 82; Geissenberger, 'Die Schuhmacherei in Leipzig und Umgegend', p. 169; Watteroth, 'Die Erfurter Schuharbeiterschaft', p. 15.

76. In Santiago and Valparaiso provinces in 1854 there were 5,865 of them, compared to 3,720 carpenters, 1,615 tailors, 1,287 masons and bricklayers and 1,088 smiths and farriers: L.A. Romero, *La Sociedad de la Igualdad: los artesanos de Santiago de Chile y sus primeras experiencias politicas, 1820–1851* (Buenos Aires, 1978), p. 14. See also A. Bernal, A. Collantes de Teran and A. Garcia-Baquero, 'Sevilla: de los gremios a la industrialización', *Estudios de historia social* [Madrid], nos. 5-6 (1978), pp. 7-310, esp. Cuadro 8.

77. Griessinger, *Das symbolische Kapital der Ehre*, pp. 87-90.

78. J.A. Faber, *Drie Eeuwen Friesland*, 2 cols. (A.A.G. Bijdragen, xvii, Wageningen, 1972), ii, tables 111.8, 111.9, at pp. 444-5, 446-7.

79. Griessinger, *Das symbolische Kapital der Ehre*, pp. 90-5.

80. Thus Winks discusses the problem of the intellectual distinction of shoemakers under the heading 'A Constellation of Celebrated Cobblers': Winks, *Lives of Illustrious Shoemakers*, pp. 229 ff. For interchangeability, see also *Scottish National Dictionary*, under 'souter'.

81. C.N.R.S., *Trésor de la langue française* (Paris, 1978), under 'cordonnier'; *Grimms Wörterbuch*, under 'Schuster'.

82. Geissenberger, 'Die Schuhmacherei in Leipzig und Umgegend', p. 175. In the Germany of 1882 46.5% of all independent shoemakers were in villages of less than 2,000 inhabitants (two-thirds of them having another by-employment). Two thirds of all independent shoemakers were found in centres of less than 5,000 inhabitants. (*Statistik des Deutschen Reiches* NF Bd4. 1-2, p. 1194 and NF Bd 111, p. 104 f.)

83. Utz Jaeggle, *Kiebingen: Eine Heimatgeschichte* (Tübingen, 1977), p. 249. Hardly any of the local shoemakers belonged to the upper stratum of the village, and the majority not even to the middle stratum. 'Even today shoemakers count for nothing in the village': *ibid*. We are obliged to Rainer Wirtz for this reference.

84. Wilhelm Weitling, *Garantien der Harmonie und Freiheit* (Berlin, 1955 edn.), p. 289.

85. Flanner, *Die Revolution von 1848 in Wiener Neustadt*, pp. 26-7. Since the city specialized in the metal industries as well as textiles, metal craftsmen (less numerous though they were than shoemakers) are omitted as likely to have been over-represented.

86. cf. the Calabrian shoemaker cited in E.J. Hobsbawm, *Primitive Rebels* (Manchester, 1959), appendix 9, who prided himself on working even for the *carabinieri*.
87. We owe this point to Dr Mikuláš Teich, who quotes the proverb from his native Czechoslovakia: 'Where there is cutting, weighing or pouring, money is to be made'.
88. Raymond Williams, *Culture and Society* (New York, 1960), p. 16, citing the *Political Register*, 14 Apr. 1821.
89. Richard Cobb, *Les armées révolutionnaires*, 2 vols. (Paris and The Hague, 1961–3), ii, pp. 486–7.
90. *Crispin Anecdotes*, pp. 154–5.
91. Dale Tomich and Anson G. Rabinbach, 'Georges Haupt, 1928–1978', *German Critique*, no. 14 (1978), p. 3.
92. Richard Schüller, 'Die Schuhmacherei in Wien', in *Untersuchungen über die Lage des Handwerks in Österreich* (Schriften des Vereins für Socialpolitik, lxxi, Leipzig, 1896), pp. 49–50.
93. J.H. Clapham, *Economic History of Modern Britain*, i, 2nd edn. (Cambridge, 1930), p. 169.
94. Geissenberger, 'Die Schuhmacherei in Leipzig und Umgegend', p. 190.
95. Tayenthal, 'Die Schuhwarenindustrie Österreichs', pp. 974–5; Heckscher, 'Über die Lage des Schuhmachergewerbes in Altona, Elmshorn, Heide, Preetz und Barmstedt', pp. 4, 6.
96. P.R. Mounfield, 'The Footwear Industry of the East Midlands', *East Midlands Geographer*, xxii (1965), pp. 293–306.
97. For the situation in Lynn, Massachusetts, see Alan Dawley, *Class and Community: The Industrial Revolution in Lynn* (Cambridge, Mass., 1976).
98. James Devlin, *The Guide to Trade: The Shoemaker*, 2 vols. (London, 1839), is the best manual of shoemaking techniques before mechanization. The author, a radical, activist and minor literary figure (he contributed to Leigh Hunt's *London Journal*) was the best craftsman in the London trade: Goodway,'Chartism in London', p. 245. For the later nineteenth century, see John Bedford Leno, *The Art of Boot- and Shoe-making . . . with a Description of the Most Approved Machinery Employed* (London, 1885). Leno, though a printer by trade and poetaster/reciter by avocation, was long associated with the craft as owner and editor of the journal *St. Crispin*; see his *The Aftermath: With Autobiography of the Author* (London, 1892). For a more recent treatment, see R.A. Church, 'Labour Supply and Innovation, 1800–1860: The Boot and Shoe Industry', *Business Hist.*, xii (1970). For Erfurt, see Watteroth, 'Die Erfurter Schuharbeiterschaft', esp. pp. 113–14.
99. Barberet, *Le travail en France*, v, pp. 71, 85, 116, 163; Émile Levasseur, *Histoire de classes ouvrières et de l'industrie en France de 1789 à 1870*, 2 vols. (Paris, 1940 edn.), ii, p. 567; Christopher Johnson, 'Communism and the Working Class before Marx: The Icarian Experience', *Amer. Hist. Rev.*, lxxvi (1971), p. 66; David Landes, *The Unbound Prometheus* (London, 1969), pp. 294–6; Direction du travail, *Les associations professionelles ouvrières*, 4 vols. (Paris, 1894–1904) ii, pp. 11–87; *The Unknown Mayhew*, ed. Yeo and Thompson, pp. 228–79.
101. Charles Poncy, 'La chanson du cordonnier', in his *La chanson de chaque métier* (Paris, 1850), pp. 80–5.
102. Thompson, *The Making of the English Working Class*, p. 704.
103. Cited in Faure and Rancière, *La parole ouvrière, 1830–1851*, p. 161.
104. *James Hawker's Journal: A Victorian Poacher*, ed. Garth Christian (Oxford, 1978), pp. 15, 16. See also Mansfield, 'John Brown: A Shoemaker's Place in

London', pp. 130–1, who cites John Brown in 1811: 'So soon as I was settled in a regular seat of work, it became necessary that I should join the trade or shops-meeting, which is a combination for the support of wages'.

105. 'The Reminiscences of Thomas Dunning (1813–1894) and the Nantwich Shoemakers' Case of 1834', ed. W.H. Chaloner, *Trans. Lancs. and Cheshire Antiq. Soc.*, lix (1947), p. 98.

106. *ibid.*

107. Based on the biographical data in Hermann Weber, *Die Wandlung des deutschen Kommunismus*, 2 vols. (Frankfurt, 1969), ii.

108. Claude Willard, *Le mouvement socialiste en France, 1893–1905: les Guesdistes* (Paris, 1965), esp. pp. 335–7. See also Tony Judt, *Socialism in Provence, 1871–1914* (Cambridge, 1979), pp. 73, 112.

109. Parti Communiste Français, *Des Français en qui la France peut avoir confiance*, 2nd edn. (Paris, 1945); Maurice Duverger (ed.), *Partis politiques et classes sociales en France* (Paris, 1955), pp. 302, 304.

110. Based on data in Jean Maitron and Georges Haupt (eds.), *Dictionnaire biographique du mouvement ouvrier international: l'Autriche* (Paris, 1971).

111. Personal information from Hungarian colleagues. M.K. Dziewanowski, 'Social Democrats Versus "Social Patriots": the Origins of the Split in the Marxist Movement in Poland' (*American Slavic and East European Review*, vol. X, 1951), p. 18.

112. Based on Joyce Bellamy and John Saville (eds.), *Dictionary of Labour Biography* (London, 1972–, in progress).

113. Maitron, *Le mouvement anarchiste en France*, i, p. 131.

## Chapter 8: The Nineteenth-Century London Labour Market

1. The term 'labour market', as used here, means an area within which the various labour conditions (insofar as they depend on the bargains between workers and employers) are distinct from comparable ones in other areas. This does not imply that a labour market is internally homogeneous, or that its borders are sharply defined, or that, measured on certain time scales, it cannot be regarded as a sub-area of wider labour markets – regional, national, perhaps even international. However, though these larger markets might in the long run modify the supply of labour and jobs in a local labour market a good deal, and in the short somewhat, in the nineteenth century the local labour market remained distinct. In London it was almost certainly the most important area affecting wages and labour conditions.

2. cf. D. Buxton, 'On the rise of the manufacturing towns of Lancashire & Cheshire', in *Proc. Hist. Soc. of Lancashire & Cheshire* vol. VIII (1855–6), pp. 199–210.

3. *Wages and Hours Enquiry 1906* (Wage Census) for the Engineers: Newcastle, Shields, Mid-Tyne. The *National Amalgamated Union of Labour* reports give: Elswick, Byker, Gateshead, Mid-Tyne, Shields.

4. H. Mayhew, *London Labour and the London Poor* (1861), vol. II, 163 ff, 416 ff, discusses the sizes of the various administrative Londons around 1850 at some length.

5. *Poor Man's Guardian*, May 3rd, 1834, *Leicester Journal*, May 4th, 1834. See also the *Rules and Orders of the Friendly Brothers, held at the Duke's Head, Great Peter Street, Westminster*, 1860, which assumes an area within the reach of personal visiting as having a 3-miles radius.

6. *Operative Bricklayers' Society*, Circular, September, 1877.

7. *Parl. Papers*, XXXI of 1868-9, Appendix, 11th Report of the Royal Commissioners ... to enquire into ... Trades Unions, p. 239. Ellic Howe and H. Waite, *The London Society of Compositors* (London, 1948), 273 ff. A.E. Musson, *The Typographical Association* (Oxford, 1954), 273 ff.

8. 'Local Variations in Wage Rates' (*Ministry of Labour Gazette* vol. LVII, 5, 1949, 157-61).

9. London and the Provinces were organized by quite distinct and sovereign unions.

10. Reports, Monthly Circulars of *Operative Bricklayers' Society; R.C. on Trade Unions* (*Parl. Papers XXXI of 1868-9*), p. 301; *Return on Trades, Hours of Work* (*Parl. Papers* LXVIII of 1890), p. 10.

11. *Amalgamated Society of Carpenters and Joiners*, monthly and annual reports.

12. This expansion is recorded in *A Biographical Sketch of Brother John Jeffrey* (British Library of Political Science, Coll. EB XXXIV, p. 5).

13. cf. C. Booth, *Life and Labour*, Second Series, vol. V (1903), pp. 266 ff.

14. Mayhew, *op. cit.*, vol. II, 246, 290-1, 292.

15. *London Trades Council: A History* (London, 1950), pp. 45, 60, 79.

16. 1889 edition, p. 649.

17. T.C. Barker and M. Robbins, *A History of London Transport*, vol. I: *The Nineteenth Century* (London, 1975), pp. 217, 220; H.J. Dyos, *Exploring the Urban Past: Essays in urban history*, edited by D. Cannadine and D. Reeder (Cambridge, 1982), pp. 90-1, 94, 97-8. For an excellent survey of cheap London transport in 1908, see Board of Trade, *Report on the Cost of Living* (P.P. CVII of 1908), pp. 27-9.

18. cf. *Royal Commission on Housing of the Working Classes* (*Parl. Papers* XXX of 1884-5), esp. Qs 39 ff., 1932-3, 9955 ff., 10455, 10596, and *Select Committee on Artizans' and Labourers' Dwellings* (*Parl. Papers* VII of 1881), esp. Qs 2397-2403, 2610-13.

19. *Royal Commission on the Depression of Trade* (Parl. Papers XXII of 1886) App. D, p. 57.

20. Travelling Laws of the *Friendly Society of Operative Stonemasons* 1852-85. The number of permitted days rose gradually from three to five.

21. The best discussions of job-finding in nineteenth-century London are N.B. Dearle, *Problems of Unemployment in the London Building Trade* (London 1908) and the *Special Committee on Unskilled Labour* of the Charity Organization Society (1908), but the Royal Commissions on Labour and on the Poor Law contain a good deal of evidence on the problem.

22. *A Biographical Sketch. . . . (loc. cit.)*

23. S. Higenbottom, *Our Society's History* (Manchester, 1939), App. 1, 298 ff.

24. 'Fifty Years' Experience of an Irish Shoemaker in London', *St Crispin*, vol. II, 1869, p. 213. (*Goldsmiths' Library*.)

25. *Minutes of Evidence of the Metropolitan Railways Commission* (*Parl. Papers* XVII of 1846) Qs 1234-6.

26. This distance varied, naturally, but would normally be three or four miles. At any rate out of a collection of 44 builders' 'working rules' for the late nineteenth century, which give precise figures for the distance beyond which workers were to be given a 'lodging allowance', 34 give three or four miles. For the conventional view see also *Amalgamated Society of Engineers*, Abstract of Council Proceedings, April 1862 to December 1863, p. 112, 'that members residing three miles and upwards from the club house to which they belong are not finable for absenting themselves from summoned meetings', and the Rules of the *General Union of Carpenters and Joiners* (1868) which

provide that anyone living within four miles of the lodge house shall sign the out-of-work book daily.

27. It will be observed that the conservative Stonemasons in the 1860's did not even consider Woolwich and Plumstead as part of their London district. (See Appendix I.) The following table (Carpenters) brings out this lag:

**Carpenters' weekly standard wages and hours**

|            | WAGES |        |          |          | HOURS |        |          |          |
| ---------- | ----- | ------ | -------- | -------- | ----- | ------ | -------- | -------- |
|            | 1865  | 1867   | 1872–3   | 1876–7   | 1865  | 1867   | 1872–3   | 1876–7   |
| London     | 35/4  | 37/8   | 39/4½    | 39/4½    | 56½   | 56½    | 52½      | 52½      |
| Greenwich  | 33    | 35/4   | 37/8     | 42/4     | 56½   | 56½    | 56½      | 56½      |
| Woolwich   | 33    | 33     | 37/8     | 40       | 58½   | 58½    | 56½      | 56½      |
| Croydon    | 33    | 35/4   | 35/4     | 40       | 56½   | 56½    | 56½      | 56½      |
| Poplar*    | 36    | 36     | 39       | 39       | 58½   | 58½    | 54       | 54       |

*Poplar has been included as the immediate neighbour of Woolwich, though it is across the river. For the fullest discussion of this part of London, see G.J. Crossick, *An Artisan Elite in Victorian Society: Kentish London 1840–1880* (London, 1978).

28. There were several types of union branch. (1) represented a 'district'. (2) was an artificial unit, drawing together members from areas without sufficient strength to form local branches; e.g. the various 'North London' or 'West London' branches. (3) represented a place of work, and doubtless often of residence, for a particular trade, but not necessarily a flourishing general working class community; or else it represented a conventional centre for finding work over a much larger area (much as today 'Archer Street' among musicians represents not simply the West End, but the market for casual gigs anywhere in the London area, or even beyond). 'Victoria Docks' among the engineers of the 1860's, or 'Manchester Square' among carpenters, or perhaps King's Cross – which has never been any kind of 'community' – are branches of this sort. Some of the multiplicity of highly localized branches, e.g., Drury Lane, Edgware Road. Tottenham Court Road, City Road, Bedford Square, Gray's Inn Road, Cromer Street (Carpenters) may also derive from the public houses which used to be the headquarters of the old craft unions, and after which the conservative masons still named their Westminster branch, though it is likely that others derive from local builders' yards or sites.

29. For an indication of districts and regions, see Appendix II, on the local press existing in London 1850–1880.

30. *Gas Light Establishments: Reports* (Parl. Papers V of 1823).

31. *Metropolitan Railway Commission, loc. cit.*, Q 457.

32. *Royal Commission on Trade Unions* (*Parl. Papers* XXXIX of 1867–8) Q 19960.

33. cf. the sociologically undervalued Billy Hill, *Boss of Britain's Underworld* (London, 1955) which sketches the criminal sub-areas of London. North of the river there are several, but 'the Elephant mob from over the water had South London running their way. That included Brixton, Camberwell and New Cross' (p. 7).

34. A.W. Humphrey, *Robert Applegarth* (Manchester and London n.d.), p. 258; F.W. Soutter, *Recollections of a Labour Pioneer* (London, 1923), p. 27.

35. *Royal Commission on Trade Unions (Parl. Papers* XXXI of 1868–9, pp. 665, 667). *Beehive*, 23rd March 1871: 'London Trades Unions and Benefit Societies'.

36. Sources as for note 35. This concentration is even more evident from the *London and Suburban Trade Union Guide ... compiled by F.B.B., a trade unionist* (London n.d., but clearly 1890–92). The firms in the builders' directory contained in this booklet were very heavily concentrated north of the river; but the Operative Bricklayers had 12 out of 28 branches in the south, the Amalgamated Carpenters 10 out of 29, the Masons and Plasterers 10 out of 36; and the centre of the London Building Trades Committee was at the Bricklayers' Hall, Southwark.

37. For the fullest discussion of the East End, Gareth Stedman Jones, *Outcast London: A Study in the Relationship between Classes in Victorian Society* (Oxford, 1971).

38. It may be no accident that while south London had only three very large street markets in the 1890's – one in Bermondsey, and the two in Lambeth Marsh and Lambeth Walk, which plainly served the same large community – the Islington-Clerkenwell-Shoreditch area had five, Bethnal Green two, Poplar, Bow, Whitechapel and St George's-in-the-East one each. (L.C.C.: *London Markets*, 1893.) I have listed only the 'super-markets' of more than eighty barrows, of which there were only eighteen in all London.

39. Sources as for notes 35 and 36.

40. For a discussion see P.G. Hall, *The Industries of London Since 1861* (London, 1962).

41. *Select Committee on Blackfriars Bridge* (Parl. Papers XX of 1836), p. 26; Charity Organization Society, *Special Committee on Unskilled Labour* (1908), p. 93.

42. *Final Report of Royal Commission on Trades Unions*, vol. II, Appendix, pp. 68, 70 *(Parl. Papers* XXXI of 1868–9).

43. *St Crispin I*, 314. For the distinction between the 'West End' lodge and the other branches, cf. E. Howe and J. Child, *The London Society of Bookbinders* (London, 1952). This union also had no South London Lodges.

44. *St Crispin, loc. cit.*, 279, 314.

45. Parl. Papers LXVIII of 1890, pp. 9, 24, 26, 28, 31, 43. Most of these data are taken from the employers, who were less likely to quote ideal all-London standard rates than the unions.

46. *Amalgamated Society of Carpenters and Joiners:* monthly reports. Thus in June 1866, six branches reported trade 'good', six 'dull', five 'steady', two 'moderate', three 'unsettled' and three 'bad'. On the other hand, in May 1868 out of forty-seven London branches reporting the state of trade, thirty-one were 'moderate' or 'improving', seven 'dull', two 'bad', one 'unsettled', three 'steady', and three (all on the southern suburban fringe) 'good'.

47. They are based on the standard rates and hours as given, for various times in the second half of the nineteenth century, by the Amalgamated Carpenters and the Operative Bricklayers (London Unity), builders' working rules for various localities, the 1900 *Report on the Earnings of Agricultural Labourers* (Parl. Papers LXXII of 1900), and the Wage Census (1906) data for builders and agricultural labourers. Local figures are available from the printers' unions (e.g. 1850, 1856, 1860 and 1867), and from some others, but the localization of their industries or the relative scarcity of towns with organized printing offices make them less valuable for our purposes.

48. For comparison: the Wage Census of 1906 collected information about the building trade from thirty places in Kent, fifteen in Surrey, fourteen in Essex and fourteen in Hertfordshire.
49. *Dockers' Record*, 1890, D.W.R.G.L.U., Annual Reports, 1890 ff.
50. **Amalgamated Society of House Decorators and Painters. Annual Report 1873–81**

| South of England branches at end of: | 1873 | 1874 | 1875 | 1876 | 1877 | 1878 | 1879 | 1880 | 1881 |
|---|---|---|---|---|---|---|---|---|---|
| London | 5 | 5 | 5 | 5 | 6 | 6 | 8 | 8 | 8 |
| Southampton | 1 | 1 | 1 | 1 | 1 | 1 | 1 | 1 | 1 |
| Mid-Surrey | | 1 | 1 | 1 | 1 | 1 | 1 | 1 | 1 |
| Portsmouth | | 1 | 1 | 1 | 1 | 1 | 1 | 1 | 1 |
| Winchester | | 1 | 1 | 1 | 1 | 1 | 1 | 1 | 1 |
| Croydon | | | 1 | 1 | 1 | 1 | 1 | 1 | 1 |
| Hastings | | | | 1 | 1 | 1 | 1 | 1 | 1 |
| Exeter | | | | 1 | 1 | 1 | 1 | 1 | 1 |
| Plymouth | | | | 1 | 1 | 1 | 1 | 1 | 1 |
| Wimbledon | | | | | 1 | 1 | 1 | 1 | 1 |
| Tunbridge Wells | | | | | 1 | 1 | 1 | 1 | 1 |
| Eastbourne | | | | | | 1 | 1 | 1 | 1 |
| Reigate | | | | | | | 1 | 1 | 1 |
| Kingston | | | | | | | | | 1 |
| Surbiton | | | | | | | | | 1 |
| West Kent | | | | | | | | | 1 |

51. cf. E.J. Hobsbawm, 'The Tramping Artisans', *Econ. Hist. Rev.* III, 1951, 317 ff., for a discussion of the problem. However, this does not apply to seasonal industries complementary to London ones, which drew their labour force largely from seasonally unemployed Londoners; e.g. the brickfields, which were largely worked by London gasworkers in their slack season.
52. The Religious Census of 1851 records congregations of this sect in the following towns, and nowhere else, except for a small group in Bristol: Plymouth, Devonport, Exeter, Southampton, Portsmouth, Brighton, Chatham, Greenwich, Lambeth, Tower Hamlets.
53. cf. the map of British waterside unionism in 1913 published by the *National Transport Workers Federation* (British Library of Political Science, Coll. EB CV 18).
54. *The Dockers Record*, 1890, *passim*.
55. *Navvies', Bricklayers' and General Labourers' Union:* Report and Balance Sheet of the first half of 1892. (Eastern branches in Norwich, Ipswich, Colchester.) *General Railway Workers' Union:* Balance Sheets 1892. (Eastern branches in Brentwood, Ipswich, King's Lynn, Norwich, Southend, Wymondham, Great Yarmouth, Beccles, Wickham Market, Loughton.)
56. D. Goodway, *London Chartism* (Cambridge, 1982), pp. 221–5.
57. cited in *ibid.*, p. 223.

### Chapter 9: The 'New Unionism' in Perspective

1. The term 'new unionism' dates back to the 1880s. cf. *A Speech by John Burns on the Liverpool Congress*, (London, 1890), p. 6.
2. Georges Haupt, 'Socialisme et syndicalisme. Les rapports entre partis et syndicats au plan international: une mutation?', in M. Réberioux ed. *Jaurès et la Classe Ouvrière* (Paris, 1981), p. 50.
3. Calculated from data in G.D.H. Cole, *British Working Class Politics, 1832 to 1914* (London, 1941).
4. G.S. Bain and R. Price, *Profiles of Union Growth: a comparative statistical portrait of eight countries* (Oxford, 1980), p. 170.
5. H.A. Clegg, Alan Fox, A.F. Thompson, *A History of British Trade Unions Since 1889*, vol. I (Oxford, 1964), chapter 7.
6. H. Pelling, *The Origins of the Labour Party 1880–1900* (2d ed. Oxford, 1965), p. 229 for estimates.
7. cf. the use of this tactic in E. Pouget, *Le Sabotage* (Bibliothèque du Mouvement Prolétarien XIII, Paris n.d.), pp. 5–8 where it is described as '*une importation anglaise*'.
8. cf. 'Economic Fluctuations and Some Social Movements' in E.J. Hobsbawm, *Labouring Men* (London, 1964), chapter 8.
9. cf. E.H. Hunt, *Regional Wage Variations in Britain 1850–1914* (Oxford, 1973), p. 354.
10. For TU membership, B.C. Roberts, *The Trades Union Congress 1868–1921* (London, 1958), p. 379; for the best strike estimates, Clegg, Fox, Thompson, p. 489.
11. Report on the Strikes and Lock-Outs of 1889. C. 6176. Parl. Papers LXVIII of 1890.
12. See my *Labouring Men*, chapter 9.
13. Clegg, Fox, Thompson, pp. 55–6.
14. John Lovell, *Stevedores and Dockers: A study of trade unionism in the Port of London, 1870–1914* (London, 1969), chapter 2. cf. also R. Brown, *Waterfront Organization in Hull 1870–1900* (Hull, 1972); E.L. Taplin, *Liverpool Dockers and Seamen, 1870–1890* (Hull, 1974), M. Daunton, 'The Cardiff Coal Trimmers' Union 1888–1914' (*Llafur* 2 (3) 1978, pp. 10–23.
15. For the Scottish railway strike of 1890 see Clegg, Fox, Thompson, pp. 232–33; Philip S. Bagwell, *The Railwaymen: The history of the National Union of Railwaymen* (London, 1963), pp. 139–49; J. Mavor, *The Scottish Railway Strike* (London, 1891). Quotations are from J. Mavor, 'The Scottish Railway Strike' (*Economic Journal* I, 1891), p. 215.
16. *What a Compulsory Eight Hour Day Means to the Workers*, cited in E.J. Hobsbawm ed. *Labour's Turning Point 1880–1900* (Brighton, 1974), p. 72.
17. R.H. Gretton, *A Modern History of the English People* (London, 2 vols, 1913), I, p. 263. The strike only affected about 100,000 workers, but the exaggeration is itself significant.
18. cf. E.J. Hobsbawm, *Labouring Men*, chapter 10.
19. R. Hyman, *The Workers Union* (Oxford, 1971), pp. 38 ff.
20. Lord Askwith, *Industrial Problems and Disputes* (London, 1920).
21. Leone Levi in 1877 specifically claimed that he had 'proved ... that up to 1873 at least the trade and industry of England had not suffered from the many disturbances which have taken place – at least not to any material extent –, and that foreign competition had not gained upon British industry.' *Work and Pay* (London, 1877), p. 94.
22. For a useful sketch of US building trade unionism, cf. H.A. Millis ed. *How*

*Collective Bargaining Works* (New York, 1942), chapter 4, pp. 183–228; for early twentieth century local general strikes, cf. Elsbeth Georgi, *Theorie und Praxis des Generalstreiks* (Jena, 1908).

23. M. Leroy, *La Coutûme Ouvrière*, 2 vols. (Paris, 1913), I, p. 387. National unions with branches, as distinct from federations of local unions, were virtually confined in the early 1900s to the French railways and postal service.

24. K.D. Buckley, *The Amalgamated Engineers in Australia, 1852–1920*, (Canberra, 1970), pp. 190, 212.

25. Edvard Bull, *The Norwegian Trade Union Movement* (Brussels, 1956), pp. 46–8, 128–30.

26. For the early difficulties of the French *métallos*, cf. P. Louis, *Histoire du Mouvement Syndical en France* (Paris, 1920), p. 191–2; for the logic of industrial unionism as seen by intelligent militants, cf. E. Dolléans, *Alphonse Merrheim* (Paris, n.d., 1939?), pp. 9–11; M. Antonioli and B. Bezza, *La FIOM dalle origini al Fascismo 1901–1924* (Bari, 1978), pp. 17–18.

27. J.B. Jefferys, *The Story of the Engineers* (London, 1945), pp. 137–8, 166.

28. For the 1906 contract, cf. P. Spriano, *Storia di Torino operaia e socialista* (Turin, 1972), pp. 136–46; Antonioli and Bezza, *op. cit.*, pp. 719–37 for pre-1914 automobile collective contracts. For France, P. Fridenson, *Histoire des usines Renault: 1. Naissance de la grande entreprise 1898/1939* (Paris, 1972), Première partie III.

29. E. Lemonon, *L'Italie Economique et Sociale (1861–1912)* (Paris, 1913), pp. 406–7.

30. For British unions, Bain and Price *op. cit.*, chapter 2.

31. cf. W. Troeltsch and P. Hirschfeld, *Die deutschen sozialdemokratischen Gewerkschaften, Untersuchungen und Materialien über ihre geographische Verbreitung, 1896–1903* (Berlin, 1907); Georges Haupt, *loc. cit.* pp. 63–4.

32. S. and B. Webb, *The History of Trade Unionism* (London, 1894), Appendix IV.

33. R. Hyman, *op. cit.*, pp. 35, 48.

34. Haupt, *loc. cit.*, pp. 33–4. For the Belgian model, see J. Destrée and J. Vandervelde, *Le Socialisme en Belgique* (Paris, 1903), I, chapter 2.

35. In Britain union leaders, particularly among miners, were habitually elected to Parliament before 1914. Leaders of cotton workers (Mawdsley, Shackleton), printers (Bowerman), Railwaymen (Bell, J.H. Thomas), Shipwrights (Wilkie), Engineers (Barnes), Steelworkers (Hodge), the Furniture Trades (O'Grady), not to mention the 'new' unions stood or were elected. (For a complete list, see G.D.H. Cole, *British Working Class Politics 1832–1914* (London, 1941, Appendix I). The reluctance of active national leaders to enter Parliament, except perhaps as the price of Cabinet office, came later.

36. W.H. Schröder, 'Sozialstruktur der sozialdemokratischen Reichstagskandidaten 1898–1912' in *Herkunft und Mandat: Beiträge zur Führungsproblematik in der Arbeiterbewegung* (Frankfurt–Cologne, 1976) esp. pp. 94–6.

37. F. Andreucci and T. Detti eds. *Il Movimento Operaio Italiano: Dizionario Biografico.* (Vol I: Buozzi, vol V: Verzi. )

38. Swedish union membership in mining and manufacturing rose from 13.7% of the labour force in 1902 to 38.6% in 1907, but fell to 16.3% by 1911 and had only risen to 18.5% in 1913. Bain, *op. cit.* p. 145.

39. cf. E. Shorter and C. Tilly, *Strikes in France 1830–1968* (Cambridge, 1974), pp. 155, 164.

40. Shorter and Tilly, *op. cit.* p. 172.

## Chapter 10: The Formation of British Working-Class Culture

1. cf. David Craig, 'Images of Factory Life' in *Gulliver: German-English Yearbook 2* (Berlin, 1977), pp. 96-112.
2. Richard Hoggart, *The Uses of Literacy* (Harmondsworth, 1957), p. 11.
3. Recent work has insisted on the persistence of Chartism, at least locally, well into the 1850s, but nationally its decline after 1848 was evident.
4. M. Tylecote, *The Mechanics' Institutes of Lancashire and Yorkshire before 1851* (Manchester, 1957), Appendix III.
5. The phenomenon of the 'labour sect' is discussed in E.J. Hobsbawm, *Primitive Rebels* (Manchester, 1959).
6. M.H. Dobb, *Studies in the Development of Capitalism* (London, 1946), pp. 264-5.
7. Charles Chaplin, *My Early Years* (London, 1979).
8. A useful guide to these differences is D. Elliston Allen, *British Tastes: an enquiry into the likes and dislikes of the regional consumer* (London, 1968).
9. The estimate is based on M. Abrams, *The Condition of the British People 1911-1945* (London, 1946). No official figures for house-ownership were regularly collected until after World War II.
10. D. Elliston Allen, *op. cit.* p. 85.
11. A.J.P. Taylor, *English History 1914-45* (Oxford, 1965), pp. 244-5.

## Chapter 11: The Making of the Working Class 1870-1914

1. E.P. Thompson, *The Making of the English Working Class* (London, 1963).
2. Martin Jacques and Francis Mulhern, eds., *The Forward March of Labour Halted?* (London, 1982).
3. *The Economic History of Modern Britain II* (Cambridge, 1932), p. 24.
4. Phyllis Deane and Alan Cole, *British Economic Growth 1688-1959* (Cambridge, 1967), pp. 142-3.
5. H.S. Jevons, *The British Coal Trade* (London, 1915): calculated from data on pp. 65, 117; *Earnings and Hours Enquiry I: Textile Trades* (P.P. LXXX/I of 1909, p. 27); J.H. Clapham, *loc. cit.* pp. 115, 117.
6. John Marshall, *The Industrial Revolution in Furness* (Barrow, 1958), p. 356; James Hinton, *The First Shop Stewards' Movement* (London, 1973), p. 28; M.C. Reed, ed., *Railways in the Victorian Economy: Studies in Finance and Economic Growth* (Newton Abbot, 1969), p. 125.
7. E.D. Hunt, *British Labour History 1815-1914* (1981), p. 17.
8. James E. Cronin, 'Strikes 1870-1914' in C.J. Wrigley, ed. *A History of British Industrial Relations 1875-1914* (Brighton, 1982) chapter 4.
9. H.A. Clegg, Alan Fox, A.F. Thompson, *A History of British Trade Unions Since 1889* (Oxford, 1964), p. 471.
10. Chris Wrigley, 'The Government and Industrial Relations' and Roger Davidson, 'Government Administration', in C.J. Wrigley ed., *op. cit.* chapters 7, 8.
11. Information about Richardson and Rust is taken from Joyce Bellamy and John Saville ed. *Dictionary of Labour Biography* (vols III, II).
12. Paul Martinez, *The French Communard Refugees in Britain 1871-1880* (Univ. of Sussex Ph.D. thesis, 1981), p. 341.
13. cf. E.J. Hobsbawm and T. Ranger, eds., *The Invention of Tradition* (Cambridge, 1983), p. 295.
14. *Victoria County History of Yorkshire* (London, 1914) II, pp. 543 ff.

15. E.H. Hunt, *Labour History*, pp. 77–9; D.A. Reid, 'The Decline of Saint Monday 1766–1876' (*Past and Present* 71, 1976), pp. 76–101.
16. T.C. Barker, J.C. McKenzie and J. Yudkin, eds., *Our Changing Fare: Two Hundred Years of British Food Habits* (London, 1966), p. 110; 'Chatchip' (W. Loftas), *The Fish Frier and His Trade: Or How To Establish and carry on an Up-to-date Fish Frying Business* (London, n.d.), pp. 15, 23–4. Of the ten firms manufacturing frying ranges mentioned or advertising in this handbook, all but two are in Lancashire and Yorkshire.
17. Tony Mason, *Association Football and English Society, 1863–1915* (Brighton, 1980).
18. C.D. Stuart & A.J. Park, *The Variety Stage* (London, 1895); G.J. Mellor, *The Northern Music Hall* (Newcastle, 1970).
19. J.B. Jefferys, *Retail Trading in Britain, 1850–1950* (Cambridge, 1954), W. Hamish Fraser, *The Coming of the Mass Market, 1850–1914* (London, 1982).
20. Cyril Ehrlich, *The Piano, A History* (London, 1976), pp. 102–3.
21. John Burnett, *Plenty and Want: A Social History of Diet in England from 1815 to the Present* (London, 1966), p. 111.
22. Geoffrey Green, *The History of the Football Association* (London, 1953), p. 125.
23. *Herapath's Railway Journal* 19 April 1884, p. 441.
24. This was under the General Pier and Harbours Act of 1861. Returns in PP LXII, 1863; LV, 1864; L, 1865; LXVI, 1866; LXIII, 1867–8; LIV, 1868–9; LIX, 1870; LX, 1871; LII, 1872; LVIII, 1873; LIX, 1874; LXVII, 1875; LXV, 1876; LXXIII, 1877; LXVII, 1878; LXIV, 1878–9; LXVI, 1880; LXXXII, 1881; LXII, 1882; LXII, 1883; LXXI, 1884; LXX, 1884–5; LIX, 1886; LXXIV, 1887; XC, 1888; LXIX, 1889; LXVI, 1890; LXXVI, 1890–1; LXXI, 1892; LXXX, 1893–4; LXXVI, 1894; LXXXVII, 1895; LXXV, 1896; LXXVIII, 1897; LXXXIII, 1898; LXXXVII, 1899. See also: *Return from the Authorities of Harbours ... Giving description of works executed within the last twenty years, distinguishing Piers, Docks ... etc* (P.P. LXII of 1883).
25. Seaside resorts, have been assigned their 'social tone' (to use H.J. Perkin's suitably Victorian phrase) in the light of general knowledge (e.g. Torquay or Skegness) and of the researches of numerous researchers, starting with E.W. Gilbert, 'The growth of inland and seaside health resorts in England' (*Scottish Geographical Magazine* LV, 1939). For a bibliography, see J. Walvin, *Leisure and Society 1830–1950* (London, 1978); also cf. H.J. Perkin, 'The "social tone" of Victorian seaside resorts in the Northwest' (in his *The Structured Crowd: Essays in English Social History*); J. Lowerson and J. Myerscough, *Time to Spare in Victorian England* (Brighton, 1977), pp. 30–44. In the latter period middle-class investment is probably overstated, partly because several large projects for loans were turned down, partly because in time even middle-class resorts recognized, sometimes reluctantly, the financial potential of the mass market.
26. For an impression of a working-class 'ghetto', see C.F.G. Masterman in *The Heart of the Empire* (London, 1901), pp. 12–13.
27. G.S. Layard, 'Family Budgets II' (*Cornhill Magazine* N.S.X., 1901), pp. 656 ff.
28. Board of Trade, Report on Cost of Living (P.P. CVII, 1908) *passim*. The quotation is from p. 655.
29. *Ibid.*, p. 406.
30. R. Roberts, *The Classic Slum*, p. 13.
31. G. Askwith, *Industrial Problems and Disputes* (London, 1920), p. 10.

32. B.S. Rowntree, *Poverty and Progress. A Second Social Survey of York* (London, 1941), p. 359–60.
33. Ross McKibbin, 'Working-Class Gambling in Britain, 1880–1939' (*Past and Present* 82, 1979), p. 172.
34. cited in H. Pelling, *Popular Politics and Society in Late Victorian Britain* (1968), p. 147.
35. Fred Reid, 'Keir Hardie's Conversion to Socialism', in Asa Briggs and John Saville, eds., *Essays in Labour History 1886–1923* (London, 1971), p. 28.
36. Julian Amery, in James L. Garvin, *The Life of Joseph Chamberlain* (London, 1932–69), vol VI, p. 791.
37,. P. Stead, 'The Language of Edwardian Politics' in D. Smith ed. *A People and a Proletariat* (London, 1980), p. 150.
38. P.J. Waller, *Democracy and Sectarianism: A political and social history of Liverpool 1868–1920* (Liverpool, 1981), chapters 7, 13–15.
39. H. Pelling and F. Bealey, *Labour and Politics, 1900–1906* (London, 1958), p. 158.
40. Ray Gregory, *The Miners and British Politics, 1906–1914* (London, 1968), p. 185.
41. Joseph L. White, *The Limits of Trade Union Militancy* (Westport-London, 1978), p. 152–155.
42. cited in David Marquand, *Ramsay Macdonald* (London, 1977), p. 84.
43. Gregory, p. 178.
44. *ibid.*, p. 188.
45. Beatrice Webb, *Diaries 1912–1924* (London, 1952), p. 45.
46. Jack Lawson, *The Man in the Cap: The Life of Herbert Smith* (London, 1941).

**Chapter 12: Debating the Labour Aristocracy**

1. This is a modified version of the paper summarized in *Bulletin of the Society for the Study of Labour History* 40, spring, 1980.
2. H. Pelling, 'The Concept of the Labour Aristocracy' in *Popular Politics and Society in Late Victorian England* (London, 1968); A.E. Musson, *British Trade Unions 1800–1875* (London, 1972); M. Piva, 'The Aristocracy of the English Working Class: Help for a Debate in Difficulties' *Histoire Sociale – Social History*, Vol 7, 14, 1974, pp. 270–92; J. Foster, *Class Struggle and the Industrial Revolution* (London, 1974); J. Foster, 'British Imperialism and the Labour Aristocracy' in J. Skelley, ed., *The General Strike 1926* (London, 1976); G. Stedman Jones, 'Class Struggle and the Industrial Revolution', *New Left Review*, 90, 1975, pp. 35–69; A.E. Musson, 'Class struggle and the labour aristocracy, 1830–1860', *Social History*, 3, 1976, pp. 335–56; H.F. Moorhouse, 'The Marxist theory of the labour aristocracy', *Social History*, 3/1, 1978, pp. 61–82; A. Reid, 'Politics and economics in the formation of the British working class: a response to H.F. Moorhouse', *Social History*, 3/3, 1978, pp. 347–61; John Field, 'British Historians and the Concept of the Labour Aristocracy', *Radical History Review*, 19, 1978–9, pp. 61–85; Bulletin of SSLH, No 37, M. Shepherd, 'The origins and incidence of the term "labour aristocracy"' (autumn, 1978), pp. 51–67; Bulletin of SSLH, No 39, (autumn, 1979), pp. 16–22; J. Melling, 'Aristocrats and Artisans'; Bulletin of SSLH, No 40, (spring, 1980), pp. 6–11; Conference Report: The Labour Aristocracy; *ibid.*, pp. 13–18; Correspondence on the same subject between John Baxter and Michael A. Shepherd. See also Editorial, pp. 2–3; Gregor

McLennan, *Marxism and the Methodology of History* (London, 1981), chapter 10, 'The Theory of the Labour Aristocracy', pp. 206–32; A. Reid, 'Intelligent artisans and aristocrats of labour: the essays of Thomas Wright' in J. Winter ed. *The Working Class in Modern British History: Essays in Honour of Henry Pelling* (Cambridge, 1983).

3. E.J. Hobsbawm, *Labouring Men* (London, 1964), chapter 15.
4. See note 2.
5. Thus the term is used both by G.v. Schulze Gaevernitz, *Britischer Imperialismus und englischer Freihandel zu Beginn d. 20. Jahrhunderts* (Leipzig, 1906), p. 365–6, and K. Kautsky, 'Die Neutralisierung d.Gewerkschaften' (*Neue Zeit* XVIII, 1899–1900 v. 2, pp. 389 ff.
6. See E.J. Hobsbawm, *Revolutionaries* (London, 1973), chapter 12.
7. Moorhouse, *op. cit.*
8. See titles under Foster in note 2 above.
9. J. Foster in J. Skelley ed. *The General Strike 1926*.
10. H. Pelling: *Popular Politics* (London, 1968), p. 36 ff; J. Vincent, *The Formation of the British Liberal Party 1857–8* (London, 1966), pp. 76–82, 96–126.
11. William Lazonick, 'Industrial relations and technical change: the case of the self-acting mule', *Cambridge Journal of Economics*, 1979, 3, pp. 231–62.
12. H. Pelling, *Popular Politics in late Victorian Society*, pp. 37–61.
13. Crossick, *An Artisan Elite in Victorian Society: Kentish London, 1840–1880* (London, 1980).
14. Charles Booth, *Life and Labour of the People of London*, First series, vol I, 1902, p. 51.
15. R. Roberts, *The Classic Slum* (Manchester, 1971), chapter 1.
16. J. White, *The Limits of Militancy: the Lancashire textile workers 1910–1914* (Westport-London, 1978), p. 35; H.A. Turner, *Trade Union Growth, Structure and Policy* (London, 1962), p. 151.
17. Lazonick, *op. cit.*
18. Keith McLelland and Alastair Reid, 'The Shipbuilding Workers 1840–1914' (unpublished paper).
19. J.F. Rowe, *Wages in Practice and Theory* (London, 1928), pp. 109–10.
20. Norman Gash, *Aristocracy and the People: Britain 1815–1865* (London, 1979), p. 18.
21. G. Crossick, *op. cit.*; 'The Labour Aristocracy and its Values', *Victorian Studies*, 19, 1976; ed. *The Lower Middle Class in Britain* (London, 1977); Robert Gray, *The Aristocracy of Labour in Nineteenth-century Britain, c.1850–1914* (London, 1981); 'Styles of life, the "Labour Aristocracy" and Class Relations in later Nineteenth-century Edinburgh', *Int. Rev. of Soc. Hist.*, 8, 1973; 'The Labour Aristocracy in the Victorian Class Structure' (F. Parkin ed. *The Social Analysis of Class Structure*, London, 1974); *The Labour Aristocracy in Victorian Edinburgh* (London, 1976).
22. H. Pelling, *Popular Politics*, pp. 56–7.
23. James Hinton, *The First Shop Stewards' Movement* (London, 1973).
24. I. Prothero, *Artisans and Politics in early Nineteenth-century London: John Gast and his Times* (Folkestone, 1979).
26. Beatrice Potter, *The Co-operative Movement in Great Britain* (London, 1899), esp. pp. 167–8.
27. R.A. Leeson, *Travelling Brothers* (London, 1978).
28. cf. Takao Matsamura, *The Labour Aristocracy Revisited: The Victorian Flint Glass Makers 1850–1880* (Manchester, 1984).

### Chapter 13: The Aristocracy of Labour Reconsidered

1. Edith Simcox in *Industrial Remuneration Conference* (London, 1885), p. 90.
2. *Interdepartmental Committee on Physical Deterioration*, PPXXXII, 1904, Q 4419. Evidence of Rev W. Rees of Salford.
3. *Report of the Departmental Committee on the Pupil-Teacher System*, vol II, Minutes of Evidence, PP XXVI, 1898, Q 12373.
4. *Saturday Review*, 6 April 1867, pp. 438–9.
5. *The Athenaeum*, 3 March 1866, p. 292.
6. *Edinburgh Review*, vol 171, 1890, pp. 211 ff.
7. B.S. Rowntree, *Poverty* (2d ed, Nelson reprint), pp. 250–3.
8. Cited in Standish Meacham, *A Life Apart* (London, 1977), p. 25.
9. I have discussed his actual views in 'Lenin and the Aristocracy of Labour', *Revolutionaries* (London, 1973), pp. 121–9.
10. G. Best, *Mid-Victorian Britain 1851–1875* (London, 1971) is a convenient introduction to the much-discussed subject of 'respectability', esp. pp. 256–63.
11. *Royal Commission on Friendly Societies* (henceforth RCFS) PP XXV, 1871, Q 6584.
12. *Royal Commission on the Militia and Volunteers*, PP XXX, 1904, Q 11926.
13. R. Gray, 'Styles of Life, the "Labour Aristocracy" and Class Relations in Later Nineteenth Century Edinburgh', *International Review of Social History*, 8, 1973, p. 445.
14. A.E. Musson, The Typographical Association (Oxford, 1954), pp. 93–4.
15. e.g. *RCFS*, PP XII, 1873, Q 25,509 for Enginemen and Firemen. cf. K. Buckley, *The Amalgamated Engineers in Australia 1852–1920* (Canberra, 1970), pp. 95–6 for members of that union who were employers.
16. R. Gray, 'Styles of Life', *loc. cit.*
17. *RCFS* XXV, 1871, Q 6211.
18. *RC Volunteers* XXX, 1904, Q 8222.
19. *ibid.*, Qs 8961, 12312.
20. cf. G.S. Layard, 'Family Budgets II: A Lower-Middle Class Budget' *Cornhill Magazine* X, 1901, p. 656' 'a class which includes all those sorts and conditions of men which range between the skilled mechanic and the curate in priest's orders.'
21. Henry Mayhew, *London Labour and the London Poor. A Cyclopaedia of the Conditions and Earnings of Those that Will Work, Those that Cannot Work, and Those that Will Not Work.* (London, 1861).
22. *The Beehive*, 2 July 1864.
23. *RCFS* XXIII/ii, 1874, Appendix to Sir G. Young's Report, p. 526.
24. A.L. Bowley, *Wages in the United Kingdom in the Nineteenth Century* (London, 1900), p. 23.
25. in G. Haw ed. *Christianity and the Working Classes* (London, 1906), p. 152.
26. Charity Organization Society, *Report on Unskilled Labour* (cited as RUL) (London, 1908), p. 14; N.B. Dearle, *Industrial Training* (London, 1914), pp. 13, 32.
27. cited in A. Marwick, 'Images of the Working Class Since 1930' in J. Winter, ed. *The Working Class in Modern British History* (Cambridge, 1983), p. 219.
28. e.g. in the *Falkirk Herald* 8 Oct. 1890. I owe this reference to Dr James Young.
29. *RCFS* XXVI, 1872, Q 16592.
30. Raphael Samuel in R. Samuel ed. *Miners, Quarrymen and Saltworkers* (London, 1977), p. 66.
31. *RUL*, Q 409, and more generally Qs 407–413.

32. cf. Mayhew III, p. 221, I. Prothero, *Artisans and Politics in Early Nineteenth Century London* (Folkestone, 1979), pp. 42 ff. David Goodway, *London Chartism 1838–1848* (Cambridge, 1982), part four: The Trades.

33. W.G. Bunn in *Industrial Remuneration Conference* 1885, pp. 168–9.

34. For the chief contributions to the debate, see note 2 to chapter 12, esp. Pelling and Reid (1983).

35. *RUL*, pp. 11, 48–49, pp. 102–3, Qs 225, 235.

36. N.B. Dearle, *Problems of Unemployment in the London Building Trade* (London, 1908), p. 93.

37. R. Samuel, 'The Workshop of the World: Steam Power and Hand Technology in mid-Victorian Britain' *History Workshop* 3, 1977, pp. 6–72.

38. *Royal Commission on Trade Unions and Employers' Associations 1965–1968: Report.* Cmnd 3623, (London, 1968), p. 87.

39. *ibid.*

40. J. White, *The Limits of Trade Union Militancy. The Lancashire Textile Workers 1910–1914* (Westport-London, 1978), p. 36 ff. For the figures, pp. 32, 38.

41. e.g. H. Stanley Jevons, *The British Coal Trade* (London, 1915), p. 856, Appendix X, clause 11, for an example: 'Persons whose duty is that of inspection and supervision, are not workmen to whom the Coal Mines (Minimum Wage) Act applies.' Dr Joseph Melling has drawn my attention to the fact that the question of distinguishing foremen from workers arose even earlier, under the legislation for workmen's compensation (Employers' Liability Act, 1880), since 'fellow-servants having superintendence or direction' could be regarded as agents of the employer for purposes of liability for injuries caused by their negligence or orders given by them.

42. 'The shop foremen will be men who are skilled in the work of their respective shops. Probably as workmen they showed especial ability and skill, which led to their promotion from the ranks.' John Macauley ed. *Modern Railway Working. A Practical Treatise by Engineering Experts*, 2 vols (London, 1912–14), vol II, pp. 57–58. For workers and foremen see Carter Goodrich, *The Frontier of Control* (1975 edn.), chapters VII–IX.

43. cited in E.J. Hobsbawm ed. *Labour's Turning Point* (London, 1948), p. 6. See also J. White (1978), *loc. cit.*

44. *Labour's Turning Point, loc. cit.*

45. R. Roberts, *The Classic Slum* (Harmondsworth, 1973), p. 92.

46. S. and B. Webb, *Industrial Democracy* (1913, edn.), p. 719.

47. For the main contributions to the debate on the labour aristocracy, see note 12 to chapter 14. A. Reid, 'Intelligent artisans and aristocrats of labour: the essays of Thomas Wright' in J. Winter ed. *The Working Class in Modern British History*, pp. 171–3 is the most succinct statement of the case against it.

48. Simcox in *Industrial Remuneration Conference*, p. 86.

49. *RCFS*, XXII, 1872, Q 24392.

50. Roberts, *Classic Slum*, p. 38.

51. See note 21 to Chapter 12.

52. *RUL*, Qs 227, 231; pp. 102,103.

53. cf. D. Douglas, 'The Durham Pitman' in R. Samuel ed. *Miners, Quarrymen*, p. 215 ff. H.S. Jevons, *Coal Trade*, p. 606. For the general question of job control, R. Price, *Masters, Unions and Men. Work Control in Building and the Price of Labour, 1830–1914* (Cambridge, 1980), Carter Goodrich, *Frontier of Control.*

54. E.J. Hobsbawm, *Labouring Men* (London, 1964), chapter 15.
55. Booth, *Life and Labour*, I, p. 161.
56. *RCFS* XXV, 1871, Q 6236.
57. Paul Johnson, 'Credit and Thrift and the British Working Class' in J. Winter ed. *The Working Class*, p. 156.
58. The Pilgrim Trust, *Men Without Work* (Cambridge, 1938), p. 189.
59. G. von Schulze Gaevernitz, *The Cotton Trade in England and on the Continent* (London, 1895), p. 175; *Britischer Imperialismus und engl.Freihandel*, pp. 365-66.
60. *RUL*, Q 252. For general discussion, Qs 245-262.
61. Mayhew, vol III, p. 221; 'as a general rule I may remark that I find the society men of every trade comprise about one tenth of the whole.'
62. S. and B. Webb, *Industrial Democracy*, pp. 475, 575.
63. H.A. Turner, *Trade Union Growth, Structure and Policy: a comparative study of the cotton unions* (London, 1962), p. 141.
64. E.H. Hunt, *Regional Wage Variations in Britain 1850-1914* (Oxford, 1973), ch. 9, esp. pp. 354, 358.
65. cf. John Burnett, *A Social History of Housing 1815-1970*, (London, 1978) and references therein.
66. For a useful survey, James Walvin, *Leisure and Society 1830-1950* (London, 1978).
67. For London, the best studied city, A.S. Wohl, 'The Housing of the Working Classes in London, 1815-1914' in Stanley D. Chapman ed. *The History of Working Class Housing* (Newton Abbot, 1971), esp. pp. 29-36. See also chapter 8 of the present book. For the provinces, Burnett, pp. 161 ff.
68. It is assumed in Rowntree. For the fullest contemporary survey of housing, see *Report of an Enquiry by the Board of Trade into Working Class Rents, Housing and Retail Prices*, PP CVII, 1908, which surveys 73 towns in England and Wales.
69. Rowntree, pp. 183-4, Board of Trade, 1908, pp. 51, 156, 167, 358.
70. Rowntree, p. 103.
71. John Foster, *Class Struggle and the Industrial Revolution* (London, 1974), G. Crossick, *An Artisan Elite* are notable attempts to analyse this.
72. Crossick (1976).
73. Gray (1973).
74. J. Bellamy and J. Saville eds. *Dictionary of Labour Biography* (1972-  ). Six volumes have been published to date.
75. Virginia Berridge, 'Popular Sunday papers and mid-Victorian society' in G. Boyce, J. Curran, P. Wingate, eds., *Newspaper History* (London-Beverly Hills, 1978), chapter 13. *Popular Journalism and Working Class Attitudes 1854-1886. A Study of Reynolds Newspaper, Lloyd's Weekly Newspaper and the Weekly Times* (Univ. of London Ph.D. thesis, 1976).
76. Board of Trade 1908, p. 790.
77. Cyril Ehrlich, *The Piano: A History* (London, 1976), p. 91.
78. *Ibid.*, p. 97.
79. *Ibid.*, p. 106.
80. Rowntree, p. 184.
81. Among them T. Tholfsen, 'The intellectual origins of mid-Victorian stability' (*Pol. Sci. Quarterly* LXXXVI, 1971), pp. 57-91, and *Working Class Radicalism in Mid-Victorian England* (London, 1977), G. Best, *op. cit.* (1971), R. Gray, *op. cit.* 1973, 1974, 1976; G. Stedman Jones, 'Working Class Culture and Working-Class Politics in London, 1870-1900: Notes on the Remaking of a Working Class' (*Journ. of Social History* VII, 1974, pp. 460-

508); G. Crossick, *op. cit.* 1976, 1978; C. Reid, 'Middle class values and working class culture in nineteenth century Sheffield – the pursuit of Respectability' (in S. Pollard and C. Holmes, eds. *Essays in the Economic and Social History of South Yorkshire* (Sheffield, 1976); P. Bailey, 'Will the Real Bill Banks Please Stand Up? Towards a Role Analysis of Mid-Victorian Working Class Respectability' (*Journ. of Social History* XII, 1979), pp. 336-353.

82. Royden Harrison, *Before the Socialists* (London, 1965), p. 32.
83. Roberts, *Classic Slum*, p. 92.
84. *ibid.*, p. 18.
85. S. and B. Webb, *Industrial Democracy*, p. 282.
86. J. White, *The Limits*, pp. 113-14.
87. *RCFS* XXIII/ii, 1874, Report of the Hon. E.L. Stanley, pp. 290 ff.
88. cf. the remarks of T. Matsamura, *The Labour Aristocracy Revisited* (Manchester, 1984), p. 4 à propos of Pelling's 'The concept of labour aristocracy' in his *Popular Politics and Society in Late Victorian Britain* (London, 1968).
89. Roberts, *op. cit.*, pp. 177-8.
90. J.B. Jefferys, *The Story of the Engineers* (London, 1945), p. 113. This was 'by far the largest vote ever cast'.
91. *RCFS* XXV, 1971, Q 6253.
92. Roberts, *op. cit.*, p. 179.
93. Neal Blewett, 'The Franchise in the United Kingdom, 1885-1918' (*Past and Present* 32, 1965), pp. 27-56; H.C.G. Mathew, R. McKibbin, J. McKay, 'The franchise factor in the rise of the Labour Party' (*English Hist. Rev.* 1976), pp. 723-52.
94. Rowntree, p. 182, Booth I, p. 36; Sidney Webb, *Facts for Socialists* (Fabian Tracts) 1915 edn.
95. Simcox, *Industrial Remuneration Conf.* pp. 86-90.
96. Booth, vol VII, p. 54.
97. Goodway, *London Chartism*, p. 174, 178.
98. *Royal Commission on Trades Unions*, PP XXXII, 1867, Q 23.
99. Simcox, *loc. cit.*, p. 90.
100. Booth, Ser I, vol I, p. 294.
101. Patrick Joyce, *Work, Society and Politics: The Culture of the Factory in Later Victorian England* (Brighton, 1980).
102. For the unresponsiveness of unions to political campaigns (except as usual, the shoemakers), cf. F.E. Gillespie, *Labour and Politics in England 1850-1867* (Durham NC 1927), p. 204.
103. P.J. Waller, *Democracy & Sectarianism: A political and social history of Liverpool, 1868-1939* (Liverpool, 1981), p. 100.
104. John Vincent, *The Formation of the British Liberal Party, 1857-1868* (Harmondsworth, 1972), p. 117.
105. *Labouring Men*, p. 303.
106. For Wright, see Alastair Reid, 'Intelligent artisans and aristocrats of labour: the essays of Thomas Wright' in J. Winter ed., *The Working Class*, pp. 171-186.
107. Denis Poulot, Question Sociale. *Le sublime ou la travailleur comme il est en 1870 et ce qu'il peut être.* (Paris, 1870). New edition with introduction by Alain Cottereau, Paris 1980.
108. Poulot, p. 291.
109. *ibid.*, pp. 135-7, 156, 170-1, 188.
110. J. Rougerie, *Paris Libre 1871* (Paris, 1971), pp. 158-9.

111. David Howell, *British Workers and the Independent Labour Party, 1888–1906* (Manchester, 1983), p. 126; see also P. Joyce, *Work, Society and Politics*, p. 331.

112. Poulot, p. 351.

**Chapter 14: Artisans and Labour Aristocrats**

1. This is the text of the Tawney Lecture to the Economic History Society, 1983. Much of it is based on the research, still largely unpublished in print, of a number of younger labour historians. Among them readers familiar with the field will recognize my debt to Nina Fishman, Gareth Stedman Jones, Wayne Lewchuk, Keith McLelland, Joe Melling, Alastair Reid, Richard Price and Jonathan Zeitlin.

2. Anon., *Working Men and Women by a Working Man* (1879), p. 62.

3. J. Zeitlin, 'The Labour Strategies of British Engineering Employers, 1890–1922' in H.C. Gospel and C. Littler, eds., *Management Strategy and Industrial Relations: An Historical and Comparative Survey* (1983). My reference is to p. 20 of the original paper at the SSRC Conference on Business and Labour History 23 March 1981.

4. *Working Men and Women*, p. 102.

5. Waldo R. Browne, *What's What in the Labor Movement: A Dictionary of Labor Affairs and Labor Terminology* (New York, 1921), p. 497.

6. Bob Gilding, *The Journeymen Coopers of East London* (Oxford, 1971), pp. 56–57.

7. N.B. Dearle, *Industrial Training: With special reference to the conditions prevailing in London* (1914), pp. 31–2; see also note 26 to chapter 12.

8. *ibid.*, p. 31.

9. *Royal Commission on Labour* (P.P. 1892 XXXVI/i) Group A, Q. 16064. Evidence of J. Cronin, Secretary of the Associated Millmen of Scotland.

10. George Howell, 'Trade Unions, Apprentices and Technical Education' (*Contemporary Review* XXX (1877), p. 854.

11. H.A. Clegg, A.J. Killick, Rex Adams, *Trade Union Officers* (Oxford, 1961), p. 50.

12. cf. Alastair Reid, 'Intelligent artisans and aristocrats of labour: the essays of Thomas Wright' in Jay Winter, ed., *The Working Class in Modern British History: Essays in Honour of Henry Pelling* (Cambridge, 1983), pp. 175–76.

13. The Registers of the Institution are preserved in Birkbeck College, University of London, to which I am obliged for access.

14. N.B. Dearle, *Industrial Training*, pp. 566–7.

15. 'Report of the Committee on the Petition of the Watchmakers, 1817' cited in A.E. Bland, P.A. Brown, R.H. Tawney, eds., *English Economic History: Select Documents* (1914), pp. 588–90.

16. A. Kidd, *History of the Tin Plate Workers and Sheet Metal Workers and Braziers Societies* (1949), p. 28.

17. cf. Andreas Griessinger, *Das symbolische Kapital der Ehre: Streikbewegungen und kollektives Bewusstsein deutscher Handwerksgesellen im 18. Jahrhundert* (Berlin, 1981) for an extensive discussion.

18. Iorwerth Prothero, *Artisans and Politics in Early Nineteenth Century London: John Gast and His Times* (Folkestone, 1979), pp. 27–28.
19. Thomas Wright, *Some Habits of the Working Classes* (1867), p. 102. See also the account by F.W. Galton in S. and B. Webb, *History of Trade Unionism* (1894), pp. 431–2, and, for the importance of rituals attached to the workplace, John Dunlop, *Artificial and Compulsory Drinking Usages of the United Kingdom* (7th edn, 1844), passim.
20. See R. Price, *Masters, Unions and Men: Work Control in Building and the Rise of Labour* (Cambridge, 1980), chapter 2, for references.
21. 'It is our duty then to exercise the same control over that in which we have a vested interest, as the physician who holds his diploma, or the author who is protected by his copyright.' Preface to the Rules of the Amalgamated Society of Engineers, 1851, cited in J.B. Jefferys ed., *Labour's Formative Years* (1948), p. 30.
22. cited in G. Stedman Jones, *Languages of Class* (Cambridge, 1983), pp. 136–137.
23. Prothero, *Artisans*, pp. 337–38. For a clear statement, see William H. Sewell Jr., *Work and Revolution in France: The Language of Labour from the Old Regime to 1848* (Cambridge, 1980), p. 283.
24. *Amalgamated Society of Carpenters and Joiners* (hereafter ASCJ) Monthly Report, January 1868, p. 25.
25. See the description of banners in W.A. Moyes, *The Banner Book* (Gateshead, 1974).
26. R. Price, *Masters, Unions and Men*, p. 62.
27. M. and J.B. Jefferys, 'The wages, hours and trade customs of the skilled engineer in 1861' (*Economic History Review* XVII, 1947), pp. 29–30; but the inclusion of members of other skilled unions would raise this percentage.
28. LSE Library, *Webb Collection* Coll. EA 31, pp. 245–9.
29. *ibid.*, pp. 311–22.
30. N.B. Dearle, *Problems of Unemployment in the London Building Trade* (1908), p. 93.
31. *ASCJ*, Monthly Report, February 1868, p. 63.
32. *Amalgamated Society of Engineers* (hereafter ASE), Monthly Record June 1911, cited in M. Holbrook-Jones, *Supremacy and Subordination of Labour* (1982), p. 78.
33. J.B. Goodman ed., *Victorian Cabinet Maker: The Memoirs of James Hopkinson 1819–1894* (1968), p. 24.
34. 'That if the Central Association of Employers carry out their threat of a Masters' strike . . . it is the duty of working men to . . . begin manufacturing for the public . . . That inasmuch as many of our members have lathes and other tools in their possession . . . it is to be hoped that they will . . . communicate their intention of lending such tools for the benefit of those persons who may be thrown out of employment by the masters' strike.' Announcement by the Council of ASE in *The Operative*, 23 December 1851.
35. Henry Broadhurst: *The Story of his Life from Stone-mason's Bench to the Treasury Bench* (1901), p. 2.
36. Harry Pollitt, *Serving My Time* (1941 edn), p. 14.
37. *ASCJ*, Monthly Report, July 1886, pp. 137–8.
38. The boilermakers appear to have had none (D.C. Cummings, *History of the United Society of Boilermakers and Iron & Steel Ship Builders* (Newcastle, 1905), pp. 36–37, 52. The ASE Annual Reports included expenditure for 'loss of tools by fire' in an item of the accounts covering miscellaneous grants, from which its relative insignificance may be inferred.

39. Following branch pressure, lists of tools stolen from members were published in the Monthly Report from October 1868 on.
40. Total benefit per member of ASCJ 1860-1889 inclusive: Funeral £3 2s 8d, Accident, £1 15s 10½d; Tool, £1 14s 6½d. (G. Howell, *The Conflicts of Capital and Labour historically and economically considered, being a history and review of the trade unions of Great Britain etc.* (2d edn 1890), p. 519.
41. Henry Mayhew, *The Morning Chronicle Survey of Labour and the Poor: The Metropolitan Districts* (Horsham 1982), vol 5, p. 225.
42. David Dougan, *The Shipwrights: The history of the Shipconstructors and Shipwrights Association, 1882-1963* (1968), pp. 19, 30. See also *Royal Commission on Labour* (P.P. 1893-4, XXXIV) Group A, Q 20,413, 21,398.
43. Mayhew, vol 5, p. 193. For data on tool costs from the *Royal Comm. on Labour* (Group A), see P.P. 1892 XXXVI/ii, Q 16,848, 19466, 19812-3, 20367-9.
44. Mayhew, *ibid.*, pp. 94, 96, 155, 167, 214 estimates the weekly cost at between 6d and 2s a week.
45. S. and B. Webb, *Industrial Democracy* (1913 edn.), p. 313.
46. Huw Benyon, *Working for Ford* (Harmondsworth, 1973), p. 145: 'On the assembly line one man is as good as the next man ... In a skilled work situation things are slightly different ... by virtue of the fact that (the men) control the tools, or the knowledge, vital to the completion of the job. The foreman *has* to ask *them*.'
47. Zeitlin, *Labour Strategies*, pp. 21, 26.
48. 'The shop foremen will be men who are skilled in the work of their respective shops. Probably as workmen they showed especial ability and skill, which led to their promotion from the ranks.' James Clayton, 'The Organization of the Locomotive Department', in John Macauley ed., *Modern Railway Working: A practical treatise by engineering experts* (1912-14), vol 2, p. 57.
49. Kenneth Hudson, *Working to Rule: Railway Workshop Rules: a study of industrial discipline* (Bath, 1970).
50. *Working Men and Women*, p. 66; ASE *Quarterly Report*, Dec 1893, pp. 48, 59; *Dearle, Industrial Training*, p. 25.
51. cf. the collection of builders' 'working rules' in the Webb Collection (LSE Library, Coll EB XXXI-XXXVI and Coll EC VI-XVIII); for instance Bridgnorth 1863, Loughborough 1892, Worcester 1891 (Coll EB XXXIV), Shrewsbury (Coll EC VII).
52. Gilding, *Journeymen Coopers*, p. 56.
53. Thomas Wright, *The Great Unwashed* (1868), p. 282: shopmates will lend a longterm tramping artisan 'their best tools'. Charity Organization Society, *Special Committee on Unskilled Labour: Report and Minutes of Evidence, June 1908*, p. 98: 'In the case of mechanics who have been out of work for any time, how far are they short of tools ...? ... There is a lot of freemasonry among them, and they lend each other tools. If you looked into their baskets you would find ten per cent of them deficient in tools.' Note that the witness, a building foreman, claims to be merely guessing. He does not look into the artisans' baskets. For the penalty of losing tools, namely lapsing into unskilled labouring, see Mayhew, *Morning Chronicle Survey*, vol 5, p. 130.
54. J.B. Jefferys, *The Story of the Engineers* (1945), p. 58 on second and third sons, and sons of fathers out of the trade, joining the trade.
55. Coll EB XXXIV: Hull, Redditch, Wakefield; Coll EC VII: Bristol, Dudley, Gornal, Kidderminster, Leicester, Rotherham, Stourbridge, Wigan.

56. Keith McLelland and Alastair Reid, '*The Shipbuilding Workers, 1840-1914*' (unpublished paper), p. 18.
57. Dearle, Industrial Training, p. 241.
58. Joyce M. Bellamy and John Saville, eds. *Dictionary of Labour Biography*, vols I-VI (1972-1982).
59. Geoffrey Crossick, *An Artisan Elite in Victorian Society: Kentish London 1840-1880* (1978), p. 116.
60. Charles More, *Skill and the English Working Class* (1980), p. 103, Table 5.13.
61. M.L. Yates, *Wages and Labour Conditions in British Engineering* (1937), p. 31, Table 6.
62. e.g. A. Reid, 'The division of labour in the British shipbuilding industry, 1880-1920' (unpublished Ph.D. thesis, Cambridge University 1980); J. Zeitlin, 'Craft regulation and the division of labour: Engineers and Compositors in Britain, 1890-1914' (unpublished Ph.D. thesis, Warwick University, 1981).
63. B.C.M. Weekes, 'The Amalgamated Society of Engineers, 1880-1914: A Study of Trade Union Government, Politics and Industrial Policy' (unpublished Ph.D. thesis, Warwick University, 1970), pp. 318-20, 322. As early as 1895 four ASE members stood as parliamentary candidates under Independent Labour Party auspices (David Howell, *British Workers and the Independent Labour Party 1888-1906*, Manchester, 1983, p. 88).
64. Kenneth Newton, *The Sociology of British Communism* (1969), Apps. II, III.
65. cf. the Resolution of the Hull TUC, 1924, in W. Milne-Bailey ed. *Trade Union Documents* (1929), p. 129: for the abandonment of systematic reform, *ibid.*, p. 133-4.
66. J. Zeitlin, 'The Emergence of Shop Steward Organisation and Job Control in the British Car Industry' (*History Workshop Journal* 10 (1980), p. 129.
67. Zeitlin, *Labour Strategies*, pp. 30-2.
68. For this part of the paper I am especially indebted to the as yet unpublished research of Ms Nina Fishman on the Communist Party and the Trade Unions in the 1930s and 1940s. See also R. Croucher, *Engineers at War 1939-1945* (1982) esp. pp. 168-74, and James Hinton, 'Coventry Communism: A Study of Factory Politics in the Second World War' (*History Workshop Journal* 10 (1980).
69. Beynon, *Working for Fords*, p. 145.
70. 'Perhaps the most interesting point about the shipwrights' powers of work control was that they did not use them to maximise their earnings or to create differentials. The shipwrights were willing to accept wages unrelated to the effort or skill of individuals and which tended towards a single rate ' (David Wilson, 'A Social History of Workers in H.M. Dockyard during the Industrial Revolution, particularly 1793-1815,' unpublished Ph.D. thesis, Warwick University, 1975, p. 188). For Edwardian skilled builders' insistence on standard rates for standard output, Charity Organisation Society, *Report on Unskilled Labour* (Q 251-272, pp. 104-5). The Webbs argued (*Industrial Democracy*, p. 719), noting the parallel with middle-class professional corporatism approvingly, that 'the progressive raising of the Common Rule, by constantly promoting the 'Selection of the Fittest', causes an increasing specialisation of function, creating a distinct group, having a Standard of Life and corporate traditions of its own which each recruit is glad enough to fall in with.'
71. In absolute numbers: 1906, 343,200 (More, *Skill*, p. 103); 1966: 271,650 (Min. of Lab. Gazette, January 1967), 1974: 66,000 (Min. of Labour Gazette, May 1974). The statutory school leaving age was raised to sixteen as from Sept.

1972. Only male figures are given, in view of the insignificance of female apprenticeship.

## Chapter 15: The 1970s: Syndicalism without Syndicalists?

1. G.D.H. Cole, *The World of Labour* (London, 1913), p. 35.
2. E. Pouget, *Le Sabotage* (Paris, n.d.), p. 29 and Maxime Leroy, *La Coutûme Ouvrière* (Paris, 1913), II, p. 628.
3. Pouget, p. 67; Leroy, *loc. cit.*

## Chapter 16: Should Poor People Organize?

1. Frances Fox Piven and Richard A. Cloward, *Poor People's Movements: Why They Succeed, How They Fail* (New York, 1977).

## Chapter 17: Labour and Human Rights

1. Barrington Moore Jr., *Injustice: The Social Bases of Obedience and Revolt* (London, 1978).
2. A.E. Bland, P.A. Brown, R.H. Tawney, eds. *English Economic History: Select Documents* (London, 1914), p. 325.
3. E.P. Thompson, 'The Moral Economy of the English Crowd in the Eighteenth Century' (*Past and Present* 50, 1971), pp. 76–136.
4. E.J. Hobsbawm and G. Rudé, *Captain Swing* (Harmondsworth, 1973), p. 61, chapter 13.
5. P.B. Munsche, *Gentlemen and Poachers: The English Game Laws 1671–1831* (Cambridge, 1981), pp. 117–19.
6. A. Pigliaru, *Il Banditismo in Sardegna: La vendetta barbaricina come ordinamento giuridico* (Milan, 1975), pp. 241–57: 'The vendetta as a juridical duty'.
7. Iorwerth Prothero, *Artisans and Politics in Early 19th Century London: John Gast and His Times* (London, 1981).
8. Gareth Stedman Jones, *Languages of Class: Studies in English working class history 1832–1982* (Cambridge, 1983), chapter 3; 'Rethinking Chartism'.
9. e.g., L. Kolakowski, 'Marxism and Human Rights' (*Daedalus*, fall, 1983, pp. 81–92).
10. Albert Laponneraye, 'Déclaration des Droits de l'Homme et du Citoyen' (1832) in Gian Mario Bravo, *Les socialistes avant Marx* (Paris, 1970), vol I: article 10.

# Index

## About the Author

ERIC HOBSBAWM was born in Alexandria, Egypt, and was educated in Vienna, Berlin, London, and Cambridge. He was a Fellow of King's College, Cambridge, from 1949 to 1955 and is at present Reader in History at Birkbeck College in the University of London. He has visited the U.S.A. several times, being visiting professor in the Department of Economics at Stanford University in the summer of 1960, at the Department of Humanities at Massachusetts Institute of Technology in 1967, and at the New School for Social Research in 1984. He has traveled widely in Europe, the Mediterranean countries, and Latin America.

He is the author of *Labour's Turning Point 1880–1900, Primitive Rebels, The Age of Revolution, Industry and Empire, Labouring Men, Bandits, Revolutionaries,* and (with George Rudé) *Captain Swing.*